LANGUAGES for PARALLEL ARCHITECTURES

Design, Semantics, Implementation Models

WILEY SERIES IN PARALLEL COMPUTING

SERIES EDITORS:

J.W. de Bakker, *Centrum voor Wiskunde en Informatica, The Netherlands*

M. Hennessy, *University of Sussex, UK*

D. Simpson, *Brighton Polytechnic, UK*

Carey (ed.): Parallel Supercomputing: Methods, Algorithms and Applications

de Bakker (ed.): Languages for Parallel Architectures: Design, Semantics, Implementation Models

Axford: Concurrent Programming: Fundamental Techniques for Real-Time and Parallel Software Design

Gelenbe: Multiprocessor Performance

Treleaven (ed.): Parallel Computers: Object-oriented, Functional and Logic

LANGUAGES for PARALLEL ARCHITECTURES

Design, Semantics, Implementation Models

EDITED BY

J.W. de Bakker

Centrum voor Wiskunde en Informatica, Amsterdam,
The Netherlands

JOHN WILEY & SONS

Chichester · New York · Brisbane · Toronto · Singapore

Other Wiley Editorial Offices

John Wiley & Sons, Inc., 605 Third Avenue,
New York, NY 10158-0012, USA

Jacaranda Wiley Ltd, G.P.O. Box 859, Brisbane,
Queensland 4001, Australia

John Wiley & Sons (Canada) Ltd, 22 Worcester Road,
Rexdale, Ontario M9W 1L1, Canada

John Wiley & Sons (SEA) Pte Ltd, 37 Jalan Pemimpin 05-04,
Block B, Union Industrial Building, Singapore 2057

Library of Congress Cataloging-in-Publication Data;

Languages for parallel architectures : design, semantics
implementation models / edited by J.W. de Bakker.
p. cm.—(Wiley series in parallel computing)
includes bibliographies.
ISBN 0 471 92177 7
1. Parallel programming (Computer science) 2. Programming
languages (Electronic computers) 3. Computer architecture.
I. Bakker, J.W. de (Jacobus Willem), 1939– . II. Series.
QA76.6.L3353 1989
004′.35—dc20 89-14705
CIP

British Library Cataloguing in Publication Data:

Languages for parallel architectures : design,
semantics, implementation models.
1. Computer systems. Parallel-processors systems.
programming languages
I. Bakker, J.W. de (Jacobus Willem), *1939* –
005.4′5

ISBN 0 471 92177 7

Printed and bound in Great Britain by Courier International, Tiptree, Essex

List of Contributors

P.H.M. America, Philips Research Laboratories, Eindhoven, The Netherlands

J.W. de Bakker, Centrum voor Wiskund en Informatica, The Netherlands.

P.G. Bosco, CSELT, Italy.

G.L. Burns, CES Research, UK.

C. Cecchi, CSELT, Italy.

W. Damm, FB Informatik, West Germany.

H. Dohmen, FB Informatik, West Germany.

E. Giovannetti, University of Turin, Italy.

Ph. Jorrand, LIFIA-IMAG, France.

C. Moiso, CSELT, Italy.

C. Palamidessi, University of Pisa, Italy.

J.J. Rutten, Centre of Mathematics & Computer Science, The Netherlands.

Ph. Schnoebelen, LIFIA-IMAG, France.

CONTENTS

Foreword xi
Preface xiii

Chapter 1 A Parallel Object-Oriented Language: Design and Semantic Foundations 1
P.H.M. America and J.J.M.M. Rutten
1. Introduction 1
2. The design of POOL2 2
2.1 Object-oriented programming 3
2.2 Introducing parallelism 5
2.3 A programming example 7
2.4 Typing and inheritance 11
3. Semantic investigation of a simple language 12
3.1 Operational semantics for $\mathcal{L}$ 15
3.2 Denotational semantics for $\mathcal{L}$ 19
3.3 Semantic correctness of $\mathcal{D}_{Pr}$ 24
4. The semantics of POOL 30
4.1 An operational semantics for POOL 33
4.2 A denotational semantics for POOL 39
4.3 Semantic correctness of $[\![\ldots]\!]_{\mathcal{D}}$ 45
5. References 45
Appendix: Mathematical definitions 47

Chapter 2 AADL: A Net-Based Specification Method for Computer Architecture Design 51
W. Damm and G. Döhmen
1. Introduction 51
2. Specifying computer architectures in AADL 56
3. Representing AADL specifications by Petri nets 66
4. An outline of further steps in AADL's net semantics 98
5. The place of AADL in the world of specification languages 104
6 Acknowledgements 106
7. References 106

Chapter 3 Deriving a Parallel Evaluation Model for Lazy Functional Languages Using Abstract Interpretation 111
G.L. Burn
1 Introduction 111
2 The evaluation model 113
2.1 Evaluators 113
2.2 Evaluation transformers 114
2.3 The parallel model 115
3. A framework for the abstract interpretation of functional languages 115
3.1 An introduction to abstract interpretation 115
3.2 The language 121

3.3 Domains, powerdomains, functions and algebraic relationships 124
3.4 The framework 126
4. A definedness abstract interpretation for determining evaluation transformers 142
4.1 Abstraction of base domains 142
4.2 Abstract interpretation of constants 146
4.3 Some example abstract interpretations 153
4.4 Two theorems 155
5. Evaluation transformers 156
5.1 Context-free evaluation transformers 156
5.2 Context-sensitive evaluation transformers 158
6. Implementing the evaluation transformer model of parallel reduction 160
7. Relationship to other work 161
8. Conclusion 163
9. Acknowledgements 163
10. References 164

Chapter 4 Using Resolution for a Sound and Efficient Integration of Logic and Functional Programming 167
P.G. Bosco, C. Cecchi, E. Giovanetti, C. Moiso and C. Palamidessi
1. Introduction: the reasons for the integration and our global approach 167
2. An IDEAL integrated language by examples 168
2.1 A simple logic simulator written in IDEAL 168
2.2 Turning the logic simulator into a fault-finder 173
3. The first-order language K-LEAF 176
3.1 The rationale 176
3.2 Syntax of K-LEAF 181
3.3 The flat LEAF 184
3.4 Clauses for equality and strict equality 185
3.5 Declarative semantics 187
3.6 Equivalence results 190
4. The IDEAL Language 191
4.1 The rationale behind IDEAL 191
4.2 The higher-order language IDEAL 193
4.3 The user level IDEAL 200
5. Execution mechanism for K-Leaf: the Outermost SLD-resolution . 202
6. Mapping IDEAL into K-LEAF 207
6.1 A partial-evaluation approach to compilation 207
6.2 Type inference 209
6.3 An actual compiler 210
7. Parallelism in IDEAL/K-LEAF 214
7.1 Completeness and OR-parallelism 216
7.2 Completeness and AND-parallelism 216
7.3 A simpler alternative: mapping AND-parallelism into OR-parallelism 217
8. The present state of IDEAL implementation and future work 218

9. References 219
Chapter 5 Principles of FP2: Term Algebras for Specification of Parallel Machines 223
Ph. Schnoebelen and Ph. Jorrand
1. Introduction 223
2. An algebra of communicating systems 225
2.1 Basic notions 225
2.2 Communicating systems 226
2.3 Combining communicating systems 228
2.4 Communicating processes 230
2.5 Some comments on communicating systems 232
3. A language for communicating systems 234
3.1 Signatures, terms and equations 234
3.2 Term rewriting 236
3.3 FP2 data types 237
3.4 FP2 processes 239
3.5 FP2 networks 242
3.6 Operational semantics of FP2 246
3.7 The 'Alternating Bit' protocol in FP2 248
3.8 Some comments on FP2 250
4. A temporal logic for communicating systems 253
4.1 Syntax of *CTL* 253
4.2 Semantics of *CTL* 254
4.3 Predicate transformers 255
4.4 Model checking 257
5. Symbolic model checking in FP2 259
5.1 Disunification 259
5.2 Constrained terms and predicates 263
5.3 A temporal logic for FP2 265
5.4 Analysis of FP2 processes: some examples 267
6. Conclusions 269
7. Acknowledgements 269
8. References 269

FOREWORD

Parallel processing is the most promising answer to the quest for increased computer performance. Already parallel processing and its use in industrial applications has become a major topic in computer science. This has resulted in the development of new programming languages and new algorithms for expressing tasks in parallel forms, and has added a new impetus to computer architectures. The foundation is being laid for new markets for the Information Technology (IT) industry.

In Europe, the focus for research into parallel computers and new programming languages is provided by the European Strategic Programme for Research and Development in Information Technology (ESPRIT). In particular, ESPRIT Project 415, entitled "Parallel Architectures and Languages for Advanced Information Processing - a VLSI-directed approach", is investigating and comparing the major approaches in designing high performance parallel computer systems. The project started in 1984 and had a duration of 5 years. ESPRIT Project 415 brought together six major European IT industries and numerous outstanding universities and research institutes. The table below shows the industrial partners, the contracted universities and research institutes, as well as the approaches to parallel computing systems chosen by each Subproject.

Partner	**Subcontractor**	**Parallel Computing System**
PHILIPS AEG	CWI, Amsterdam Technical University Aachen Technical University Berlin	Object-Oriented system
GEC	University College London Imperial College London	Functional system
BULL	ESIEE LITP University of Paris	Logic system
CSELT	University of Pisa	Logic+Functional system
NIXDORF	Stollmann Hamburg	Data Flow system
NIXDORF	LIFIA-IMAG Grenoble Technical University Munchen	Logical Connection system

The Project is organised as six Subprojects, each investigating a specific style of parallel processing, and two Working Groups that meet regularly to communicate and discuss results. The major new approaches to parallel computing are object-oriented, functional (including data flow) and logic. Each of the styles has specific advantages for applications and programming, and resulting ramifications for system architecture implementation. For example, parallelism may be explicit and under the control of the programmer or implicitly found and handled by the language's compiler.

However, there were many commonalities in the problems encountered and solutions provided by the six Subprojects. Two Working Groups facilitate a proper platform for the presentation and discussions of mutually important topics. These are: "Architectures & Applications" and "Semantics & Proof Techniques". Project 415, on behalf of ESPRIT, has organised two summer schools: Current Trends in Concurrency in 1985, and Future Parallel Computers in 1986; together with two major international conferences: Parallel Architectures and Languages Europe PARLE 87 and PARLE 89, in 1987 and 1989 respectively. All four proceedings are published by Springer-Verlag. These conferences and summer schools provided a meeting place for European researchers in parallel computing, and also a platform to disseminate the work of the six Subprojects to a wider audience. As a finale to the work on Project 415, this book has been prepared to provide a representative selection of the work performed in the Working Group on Semantics and Proof Techniques. In a companion volume also available from John Wiley and Sons, entitled Parallel Computers: Object-Oriented, Functional and Logic, edited by P.C. Treleaven, a comprehensive overview is provided of the work of Project 415 on parallel architectures.

Eddy A.M. Odijk
Manager, ESPRIT Project 415
Philips Research Laboratories, Eindhoven

PREFACE

The design of computing systems that are candidates for a future generation of parallel computers is centred around a small set of parallel programming models. Each model comprises a parallel computer architecture and a corresponding category of programming languages. There are control flow computers (e.g. SEQUENT Balance, INMOS Transputer) and procedural languages (e.g. ADA, OCCAM). Next are object-oriented computers (e.g. PHILIPS' DOOM) and object-oriented languages (e.g. SMALLTALK, POOL). Then there are data flow computers (e.g. Manchester University) and single-assignment languages (e.g. ID, LUCID, SISAL). There are reduction computers (e.g. UCL GRIP, ICL FLAGSHIP) and applicative languages (e.g. Pure LISP, MIRANDA, FP). Next there are logic computers (e.g. ICOT PIM) and predicate logic languages (e.g. GHC). There are rule-based computers (e.g. Columbia University NON-VON & DADO) and production system languages (e.g. Carnegie Mellon's OPS5). Lastly, there are connectionist computers (e.g. Connection Machine) and semantic net languages (e.g. NETL).

ESPRIT Project 415, as discussed in the Foreword, is a systematic study of these candidate parallel architectures and languages. Subproject A, comprising Philips in Eindhoven and AEG in Berlin, have investigated object-oriented systems. Philips has developed a parallel object-oriented language called POOL and an associated processor architecture DOOM. Subproject B, GEC in London, investigated parallel functional - reduction - systems, and made use of the MIRANDA functional programming language. Subproject C, BULL in Paris, developed a parallel logic processor primarily for database applications, using PROLOG as the programming language. Subproject D, CSELT in Turin, investigated parallel systems integrating logic and functional programming. Two languages have been produced: a programming language IDEAL - combining logic and functional concepts, and its support language KLEAF - based on the Horn Clause subset of logic. Subproject E, STOLLMANN in Hamburg (on behalf of NIXDORF), developed a data flow machine implemented on a fast bus, multiprocessor architecture. Subproject F, NIXDORF in Munich, investigated a full first-order logic system called the Logical Connection Machine (LCM). The LCM is programmed in LOP, which itself is supported by the functional and parallel programming language FP2.

The present volume contains a number of studies which are in particular devoted to design, semantics and implementation models for several of the above mentioned languages. (In a companion volume, entitled Parallel Computers: Object-oriented, Functional and Logic, and edited by P.C. Treleaven, a comprehensive review of the architectural work of Project 415 is provided.) The five chapters collected below constitute a major part of the work done by the Working Group on Semantics and Proof Techniques of Project 415. Three out of the five chapters (1,3,4) are concerned directly with the programming styles which underly the architectural designs of the corresponding subprojects (A,B,D). Chapter 2 presents design and semantics of a general specification formalism for architecture design, and chapter 5 is devoted to a specification language for systems of parallel processes based on term rewriting.

Brief outlines of the five chapters follow:

Chapter 1. *A Parallel Object-Oriented Language: Design and Semantic Foundations*

(P.H.M. America, J.J.M.M. Rutten). This chapter introduces the language POOL, Philips' parallel object-oriented language. POOL integrates the structuring mechanisms of object-oriented programming with facilities for parallel programming. Furthermore, the most important issues in the design of POOL are discussed, and several different ways of combining object-oriented programming with parallelism are reviewed. Next, operational and denotational semantic models for POOL are presented, and the relationship between the two models is established: the operational semantics of a program can be recovered from its denotational semantics by applying an abstraction operation.

Chapter 2. *AADL: a Net-based Specification Method for Computer Architecture Design* (W. Damm, G. Doehmen). A specification language for computer architecture design together with its formal semantics is presented. AADL (short for axiomatic architecture description language) allows a modular and concise specification of multiprocessor architectures at levels of abstraction ranging from compiler/operating system interfaces down to chip level. The main part of the paper develops a compositional semantics for AADL. A two-stage approach is adopted: first an AADL specification is translated into a certain type of Petri net, and next for each process of the Petri net a mapping is defined from its places to states of the architecture.

Chapter 3. *Deriving a Parallel Evaluation Model for Lazy Functional Languages Using Abstract Interpretation* (G. Burn). Functional languages have the Church-Rosser property. The languages are therefore implictly parallel, making them suitable for parallel architectures. However, the Church-Rosser property is only a correctness result modulo termination. For this reason, a model is developed for the parallel implementation of lazy functional languages which preserves their denotational properties. The model does not need a special scheduling strategy for parallel tasks, and never does more work than it needs in order to get a result from a program. In these respects, and from how it is defined, it is a natural extension of lazy evaluation to the parallel world. In order to determine the information needed by the model, a framework for the abstract interpretation of functional programs is developed and applied in the determination of so-called evaluation transformers.

Chapter 4. *Using Resolution for a Sound and Efficient Integration of Logic and Functional Programming* (P.G. Bosco, C. Cecchi, E. Giovanetti, C. Moiso, C. Palamidessi). The approach to integration adopted in this chapter is based on two levels. The upper level, or user interface, represented by the experimental language IDEAL, is a sort of extension of a MIRANDA-like functional language with logical operators (where the absence of negation prevents the occurrence of Curry's paradox) or, equivalently, a higher-order extension of a Horn-clause logic language. Some theoretical aspects of this language, which is subject to evolution, still have to be considered further, in particular concerning a satisfactory definition and semantic characterization of the programming problems to be solved with IDEAL. The lower level is the language K-LEAF, a Prolog-like language augmented with directed equality. K-LEAF has a clear and original declarative semantics, and a sound and complete operational semantics, namely flattening plus outermost SLD-resolution.

Chapter 5. *Principles of FP2: Term Algebras for Specification of Parallel Machines* (Ph. Schnoebelen, Ph. Jorrand). This chapter presents the principles of FP2 (Functional Parallel Programming), a language where systems of parallel processes are described by means of a form of term rewrite rules. FP2 uses an algebraic framework and describes nondeterministic systems by means of transition rules, which are clauses stating what the possible changes of state are. An FP2 process has some named communication ports (or connectors), and its transitions may involve communications along these connectors using a form of the rendez-vous mechanism. FP2 processes can be combined to form networks of parallel processes, and the connectors of these processes can be linked. Another important feature is the possibility to flatten combinations of processes. Theoretical properties are investigated using a branching time temporal logic, and a model checker for FP2 processes is defined and an appropriate calculus developed.

I am especially grateful to the authors of the five chapters of this volume, all members or former members of Project 415's Working Group on Semantics. Much of the material was discussed intensively in various meetings of the Group, and the contributions of all participants in these discussions are sincerely acknowledged. I am in particular indebted to Werner Damm for his vital contribution to the work of the Group. Finally, I want to extend my thanks to Eddy Odijk, the current project leader of ESPRIT 415, and to Loek Nijman who recognized the importance of semantic research in the area of parallel architectures and languages at the moment Project 415 was conceived.

J.W. de Bakker
CWI, Amsterdam

Chapter 1

A Parallel Object-Oriented Language: Design and Semantic Foundations

P.H.M. America
Philips Research Laboratories,
P.O. Box 80.000, 5600 JA Eindhoven,
The Netherlands

and

J.J.M.M. Rutten
Centre for Mathematics and Computer Science,
P.O. Box 4079, 1009 AB Amsterdam,
The Netherlands

The language POOL2 integrates the structuring mechanisms of object-oriented programming with facilities for parallel programming. We discuss the most important issues in the design of this language. In particular, we give an overview of the basic principles of object-oriented programming, and we compare several different ways of combining them with parallelism. The language is illustrated by a programming example. Then we define two kinds of formal semantics: an operational semantics based on transition systems and a denotational semantics, which uses the framework of complete metric spaces. These two semantic models are found to be equivalent, in the sense that the operational semantics of a program can be recovered from its denotational semantics by applying an abstraction operation. The semantic techniques are introduced by applying them first to a simplified language.

1. Introduction

The use of parallelism offers the theoretical possibility of a significant increase in the performance of computer systems. However, after decades of intensive study, the effective exploitation of parallelism is still a very difficult problem. Whereas in the area of numeric computation impressive advances have been achieved, symbolic applications, with their more irregular and data-dependent structure, have not shown much progress. The most important difficulties seem to lie in programming such complex applications for execution on a parallel machine. What is needed here is a programming notation that serves as an intermediary between human insight and intuition, on the one hand, and the parallel machine architecture, on the other. At the same time it should be the subject of a body of mathematical knowledge, so that formal methods can supplement informal understanding in the design of programs.

In this chapter we present the parallel object-oriented language POOL2 (America, 1988a). This language has been designed for programming symbolic applications such that they can be executed on DOOM, a Decentralized Object-Oriented Machine (Odijk, 1987). It is, however, general enough to be suitable for a large class of machine architectures. The starting point of the language design is the idea of object-oriented programming, as exemplified by Smalltalk-80 (Goldberg and Robson, 1983). Parallelism is integrated in this model by supplying each object with a *body,* an independent parallel process, so that objects are now active entities instead of passive ones. More details on POOL2 are given in section 2.

The rest of the chapter is devoted to a formal semantic study of POOL. This is a syntactically simplified version of POOL2, which retains all the semantic essentials. Since the techniques used are quite complicated, they are first illustrated, in section 3, by applying them to a language $\mathcal{L}$, which is much simpler than POOL. First we define for this language $\mathcal{L}$ an *operational semantics* $\mathcal{O}_{Pr}$, which assigns to each program and initial state a set containing all the sequences of states that occur during a possible execution of this program from the initial state. This operational semantics is defined by a *transition system* (in the style of Plotkin (1981, 1983)), which describes the possible transitions that the whole system can make from one configuration to another.

Next we give a *denotational semantics* $\mathcal{D}_{Pr}$ for $\mathcal{L}$, which assigns to each program an element of the domain $\bar{P}$ of *processes.* This domain $\bar{P}$ is a complete metric space, defined by a domain equation. (The required concepts and properties of complete metric spaces are summarized in the appendix to this chapter.) The processes in $\bar{P}$ are tree-like structures that can describe the execution of a single statement up to a whole system. The main point of such a denotational semantics is its *compositionality:* the meaning of a composite construct can be determined from the semantics of its constituent parts.

Then we prove that the denotational semantics is correct with respect to the operational semantics, or in other words, that the two kinds of semantics are essentially equivalent. We do this by defining an abstraction operation *abstr*, which maps a process $p \in \bar{P}$ to a function from initial states to sets of sequences of states. The relationship between the operational and the denotational semantics can then be described by $\mathcal{O}_{Pr} = abstr \circ \mathcal{D}_{Pr}$.

Finally, in section 4, we do the same for POOL. Using mainly the same techniques as in section 3, we define an operational semantics and a denotational semantics. Again, this denotational semantics is correct with respect to the operational semantics.

2. The design of POOL2

In this section we give an overview of the most important issues that have played a part in the design of the language POOL2. A more extensive discussion can be found in America (1988c). The design of POOL2 is based to a large extent on its predecessor POOL-T, and many of the considerations given in America (1987a) are still valid for POOL2.

The structure of this section is as follows: First, in section 2.1 we give an overview of the principles of object-oriented programming as they have been incorporated into POOL2. Then section 2.2 describes how parallelism is integrated into the language. Section 2.3 presents a programming example and finally section 2.4 discusses some additional issues.

2.1 Object-oriented programming

In the object-oriented programming style a system is described as a collection of *objects*. An object is best defined as an integrated unit of *data* and *procedures* acting on these data. One can think of it as a box that stores some data and has the possibility of acting on these data. The data in an object are stored in *variables*. The contents of a variable can be changed by executing an assignment statement.

A very important principle is that one object's variables are not accessible to other objects: they are strictly private. In other words, the box has a thick wall around it, which separates the inside from the outside. The only way in which objects can interact is by sending *messages* to each other. Such a message is in fact a request from the sender for the receiver to execute a procedure. In POOL these procedures, which are executed in response to messages, are called *methods*. The receiver decides whether and when it executes such a method, and in some cases it even depends on the receiver which method is executed (see section 2.4). In general, the sender of the message can include some parameters to be passed to the method and the method can return a result, which is passed back to the receiver (see Figure 1). In this way objects can co-operate and communicate. It is important to note that this interaction between objects can only occur according to this precisely determined message interface. Thus every object has the possibility and the responsibility of maintaining its own local data in a consistent state.

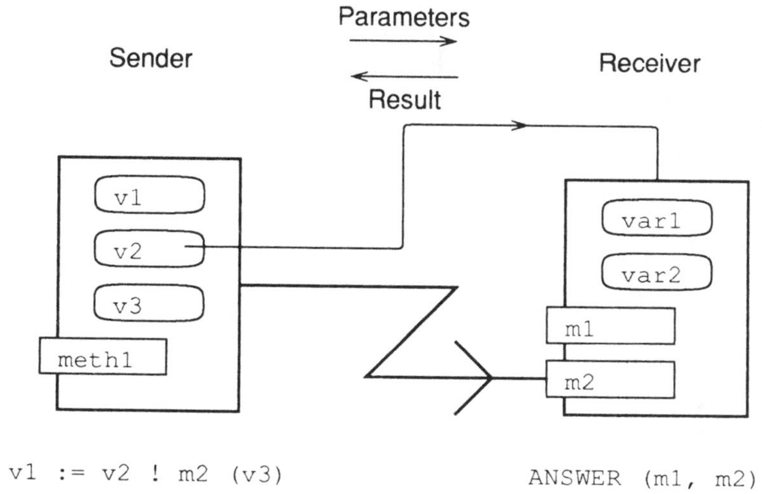

Figure 1: Sending a message

Objects are entities of a dynamic nature. At any point in the execution of a program a new object can be created, so that an arbitrarily large number of objects can come into existence. (Objects are never destroyed explicitly. However, they can be removed by garbage collection if it is certain that this will not influence the correct execution of the program.) In order to describe such systems with many objects, the objects are grouped into *classes*. All the elements (the *instances*) of a class have the same names and types for their variables (although each object has its own set of variables) and they all execute the same code for their methods. In this way, a class can serve as a blueprint for the creation of its instances.

Several object-oriented programming languages use different mechanisms to describe object creation. In general it is agreed that creating new objects is not a natural task for the existing instances of the same class (where would the first instance come from?) but rather for the class itself. In Smalltalk-80 (Goldberg and Robson, 1983) classes are considered to be objects themselves: they can also be created and changed dynamically. Therefore it is natural to describe object creation in *class methods:* a new object can be created by sending an appropriate message to the class. In POOL2 it is not natural to consider classes as objects, because we do not want them to be created or to change during program execution. Therefore in POOL2 the creation of new objects is done by *routines,* a kind of procedure different from methods. Routines are not associated with certain objects and they do not have direct access to any object's variables. Instead, a routine is associated with a *class,* and it can be executed by any object that knows it. By encapsulating the creation of new objects in routines it can be ensured that such a new object is properly initialized before it is used.

Let us now briefly discuss the nature of the data that are stored and manipulated in the objects. In general, a variable contains a *reference* to some object. Also in parameters and results of methods, references are transferred. Some languages, like C++ (Stroustrup, 1986) and Eiffel (Meyer, 1988), also have other built-in data types, like integers and characters, that can be manipulated by the objects. These languages are sometimes called *hybrid* object-oriented. In contrast, in *pure* object-oriented languages, like Smalltalk-80 and POOL2, every data item is represented by (a reference to) an object. In these languages, even very simple items such as integers are conceptually modelled as objects. For example, the addition 3+4 is performed by sending to object 3 a message mentioning the method `add` and having (a reference to) object 4 as a parameter (in POOL2, the expression `3+4` is considered as a shorter notation for the message-sending expression `3 ! add (4)`). In response to this message, object 3 somehow knows how to add itself to the parameter object and it returns the result, a reference to object 7, to the sender of this message. Of course, this is just a conceptual view: in an actual implementation some optimizations will take place so that these operations can be performed much more efficiently using the hardware facilities for integer addition.

The most important contribution of object-oriented programming in the direction of better software development methods stems from the fact that it is a refinement of programming with abstract data types. It encourages the grouping together of all the information pertinent to a certain kind of entity and it enforces the encapsulation of this information according to an explicit interface with the outside world. For users of a certain class, the set of available methods and routines, together with a description of their behaviour (including at least the types of parameters and results), is all that is relevant. The interior of the objects, the variables and the code of methods and routines, is completely inaccessible to them.

Two important quality aspects of software are addressed by this technique. The first is *adaptability:* If a piece of software must be modified (a frequently occurring phenomenon), it is very often the case that many of the relevant pieces of code are inside one class definition instead of spread out over the whole program. Moreover, if the interface of such a class is unchanged or only extended (new methods are added, but the old ones retain their functionality), it is clear that the rest of the program will not be affected by the change. Another aspect is *re-usability:* A class that is well designed and validated by testing or verification can be used repeatedly in different programs. In order to be able to use a class one need only to consider the external interface; the internal details are irrelevant.

Object-oriented programming also leads to a different way of designing software. The common technique of top-down functional design starts from the required end-to-end functionality of a complete program and divides this iteratively into subfunctions until basic language primitives are obtained. The resulting software is not very adaptable to changing requirements, because in practice the changes mostly pertain exactly to this end-to-end functionality. Moreover, it is very unlikely that the subfunctions into which the program is divided coincide precisely with subfunctions in another program, which would allow re-use of software, because these subfunctions are obtained seperately in an *ad hoc* way for each program. In contrast, object-oriented design initially focuses on the basic entities (objects) manipulated by the program and it grows towards the required end-to-end functionality in a rather bottom-up way. The resulting software is often easier to adapt to changing circumstances, because these basic entities are not very likely to change. Moreover, this way of designing software leads more often to meaningful software components that can be re-used. A more extensive discussion of these issues can be found in (Meyer, 1988).

2.2 Introducing parallelism

Despite the terminology of "message passing", most existing object-oriented languages are sequential in nature. This can be explained by the fact that they observe the following restrictions:

(1) Execution starts with exactly one object being active.
(2) Whenever an object sends a message, it does not do anything before the result of that message has arrived.
(3) An object is only active when it is executing a method in response to an incoming message.

Under these conditions we can see that at any moment there is exactly one active object, although very often control is transferred from one object to another.

Now one can think of several ways of introducing parallelism to object-oriented languages. One possibility is to add processes as an orthogonal concept to the language. In some sense this can be seen as eliminating restriction (1). Several processes can be active at the same time, each executing an object-oriented program in the way described in section 2.1. These processes act on the same collection of objects; it is even possible that they are executing the same method in the same object at the same time. This way of dealing with parallelism has been adopted by some languages that were initially meant to be purely sequential, such as Smalltalk-80.

While this approach seems appealing theoretically, it is not so attractive in practice. The point is that it does not solve the problems associated with parallelism. The most important problem of parallel programming is dealing with *non-determinism*. The relative execution speed of the several processes in the system is unknown and can even vary from one execution of a program to another. In this way different program executions can lead to different results in a non-reproducible fashion. The number of possible executions increases very quickly with the number of processes and of places where these can interact. Now a certain amount of non-determinism is necessary in order to flexibly exploit the available hardware parallelism, but too much of it makes it almost impossible to ensure the correctness of a program. The main principles of reducing non-determinism are *synchronization* and *mutual exclusion.* Languages that have processes as orthogonal concepts need extra facilities to achieve synchronization and mutual exclusion. To this end, such languages provide some built-in classes (for example, semaphores). However, the programmer must remember to use these, and use them correctly.

More promising approaches can be obtained by relaxing the other above restrictions. By omitting restriction (2), the sender of a message can immediately continue with its own activities without waiting for a result. This is called *asynchronous communication.* In this way the sender can execute in parallel with the receiver of the message. It is possible to obtain a large degree of parallelism after a number of messages have been sent. This scheme has been adopted most notably by the family of *actor languages* (Agha, 1986). One can say that this provides a convenient mechanism for mutual exclusion, because an object only processes one message at a time. However, the facilities for synchronization are not yet satisfactory in this model.

Therefore POOL2 uses yet another approach, which can be characterized by relaxing restriction (3) above. Every object has a *body,* a local independent process, which is started as soon as the object is created and executes in parallel with all the other objects in the system. At arbitrary places in this body it can be indicated explicitly that the object wants to send or receive a message. In this approach, too, a large degree of parallelism can be obtained by creating a sufficient number of objects, whose bodies can execute in parallel.

The basic communication mechanism in POOL2 is *synchronous message passing.* The sender executes a so-called send expression, which has the form

```
destination ! method (arg1, ..., argn)
```

We see that it explicitly indicates the receiver, the method name, and a number of arguments to be handed over to the method. The receiver executes an answer statement, which is of the following form:

```
ANSWER (method1, ..., methodn)
```

This indicates that exactly one message should be answered, where the method name should be among the ones in the list. Now the actual communication takes place in the form of a rendezvous: the sender and the receiver synchronize (the one that is first willing to communicate waits until the other is ready), and the parameters are passed to the receiver's method, which is then executed. As soon as the method returns a result, this result is passed back to the sender of the message. Now the rendezvous ends and both objects continue independently with their computation. Returning the result is not necessarily done at the end of the method: it is possible that the method still continues after the end of the rendezvous. In any case, the answer statement terminates when the method invocation has ended.

POOL2 also offers an asynchronous communication mechanism. In this case, no result is returned, and the sender continues immediately after having sent the message on its way to the receiver. This mechanism is considered as being *derived* from the synchronous one: its meaning can be described exactly by creating for each asynchronous message a buffer object to which the message is first sent synchronously and which then passes the message to the end destination, again synchronously.

Together the mechanisms available in POOL2 for dealing with parallelism offer a great deal of flexibility in programming while allowing the construction of very reliable programs. In fact very few classes tend to have an elaborate body: only objects that actively pursue a certain task and objects that wish to impose an explicit ordering on the messages they receive need such a body. The rest of the objects use the default body, which answers all incoming messages in sequence. Even for these objects a significant amount of parallelism can be obtained by letting the methods return their results as soon as possible. In this way the safety of synchronous message passing is retained. Asynchronous communication is mainly used where it is necessary to avoid deadlock. By the encapsulation of data and the associated operations in an object that is strictly sequential internally, mutual exclusion in accessing these data is automatically guaranteed and destructive interference of processes acting on the same data is seldom a problem in POOL2 programming.

2.3 A programming example

We will now illustrate the above principles by a brief example. This also gives us the opportunity of introducing a few additional language constructs. In our example we implement a parallel version of a priority queue that can store integers. These integers can be input in an arbitrary order; when they are retrieved from the queue the largest one is always output first. We first give a *specification unit,* in which the class `PQ` and its interface with the outside world is described. Such a specification unit gives all the information that is needed to *use* a class or collection of classes.

```
SPEC UNIT Prio_Queue

CLASS PQ
%% Instances of this class are priority queues that store integers.

ROUTINE new () : PQ
%% Creates and returns a new, empty priority queue.

METHOD put (n : Int) : PQ
%% Stores the integer n in the queue; returns SELF.

METHOD get () : Int
%% Deletes the largest integer from the queue and returns it.
%% This method will not be answered if the queue is empty.

END PQ
```

This means that we have a class `PQ` with a routine `new` to create fresh priority queues and methods `put` and `get` to insert and retrieve integers. (The method `put` does not yield a meaningful result to return but, being a synchronous method, it should return some result. In this situation we have the convention that the method returns a reference to the receiver itself.) Therefore we can create a new instance of the class `PQ` by a statement such as

```
q := PQ.new (),
```

we can insert a new element by

```
q ! put (i),
```

and we can extract an element by

```
j := q ! get ().
```

Let us now consider the corresponding *implementation unit,* which gives the actual implementation details of the class `PQ`:

```
IMPL UNIT Prio_Queue

CLASS PQ
%% Instances of this class are priority queues that store integers.

%% The routine new, which creates and returns an empty priority queu
%% is defined automatically. An explicit definition is not necessary


VAR max : Int     %% the largest element in the queue
    rest : PQ     %% a PQ that stores all the other elements
    %% Both variables are automatically initialized to NIL.

%% Invariant: max == NIL  <==> queue is empty
%%            max ~== NIL ==> rest ~== NIL


METHOD put (n : Int) : PQ
%% Stores the integer n in the queue; returns SELF.
BEGIN
   RESULT SELF;    %% end of rendezvous: sender can continue
   IF max == NIL
   THEN max := n;
        IF rest == NIL THEN rest := PQ.new () FI
   ELSIF max >= n
   THEN rest ! put (n)
   ELSE rest ! put (max);
        max := n
   FI
END put


METHOD get () : Int
%% Deletes the largest integer from the queue and returns it.
%% This method will not be answered if the queue is empty.
BEGIN              %% We know that max ~== NIL, so rest ~== NIL
   RESULT max;     %% end of rendezvous: sender can continue
   max := rest ! get_largest_or_NIL ()
END get
```

```
METHOD get_largest_or_NIL () : Int
%% Returns NIL if the queue is empty. Otherwise it deletes
%% the largest element and returns it.
BEGIN
   RESULT max;     %% end of rendezvous: sender can continue
   IF max ~== NIL
   THEN max := rest ! get_largest_or_NIL ()
   FI
END get_largest_or_NIL


BODY
   DO     %% forever
      IF max == NIL
      THEN ANSWER (put, get_largest_or_NIL)
      ELSE ANSWER (put, get, get_largest_or_NIL)
      FI
   OD
YDOB

END PQ
```

Figure 2 shows a number of instances of the class **PQ**. We see that each instance stores, at most, one integer itself; for the rest of the contents it uses another instance. All the methods in this class return their result immediately at the beginning. In this way the sender can continue its own activities while the method is still processing the message. This is the source of parallelism in the current example: While a newly input integer is propagating throughout the whole queue, the next can already have been entered, and the same holds for requests for output.

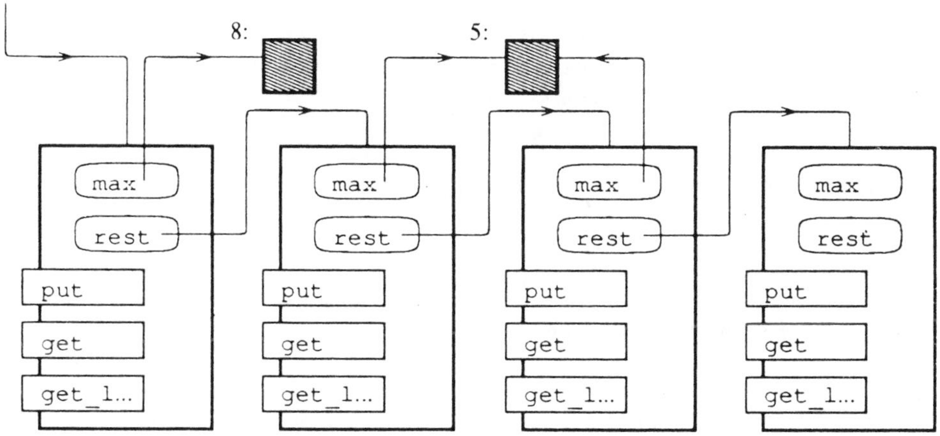

Figure 2: A priority queue containing the number 8 and twice the number 5

The method **get_largest_or_NIL** does not appear in the specification unit. Therefore it cannot be used by other units. In the current unit we need it because the blocking behaviour of the method `get` is undesirable when we ask the `rest` queue for its largest element: this would block the requesting queue even for `put` messages. Instead, the method `get_largest_or_NIL` does not block if the queue is empty but it returns the special value `NIL`, which is a reference to *no* object. (One may argue that this method `get_largest_or_NIL` would be quite useful to put in the specification unit for external use as well. We have not done so in order to illustrate the possibility of hiding certain methods.)

The body of the class `PQ` makes sure that the method `get` is only answered when the queue is not empty. The loop is never terminated explicitly, but the object may nevertheless be discarded by a garbage collector as soon as no other object no longer has a reference to it.

The example shows quite a few expressions that use operators. Most of these are in fact shorthand notations for send expressions. For example, the expression `max >= n` is another form of writing `max ! greater_or_equal (n).` The operator `==` is an exception, in the sense that it represents a routine call instead of a send expression. For example, the expression `max == NIL` is equivalent to `Int.id (max, NIL).` In POOL2, every class automatically gets such a routine `id`. Without sending a message, it checks whether its two arguments refer to the same object (or both refer to no object, `NIL`).

The unit `Prio_Queue` shown above can be used for different purposes. For example, it can sort a sequence of integers, as shown in the following unit:

```
IMPL UNIT Sorting

USE File_IO, Prio_Queue

GLOBAL root := Sorter.new()

CLASS Sorter
%% An instance of this class will read integers from the standard inp
%% file until a negative one is encountered. Then it will print the
%% nonnegative ones in descending order.

VAR pq := PQ.new ()
    n : Int := standard_in ! read_Int ()

BODY
   WHILE n >= 0
   DO pq ! put (n);
      n := standard_in ! read_Int ()
   OD;
   DO   %% until deadlock
      standard_out ! write_Int (pq ! get (), 0) ! new_line ()
   OD
YDOB
END Sorter
```

We also see how the execution of a POOL2 program is initiated: The global name `root` is declared, and in order to initialize it, a new element of the class `Sorter` is created. (In principle, any object in the system can now refer to this `Sorter` object under the name `root`.) This `Sorter` object then creates other objects, in this case a priority queue, and sets the whole system running. The program ends in a deadlock, where the `Sorter` object tries to get an integer from an empty queue. This is quite a normal way of termination for a POOL program (it is detected by the run-time system and all the objects are removed). It could be avoided by also inserting the last, negative integer into the queue and terminating when it emerges. Note that this program can, in principle, sort a sequence of integers in linear time, while a sequential program would always need $O(N\log N)$ time for this task.

Another possibility of using the unit `Prio_Queue` would be to share such a priority queue among several other objects. It could serve as a repository between a number of producers and a number of consumers of information, such that a consumer asking for new input always gets the item with the highest priority. (Note that items with equal priority are handled in a first-in first-out way, which is not interesting for integers but can be important for generalizations.) The message interface of such a `PQ` object ensures that requests from consumers and producers are processed in sequence (mutual exclusion is guaranteed) and that consumers are automatically blocked until more input for them is available.

2.4 Typing and inheritance

As can be seen from the above example, POOL2 is a strongly typed language: Every variable, parameter and result has a type associated with it, indicating the class of the object it represents. First, this allows the compiler to check, for example, whether the destination object of a message indeed has the indicated method, so that a certain class of programming errors can be detected even before the program is run. In addition, this typing information constitutes an important kind of documentation of the program, which is now automatically included.

In some cases the strong typing rules might decrease the flexibility of the programmer to construct widely usable classes. More advanced typing schemes are then needed. For example, POOL2 offers the possibility of defining *generic* classes, where some of the types used in the definition are parameters which need only be filled in when the class is actually used. Operations on such types can also be passed as parameters, because in POOL2 routines are considered as objects, so that they can be stored in variables and passed as arguments or results of methods and routines.

In connection with typing there is the concept of *inheritance,* which plays an important role in many object-oriented languages. Its basic principle is that in defining a new class it is often convenient to take over all the variables and methods of an existing class and only add or redefine a few of them. The new class is then said to inherit these variables and methods from the old one. The advantage of this mechanism is the possibility of code sharing: duplication of code is avoided and both the programmer and the implementation can profit from this.

In many cases, the new class is intended to be a specialized version of the old one, in the sense that an instance of the new class can be used whenever an instance of the old one is expected. Therefore the new class is often called a *subclass* of the old one. In typed object-oriented languages this is often reflected by considering the type associated with this new class as a subtype of the old one, which means that, for example, an expression of the new type may be assigned to a variable of the old one.

There are, however, problems with this connection between inheritance and subtyping (America (1987b)). The most important point is that by just taking over the variables and methods of an existing class, even if redefinition is not allowed, it is not automatically the case that the new class is really a specialized version, nor is this the only way in which specialization in behaviour can be obtained. Whereas code sharing is a fairly straightforward mechanism, subtyping should be based on a thorough semantic understanding of the behaviour of objects. In POOL2 the decision has been made not to include inheritance or subtyping until a satisfactory body of fundamental knowledge of these issues has been obtained.

3. Semantic investigation of a simple language

In this section we investigate the semantics of a language $\mathcal{L}$, which, on the one hand, is simple enough to give a formal treatment of its semantics in full detail and, on the other, has enough in common with POOL to be of relevance for the study of the latter's semantics.

After having introduced the language $\mathcal{L}$ and briefly explained its informal semantics, we shall define an *operational* and a *denotational* semantics for $\mathcal{L}$. Next we shall prove that the operational semantics equals the (functional) composition of the denotational semantics with a so-called *abstraction* operation. From this, the semantic *correctness* (a notion we shall shortly introduce formally) of the denotational semantics with respect to the operational semantics follows.

A semantics for a programming language $\mathcal{L}$ is a mapping $\mathcal{M}:\mathcal{L}\to D$, where D is some mathematical domain (a set, a complete partial ordering, a complete metric space), which we call the semantic *universe* of $\mathcal{M}$. Sometimes $\mathcal{M}$ is called a model for $\mathcal{L}$. Traditionally, two main types of semantics are distinguished: *operational* and *denotational.* Without wishing to become involved in a discussion of the precise definitions, we state that the main characteristic of the former is that its definition is based on a *transition system*, or *abstract machine*, in the style of Hennessy and Plotkin (1979) and Plotkin (1981, 1983). A denotational semantics is characterized by the fact that it is defined in a *compositional* manner: the denotational semantics of a composite statement is given in terms of the denotational semantics of its components. (As a second distinctive property one often considers the way in which recursion is treated. The usual view is that an operational semantics treats recursion by means of so-called *syntactic environments* (or body replacement), whereas a denotational semantics uses *semantic environments*, in combination with some fixed-point argument.)

Now consider an operational semantics $\mathcal{O}:\mathcal{L}\to D$ and a denotational semantics $\mathcal{D}:\mathcal{L}\to D'$. Ideally, one would wish both models to coincide; then $\mathcal{D}$ could be regarded as a compositional reformulation of $\mathcal{O}$. Often, however, this is not the case. The requirement for $\mathcal{D}$ to be compositional in general implies that it must distinguish more statements than $\mathcal{O}$ does. (Therefore, its semantic universe D' is often more involved than the semantic universe D of $\mathcal{O}$.) A natural question is whether such a denotational semantics $\mathcal{D}$ distinguishes *at least* the same statements as $\mathcal{O}$; in other words, whether for all statements s and t: if $\mathcal{O}[\![s]\!]\neq\mathcal{O}[\![t]\!]$ then $\mathcal{D}[\![s]\!]\neq\mathcal{D}[\![t]\!]$. In that case, we call $\mathcal{D}$ *correct* with respect to $\mathcal{O}$. If we define for a semantics $\mathcal{M}:\mathcal{L}\to D''$ an equivalence relation $\equiv_{\mathcal{M}}$ by

$$s\equiv_{\mathcal{M}} t \Leftrightarrow \mathcal{M}[\![s]\!]=\mathcal{M}[\![t]\!],$$

for all s, $t\in\mathcal{L}$, then the correctness of $\mathcal{D}$ with respect to $\mathcal{O}$ can be expressed formally by the condition

$$\equiv_{\mathcal{D}}\subset\equiv_{\mathcal{O}}.$$

One way to prove the correctness of $\mathcal{D}$ is to introduce a so-called *abstraction* operator $\alpha: D' \rightarrow D$, which relates the denotational semantic universe with the operational one. If one can prove that

$$\mathcal{O} = \alpha \circ \mathcal{D}$$

then a precise relationship between $\mathcal{O}$ and $\mathcal{D}$ has been established, which moreover implies the correctness of $\mathcal{D}$ with respect to $\mathcal{O}$.

As a mathematical framework for our semantic descriptions we have chosen *complete metric spaces*. (For the basic definitions of metric topology see Dugundji (1966) or Engelking (1977) and the appendix to this chapter.) In this we follow and generalize De Bakker and Zucker (1982). (For other applications of this type of semantic framework see De Bakker *et al* (1986).) We follow Kok and Rutten (1988) in using contractions on complete metric spaces as our main mathematical tool, exploring the fact that contractions have *unique* fixed points (Banach's theorem). We shall define both operators on our semantic universes and the semantic models themselves as fixed points of suitably defined contractions. In this way, we are able to use a general method for proving semantic correctness. Suppose we have defined $\mathcal{O}$ as the fixed point of a contraction

$$\Phi: (\mathcal{L} \rightarrow D) \rightarrow (\mathcal{L} \rightarrow D).$$

If we next show that also $\alpha \circ \mathcal{D}$ is a fixed point of Φ then Banach's theorem implies that $\mathcal{O} = \alpha \circ \mathcal{D}$.

It will be precisely the scheme outlined above that we shall apply to the language $\mathcal{L}$, which we introduce next. First some notation: Throughout this chapter we shall write $(x, y \in) X$ when a set X is introduced that has x and y as typical elements. For the definition of $\mathcal{L}$, we need the following sets: a set of *variables* $(x, y \in) Var$; a set of *expressions* $(e \in) Exp$, which here will have no internal structure (as opposed to the expressions in POOL); a set $(m \in) MName$ of *method names;* and a set $(\alpha, \beta \in) SLabel$ of *statement labels* (which will also be called *object names*). The definition of $\mathcal{L}$ consists of three parts. First, we introduce the set of *statements* $\mathcal{L}_S$, next the set of *labelled statements* $\mathcal{L}_{LS}$, and finally the set of *programs* $\mathcal{L}_{Pr}$.

Definition 3.1 ($\mathcal{L}_S$, $\mathcal{L}_{LS}$, $\mathcal{L}_{Pr}$)
We defined the set $(s, t \in) \mathcal{L}_S$ of statements by

$$s ::= x := e \mid \alpha!m \mid \textbf{answer} \mid s_1; s_2 \mid s_1 + s_2 \mid \textbf{release}(\alpha, s)$$

As a special element, the set $\mathcal{L}_S$ contains the *empty* statement E, which stands for termination. The set $((\alpha, s) \in) \mathcal{L}_{LS}$ of labelled statements is given by

$$\mathcal{L}_{LS} = SLabel \times \mathcal{L}_S.$$

Finally, we introduce the set $((X, \delta) \in) \mathcal{L}_{Pr}$ of programs:

$$\mathcal{L}_{Pr} = \mathcal{P}_{fin}(\mathcal{L}_{LS}) \times Decl,$$

where *Decl* is the set of declarations, defined below. If a set $X \in \mathcal{P}_{fin}(\mathcal{L}_{LS})$ contains only pairs with E as a statement then we call it *final*:

$$final(X) \Leftrightarrow \forall \alpha \forall s \; [(\alpha, s) \in X \Rightarrow s = E].$$

Definition 3.2 (Declarations)
The set $(\delta \in)$ *Decl* of declarations is given by

$$\delta ::= <m_1 \Leftarrow s_1, \ldots, m_n \Leftarrow s_n>,$$

for $n \geqslant 0$. If $\delta = < \cdots, m \Leftarrow s, \cdots >$ we sometimes write $\delta(m) = s$.

A program is a pair (X, δ): X is a finite set of labelled statements, which are executed in parallel and can communicate with each other by sending messages; δ is a declaration, giving for each method name a corresponding statement. A labelled statement (α, s) consists of a label α and a statement s. Facilitating an understandable explanation of $\mathcal{L}$ and its semantics, and following the object-oriented terminology that we use in the description of POOL, we shall say that the *object* α executes the statement s. This statement s is the part of the *body* (the statement with which α starts at the beginning of the program) of the object α that still has to be executed. When describing the communication in $\mathcal{L}$, this convention is found to be particularly useful.

A statement can be an assignment $x := e$, the execution of which is considered to be atomic; that is, both the evaluation of the expression e and the assignment of the result to the variable x take place in one step.

There are two statements for communication: a send statement $\alpha!m$ and an answer statement **answer.** The form of communication we have here is a simplified version of the POOL rendezvous. A send statement specifies an address to which the message is sent together with the name of the method that should be executed, but no parameters. An answer statement does not specify a method name; it indicates that any method can be executed. Successful communication results in the suspension of the sender until the receiver has executed the requested method. Then both the sender and the receiver continue with their own bodies. Note that we do not have value passing here: The execution of a method consists of the execution of the corresponding statement, given by a declaration; no result is sent back to the sender.

Next we have the sequential composition $s_1;s_2$ of two statements with its usual interpretation, and the non-deterministic choice $s_1 + s_2$ between two statements, also called *global* non-determinism. The execution of $s_1 + s_2$ consists of the execution of either s_1 or s_2; since both s_1 and s_2 can begin with a communication statement this choice may be influenced by the environment, that is, by other labelled statements present in the same program.

Finally, there is the release statement **release** (α, s), which is added only to enable an elegant description of the operational semantics of communication. When it is executed, the object α is put to work again and resumes execution with s. Its use will become clear below.

Obviously, there are many differences between POOL and $\mathcal{L}$, which is much simpler than POOL. However, for the semantic description of in particular the communication in $\mathcal{L}$, we need almost all technical tools that we shall use for the semantics of the full language POOL itself. This fact motivates our choice of $\mathcal{L}$ as a starting point for the semantic study of POOL. (There is one aspect of the methods used in this section that is not really necessary here: since the number of objects for a given program is always finite, and since we do not have a construct for recursion, we are not able to model infinite behavior. Therefore, we could use sets and structural induction rather than complete metric spaces and contractions. We introduce these notions here because we need them in the next section (since in POOL one *can* model infinite behavior).)

3.1 Operational semantics for $\mathcal{L}$

We assume given a set of *states* $(\sigma\in)\Sigma$, defined by

$$\Sigma = Var \rightarrow Val,$$

where *Val* is some set of values. We shall use $\sigma\{\nu/x\}$ to denote the state that is like σ but for its value in x, which is ν. For the evaluation of expressions, we stipulate an interpretation function

$$\mathcal{E}: Exp \rightarrow \Sigma \rightarrow Val.$$

The operational semantics of $\mathcal{L}$ will be based on the *labelled transition system* $<Conf, \Lambda, \rightarrow>$ defined below. It consists of a set *Conf* of *configurations*, a set Λ of *transition labels*, and a *transition relation* $\rightarrow$. The transition relation specifies transitions between configurations:

$$\rightarrow \subseteq Conf \times \Lambda \times Conf.$$

The label of such a transition gives some information on the kind of step that is is modelled (e.g., a computation step or a communication one). Using a transition system, we can model each of the possible executions of a program as a sequence of transitions, starting in some initial configuration. The transition system is defined as follows.

Definition 3.3 (Transition system)
Let $\delta \in Decl$ be fixed. We define a labelled transition system $<Conf, \Lambda, \rightarrow>$, where the sets $(<X,\sigma>\in)Conf$ of configurations and $(\lambda\in)\Lambda$ of transition labels are given by

$$Conf = \mathcal{P}_{fin}(\mathcal{L}_{LS}) \times \Sigma,$$

$$\Lambda = \{\tau\} \cup \{(\alpha, \beta!m): \alpha,\beta \in SLabel,\ m \in MName\} \cup \{\alpha?: \alpha \in SLabel\}.$$

The label τ will be used to denote a computation step; $(\alpha,\beta!m)$ and $\alpha?$ will denote send and answer steps. We define $\rightarrow$ as the smallest relation satisfying the following axioms and rules:

Axioms

(A1) $<\{(\alpha, x:=e)\}, \sigma> \xrightarrow{\tau} <\{(\alpha,E)\}, \sigma\{\mathcal{E}[\![e]\!](\sigma)/x\}>$

(A2) $<\{(\alpha,\beta!m)\}, \sigma> \xrightarrow{(\alpha,\ \beta!m)} <\{(\alpha,E)\}, \sigma>$

(A3) $<\{(\alpha, \textbf{answer})\}, \sigma> \xrightarrow{\alpha?} <\{(\alpha,E)\}, \sigma>$

Rules

(R1) If $<\{(\alpha,s)\}, \sigma> \xrightarrow{\lambda} <\{(\alpha,s')\}, \sigma'>$

then $<\{(\alpha,s;t)\}, \sigma> \xrightarrow{\lambda} <\{(\alpha,s';t)\}, \sigma'>$

(read t instead of $s';t$ if $s'=E$)

$<\{(\alpha,s+t)\}, \sigma> \xrightarrow{\lambda} <\{(\alpha,s')\}, \sigma'>$

$<\{(\alpha,t+s)\}, \sigma> \xrightarrow{\lambda} <\{(\alpha,s')\}, \sigma'>$

(R2) If $<\{(\beta,t), (\alpha,s)\}, \sigma> \xrightarrow{\lambda} <X, \sigma'>$

then $<\{(\beta, \mathbf{release}(\alpha,s);t)\}, \sigma> \xrightarrow{\lambda} <X, \sigma'>$

(R3) If $<X, \sigma> \xrightarrow{\lambda} <X', \sigma'>$

then $<X \cup Y, \sigma> \xrightarrow{\lambda} <X' \cup Y, \sigma'>$

(R4) If $<X, \sigma> \xrightarrow{(\alpha,\beta!m)} <\{(\alpha,s)\} \cup X', \sigma>$ and

$<Y, \sigma> \xrightarrow{\beta?} <\{(\beta,t)\} \cup Y', \sigma>$

then $<X \cup Y, \sigma> \xrightarrow{\tau} <\{(\beta, \delta(m); \mathbf{release}(\alpha,s); t)\} \cup X' \cup Y', \sigma>$

(Note that the fixed declaration δ occurs only in rule R4.)

The label $(\alpha,\beta!m)$ used in axiom A2 indicates that the object α sends a message to object β, requesting the execution of method m. In A3, the label $\alpha?$ indicates that object α is willing to answer any message.

The interpretation of R1 is straightforward. In R2, it is expressed that the execution of **release**(α,s) amounts to the extension of the current set of labelled statements with (α,s). Labelled statements are executed in an interleaved way, according to R3: A set of labelled statements is evaluated by repeatedly performing a step of one of its elements.

In rule R4, communication is described. If object α is sending a message to object β, requesting the execution of method m, and if object β is willing to answer a message, then the following happens. Object β starts executing the statement $\delta(m)$, which corresponds to the definition of method m according to the declaration δ. Next, the statement **release**(α,s) is executed, reactivating object α, which will continue with s, the remainder of its body. Finally, object β proceeds with t, the remainder of its own body. Note that during the execution of method m, that is, the statement $\delta(m)$, object α is non-active, as can be seen from the fact that α does not occur as the name of any labelled statement in the configuration resulting from this transition.

Now we are almost ready to define the operational semantics for $\mathcal{L}$. First, we introduce its *semantic universe.*

Definition 3.4 (Semantic universe *P*)
Let $(w\in)\Sigma_\partial^\infty = \Sigma^* \cup \Sigma^*\cdot\{\partial\} \cup \Sigma^\omega$. We put

$$(p,q\in)\ P = \Sigma \rightarrow \mathcal{P}(\Sigma_\partial^\infty),$$

where $\mathcal{P}(\Sigma_\partial^\infty)$ denotes the set of all subsets of Σ_∂^∞, and the symbol ∂ denotes *deadlock.*

The elements of P will be used to represent the operational meanings of statements and units. For a given state $\sigma\in\Sigma$, the set $p(\sigma)$ contains streams $w\in\Sigma_\partial^\infty$, which are sequences of states representing possible computations. They can be of one of three forms: If $w\in\Sigma^*$, it stands for a finite normally terminating computation. If $w\in\Sigma^\omega$, it represents an infinite computation. Finally, if $w\in\Sigma^*\cdot\{\partial\}$, it reflects a finite abnormally terminating computation, which is indicated by the symbol ∂ for deadlock.

Definition 3.5 (Operational semantics for $\mathcal{L}$)
We define

$$\mathcal{O}_{Pr}: Prog \rightarrow P$$

as follows. Let $(X,\delta)\in Prog$ and $\sigma\in\Sigma$. For a word $w\in\Sigma_\partial^\infty$ we put

$$w \in \mathcal{O}_{Pr}[\![(X,\delta)]\!](\sigma)$$

if and only if one of the following conditions is satisfied:

(1) $w = \sigma_0 \cdots \sigma_n$ $(n \geqslant 0)$ and there exist $X_0, \ldots, X_n$ such that $<X_0,\sigma_0> = <X,\sigma>$ and

$$<X_0,\sigma_0> \xrightarrow{\tau} <X_1,\sigma_1> \xrightarrow{\tau} \cdots \xrightarrow{\tau} <X_n,\sigma_n> \text{ and } \mathit{final}(X_n)$$

(2) $w = \sigma_0\sigma_1 \cdots$ and there exist $X_0, X_1, \ldots$ such that $<X_0,\sigma_0> = <X,\sigma>$ and

$$<X_0,\sigma_0> \xrightarrow{\tau} <X_1,\sigma_1> \xrightarrow{\tau} <X_2,\sigma_2> \xrightarrow{\tau} \cdots$$

(3) $w = \sigma_0 \cdots \sigma_n \cdot \partial$ $(n \geqslant 0)$ and there exist $X_0, \ldots, X_n$ such that $<X_0,\sigma_0> = <X,\sigma>$ and

$$<X_0,\sigma_0> \xrightarrow{\tau} <X_1,\sigma_1> \xrightarrow{\tau} \cdots \xrightarrow{\tau} <X_n,\sigma_n>$$

with $\neg\, \mathit{final}(X_n)$ and $\neg <X_n,\sigma_n> \xrightarrow{\tau}$.

Here $\neg <X_n,\sigma_n> \xrightarrow{\tau}$ is an abbreviation for $\neg \exists <X',\sigma'> [<X_n,\sigma_n> \xrightarrow{\tau} <X',\sigma'>]$. (Note that in the transition sequences above we consider only computation steps that are labelled by τ.)

Case (1) represents a normally terminating computation and case (2) stands for an infinite computation. In case (3), a deadlocking computation is described: If after a number of computation steps a configuration $<X_n,\sigma_n>$ is reached which is not final and from which no computation steps are possible, this implies that from there only single-sided communication steps are possible, for which there is no matching communication partner present. This we consider as a case of deadlock, which is indicated by ∂.

Anticipating the definition of a denotational semantics for $\mathcal{L}$ and the proof of its correctness with respect to $\mathcal{O}_{Pr}$, we next give a fixed-point characterization of $\mathcal{O}_{Pr}$. As indicated at the beginning of this section, this will happen in the context of complete metric spaces. Therefore, we first turn P into a complete metric space.

Definition 3.6 (P as a complete metric space)
We redefine the semantic universe P by putting

$$P = \Sigma \rightarrow \mathcal{P}_{ncompact}(\Sigma_\partial^\infty),$$

where $\mathcal{P}_{ncompact}(\Sigma_\partial^\infty)$ is the set of all non-empty and compact subsets of Σ_∂^∞. This set is a complete metric space when supplied with the so-called *Hausdorff* metric, induced by the usual metric on Σ_∂^∞ (see Example A.1.1 and Definition A.6(d) of the appendix to this chapter). The metric on P is then defined according to Definition A.6(a).

Definition 3.7 (Φ)
We define a function

$$\Phi : (\mathit{Prog} \rightarrow P) \rightarrow (\mathit{Prog} \rightarrow P).$$

Let $F \in \mathit{Prog} \rightarrow P$, $(X,\delta) \in \mathit{Prog}$, and $\sigma \in \Sigma$. We put

$$\Phi(F)((X,\delta))(\sigma) = \begin{cases} \{\epsilon\} & \text{if } \mathit{final}(X) \\ \{\partial\} & \text{if } \neg <X,\sigma> \xrightarrow{\tau} \wedge \neg\, \mathit{final}(X) \\ \bigcup \{\sigma' \cdot F((X',\delta))(\sigma') : <X,\sigma> \xrightarrow{\tau} <X',\sigma'>\} & \text{otherwise} \end{cases}$$

It is straightforward to prove that Φ is contracting and thus has a unique fixed point. In fact, this fixed point is $\mathcal{O}_{Pr}$:

Theorem 3.8: $\Phi(\mathcal{O}_{Pr}) = \mathcal{O}_{Pr}$

Proof

The proof consists of two parts. First, we show that for every program (X,δ) we have that $\mathcal{O}_{Pr}[\![(X,\delta)]\!]$ is in P, that is, for every state σ the set $\mathcal{O}_{Pr}[\![(X,\delta)]\!](\sigma)$ is *compact*. Second, we prove that $\Phi(\mathcal{O}_{Pr})=\mathcal{O}_{Pr}$.

So let $(X,\delta)\in$ *Prog* and $\sigma\in\Sigma$. Let $(w_i)_i$ be a sequence of words in $\mathcal{O}_{Pr}[\![(X,\delta)]\!](\sigma)$ $(\subseteq\Sigma_\partial^\infty)$, say,

$$w_i = \sigma_i^1\sigma_i^2\sigma_i^3 \cdots .$$

We show that $(w_i)_i$ has a converging subsequence with its limit in $\mathcal{O}_{Pr}[\![(X,\delta)]\!](\sigma)$. Assume for simplicity that all words w_i are infinite. Since $w_i\in\mathcal{O}_{Pr}[\![(X,\delta)]\!](\sigma)$ for every i, there exist infinite transition sequences such that

$$<X,\sigma>\rightarrow<X_i^1,\sigma_i^1>\rightarrow<X_i^2,\sigma_i^2>\rightarrow \cdots$$

(omitting the labels τ). From the definition of $\rightarrow$ it follows that the set

$$\{<X',\sigma'>: <X,\sigma>\rightarrow<X',\sigma'>\}$$

is finite. Thus there exists a pair $<X_1,\sigma_1>$ such that for infinitely many i's:

$$<X_i^1,\sigma_i^1> = <X_1,\sigma_1>.$$

Let $f_1:\mathbb{N}\rightarrow\mathbb{N}$ be a monotonic function with, for all i,

$$<X_{f(i)}^1,\ \sigma_{f(i)}^1> = <X_1,\sigma_1>.$$

Next we proceed with the subsequence $(w_{f_1(i)})_i$ of $(w_i)_i$ and repeat the above argument, now with respect to the set

$$\{<X',\sigma'>:\ <X_1,\sigma_1>\rightarrow<X',\sigma'>\}.$$

Continuing in this way we find a sequence of monotonic functions $(f_k)_k$, defining a sequence of subsequences of $(w_i)_i$, and a sequence of configurations $(<X_k,\sigma_k>)_k$ such that

$$\forall k\ \forall j\ \forall i\leqslant k\ [\,\sigma_{f_k(j)}^i = \sigma_i\,]$$

and

$$<X,\sigma>\rightarrow<X_1,\sigma_1>\rightarrow<X_2,\sigma_2>\rightarrow \cdots$$

and moreover such that the sequence $(w_{f_{k+1}(i)})_i$ is a subsequence of the sequence of $(w_{f_k(i)})_i$. Now we define

$$g(i) = f_i(i).$$

Then we have

$$\lim_{i\rightarrow\infty} w_{g(i)} = \sigma_1\sigma_2\sigma_3 \cdots .$$

Thus we have constructed a converging subsequence of $(w_i)_i$ with its limit in $\mathcal{O}_{Pr}[\![(X,\delta)]\!](\sigma)$. (In case not all w_i are infinite a similar argument can be given.)

Second, we show that $\Phi(\mathcal{O}_{Pr})=\mathcal{O}_{Pr}$. Let $(X,\delta)\in$*Prog* with $\neg$ *final*(X), let $\sigma\in\Sigma$ and let $w \in \Sigma_\partial^\infty$. If $w = \partial$ then

$$w \in \Phi(\mathcal{O}_{Pr})((X, \delta))(\sigma) \Leftrightarrow w \in \mathcal{O}_{Pr}[\![(X, \delta)]\!](\sigma).$$

Now suppose $w \neq \partial$. We have

$$\begin{aligned} w \in \mathcal{O}_{Pr}[\![(X, \delta)]\!](\sigma) &\Leftrightarrow \exists \sigma' \in \Sigma\, \exists X' \in \mathcal{P}_{fin}(LStat)\, \exists w' \in \Sigma_\partial^\infty \\ &\qquad [<X,\sigma> \rightarrow <X',\sigma'> \wedge w = \sigma' \cdot w' \wedge w' \in \mathcal{O}_{Pr}[\![(X', \delta)]\!](\sigma)] \\ &\Leftrightarrow [\text{definition } \Phi] \\ &\qquad w \in \Phi(\mathcal{O}_{Pr})((X, \delta))(\sigma). \end{aligned}$$

So we see: $\mathcal{O}_{Pr} = \Phi(\mathcal{O}_{Pr})$. (End of proof.)

3.2 Denotational semantics for $\mathcal{L}$

The domain that we shall take as the semantic universe of our denotational model is defined by a reflexive domain equation. In De Bakker and Zucker (1982) solving these equations in a metric setting was first described. Then, in America and Rutten (1988), this approach was generalized in order to deal with equations in which P occurs at the left-hand side of a function space constructor, as in $P \cong P \rightarrow P$; this case that was not covered by De Bakker and Zucker. For a quick overview of the main results of America and Rutten (1988), the reader may wish to read section 2 of America *et al* (1986b).

Further, our model is based on the use of *continuations*. For an extensive introduction to continuations and expression continuations, which we shall also use, we refer to Gordon (1979); see also De Bruin (1986).

We start with the definition of a domain $\bar{P}$, the elements of which we shall call *processes* from now on. Such a process represents the whole or a part of the execution of a program.

Definition 3.9 (Semantic process domain $\bar{P}$)
Let $(p, q \in)\bar{P}$ be a complete ultra-metric space satisfying the following reflexive domain equation:

$$\bar{P} \cong \{p_0\} \cup id_{1/2}(\Sigma \rightarrow \mathcal{P}_{compact}(Step_{\bar{P}})),$$

where $(\pi, \rho \in) Step_{\bar{P}}$ is

$$Step_{\bar{P}} = Comp_{\bar{P}} \cup Send_{\bar{P}} \cup Answer_{\bar{P}},$$

with

$$\begin{aligned} Comp_{\bar{P}} &= \Sigma \times \bar{P}, \\ Send_{\bar{P}} &= SLabel \times MName \times \bar{P} \times \bar{P}, \\ Answer_{\bar{P}} &= SLabel \times (MName \rightarrow \bar{P} \rightarrow^1 \bar{P}). \end{aligned}$$

(The sets $\{p_0\}$, Σ, *SLabel*, and *MName* become complete ultra-metric spaces by supplying them with the discrete metric (see Example A.1.1 of the appendix to this chapter); $\bar{P} \rightarrow^1 \bar{P}$ denotes the set of all non-expansive functions (A.3.(c)) from $\bar{P}$ to itself.)

America and Rutten (1988) describe how to find for such an equation a solution, which is unique up to isomorphy. Let us try to explain intuitively the intended interpretation of the domain $\bar{P}$. First, we observe that in the equation above the operation $id_{1/2}$ is necessary only to guarantee that the equation is solvable by defining a contracting functor on $\mathcal{C}$, the category of complete metric spaces. For a, say, more operational understanding of the equation this is not important.

A process $p \in \bar{P}$ is either p_0 or a function from Σ to $\mathcal{P}_{compact}(Step_{\bar{P}})$, the set of all *compact* subsets of $Step_{\bar{P}}$. The process p_0 is the terminated process. For $p \neq p_0$, the process p has the choice, depending on the current state σ, among the *steps* in the set $p(\sigma)$. If $p(\sigma) = \emptyset$, then no further action is possible, which is interpreted as abnormal termination (deadlock). For $p(\sigma) \neq \emptyset$, each step $\pi \in p(\sigma)$ consists of some action (for instance, a change of the state σ or an attempt at communication) and a *resumption* of this action, that is, the remaining actions to be taken after this action. There are three different types of steps $\pi \in Step_{\bar{P}}$.

First, a step may be an element of $\Sigma \times \bar{P}$, say

$$\pi = <\sigma', p'>.$$

The only action is a change of state: σ' is the new state. Here the process p' is the resumption, indicating the remaining actions process p can do. (When $p' = p_0$ no steps can be taken after this step π.)

Second, π might be a *send step*, $\pi \in Send_{\bar{P}}$. In this case we have, say

$$\pi = <\alpha, m, p_1, p_2>,$$

with $\alpha \in SLabel$, $m \in MName$, and $p_1, p_2 \in \bar{P}$. The action involved here consists of an attempt at communication, in which a message is sent to the object α, specifying the method m. This is the interpretation of the first two components α and m. The third component p_1, called the *dependent* resumption of this send step, indicates the steps that will be taken when the sender becomes active again, that is, after the execution of the method. The last component p_2, called the *independent* resumption of this send step, represents the steps to be taken after this send step that need *not* wait for the result of the method execution. In general, this process p_2 is the result of the parallel composition of this send step with some other process (see Definition 3.10 below).

Finally, π might be an element of $Answer_{\bar{P}}$, say

$$\pi = <\alpha, g>$$

with $\alpha \in SLabel$, and $g \in (MName \to \bar{P} \to^1 \bar{P})$. It is then called an *answer step*. The first component of π expresses that object α is willing to accept a message. The last component g, the resumption of this answer step, specifies what should happen when an appropriate message actually arrives. The function g is then applied to the method name specified in this message and to the dependent resumption of the sender (specified in its corresponding send step). It then delivers a process which is the resumption of the sender and the receiver *together*, which is to be composed in parallel with the independent resumption of the send step.

We now define a semantic operator for the *parallel composition* (or *merge*) of two processes, for which we shall use the symbol $\|$. It is *auxiliary* in the sense that it does not correspond to a syntactic operator in the language $\mathcal{L}$.

Definition 3.10 (Parallel composition)

Let $\| : \bar{P} \times \bar{P} \to \bar{P}$ be such that it satisfies the following equation:

$$p \| q = \lambda\sigma \cdot ((p(\sigma) \mathbin{\|\!\!\_} q) \cup (q(\sigma) \mathbin{\|\!\!\_} p) \cup (p(\sigma) \,|_\sigma\, q(\sigma))),$$

for all $p, q \in \bar{P} \setminus \{p_0\}$, and such that $p_0 \| q = q \| p_0 = p_0$. Here, $X \mathbin{\|\!\!\_} q$ and $X \,|_\sigma\, Y$ are defined by:

$$X \lfloor\!\lfloor q = \{\pi \hat{\|} q \colon \pi \in X\},$$

$$X \,|_\sigma Y = \bigcup \{\pi \,|_\sigma \rho \colon \pi \in X,\ \rho \in Y\},$$

where $\pi \hat{\|} q$ is given by

$$<\sigma',p'> \hat{\|} q = <\sigma',p' \| q>,$$

$$<\alpha,m,p_1,p_2> \hat{\|} q = <\alpha,m,p_1,p_2 \| q>, \text{ and}$$

$$<\alpha,g> \hat{\|} q = <\alpha,\lambda m \cdot \lambda p \cdot (g(m)(p) \| q)>,$$

and $\pi|_\sigma \rho$ by

$$\pi|_\sigma \rho = \begin{cases} \{<\sigma,\ g(m)(p_1) \| p_2>\} & \text{if } \pi = <\alpha,m,p_1,p_2> \text{ and } \rho = <\alpha,g> \\ & \text{or } \rho = <\alpha,m,p_1,p_2> \text{ and } \pi = <\alpha,g> \\ \emptyset & \text{otherwise.} \end{cases}$$

We observe that this definition is self-referential, since the merge operator occurs at the right-hand side of the definition. For a formal justification of this definition see the appendix of America *et al* (1986b), where a similar merge operator is given as the unique fixed point of a contraction on $\overline{P} \times \overline{P} \rightarrow^1 \overline{P}$.

Since we intend to model parallel composition by interleaving, the merge of two processes p and q consists of three parts. The first part contains all possible first steps of p followed by the parallel composition of their respective resumptions with q. The second part similarly contains the first steps of q. The last part contains the communication steps that result from two matching communication steps taken simultaneously by processes p and q. For $\pi \in Step_{\overline{P}}$ the definition of $\pi \hat{\|} q$ is straightforward. The definition of $\pi|_\sigma \rho$ is more involved. It is the empty set if π and ρ do not match. Now suppose they do match, say $\pi = <\alpha,m,p_1,p_2>$ and $\rho = <\alpha,g>$. Then π is a *send* step, denoting a request to object α to execute method m, and ρ is an *answer* step, denoting that object α is willing to accept a message. In $\pi \,|_\sigma \rho$, the state σ remains unaltered. The function g, the second component of ρ, needs as an argument the method name m. Moreover, g depends on the dependent resumption p_1 of the send step π. This explains why both m and p_1 are supplied as arguments to the function g. Now it can be seen that $g(m)(p_1) \| p_2$ represents the resumption of the sender and the receiver together. (In order to obtain more insight into this definition it is advisable to return to it after having seen the definition of the semantics of an answer statement.)

The merge operator is associative, which can easily be proved as follows. Define

$$\epsilon = \sup_{p,q,r \in \overline{P}} \{d_{\overline{P}}((p \| q) \| r, p \| (q \| r))\}$$

Then, using the fact that the operator $\|$ satisfies the equation above, one can show that $\epsilon \leqslant \frac{1}{2} \cdot \epsilon$, hence $\epsilon = 0$.

Now we come to the definition of the semantics of $\mathcal{L}$. First, we introduce the semantics $\mathcal{D}_S$ of statements; next, the semantics $\mathcal{D}_{Pr}$ of programs is defined.

The semantics of statements will be given by a function

$$\mathcal{D}_S : \mathcal{L}_S \rightarrow SLabel \rightarrow Decl \rightarrow Cont \rightarrow \overline{P},$$

where the set of continuations *Cont* is given by

$$Cont = \bar{P}.$$

Let $s \in \mathcal{L}_S$, $\alpha \in SLabel$, $\delta \in Decl$, and $p \in \bar{P}$. The semantic value of the statement s is given by

$$\mathcal{D}_S[\![s]\!](\alpha)(\delta)(p).$$

The statement label α is of importance in case s contains some communication statement. Second, the semantic value of s depends on the declaration δ. Finally, the last argument for $\mathcal{D}_S$ is the continuation p: the semantic value of everything that will happen after the execution of s. The use of continuations enables us to describe the semantics of $\mathcal{L}$ compositionally and, moreover, in a concise and elegant way.

Please note the difference between the notions of *resumption* and *continuation*. A resumption is a part of a semantic step $\pi \in Step_{\bar{P}}$, indicating the remaining steps to be taken after the current one. A continuation, on the other hand, is an argument to a semantic function. It may appear as a resumption in the result. A good example of this is the definition of $\mathcal{D}_S[\![x:=e]\!](\alpha)(\delta)(p)$ below.

Definition 3.11 (Denotational semantics of statements)
We define

$$\mathcal{D}_S: \mathcal{L}_S \to SLabel \to Decl \to Cont \to^1 \bar{P},$$

with $Cont = \bar{P}$, as follows:

$$
\begin{aligned}
&(0)\ \ \mathcal{D}_S[\![E]\!](\alpha)(\delta)(p) = p\\
&(1)\ \ \mathcal{D}_S[\![x:=e]\!](\alpha)(\delta)(p) = \lambda\sigma\cdot\{<\sigma\{\mathcal{E}[\![e]\!](\sigma)/x\},\ p>\}\\
&(2)\ \ \mathcal{D}_S[\![\beta!m]\!](\alpha)(\delta)(p) = \lambda\sigma\cdot\{<\beta,m,p,p_0>\}\\
&(3)\ \ \mathcal{D}_S[\![\mathbf{answer}]\!](\alpha)(\delta)(p) = \lambda\sigma\cdot\{<\alpha,\ \lambda m\cdot\lambda q\cdot\mathcal{D}_S[\![\delta(m)]\!](\alpha)(\delta)(p \,\|\, q)>\}\\
&(4)\ \ \mathcal{D}_S[\![s_1;s_2]\!](\alpha)(\delta)(p) = \mathcal{D}_S[\![s_1]\!](\alpha)(\delta)(\mathcal{D}_S[\![s_2]\!](\alpha)(\delta)(p))\\
&(5)\ \ \mathcal{D}_S[\![s_1+s_2]\!](\alpha)(\delta)(p) = \lambda\sigma\cdot(\mathcal{D}_S[\![s_1]\!](\alpha)(\delta)(p)(\sigma) \cup \mathcal{D}_S[\![s_2]\!](\alpha)(\delta)(p)(\sigma))\\
&(6)\ \ \mathcal{D}_S[\![\mathbf{release}(\beta,s)]\!](\alpha)(\delta)(p) = \mathcal{D}_S[\![s]\!](\beta)(\delta)(p_0) \,\|\, p
\end{aligned}
$$

This definition needs some justification since it cannot be defined by a simple induction on the complexity of statements, as is apparent from case (3) above. We can give a formally correct definition as follows. If we put

$$S = \mathcal{L}_S \to SLabel \to Decl \to Cont \to^1 \bar{P}$$

we can define $\mathcal{D}_S$ as the fixed point of a contraction

$$\Psi: S \to S$$

given, for $F \in S$, $\alpha \in SLabel, \delta \in Decl$, and $p \in Cont$, by

$$
\begin{aligned}
&(0)\ \ \Psi(F)(E)(\alpha)(\delta)(p) = p\\
&(1)\ \ \Psi(F)(x:=e)(\alpha)(\delta)(p) = \lambda\sigma\cdot\{<\sigma\{\mathcal{E}[\![e]\!](\sigma)/x\},\ p>\}\\
&(2)\ \ \Psi(F)(\beta!m)(\alpha)(\delta)(p) = \lambda\sigma\cdot\{<\beta,m,p,p_0>\}\\
&(3)\ \ \Psi(F)\ (\mathbf{answer})\ (\alpha)(\delta)(p) = \lambda\sigma\cdot\{<\alpha,\ \lambda m\cdot\lambda q\cdot F(\delta(m))(\alpha)(\delta)(p \,\|\, q)>\}\\
&(4)\ \ \Psi(F)(s_1;s_2)(\alpha)(\delta)(p) = \Psi(F)(s_1)(\alpha)(\delta)(\Psi(F)(s_2)(\alpha)(\delta)(p))\\
&(5)\ \ \Psi(F)(s_1+s_2)(\alpha)(\delta)(p) = \lambda\sigma\cdot(\Psi(F)(s_1)(\alpha)(\delta)(p)(\sigma) \cup \Psi(F)(s_2)(\alpha)(\delta)(p)(\sigma))\\
&(6)\ \ \Psi(F)\ (\mathbf{release}(\beta,s))(\alpha)(\delta)(p) = \Psi(F)(s)(\beta)(\delta)(p_0) \,\|\, p.
\end{aligned}
$$

We give some motivation for the definition of $\mathcal{D}_S$. In case (1), the expression e is evaluated and its result is at once assigned to x.

The evaluation of a send statement, in case (2), results in a process containing a send step $<\beta,m,p,p_0>$. Here β refers to the object to which a message is sent, which requests the execution of the method m. The dependent resumption of this send step consists of the continuation p, indicating that the activity of object α, which is executing the send statement, is suspended until the message has been answered and the method has been executed. The independent resumption of this sent step is initialized to p_0.

The function g in the answer step in case (3) represents the execution of an arbitrary method followed by its continuation. It takes as arguments a method name m, indicating the method that will be executed, and a continuation q, both to be received from an object sending a message to α. The execution of method m consists of the execution of the statement $\delta(m)$. Next, both the continuation q of the sending object and the given continuation p are to be executed in parallel. This explains the continuation $p\|q$ in $\mathcal{D}_S[\![\delta(m)]\!]$.

Let us look more closely at the definition of $\pi|_\sigma\rho$ (Definition 3.10) now that we have defined the semantics of send and answer statements. Let $\pi=<\alpha,m,p_1,p_2>$ be the result of the evaluation of a send statement and let $<\alpha,g>$ stem from an answer statement. We have that

$$\pi|_\sigma\rho = \{<\sigma,\ g(m)(p_1)\ \|\ p_2>\}.$$

The execution of the method m proceeds in parallel with the independent resumption p_2 of the sender. From the definition of the semantics of an answer step it follows that

$$g(m)(p_1) = \mathcal{D}_S[\![\delta(m)]\!](\alpha)(p_1\|q),$$

for some continuation q. The continuation of the execution of m is given by $p_1\|q$, the parallel composition of continuations p_1 and q, reflecting the fact that after the rendezvous both the sender and the receiver of the message can proceed in parallel again. (Of course, the independent resumption p_2 may still be executing at this point.)

Continuing with the explanation of Definition 3.11 above, we come to case (6), since the semantics of $s_1;s_2$ and s_1+s_2 is defined straightforwardly. In the definition of the semantics of a release statement, the process $\mathcal{D}_S[\![s]\!](\beta)(\delta)(p_0)$ represents the meaning of the execution of s by object β with the empty continuation p_0, indicating that after s nothing remains to be done. This process is put in parallel with p, the continuation of the release statement.

Note that the function $\mathcal{D}_S$ is compositional, which follows from the observation that it is defined in a compositional manner.

Next, we introduce the denotational semantics of programs.

Definition 3.12 (Denotational semantics of programs)
We define

$$\mathcal{D}_{Pr}\colon Prog \rightarrow \overline{P}$$

as follows. Let $(X,\delta)\in Prog$, with $X=\{(\alpha_1,s_1),\ldots,(\alpha_n,s_n)\}$. We put

$$\mathcal{D}_{Pr}[\![(X,\delta)]\!] = \mathcal{D}_S[\![s_1]\!](\alpha_1)(\delta)(p_0)\|\cdots\|\mathcal{D}_S[\![s_n]\!](\alpha_n)(\delta)(p_0).$$

Given a set X of labelled statements, the value of $\mathcal{D}_{Pr}[\![(X,\delta)]\!]$ is obtained by first computing the semantics of every labelled statement $(\alpha_i, s_i) \in X$, which is given by $\mathcal{D}[\![s_i]\!](\alpha_i)(\delta)(p_0)$; here p_0 indicates that after s_i nothing remains to be done. Next, the resulting processes are put in parallel.

3.3 Semantic correctness of $\mathcal{D}_{Pr}$

In this section we prove that

$$\mathcal{O}_{Pr} = abstr \circ \mathcal{D}_{Pr},$$

where $abstr : \bar{P} \to P$ is an *abstraction* operation (to be defined below), which relates the semantic universes of $\mathcal{D}_{Pr}$ and $\mathcal{O}_{Pr}$. To this end, we shall introduce an intermediate semantics

$$\mathcal{I}: Prog \to \bar{P},$$

which will be related to both $\mathcal{O}_{Pr}$ and $\mathcal{D}_{Pr}$. The equality mentioned above then follows.

The intermediate semantics $\mathcal{I}$ is defined as the fixed point of a contraction Γ, the definition of which is based on the transition relation given in Definition 3.3.

Definition 3.13 (Intermediate semantics $\mathcal{I}$)
Let

$$\Gamma: (Prog \to \bar{P}) \to (Prog \to \bar{P})$$

be defined as follows. Let $F \in Prog \to \bar{P}$ and $(X, \delta) \in Prog$. If *final*(X) we put

$$\Gamma(F)((X, \delta)) = p_0.$$

Otherwise,

$$\Gamma(F)((X, \delta)) = \lambda\sigma \cdot (C_F \cup S_F \cup A_F)$$

where

$$C_F = \{<\sigma', F((X', \delta))>: <X, \sigma> \xrightarrow{\tau} <X', \sigma'>\}$$

$$S_F = \{<\beta, m, F((\{(\alpha, s)\}, \delta)), F((X', \delta))>: <X, \sigma> \xrightarrow{(\alpha, \beta!m)} <\{(\alpha, s)\} \cup X', \sigma>\}$$

$$A_F = \{<\alpha, g>: <X, \sigma> \xrightarrow{\alpha\,?} <\{(\alpha, s)\} \cup X', \sigma>\},$$

with

$$g = \lambda m \cdot \lambda p \cdot (\mathcal{D}_S[\![\delta(m)]\!](\alpha)(p \,\|\, F((\{(\alpha, s)\}, \delta))) \,\|\, F((X', \delta))).$$

It is easy to show that Γ is a contraction, so we can define a function $\mathcal{I}: Prog \to \bar{P}$ by

$$\mathcal{I} = \text{fixed point } (\Gamma).$$

The function Γ closely resembles the function Φ, given in Definition 3.7. The main difference is that Γ is a contraction on $Prog \to \bar{P}$, whereas Φ is a contraction on $Prog \to P$.

Let $(X, \delta) \in Prog$ and $\sigma \in \Sigma$. The set $\mathcal{I}((X, \delta))(\sigma)$ contains not only computation steps but also single-sided communication steps: Corresponding with every send transition of the form

$$<X, \sigma> \xrightarrow{(\alpha, \beta!m)} <\{(\alpha, s)\} \cup X', \sigma>,$$

it contains a send step

$$<\beta,\ m,\ \mathcal{I}((\{(\alpha,s)\},\delta)),\ \mathcal{I}((X',\delta))>.$$

Here β and m indicate that a message specifying method m is sent to the object β. The dependent resumption of this step is $\mathcal{I}((\{(\alpha,s)\},\delta))$: the meaning of the statement that will be executed by α as soon as method m has been executed. The last component of this send step, the independent resumption, consists of $\mathcal{I}((X',\delta))$, which is the meaning of all the statements executed by objects other than α. Thus it is reflected that these objects need not wait until the message is answered; they may proceed in parallel.

Next, $\mathcal{I}((X,\delta))(\sigma)$ can contain some answer steps. For every answer transition

$$<X,\sigma> \xrightarrow{\alpha\ ?} <\{(\alpha,s)\}\cup X',\sigma>$$

the set $\mathcal{I}((X,\delta))(\sigma)$ includes an answer step

$$<\alpha,g>,$$

with

$$g = \lambda m\cdot\lambda p\cdot (\mathcal{D}_S[\![\delta(m)]\!](\alpha)(p\,\|\,\mathcal{I}((\{(\alpha,s)\},\delta)))\ \|\ \mathcal{I}((X',\delta))).$$

This indicates that object α is willing to answer a message, while the resumption g indicates what should happen when an appropriate message arrives. This function g, when supplied with a method name m and a dependent resumption p (both to be received from the sending object), consists of the parallel composition of the process $\mathcal{I}((X',\delta))$ together with the process

$$\mathcal{D}_S[\![\delta(m)]\!](\alpha)(p\ \|\ \mathcal{I}((\{(\alpha,s)\},\delta))).$$

(Note that we have used the function $\mathcal{D}_S$ here; the definition of $\mathcal{I}$ therefore depends on its definition.) The process $\mathcal{I}((X',\delta))$ represents the meaning of all the statements executed by objects other than object α: these objects may proceed in parallel with the execution of method m, the meaning of which is indicated by the second process. Its interpretation is the same as in the definition of $\mathcal{D}_S[\![$ **answer** $]\!](\alpha)(\delta)(p)$ in the previous section but for the fact that here the last resumption of this process consists of $p\,\|\,\mathcal{I}((\{(\alpha,s)\},\delta))$: the parallel composition of the dependent resumption of the sender and the meaning of the statement s, with which object α will continue after it has answered the message.

The abstraction operation $abstr: \bar{P}\rightarrow P$ is given below.

Definition 3.14 (Abstraction operation *abstr***)**
Let $p\in\bar{P}$, $\sigma\in\Sigma$, and $w\in\Sigma_\partial^\infty$.

(1) We call w a *finite stream* in $p(\sigma)$ if there exist $<\sigma_1,p_1>, \ldots, <\sigma_n,p_n>$ such that

$$w=\sigma_1\cdots\sigma_n \wedge <\sigma_1,p_1>\in p(\sigma) \wedge \forall 1\leqslant i<n\ [<\sigma_{i+1},p_{i+1}>\in p_i(\sigma_i)] \wedge p_n=p_0$$

(2) We call w an *infinite stream* in $p(\sigma)$ if there exist $<\sigma_1,p_1>,<\sigma_2,p_2>, \ldots$ such that

$$w=\sigma_1\sigma_2\cdots \wedge <\sigma_1,p_1>\in p(\sigma) \wedge \forall i\geqslant 1\ [<\sigma_{i+1},p_{i+1}>\in p_i(\sigma)].$$

(3) We call w a *deadlocking stream* in $p(\sigma)$ if there exist $<\sigma_1,p_1>, \ldots, <\sigma_n,p_n>$ such that

$$w = \sigma_1\cdots\sigma_n\cdot\partial \wedge <\sigma_1,p_1>\in p(\sigma) \wedge \forall 1\leqslant i<n\ [<\sigma_{i+1},p_{i+1}>\in p_i(\sigma_i)] \wedge$$
$$p_n\neq p_0 \wedge p_n(\sigma_n)\cap(\Sigma\times\bar{P})=\varnothing.$$

Now we define a function *abstr*: $\bar{P} \to P$ by $abstr(p_0) = \lambda\sigma\cdot\{\epsilon\}$ and, for $p \neq p_0$, by

$$abstr(p) = \lambda\sigma\cdot\{w: w \text{ is a stream in } p(\sigma)\}.$$

The function *abstr* transforms a process $p \in \bar{P}$ into a function $abstr(p) \in P = \Sigma \to \mathcal{P}_{compact}(\Sigma_\partial^\infty)$, which yields for every $\sigma \in \Sigma$ a set $abstr(p)(\sigma)$ of streams. (If one regards the process p as a tree-like structure, these streams can be considered the branches of p.) There are three kinds of streams: finite, infinite and deadlocking streams, which all correspond to a similar type of computation. A stream in p for a given state σ is computed as follows. If $p = p_0$, we have finished; we have found a finite stream. If $p(\sigma) \cap Comp_{\bar{P}} = \emptyset$ we cannot proceed because single-sided communication is not possible. In that case, a symbol ∂ is delivered, for deadlock. If $p(\sigma)$ does contain a computation step, say $<\sigma_1, p_1>$, the new state σ_1 is taken as the first element of the stream and is passed on as an argument to the resumption p_1. Next, we look for a second computation step in $p_1(\sigma_1)$. Continuing this way, we can construct all streams in $p(\sigma)$.

Now we want to prove

$$\mathcal{O}_{Pr} = abstr \circ \mathcal{G}.$$

It is found to be convenient to use the fixed-point characterizations $\mathcal{O}_{Pr} = \Phi(\mathcal{O}_{Pr})$ and $\mathcal{G} = \Gamma(\mathcal{G})$ for the proof; moreover, we shall also use a fixed-point property for *abstr*, which we prove next.

Theorem 3.15
We define $\Xi: (\bar{P} \to^1 P) \to (\bar{P} \to^1 P)$. Let $F \in \bar{P} \to^1 P$, $P \in \bar{P}$ and $\sigma \in \Sigma$. We put

$$\Xi(F)(p_0)(\sigma) = \{\epsilon\},$$

$$\Xi(F)(p)(\sigma) = \{\partial\}, \quad \text{if } p(\sigma) \cap Comp_{\bar{P}} = \emptyset.$$

(Recall that $Comp_{\bar{P}} = \Sigma \times \bar{P}$.) Otherwise, we set

$$\Xi(F)(p)(\sigma) = \bigcup \{\sigma' \cdot F(p')(\sigma'): <\sigma', p'> \in p(\sigma)\}.$$

Now we have:

$$abstr = \Xi(abstr).$$

Proof
First, we have to verify that Ξ is well defined, that is, that for every $F \in \bar{P} \to^1 P$, $p \in \bar{P}$, and $\sigma \in \Sigma$ the set $\Xi(F)(p)(\sigma)$ is compact. This is proved in Appendix II of Rutten (1988). Second, we have to show, similarly to the proof of Theorem 3.8, that

(1) For every $p \in \bar{P}$, and $\sigma \in \Sigma$: $abstr(p)(\sigma)$ is a compact set.
(2) $\Xi(abstr) = abstr$.

For the proof of part (1), which is not trivial, we refer once again to Appendix II of Rutten (1988). Here we show only part (2). Consider $p \in \bar{P} - \{p_0\}$ and $\sigma \in \Sigma$ such that $p(\sigma) \cap (\Sigma \times \bar{P}) \neq \emptyset$. Then:

$$w \in abstr(p)(\sigma) \Leftrightarrow [\text{definition } abstr]$$

$$\exists \sigma' \in \Sigma\, \exists w' \in \Sigma_\partial^\infty\, \exists p' \in \bar{P}\ [w = \sigma' \cdot w' \wedge w' \in abstr(p')(\sigma')]$$

$$\Leftrightarrow [\text{definition } \Xi]$$

$$w \in \Xi(abstr)(p)(\sigma).$$

The other cases are easy. We see: $abstr = \Xi(abstr)$.

Now we are ready to prove the following theorem.

Theorem 3.16: $\forall F \in Prog \rightarrow \bar{P}\ [\Phi(abstr \circ F) = abstr \circ (\Gamma(F))]$

Proof

Let $F \in Prog \rightarrow \bar{P}$, $(X,\delta) \in Prog$, and $\sigma \in \Sigma$. Suppose $\neg final(X)$. If $\neg <X,\sigma> \xrightarrow{T}$, then

$$\Phi(abstr \circ F)((X,\delta))(\sigma) = \{\partial\}$$
$$= abstr(\Gamma(F)((X,\delta)))(\sigma)$$

since $\Gamma(F)((X,\delta))(\sigma) \cap Comp_{\bar{P}} = \emptyset$. If $<X,\sigma> \xrightarrow{T}$ we have

$$\begin{aligned}\Phi(abstr \circ F)((X,\delta))(\sigma) &= \bigcup \{\sigma' \cdot (abstr \circ F)((X',\delta))(\sigma') \colon <X,\sigma> \xrightarrow{T} <X',\sigma'>\} \\ &= \bigcup \{\sigma' \cdot (abstr(F((X',\delta)))(\sigma')) \colon <X,\sigma> \xrightarrow{T} <X',\sigma'>\} \\ &= [\text{Theorem 3.15, Definition 3.13}] \\ &\quad abstr(\lambda\sigma \cdot C_F)(\sigma) \\ &= abstr(\lambda\sigma \cdot (C_F \cup S_F \cup A_F))(\sigma) \\ &= abstr(\Gamma(F)((X,\delta)))(\sigma) \\ &= (abstr \circ \Gamma(F))((X,\delta))(\sigma).\end{aligned}$$

Since Φ and Γ are contractions and thus have unique fixed points, the following corollary is immediate.

Corollary 3.17: $\mathcal{O}_{Pr} = abstr \circ \mathcal{I}$

Finally, we shall show that $\mathcal{D}_{Pr}$ and $\mathcal{I}$ are equal. This follows from the following theorem.

Theorem 3.18: $\Gamma(\mathcal{D}_{Pr}) = \mathcal{D}_{Pr}$

Proof

We prove: For every $(X,\delta) \in Prog$

$$\Gamma(\mathcal{D}_{Pr})((X,\delta)) = \mathcal{D}_{Pr}[\![(X,\delta)]\!],$$

using induction on the number of elements in X.

Case (1): $X = \{(\alpha,s)\}$

(1.1) $s = x := e$

$$\begin{aligned}\Gamma(\mathcal{D}_{Pr})((\{(\alpha,x:=e)\},\delta)) &= \lambda\sigma \cdot \{<\sigma\{\mathcal{E}[\![e]\!](\sigma)/x\},p_0>\} \\ &= \mathcal{D}_S[\![x:=e]\!](\alpha)(\delta)(p_0) \\ &= \mathcal{D}_{Pr}[\![(\{(\alpha,x:=e)\},\delta)]\!]\end{aligned}$$

(1.2) $s = \beta!m$

$$\begin{aligned}\Gamma(\mathcal{D}_{Pr})((\{\alpha,\beta!m)\},\delta)) &= \lambda\sigma\cdot\{<\beta,m,p_0,p_0>\}\\ &= \mathcal{D}_S[\![\beta!m]\!](\alpha)(\delta)(p_0)\\ &= \mathcal{D}_{Pr}[\![(\{a,\beta!m)\},\delta)]\!]\end{aligned}$$

(1.3) $s =$ **answer**

$\Gamma(\mathcal{D}_{Pr})((\{(\alpha,\ \textbf{answer})\},\ \delta)) = \lambda\sigma\cdot\{<\alpha,g>\}$,

$$\begin{aligned}\text{where } g &= \lambda m\cdot\lambda p\cdot \mathcal{D}_S[\![\delta(m)]\!](\alpha)(\delta)(p \,\|\, \mathcal{D}_{Pr}((\{(\alpha,E)\},\ \delta))\\ &= \lambda m\cdot\lambda p\cdot\mathcal{D}_S[\![\delta(m)]\!](\alpha)(\delta)(p)\end{aligned}$$

$$\begin{aligned}\text{Now } \lambda\sigma\cdot\{<\alpha,g>\} &= \mathcal{D}_S[\![\textbf{answer}]\!](\alpha)(\delta)(p_0)\\ &= \mathcal{D}_{Pr}[\![(\{(\alpha,\ \textbf{answer})\},\ \delta)]\!].\end{aligned}$$

(1.4) $s = s_1;s_2$: case analysis for s_1. We give two examples.

(1.4.1) $s_1 = x := e$. Let $\sigma' = \sigma\{\mathcal{E}[\![e]\!](\sigma)/x\}$, then

$$\begin{aligned}\Gamma(\mathcal{D}_{Pr})((\alpha,\ x:=e\,;s_2)\},\ \delta)) &= \lambda\sigma\cdot\{<\sigma',\mathcal{D}_{Pr}[\![(\{(\alpha,\ s_2)\},\delta)]\!]>\}\\ &= \lambda\sigma\cdot\{<\sigma',\mathcal{D}_S[\![s_2]\!](\alpha)(\delta)(p_0)>\}\\ &= \mathcal{D}_S[\![x:=e]\!](\alpha)(\delta)(\mathcal{D}_S[\![s_2]\!](\alpha)(\delta)(p_0))\\ &= \mathcal{D}_S[\![x:=e;s_2]\!](\alpha)(\delta)(p_0)\\ &= \mathcal{D}_{Pr}[\![(\{(\alpha,\ x:=e;s_2)\},\delta)]\!]\end{aligned}$$

(1.4.2) $s_1 =$ **release**(β,t)

$$\begin{aligned}\Gamma(\mathcal{D}_{Pr})((\{(\alpha,\ \textbf{release}(\beta,t);s_2)\},\delta)) &= [\,\text{Definition 3.3}(R2)\,]\\ &\quad\ \Gamma(\mathcal{D}_{Pr}((\{(\alpha,s_2),(\beta,t)\},\delta))\\ &= [\,\text{induction, Case (2) below}\,]\\ &\quad\ \mathcal{D}_{Pr}[\![(\{(\alpha,s_2),\ (\beta,t)\},\delta)]\!]\\ &= \mathcal{D}_S[\![s_2]\!](\alpha)(\delta)(p_0) \,\|\, \mathcal{D}_s[\![t]\!](\beta)(\delta)(p_0)\\ &= \mathcal{D}_S[\![\textbf{release}(\beta,t)]\!](\alpha)(\delta)(\mathcal{D}_S[\![s_2]\!](\alpha)(\delta)(p_0))\\ &= \mathcal{D}_s[\![\textbf{release}(\beta,t);s_2]\!](\alpha)(\delta)(p_0)\\ &= \mathcal{D}_{Pr}[\![(\{(\alpha,\ \textbf{release}(\beta,t);s_2)\},\delta)]\!]\end{aligned}$$

The other subcases of Case (1), $s = s_1 + s_2$ and $s =$ **release**(β,t), are easy.

Case (2): $|X| > 1$
Suppose we have two disjoint sets X_1 and X_2 in $\mathcal{P}_{fin}(\mathcal{L}_{LS})$ with $\neg$ *final*(X_1) and $\neg$ *final*(X_2), and assume that

$$\Gamma(\mathcal{D}_{Pr})((X_1,\delta)) = \mathcal{D}_{Pr}[\![(X_1,\delta)]\!]$$

and

$$\Gamma(\mathcal{D}_{Pr})((X_2,\delta)) = \mathcal{D}_{Pr}[\![(X_2,\delta)]\!].$$

We show that from this induction hypothesis it follows that

$$\Gamma(\mathcal{D}_{Pr})((X_1 \cup X_2,\delta)) = \mathcal{D}_{Pr}[\![(X_1 \cup X_2,\delta)]\!].$$

From the definition of $\rightarrow$ (Definition 3.3) we have

$$\Gamma(\mathcal{D}_{Pr})((X_1 \cup X_2,\delta)) = \lambda\sigma\cdot(V_1 \cup V_2 \cup W).$$

Here

$$\begin{aligned} V_1 = \{&<\sigma',\mathcal{D}_{Pr}[\![(X'_1 \cup X_2,\delta)]\!]>: <X_1,\sigma> \xrightarrow{\tau} <X_1',\sigma'>\} \\ \cup \{&<\beta, m, \mathcal{D}_{Pr}[\![(\{(\alpha,s)\},\delta)]\!], \mathcal{D}_{Pr}[\![(X_1' \cup X_2,\delta)]\!]>: \\ &<X_1,\sigma> \xrightarrow{(\alpha,\beta!m)} <\{(\alpha,s)\} \cup X_1', \sigma>\} \\ \cup\{&<\alpha,g>: <X_1,\sigma> \xrightarrow{\alpha?} <\{(\alpha,s)\} \cup X_1',\sigma>\} \end{aligned}$$

with

$$g = \lambda m\cdot\lambda p\cdot (\mathcal{D}_S[\![\delta(m)]\!](\alpha)(\delta)(p \| \mathcal{D}_{Pr}[\![(\{\alpha,s)\},\delta)]\!]) \| \mathcal{D}_{Pr}[\![(X_1' \cup X_2,\delta)]\!]).$$

The set V_2 is like V_1 but with the roles of X_1 and X_2 interchanged. Finally,

$$\begin{aligned} W = \{&<\sigma,\mathcal{D}_{Pr}[\![(\{(\beta,u)\} \cup X'_1 \cup X_2',\delta)]\!]>: \\ &<X_i,\sigma> \xrightarrow{(\alpha,\beta!m)} <\{(\alpha,s)\} \cup X_i',\sigma> \text{ and} \\ &<X_j,\sigma> \xrightarrow{\beta?} <\{(\beta,t)\} \cup X_j',\sigma>, \\ &\text{for } i=1,\ j=2 \text{ or } i=2,\ j=1\}, \end{aligned}$$

with

$$u = \delta(m);\ \textbf{release}(\alpha,s);\ t.$$

The steps in V_1 correspond to the transition steps that can be made from $X_1 \cup X_2$ stemming from X_1. Similarly for V_2. The set W contains those steps that correspond with a communication transition from $X_1 \cup X_2$ stemming, by an application of rule (R4) of Definition 3.3, from a send step from X_i and an answer step from X_j (for $i=1$, $j=2$ or $i=2$, $j=1$). Now the following holds:

$$\begin{aligned} V_1 &= \Gamma(\mathcal{D}_{Pr})((X_1,\delta))(\sigma) \mathbin{\|\!\!\_} \mathcal{D}_{Pr}[\![(X_2,\delta)]\!] \\ V_2 &= \Gamma(\mathcal{D}_{Pr})((X_2,\delta))(\sigma) \mathbin{\|\!\!\_} \mathcal{D}_{Pr}[\![(X_1,\delta)]\!] \\ W &= \Gamma(\mathcal{D}_{Pr})((X_1,\delta))(\sigma) \mid_\sigma \Gamma(\mathcal{D}_{Pr})((X_2,\delta))(\sigma). \end{aligned}$$

We prove only the first equality, the other two cases being similar:

$$\begin{aligned} V_1 = \{&<\sigma',\mathcal{D}_{Pr}[\![(X_1',\delta)]\!] \| \mathcal{D}_{Pr}[\![(X_2,\delta)]\!]>: <X_1,\sigma> \xrightarrow{\tau} <X_1',\sigma'>\} \\ \cup\{&<\beta, m, \mathcal{D}_{Pr}[\![(\{(\alpha,s)\}, \delta)]\!], \mathcal{D}_{Pr}[\![(X_1',\delta)]\!] \| \mathcal{D}_{Pr}[\![(X_2,\delta)]\!]>: \\ &<X_1,\sigma> \xrightarrow{(\alpha,\beta!m)} <\{(\alpha,s)\} \cup X_1',\sigma>\} \\ \cup\{&<\alpha,g'>: <X_1,\sigma> \xrightarrow{\alpha?} <\{(\alpha,s)\} \cup X_1',\sigma>\} \\ &[\text{with } g' = \lambda m\cdot\lambda p\cdot(\mathcal{D}_S[\![\delta(m)]\!](\alpha)(\delta)(p \| \mathcal{D}_{Pr}[\![(\{(\alpha,s)\},\delta)]\!]) \\ &\| \mathcal{D}_{Pr}[\![(X_1',\delta)]\!] \| \mathcal{D}_{Pr}[\![(X_2,\delta)]\!]] \\ = &\ [\text{according to the definition of } \mathbin{\|\!\!\_} (3.10)] \\ &(\{<\sigma',\mathcal{D}_{Pr}[\![(X_1',\delta)]\!]>: <X_1,\sigma> \xrightarrow{\tau} <X_1',\sigma'>\} \\ &\cup\{<\beta,m,\mathcal{D}_{Pr}[\![\{(\alpha,s)\},\delta)]\!],\mathcal{D}_{Pr}[\![(X_1',\delta)]\!]>: \end{aligned}$$

$$<X_1,\sigma> \xrightarrow{(\alpha,\beta!m)} <\{(\alpha,s)\}\cup X_1',\sigma>\}$$

$$\cup <\alpha,g''>: <X_1,\sigma> \xrightarrow{\alpha?} <\{(\alpha,s)\}\cup X_1',\sigma>\}) \mathbin{\|\!\!\_} \mathcal{D}_{Pr}[\![(X_2,\delta)]\!]$$

$$[\text{ with } g'' = \lambda m\cdot\lambda p\cdot \mathcal{D}[\![\delta(m)]\!](\alpha)(\delta)(p \,\|\, \mathcal{D}_{Pr}[\![(\{(\alpha,s)\},\delta)]\!]) \,\|\, \mathcal{D}_{Pr}[\![(X_1',\delta)]\!] \;]$$

$$= \Gamma(\mathcal{D}_{Pr})((X_1,\delta))(\sigma) \mathbin{\|\!\!\_} \mathcal{D}_{Pr}[\![(X_2,\delta)]\!].$$

From these equalities we deduce:

$$\begin{aligned}
\Gamma(\mathcal{D}_{Pr})((X_1\cup X_2,\delta)) &= \lambda\sigma\cdot(V_1\cup V_2\cup W) \\
&= \lambda\sigma\cdot(\Gamma(\mathcal{D}_{Pr})((X_1,\delta))(\sigma) \mathbin{\|\!\!_} \mathcal{D}_{Pr}[\![(X_2,\delta)]\!] \cup \\
&\qquad \Gamma(\mathcal{D}_{Pr})((X_2,\delta))(\sigma) \mathbin{\|\!\!_} \mathcal{D}_{Pr}[\![(X_1,\delta)]\!] \cup \\
&\qquad \Gamma(\mathcal{D}_{Pr})((X_1,\delta))(\sigma) \mid_\sigma \Gamma(\mathcal{D}_{Pr})((X_2,\delta))(\sigma)) \\
&= [\text{ induction hypothesis}] \\
&\quad \lambda\sigma\cdot(\mathcal{D}_{Pr}((X_1,\delta))(\sigma) \mathbin{\|\!\!_} \mathcal{D}_{Pr}[\![(X_2,\delta)]\!] \cup \\
&\qquad \mathcal{D}_{Pr}((X_2,\delta))(\sigma) \mathbin{\|\!\!_} \mathcal{D}_{Pr}[\![(X_1,\delta)]\!] \cup \\
&\qquad \mathcal{D}_{Pr}((X_1,\delta))(\sigma) \mid_\sigma \mathcal{D}_{Pr}((X_2,\delta))(\sigma)) \\
&= [\text{definition } \| \text{ (3.10)}] \\
&\quad \mathcal{D}_{Pr}(X_1,\delta)]\!] \,\|\, \mathcal{D}_{Pr}[\![(X_2,\delta)]\!] \\
&= \mathcal{D}_{Pr}[\![(X_1\cup X_2,\delta)]\!].
\end{aligned}$$

This concludes the proof of Theorem 3.18.

Since $\mathcal{I}$ and $\mathcal{D}_{Pr}$ are both fixed points of the same contraction Γ, they must be equal:

Corollary 3.19: $\mathcal{I} = \mathcal{D}_{Pr}$

From Corollaries 3.19 and 3.17, stating that $\mathcal{O}_{Pr} = abstr \circ \mathcal{I}$, the following theorem, which implies the correctness of $\mathcal{D}_{Pr}$ with respect to $\mathcal{O}_{Pr}$, is immediate.

Theorem 3.20: $\mathcal{O}_{Pr} = abstr \circ \mathcal{D}_{Pr}$

4. The semantics of POOL

Now we come to the semantic description of POOL, which is a syntactically simplified version of POOL2 that retains all the essential semantic features of the latter. We shall now introduce its abstract syntax and next compare POOL and POOL2 in some detail. We need the following sets of syntactic elements:

$(x \in) IVar$ (instance variables)

$(u \in) TVar$ (temporary variables)

$(C \in) CName$ (class names)

$(m \in) MName$ (method names).

We define the set $(\gamma\in)SObj$ of standard objects by

$$SObj = \mathbb{Z} \cup \{tt, ff\} \cup \{nil\}.$$

($\mathbb{Z}$ is the set of all integers.)

We introduce the sets of POOL expressions (L_E), statements (L_S) and programs (*Unit*).

Definition 4.1 (L_E, L_S, *Unit*)
We define the set $(e\in)L_E$ of expressions:

$$\begin{array}{lll} e & ::= & x \\ & | & u \\ & | & e \;!\; m\,(e_1, \ldots, e_n) \\ & | & m\,(e_1, \ldots, e_n) \\ & | & \mathbf{new}\,(C) \\ & | & e_1 \equiv e_2 \\ & | & s\;;\;e \\ & | & \mathbf{self} \\ & | & \gamma \end{array}$$

The set $(s\in)L_S$ of statements:

$$\begin{array}{llll} s & ::= & x \leftarrow e & \\ & | & u \leftarrow e & \\ & | & \mathbf{answer}\; V & (V \subseteq MName,\; V \neq \varnothing) \\ & | & e & \\ & | & s_1\;;\;s_2 & \\ & | & \mathbf{if}\; e\; \mathbf{then}\; s_1\; \mathbf{else}\; s_2\; \mathbf{fi} & \\ & | & \mathbf{while}\; e\; \mathbf{do}\; s\; \mathbf{od} & \end{array}$$

The set $(U\in)Unit$ of units:

$$U ::= \;< C_1 \Leftarrow d_1, \ldots, C_n \Leftarrow d_n > \qquad (n \geqslant 1).$$

The set $(d\in)ClassDef$ of class definitions:

$$d ::= \;< (\, m_1 \Leftarrow \mu_1, \ldots, m_n \Leftarrow \mu_n \,)\,,\, s >$$

and finally the set $(\mu\in)MethDef$ of method definitions:

$$\mu ::= \;< (\, u_1, \ldots, u_n \,)\,,\, e >, \text{ with } n \geqslant 0.$$

Let us briefly explain the intended meaning of these syntactic constructs. An expression of the form x or u delivers the value (a reference to an object) that is currently stored in the variable of that name. The send expression $e\;!\;m(e_1, \ldots, e_n)$ is evaluated by first evaluating the expressions $e, e_1, \ldots, e_n$ in that order and then sending a (synchronous) message to the object resulting from expression e, mentioning method m and carrying as parameters the values resulting from $e_1, \ldots, e_n$. When the method is executed by the receiver of the message and it returns a result, this result will be the value of the whole send expression. The call expression $m(e_1, \ldots, e_n)$ is evaluated by executing method m without sending a message. The expression **new**(C) indicates the creation of a new object of class C, the body of which will execute in parallel with the other objects from now on. The value of this expression is a reference to this newly created object. The expression $e_1 \equiv e_2$ checks whether the expressions e_1

and e_2 result in a reference to the same object (cf. the routine `id` in section 2). Evaluating the expression s ; e is done by first executing statement s and then evaluating expression e. Finally the expression **self** results in the name of the object that evaluates this expression, and an expression that has the form of a standard object γ represents this standard object itself.

Next we come to the statements. An assignment statement $x \leftarrow e$ or $u \leftarrow e$ is executed by first evaluating expression e and storing the resulting value in the variables x or u, respectively. The answer statement **answer** V indicates that the object is willing to accept one message mentioning a method name contained in the set V. If no such message has yet been sent to this object, it waits until such a message arrives. Then the appropriate method is executed and the result of this method is sent back to the sender. If a statement consists simply of an expression e, then this statement is executed by evaluating expression e and discarding the result (among others, this is useful for sending a message if one is not interested in the result). The meaning of a sequential composition s_1 ; s_2, a conditional **if** e **then** s_1 **else** s_2 **fi**, and a loop **while** e **do** s **od** is as usual.

Next we see that a unit U associates several class names C_i with class definitions d_i. A class definition d associates several method names m_i with method definitions μ_i and it gives the body s to be executed by every instance of the class. A method definition μ gives the names of the temporary variables that will contain the parameters for the method and an expression e that will be evaluated when the method is invoked. The result of this expression will be the result of the method. (Note that quite complicated expressions are possible here, because an expression can have the form s ; e among others.)

The execution of a unit U starts with the implicit creation of one instance of the last class C_n defined in this unit. This so-called *root object* may create others, which can run in parallel with it, and in this way a whole system can be set to work.

It is clear that the abstract syntax given above is a considerably simplified version of the actual syntax of POOL2. In this way the formal semantic treatment is much easier to understand. Nevertheless, all the essential elements of POOL programs are present and therefore there is a quite straightforward translation from POOL2 to this abstract syntax. This translation comprises the following steps:

- All the units of the POOL2 program are merged into one unit. Clashes between class identifiers can be removed by renaming the appropriate classes.
- Generic class definitions are expanded so that there is a separate class definition for each set of class parameters that was used for the generic class in the original program.
- Each routine definition is replaced by a corresponding method definition in every class that calls the routine. Now every call of such a routine can be replaced by a method call. Calls of the standard routines `new` and `id` are replaced by expressions of the form **new**(C) and $e_1 \equiv e_2$, respectively.
- If there is only one global name, and this is not used in the rest of the program, this becomes the new root object.
- All the typing information is discarded. This is of no consequence, since we can assume that the original POOL2 program was correct with respect to typing.

For more complicated (and less frequently used) constructs in POOL2, such as asynchronous communication, routines treated as objects, and multiple globals, it is also possible to find an equivalent in our simplified language POOL above. More details on this can be found in America (1988b).

4.1 An operational semantics for POOL

In this section we give the definition of an operational semantics for POOL, which is a modified version of that given in America *et al* (1986a). It is very similar to the operational semantics of the language $\mathcal{L}$ of the previous section, and is again based on a transition system. First, we introduce a number of syntactic and semantic concepts.

Definition 4.2 (Objects)
We assume a set $AObj$ of names for active objects together with a function

$$T: AObj \rightarrow CName,$$

which assigns to each object $\alpha \in AObj$ the class to which it belongs. Furthermore, we assume a function

$$\nu: \mathcal{P}_{fin}(AObj) \times CName \rightarrow AObj,$$

such that $\nu(X,C) \notin X$ and $T(\nu(X,C))=C$, for finite $X \subseteq AObj$ and $C \in CName$. The function ν gives for a finite set X of object names and a class name C a new name of class C, not in X. (A possible example of such a set $AObj$ and functions T and ν could be obtained by setting:

$$AObj = CName \times \mathbb{N},$$

$$T(<C,n>) = C, \text{ and}$$

$$\nu(X,C) = <C, \max\{n: <C,n> \in X\}+1>.)$$

The set $AObj$ and the set of standard objects $SObj$ together form the set Obj of *object names,* with typical elements α and β:

$$\begin{aligned} Obj &= AObj \cup SObj \\ &= AObj \cup \mathbb{Z} \cup \{tt, ff\} \cup \{nil\}. \end{aligned}$$

Next, it is convenient to extend the sets L_E of expressions and L_S of statements by adding some auxiliary syntactic constructs.

Definition 4.3 ($L_{E'}$, $L_{S'}$)
Let $(e \in) L_{E'}$ and $(s \in) L_{S'}$ be defined by

$$\begin{aligned} e \quad ::= \quad & x \\ | \quad & u \\ | \quad & e \,!\, m\,(e_1, \ldots, e_n) \\ | \quad & m\,(e_1, \ldots, e_n) \\ | \quad & \mathbf{new}\,(C) \\ | \quad & e_1 \equiv e_2 \\ | \quad & s\,;\,e \\ | \quad & \mathbf{self} \\ | \quad & \gamma \\ | \quad & \alpha \\ | \quad & (e, \phi) \end{aligned}$$

The set $(s \in) L_{S'}$ of statements:

$$s \quad ::= \quad x \leftarrow e$$

| $u \leftarrow e$
| **answer** $V \quad (V \subseteq MName,\ V \neq \varnothing)$
| e
| $s_1\ ;\ s_2$
| **if** e **then** s_1 **else** s_2 **fi**
| **while** e **do** s **od**
| **release**$(\alpha,\ s)$
| (e, ψ)

with $\alpha \in AObj$, $\gamma \in SObj$, $\phi \in L_{PE}$, and $\psi \in L_{PS}$. Here the sets of *parameterized expressions* $(\phi \in) L_{PE}$ and *parameterized statements* $(\psi \in) L_{PS}$ are given, taking $e \in L_{E'}$ and $s \in L_{S'}$, by

$$\phi ::= \lambda u \cdot e$$

$$\psi ::= \lambda u \cdot s,$$

with the restriction that u does not occur at the left-hand side of an assignment in e or s. For $\alpha \in Obj$, $\phi = \lambda u \cdot e$, and $\psi = \lambda u \cdot s$ we shall use $\phi(\alpha)$ and $\psi(\alpha)$ to denote the expression and the statement obtained by syntactically substituting α for all free occurrences of u in ϕ and ψ, respectively. The restriction mentioned above ensures that the result of this substitution is again a well-formed expression or statement.

Let us explain the new syntactic constructs. In addition to what we already had in L_E, an expression $e \in L_{E'}$ can be an *active* object α or a pair (e, ϕ) of an expression e and a parameterized expression ϕ. The latter will be executed as follows. First, the expression e is evaluated, then the result β is substituted in ϕ and $\phi(\beta)$ is executed. As new statements we have release statements **release**(β,s) and parameterized statements (e,ψ). If the statement **release**(β,s) is executed, the active object β will start executing the statement s (in parallel to the objects that are already executing). The release statement plays a similar role as in section 3; it will be used in the description of the communication between two objects (see Definition 4.9(R11) below). The interpretation of (e,ψ) is similar to that of (e,ϕ).

Definition 4.4 (Empty statement)
The set $L_{S'}$, as given in the definition above, is extended with a special element E, denoting the *empty statement*. This extended set is again called $L_{S'}$. Note that we do *not* have elements like $s;E$ or **while** e **do** E **od** in $L_{S'}$. (There is, however, one exception: We *do* allow E in **if** e **then** s **else** E **fi**, which is needed in Definition 4.9 below.)

Definition 4.5 (States)
The set of states $(\sigma \in) \Sigma$ is defined by

$$\begin{aligned}\Sigma = & (AObj \rightarrow IVar \rightarrow Obj) \\ & \times (AObj \rightarrow TVar \rightarrow Obj) \\ & \times \mathcal{P}_{fin}(AObj).\end{aligned}$$

The three components of σ are denoted by $<\sigma_1,\ \sigma_2,\ \sigma_3>$. The first and second component of a state store the values of the instance variables and the temporary variables of each active object. The third component contains the object names currently in use. We need it in order to give unique names to newly created objects.

We shall use the following variant notation. By $\sigma\{\beta/\alpha, x\}$ (with $x \in IVar$) we shall denote the state σ' that is as σ but for the value of $\sigma_1'(\alpha)(x)$, which is β. Similarly, we denote by $\sigma\{\beta/\alpha, u\}$ (with $u \in TVar$) the state σ' that is as σ but for the value of $\sigma_2'(\alpha)(u)$, which is β.

Definition 4.6 (Labelled statements)
The set of *labelled statements* $((\alpha, s) \in) LStat$ is given by

$$LStat = (AObj \times L_{S'}) \cup \{S_t\}.$$

A labelled statement (α, s) should be interpreted as a statement s which is going to be executed by the active object α. The statement S_t will be used to model the operational behavior of standard objects.

Sometimes we also need labelled parameterized statements. Therefore, we extend *LStat*:

$$LStat' = LStat \cup (AObj \times L_{PS}).$$

A pair (α, ψ) indicates that the active object α will execute the statement ψ as soon as it receives a value which it can supply to ψ as an argument.

We call a set of labelled statements *final* (notation *final*(X)) if

$$X \subset (AObj \times \{E\}) \cup S_t.$$

Before we can give the definition of a transition system for POOL, we first have to explain which *configurations* and *transition labels* we are going to use.

Definition 4.7 (Configurations)
The set of configurations $(\rho \in) Conf$ is given by

$$Conf = \mathcal{P}_{fin}(LStat) \times \Sigma.$$

We also introduce:

$$Conf' = \mathcal{P}_{fin}(LStat') \times \Sigma.$$

Typical elements of *Conf* and *Conf'* will also be indicated by $<X,\sigma>$ and $<Y,\sigma>$.

We shall consider only configurations $<X,\sigma>$ that are *consistent* in the following sense. For $X = \{(\alpha_1, s_1), \ldots, (\alpha_k, s_k)\}$, we call $<X,\sigma>$ consistent if the following conditions are satisfied:

$$\forall i,j \in \{1, \ldots, k\}\ [i \neq j \Rightarrow \alpha_i \neq \alpha_j], \text{ and}$$

$$\{\alpha_1, \ldots, \alpha_k\} \subseteq \sigma_3.$$

Whenever we introduce a configuration $<X, \sigma>$, it will be tacitly assumed that it is consistent.

A configuration $<X, \sigma>$, consisting of a finite set X of labelled statements and a state σ, represents a "snapshot" of the execution of a POOL program. It shows what objects are active and what statements they are executing. Furthermore, it contains a state σ, in which the values of the variables of the active objects as well as the set of object names currently in use are stored.

Definition 4.8 (Transition labels)
The set of *transition labels* $(\lambda\in)\Lambda$ is given by

$$\Lambda = \{\tau\} \cup \{(\alpha,\ \beta_1!m(\beta_2)):\ \alpha,\beta_1\in AObj,\ \beta_2\in Obj\} \cup \{(\beta?V):\ \beta\in AObj\}.$$

These labels will be used in the definition of the transition relation below and are to be interpreted as follows. The label τ indicates a so-called *computation* step. Next, $(\alpha,\ \beta_1!m(\beta_2))$ indicates that object α sends a message to object β_1 requesting the execution of the method m with parameter β_2. (We shall only consider send expressions with one parameter expression.) Finally, $(\beta?V)$ indicates that object β is willing to answer a message specifying one of the methods in V.

Now we are ready to define a transition system for POOL (cf. Definition 3.3).

Definition 4.9 (Transition relation for POOL)
Let $U\in Unit$ be fixed. We define a *labelled transition system* $<Conf,\Lambda,\rightarrow>$, consisting of a set $Conf$ of configurations, a set Λ of labels, and a *transition relation*

$$\rightarrow\ \subseteq Conf \times\Lambda\times Conf.$$

Triples $<\rho_1,\ \lambda,\ \rho_2>\in\rightarrow$ will be called *transitions* and are denoted by

$$\rho_1 \xrightarrow{\lambda} \rho_2.$$

The relation $\rightarrow$ is defined as the smallest relation satisfying the following properties:

Axioms

(A1) $<\{(\alpha,\ (x,\ \psi))\},\ \sigma> \xrightarrow{\tau} <\{(\alpha,\ (\sigma_1(\alpha)(x),\ \psi))\},\ \sigma>$

(A2) $<\{(\alpha,\ (u,\ \psi))\},\ \sigma> \xrightarrow{\tau} <\{(\alpha,\ (\sigma_2(\alpha)(u),\ \psi))\},\ \sigma>$

(A3) $<\{(\alpha,\ (\beta_1!m(\beta_2),\ \psi)\},\ \sigma> \xrightarrow{(\alpha,\ \beta_1!m(\beta_2))} <\{(\alpha,\ \psi)\},\ \sigma>$

(A4) $<\{(\alpha,\ (\mathbf{new}\ (C),\ \psi))\},\ \sigma> \xrightarrow{\tau} <\{(\alpha,\ (\beta,\ \psi)),\ (\beta,\ s_C)\},\ \sigma'>$, where:
$C\Leftarrow<\ldots,\ s_C>\in U,\ \beta=\nu(\sigma_3,C),\ \sigma'=<\sigma_1,\ \sigma_2,\ \sigma_3\cup\{\beta\}>.$

(A5) $<\{(\alpha,z\leftarrow\beta)\},\sigma> \xrightarrow{\tau} <\{(\alpha,E)\},\sigma\{\beta/\alpha,z\}>$, for $z\in IVar\cup TVar$.

(A6) $<\{(\alpha,\ \mathbf{answer}\ V)\},\ \sigma> \xrightarrow{(\alpha?V)} <\{(\alpha,E)\},\sigma>$

(A7) $<\{(\alpha,\ \mathbf{while}\ e\ \mathbf{do}\ s\ \mathbf{od}\ )\},\sigma> \xrightarrow{\tau}$
$<\{(\alpha,\ \mathbf{if}\ e\ \mathbf{then}\ (s;\ \mathbf{while}\ e\ \mathbf{do}\ s\ \mathbf{od}\ )\ \mathbf{else}\ E\ \mathbf{fi}\ )\},\sigma>$

Rules

(R1) If $<\{(\alpha,\ (e,\lambda u\cdot z\leftarrow u))\},\sigma> \xrightarrow{\lambda} \rho$,
then $<\{(\alpha,\ z\leftarrow e)\},\sigma> \xrightarrow{\lambda} \rho$, for $z\in IVar\cup TVar$, and $u\neq z$.

(R2) If $<\{(\alpha,\ s)\},\sigma> \xrightarrow{\lambda} <\{(\alpha,\ s')\}\cup X,\sigma'>$,
then $<\{(\alpha,\ s\,;t)\},\sigma> \xrightarrow{\lambda} <\{(\alpha,\ s';t)\}\cup X,\sigma'>$
(read t instead of $s';t$ if $s'=E$).
If $<\{(\alpha,\ s)\},\sigma> \xrightarrow{\lambda} <\{(\alpha,\ \psi)\}\cup X,\sigma'>$,

then $<\{(\alpha,\ s\,;t)\},\sigma> \xrightarrow{\lambda} <\{(\alpha,\ \lambda u\cdot(\psi(u);t))\}\cup X,\sigma'>$.

Here u should not occur in ψ and t (we call u fresh).

(R3) If $<\{(\alpha,\ s_i)\},\sigma> \xrightarrow{\lambda} \rho$, then $<\{(\alpha,\ \textbf{if}\ \beta\ \textbf{then}\ s_1\ \textbf{else}\ s_2\ \textbf{fi}\ )\},\sigma> \xrightarrow{\lambda} \rho$,

where $s_i = \begin{cases} s_1 & if\ \beta = tt \\ s_2 & if\ \beta = ff. \end{cases}$

(R4) If $<\{(\alpha,\ t),(\beta,s)\},\sigma> \xrightarrow{\lambda} \rho$, then $<\{(\alpha,\ \textbf{release}\ (\beta,s);t)\},\sigma> \xrightarrow{\lambda} \rho$

(read **release**(β,s) instead of **release**$(\beta,s);t$ if $t=E$).

(R5) If $<\{(\alpha,\ (e,\lambda u\cdot\textbf{if}\ u\ \textbf{then}\ s_1\ \textbf{else}\ s_2\textbf{fi}\ ))\},\sigma> \xrightarrow{\lambda} \rho$,

then $<\{(\alpha,\ \textbf{if}\ e\ \textbf{then}\ s_1\ \textbf{else}\ s_2\ \textbf{fi}\ )\},\sigma> \xrightarrow{\lambda} \rho$ with u fresh.

(Here s_2 is allowed to be E.)

(R6) If $<\{(\alpha,\ ((e_1,\lambda u_1\cdot(e_2,\lambda u_2\cdot u_1!m(u_2))),\psi))\},\sigma> \xrightarrow{\lambda} \rho$,

then $<\{(\alpha,\ (e_1!m(e_2),\psi))\},\sigma> \xrightarrow{\lambda} \rho$, with u_1 and u_2 fresh and $u_1 \neq u_2$.

(R7) If $<\{(\alpha,\ s\,;(e,\psi))\},\sigma> \xrightarrow{\lambda} \rho$, then $<\{(\alpha,\ (s\,;e,\psi))\},\sigma> \xrightarrow{\lambda} \rho$.

(R8) If $<\{(\alpha,\ (e,\lambda u\cdot(\phi(u),\psi)))\},\sigma> \xrightarrow{\lambda} \rho$, then $<\{(\alpha,\ ((e,\phi),\psi))\},\sigma> \xrightarrow{\lambda} \rho$,

with u fresh.

(R9) If $<\{(\alpha,\ \psi(\beta))\},\sigma> \xrightarrow{\lambda} \rho$, then $<\{(\alpha,\ (\beta,\psi))\},\sigma> \xrightarrow{\lambda} \rho$, for $\beta \in Obj$.

If $<\{(\alpha,\ \psi(\alpha))\},\sigma> \xrightarrow{\lambda} \rho$, then $<\{(\alpha,\ (\textbf{self},\psi))\},\sigma> \xrightarrow{\lambda} \rho$.

(R10) If $<X,\sigma> \xrightarrow{\lambda} <X',\sigma'>$, then $<X\cup Y,\sigma> \xrightarrow{\lambda} <X'\cup Y,\sigma'>$.

(R11) If $<X,\sigma> \xrightarrow{(\alpha,\ \beta_1!m(\beta_2))} <\{(\alpha,\ \psi)\}\cup X',\sigma>$ and

$<Y,\sigma> \xrightarrow{\beta_1?V} <\{(\beta_1,s)\}\cup Y',\sigma>$, and if $m \in V$

then $<X\cup Y,\sigma> \xrightarrow{\tau}$

$<\{(\beta_1,(e_m,\lambda u\cdot(u_m \leftarrow \sigma_2(\beta_1)(u_m);\ \textbf{release}(\alpha,\ \psi(u));s)))\}\cup X'\cup Y',\sigma'>$,

where

$T(\beta_1) = C$

$C \Leftarrow <\ldots,\ m \Leftarrow \mu,\ \ldots> \in U$

$\mu\ =\ <(u_m),\ e_m>$

$\sigma' = \sigma\{\beta_2/\beta_1,u_m\}$.

Transitions for standard objects. The following transitions are possible from S_t:

$<\{S_t\},\ \sigma> - n?\{\texttt{add},\ \texttt{sub}\} \rightarrow <\{S_t\},\ \sigma>$

$<\{S_t\},\ \sigma> - b?\{\texttt{and},\ \texttt{or},\ \texttt{not}\} \rightarrow <\{S_t\},\ \sigma>$

for every $n \in \mathbb{Z}$ and $b \in \{tt,\ ff\}$. (This list can be extended with transitions for other operations.) Communication with a standard object is now modelled by the following transitions:

If $<\{(\alpha,s)\},\ \sigma> \xrightarrow{\alpha}) <\{(\alpha,\psi)\},\ \sigma>$

then $<\{(\alpha,s),\ S_t\},\ \sigma> \xrightarrow{\tau} <\{(\alpha,\ \psi(n+m)),\ S_t\},\ \sigma>$.

If $<\{(\alpha,s)\},\ \sigma> \xrightarrow{(\alpha,\ b_1!\mathsf{and}(b_2))} <\{(\alpha,\psi)\},\ \sigma>$

then $<\{(\alpha,s),\ S_t\},\ \sigma> \xrightarrow{\tau} <\{(\alpha,\psi(b_1 \wedge b_2)),\ S_t\},\ \sigma>$,

and by similar transitions for the other operations. (End of definition.)

Note that we have omitted the axioms and rules for some syntactic constructs (e.g., the method call). Moreover, we have made some simplifications; for example, we assume that a send expression contains only one parameter expression. However, we have omitted only what is either straightforward or similar to a clause that we *have* included in the definition above.

The general scheme for the evaluation of an expression closely resembles the approach taken in America and De Bakker (1988). Expressions always occur in the context of a (possibly parameterized) statement (for example, $x \leftarrow e$). A statement containing e as a subexpression is transformed into a pair (e,ψ) of the expression e and a parameterized statement ψ by application of one of the rules. (In our example, $x \leftarrow e$ becomes $(e,\ \lambda u \cdot x \leftarrow u)$ by an application of (R1).) Then e is evaluated, using the axioms and rules, and results in some value $\beta' \in Obj$. (In our example, $(x,\ \lambda u \cdot x \leftarrow u)$ will eventually yield $(\beta',\ \lambda u \cdot x \leftarrow u)$, for some $\beta' \in Obj$.) Next, an application of (R9) will put the resulting object β' back into the original context ψ (yielding $x \leftarrow \beta'$ in our example). Finally, the statement $\psi(\beta')$ is further evaluated by using the axioms and the rules. (The evaluation of $x \leftarrow \beta'$ results, by using (A6), in a transformation of the state.)

Let us briefly explain some of the axioms and rules above. In (A4) a new object is created. Its name β is obtained by applying the function ν to the set σ_3 of the active object names currently in use and the class name C, and is delivered as the result of the evaluation of **new**(C). The body s_C of class C, defined in the unit U, is going to be evaluated by β. Note that the state σ is changed by extending σ_3 with β.

In (R8), the evaluation of an expression pair (e,ϕ), where ϕ is a parameterized expression, in the context of a parameterized statement ψ is reduced to the evaluation of the expression e in the context of the adapted parameterized statement $\lambda u \cdot (\phi(u),\psi)$.

(R11) describes the communication rendezvous of POOL. If object α is sending a message to object β_1, requesting the execution of method m and if object β_1 is willing to answer such a message, then the following happens. Object β_1 starts executing the expression e_m, which corresponds to the definition of method m in U, while its state $\sigma_2(\beta_1)$ is changed by setting u_m, the formal parameter belonging to m, to β_2, the parameter sent by object α to β_1. After the execution of e_m, object β_1 continues by executing $u_m \leftarrow \sigma_2(\beta_1)(u_m)$, which restores the old value of u_m, followed by the statement **release**$(\alpha,\psi(u))$;s. The execution of **release**$(\alpha,\psi(u))$ will reactivate object α, which starts executing $\psi(u)$, the statement obtained by substituting the result u of the execution of e_m into ψ. Note that during the execution of e_m object α is non-active, as can be seen from the fact that α does not occur as the name of any labelled statement in the configuration resulting from this transition. Finally, object β_1 proceeds with the execution of the statement s which is the remainder of its body.

Now we are ready for the definition of the operational semantics of POOL. It will use the following semantic universe.

Definition 4.10 (Semantic universe P)
Let $(w\in)\Sigma_\partial^\infty=\Sigma^*\cup\Sigma^\omega\cup\Sigma^*\cdot\{\partial\}$, the set of *streams*, with Σ as in Definition 4.5. We define

$$(p,q\in)P=\Sigma\rightarrow\mathcal{P}(\Sigma_\partial^\infty)\ ,$$

where $\mathcal{P}(\Sigma_\partial^\infty)$ is the set of all subsets of Σ_∂^∞, and the symbol ∂ denotes deadlock. (The universe P is the same as that given in Definition 3.4 but for the use of a different set of states.)

Next, we introduce the operational semantics for POOL (cf. Definition 3.5).

Definition 4.11 (Operational semantics for POOL)
Let, for a $U\in Unit$, the function

$$\mathcal{O}_U\colon\ \mathcal{P}_{fin}(LStat)\rightarrow P$$

be given as follows. Let $X\in\mathcal{P}_{fin}(LStat)$ and $\sigma\in\Sigma$. We put for a word $w\in\Sigma_\partial^\infty$:

$$w\in\mathcal{O}_U[\![X]\!](\sigma)$$

if and only if one of the following conditions is satisfied:

(1) $w=\sigma_0\cdots\sigma_n$ $(n\geqslant 0)$ and there exist $X_0,\ldots,X_n$ such that $<X_0,\sigma_0>=<X,\sigma>$ and

$$<X,\sigma>\xrightarrow{T}<X_1,\sigma_1>\xrightarrow{T}\cdots\xrightarrow{T}<X_n,\sigma_n>\ \text{and}\ final(X_n)$$

(2) $w=\sigma_0\sigma_1\cdots$ and there exist $X_0,X_1,\ldots$ such that $<X_0,\sigma_0>=<X,\sigma>$ and

$$<X_0,\sigma_0>\xrightarrow{T}<X_1,\sigma_1>\xrightarrow{T}<X_2,\sigma_2>\xrightarrow{T}\cdots$$

(3) $w=\sigma_0\cdots\sigma_n\cdot\partial$ $(n\geqslant 0)$ and there exist $X_0,\ldots,X_n$ such that $<X_0,\sigma_0>=<X,\sigma>$ and

$$<X,\sigma>\xrightarrow{T}<X_1,\sigma_1>\xrightarrow{T}\cdots\xrightarrow{T}<X_n,\sigma_n>$$

$$\text{and}\ \neg final(X_n)\ \text{and}\ \neg<X_n,\sigma_n>\xrightarrow{T}$$

Finally, we can give the operational semantics of a unit.

Definition 4.12 (Operational semantics of a unit)
Let $[\![\ \cdots\ ]\!]_{\mathcal{O}}\colon Unit\rightarrow P$ be given, for a unit $U=<\ldots,C_n\Leftarrow<\ldots s_n>>$, by

$$[\![U]\!]_{\mathcal{O}}=\mathcal{O}_U[\![\{(\nu(\varnothing,C_n),s_n),\ S_t\}]\!].$$

The execution of the unit U consists of the creation of an object of class C_n and the execution of its body in parallel with the statement S_t, which represents the activity of the standard objects. The name of the new object is given by $\nu(\varnothing,C_n)$.

4.2 A denotational semantics for POOL

We start with the definition of the universe for the denotational semantics, which we shall again call $\bar{P}$ and which will be again a solution of a reflexive domain equation.

Definition 4.13 (Semantic process domain $\bar{P}$)
Let $(p,q\in)\bar{P}$ be a complete ultra-metric space satisfying the following reflexive domain equation:

$$\bar{P} \cong \{p_0\} \cup id_{1/2}(\Sigma \to \mathcal{P}_{compact}(Step_{\bar{P}})),$$

where $(\pi,\rho\in)Step_{\bar{P}}$ is

$$Step_{\bar{P}} = Comp_{\bar{P}} \cup Send_{\bar{P}} \cup Answer_{\bar{P}},$$

with

$$Comp_{\bar{P}} = \Sigma \times \bar{P},$$

$$Send_{\bar{P}} = Obj \times MName \times Obj \times (Obj \to \bar{P}) \times \bar{P},$$

$$Answer_{\bar{P}} = Obj \times MName \times (Obj \to (Obj \to \bar{P}) \to^1 \bar{P}).$$

The interpretation of the domain $\bar{P}$ is almost the same as that of the domain $\bar{P}$ defined in the previous section (Definition 3.9). There are some differences, however, which concern the definition of the set of send and answer steps.

To begin with, the set *SLabel* of statement labels has been replaced by the set *Obj* of object names. Since we have value passing in the communication rendezvous of POOL, a send step consists of an additional component (the third in the definition above), which is used for the parameter that is specified in the send message. The dependent resumption of a send step (the fourth component) is now a function from *Obj* to $\bar{P}$, because it depends on the result of the execution of the requested method, which is returned to the sender after this execution is finished.

An answer step $<\alpha, m, g>$ now expresses that object α is willing to answer any message that specifies method m. The type of the resumption g of this answer step is somewhat different from that in Definition 3.9: It takes as arguments first, the parameter that is specified in the message and second, the dependent resumption of the sender (which here is a function).

Because of these differences, the definition of the operator for parallel composition is a slight variant of that given in Definition 3.10.

Definition 4.14 (Parallel composition)
Let $\| : \bar{P} \times \bar{P} \to \bar{P}$ be such that it satisfies the following equation:

$$p \| q = \lambda\sigma \cdot ((p(\sigma) \mathbin{\|\!\_} q) \cup (q(\sigma) \mathbin{\|\!\_} p) \cup (p(\sigma) \mid_\sigma q(\sigma))),$$

for all $p,q \in \bar{P} \setminus \{p_0\}$, and such that $p_0 \| q = q \| p_0 = p_0$. Here, $X \mathbin{\|\!\_} q$ and $X \mid_\sigma Y$ are defined by:

$$X \mathbin{\|\!\_} q = \{\pi \hat{\|} q : \pi \in X\},$$

$$X \mid_\sigma Y = \bigcup \{\pi \mid_\sigma \rho : \pi \in X, \rho \in Y\},$$

where $\pi \hat{\|} q$ is given by

$$<\sigma', p'> \hat{\|} q = <\sigma', p' \| q>,$$

$$<\alpha, m, \beta, f, p> \hat{\|} q = <\alpha, m, \beta, f, p \| q>, \text{ and}$$

$$<\alpha, m, g> \hat{\|} q = <\alpha, m, \lambda\beta \cdot \lambda h \cdot (g(\beta)(h) \| q)>,$$

and $\pi |_\sigma \rho$ by

$$\pi|_\sigma\rho = \begin{cases} \{<\sigma,\ g(\beta)(f)\|p>\} & \text{if } \pi=<\alpha,m,\beta,f,p> \text{ and } \rho=<\alpha,m,g> \\ & \text{or } \rho=<\alpha,m,\beta,f,p> \text{ and } \pi=<\alpha,m,g> \\ \emptyset & \text{otherwise.} \end{cases}$$

Now we come to the definition of the semantics of expressions and statements. We specify a pair of functions $<\mathfrak{D}_E,\mathfrak{D}_S>$ of the following type:

$$\mathfrak{D}_E\colon L_E \to AObj \to Cont_E \to^1 \overline{P},$$

$$\mathfrak{D}_S\colon L_S \to AObj \to Cont_S \to^1 \overline{P}$$

where $Cont_E = Obj \to \overline{P}$ and $Cont_S = \overline{P}$. The semantic value of an expression $e \in L_E$, for an object α and an expression continuation $f \in Cont_E$, is given by

$$\mathfrak{D}_E[\![e]\!](\alpha)(f).$$

The evaluation of an expression e always results in a value (an element of Obj) upon which the continuation of such an expression generally depends. The function f, when applied to the result β of e, will yield a process $f(\beta) \in P$ that is to be executed after the evaluation of e.

Definition 4.15 (Semantics of expressions and statements)
Let

$$Q_E = L_E \to AObj \to Cont_E \to^1 \overline{P}$$

$$Q_S = L_S \to AObj \to Cont_S \to^1 \overline{P}.$$

For every unit $U \in Unit$ we define a pair of functions $\mathfrak{D}_U = <\mathfrak{D}_E,\ \mathfrak{D}_S>$ by

$$\mathfrak{D}_U = \text{Fixed Point } (\Psi_U),$$

where

$$\Psi_U\colon (Q_E \times Q_S) \to (Q_E \times Q_S)$$

is defined by induction on the structure of L_E and L_S by the following clauses. For $F=<F_E,\ F_S>$ we denote $\Psi_U(F)$ by $\hat{F}=<\hat{F}_E,\ \hat{F}_S>$. Let $p \in Cont_S = \overline{P}$, $f \in Cont_E = Obj \to \overline{P}$ and $\alpha \in AObj$. Then:

Expressions

(E1, instance variable)

$$\hat{F}_E(x)(\alpha)(f) = \lambda\sigma \cdot \{<\sigma, f(\sigma_1(\alpha)(x))>\}.$$

The value of the instance variable x is searched in the first component of the state σ supplied with the name α of the object that is evaluating the expression. The continuation f is then applied to the resulting value.

(E2, temporary variable)

$$\hat{F}_E(u)(\alpha)(f) = \lambda\sigma \cdot \{<\sigma, f(\sigma_2(\alpha)(u))>\}$$

(E3, send expression)

$$\hat{F}_E(e_1!m(e_2))(\alpha)(f) = \hat{F}_E(e_1)(\alpha)(\lambda\beta_1 \cdot \hat{F}_E(e_2)(\alpha)(\lambda\beta_2 \cdot \lambda\sigma \cdot \{<\beta_1, m, \beta_2, f, p_0>\})).$$

The expressions e_1 and e_2 are evaluated successively. Their results correspond to the formal parameters β_1 and β_2 of their respective continuations. Finally, a send step is performed. The object name β_1 refers to the object to which the message is sent; β_2 represents the parameter for the execution of method m. Besides these values and the method name m, the final step $<\beta_1, m, \beta_2, f, p_0>$ also contains the expression continuation f of the send expression as the dependent resumption. If the attempt at communication succeeds, this continuation will be supplied with the result of the method execution. The independent resumption of this send step is initialized to p_0.

(E4, new-expression)

$$\hat{F}_E(\textbf{ new } (C))(\alpha)(f) = \lambda\sigma\cdot\{<\sigma', f(\beta) \| F_S(s_C)(\beta)(p_0)>\},$$

where

$$\beta = \nu(\sigma_3, C),$$

$$\sigma' = <\sigma_1, \sigma_2, \sigma_3 \cup \{\beta\}>, \quad C \Leftarrow <\ldots, s_C> \in U.$$

A new object of class C is created. It is called $\nu(\sigma_3, C)$: the function ν applied to the set of all object names currently in use and the class name C yields a name that is not yet being used. The state σ is changed by expanding the set σ_3 with the new name β. The process $F_S(s_C)(\beta)(p_0)$ is the meaning of the body of the new object β with p_0 as a nil continuation. It is composed in parallel with $f(\beta)$, the process resulting from the application of the continuation f to β, the result of the evaluation of this new-expression. We are able to perform this parallel composition because we know from f what should happen after the evaluation of this new-expression, so here the use of continuations is essential.

(E5, sequential composition)

$$\hat{F}_E(s\,;e)(\alpha)(f) = \hat{F}_S(s)(\alpha)(\hat{F}_E(e)(\alpha)(f)).$$

The continuation of s is the execution of e followed by f. Note that a semantic operator for sequential composition is absent: the use of continuations has made it superfluous.

(E6, **self**)

$$\hat{F}_E(\textbf{ self })(\alpha)(f) = f(\alpha).$$

The continuation of f is supplied with the value of the expression **self**, that is, the name of the object executing this expression. We use $f(\alpha)$ instead of $\lambda\beta\cdot\{<\sigma, f(\alpha)>\}$ in this definition because we wish to express that the value of self is immediately present: it does not take a step to evaluate it.

(E7, objects)

$$\hat{F}_E(\beta)(\alpha)(f) = f(\beta), \quad \text{for } \beta \in Obj.$$

(E8, parameterized expression)

$$\hat{F}_E((e, \phi))(\alpha)(f) = \hat{F}_E(e)(\alpha)(\lambda\beta\cdot \hat{F}_E(\phi(\beta))(\alpha)(f))$$

The expression e is evaluated and the result will be passed through to the continuation, which consists of the meaning of the parameterized expression ϕ.

Statements

(S1, assignment to an instance variable)

$$\hat{F}_S(x \leftarrow e)(\alpha)(p) = \hat{F}_E(e)(\alpha)(\lambda\beta\cdot\lambda\sigma\cdot\{<\sigma', p>\}),$$

where $\sigma' = \sigma\{\beta/\alpha, x\}$. The expression e is evaluated and the result β is assigned to x.

(S2, assignment to a temporary variable)

$$\hat{F}_S(u \leftarrow e)(\alpha)(p) = \hat{F}_E(e)(\alpha)(\lambda\beta\cdot\lambda\sigma\cdot\{<\sigma', p>\}),$$

where $\sigma' = \sigma\{\beta/\alpha, u\}$.

(S3, answer statement)

$$\hat{F}_S(\textbf{ answer } V)(\alpha)(p) = \lambda\sigma\cdot\{<\alpha, m, g_m>: m \in V\},$$

where

$$g_m = \lambda\beta\cdot\lambda f\cdot\lambda\sigma\cdot\{<\sigma', F_E(e_m)(\alpha)(\lambda\beta'\cdot\lambda\bar{\sigma}\cdot\{<\bar{\sigma}', f(\beta')\| p>\})>\},$$

with

$$\sigma' = \sigma\{\beta/\alpha, u_m\},$$

$$\bar{\sigma}' = \bar{\sigma}\{\sigma_2(\alpha)(u_m)/\alpha, u_m\},$$

$$m \Leftarrow <(u_m), e_m> \in U.$$

The function g_m represents the execution of method m followed by its continuation. This function g_m expects a parameter β and an expression continuation f, both to be received from an object sending a message specifying method m. The execution of method m consists of the evaluation of the expression e_m, which is used in the definition of m, preceded by a state transformation in which the temporary variable u_m is initialized at the value β. After the execution of e, this temporary variable is set back to its old value. Next, both the continuation of the sending object, supplied with the result β' of the execution of the method m, and the given continuation p are to be executed in parallel. This explains the last resumption: $f(\beta')\|p$.

(S4, sequential composition)

$$\hat{F}_S(s_1; s_2)(\alpha)(p) = \hat{F}_S(s_1)(\alpha)(\hat{F}_S(s_2)(\alpha)(p)).$$

(S5, conditional)

$$\begin{aligned}
&\hat{F}_S(\textbf{ if } e \textbf{ then } s_1 \textbf{ else } s_2 \textbf{ fi })(\alpha)(p) = \\
&\quad \hat{F}_E(e)(\alpha)(\lambda\beta\cdot \text{ if } \beta = tt \\
&\qquad\qquad \text{then } \hat{F}_S(s_1)(\alpha)(p) \\
&\qquad\qquad \text{else } \hat{F}_S(s_2)(\alpha)(p) \\
&\qquad\qquad \text{fi }).
\end{aligned}$$

(S6, loop statement)

$$\begin{aligned}
&\hat{F}_S(\textbf{ while } e \textbf{ do } s \textbf{ od })(\alpha)(p) = \\
&\quad \lambda\sigma\cdot\{<\sigma,\ \hat{F}_E(e)(\alpha)(\lambda\beta \cdot \text{ if } \beta = tt \\
&\qquad\qquad \text{then } \hat{F}_S(s)(\alpha)(F_S(\textbf{ while } e \textbf{ do } s \textbf{ od })(\alpha)(p)) \\
&\qquad\qquad \text{else } p
\end{aligned}$$

fi)>}.

(S7, parameterized statement)

$$\hat{F}_S((e,\psi))(\alpha)(p) = \hat{F}_E(e)(\alpha)(\lambda\beta\cdot \hat{F}_S(\psi(\beta))(\alpha)(p))$$

(End of definition 4.15.)

(In the above definition, we have applied simplifications similar to those in the definition of the operational semantics for POOL; see the comment following Definition 4.8.)

It is not difficult to prove that Ψ_U is a contraction and hence has a unique fixed point $\mathfrak{D}_U$. In fact, we have defined Ψ_U such that it satisfies this property. Note that the original functions F_E and F_S have been used in only three places: in the definition of the semantics of a new-expression, of an answer statement, and of a loop statement. Here the syntactic complexity of the defining part is not necessarily less than that of what is being defined. At those places, we have ensured that the definition is "guarded" by some step $\lambda\sigma\cdot\{<\sigma', \ldots >\}$. It is easily verified that in this way the contractiveness of Ψ_U is indeed implied.

Before we can define the denotational semantics of a unit we first have to give a denotational interpretation of standard objects. We introduce a *standard* process p_{St}, which represents the activity of the standard objects. In order to let this standard process p_{St} fit into our semantic domain, we are forced to use closed subsets of steps rather than compact ones. Let us indicate the process domain given in Definition 4.13 by $\bar{P}_{co}$. We introduce here $\bar{P}_{cl}$, which satisfies:

$$\bar{P}_{cl} \cong \{p_0\} \cup id_{1/2}(\Sigma \rightarrow \mathcal{P}_{closed}(Step_{\bar{P}_{cl}})).$$

We have, via an obvious embedding, that $\bar{P}_{co} \subseteq \bar{P}_{cl}$.

Next we introduce $p_{St} \in \bar{P}_{cl}$, which represents the meaning of all standard objects. It satisfies the following equation:

$$\begin{aligned} p_{St} = \lambda\sigma\cdot\ (&\{<n, \mathsf{add},\ g_n^+>: n \in \mathbb{Z}\} \cup \\ &\{<n, \mathsf{sub},\ g_n^->: n \in \mathbb{Z}\} \cup \\ &\{<b, \mathsf{and},\ g_b^\wedge>: b \in \{tt, ff\}\} \cup \\ &\{<b, \mathsf{or},\ g_b^\vee>: b \in \{tt, ff\}\} \cup \\ &\{<b, \mathsf{not},\ g_b^\neg>: b \in \{tt, ff\}\}), \end{aligned}$$

where

$$\begin{aligned} g_n^+ &= \lambda\beta \in Obj\cdot\lambda f \in Obj \rightarrow \bar{P}\cdot (\text{if } \beta \in \mathbb{Z} \text{ then } f(n+\beta) \| p_{St} \text{ else } p_{St} \text{ fi}), \\ g_n^- &= \lambda\beta \in Obj\cdot\lambda f \in Obj \rightarrow \bar{P}\cdot (\text{if } \beta \in \mathbb{Z} \text{ then } f(n-\beta) \| p_{St} \text{ else } p_{St} \text{ fi}), \\ g_b^\wedge &= \lambda\beta \in Obj\cdot\lambda f \in Obj \rightarrow \bar{P}\cdot (\text{if } \beta \in \{tt, ff\} \text{ then } f(b \wedge \beta) \| p_{St} \text{ else } p_{St} \text{ fi}) \\ g_b^\vee &= \lambda\beta \in Obj\cdot\lambda f \in Obj \rightarrow \bar{P}\cdot (\text{if } \beta \in \{tt, ff\} \text{ then } f(b \vee \beta) \| p_{St} \text{ else } p_{St} \text{ fi}) \\ g_b^\neg &= \lambda\beta \in Obj\cdot\lambda f \in Obj \rightarrow \bar{P}\cdot f(\neg b) \| p_{St}. \end{aligned}$$

This definition is self-referential since p_{St} occurs at the right-hand side of the definition. Formally, p_{St} can be given as the fixed point of a suitably defined contraction on $\bar{P}_{cl}$.

We observe that p_{St} is an infinitely branching process, which is an element of $\bar{P}_{cl}$

but not of $\bar{P}_{co}$. This explains the introduction of $\bar{P}_{cl}$.

The operational intuition behind the definition of p_{St} is the following. For every $n \in \mathbb{Z}$ the set $p_{St}(\sigma)$ contains, among others, two elements, namely $<n, \mathsf{add}, g_n^+>$ and $<n, \mathsf{sub}, g_n^->$. These steps indicate that the integer object n is willing to execute its methods **add** and **sub**. If, for example by evaluating n!add(n'), a certain active object sends a request to integer object n to execute method **add** with parameter n', then g_n^+, supplied with n' and the continuation f of the active object, is executed. We have that $g_n^+(n')(f)$ is, by definition, the parallel composition of f supplied with the immediate result of the execution of method **add**, namely $n+n'$, and the process p_{St}, which remains unaltered: $g_n^+(n')(f) = f(n+n') \| p_{St}$. (A similar explanation applies to the presence in $p_{St}(\sigma)$ of the triples representing the booleans.)

The standard objects are assumed to be present at the execution of every unit U. Therefore, the definition of the denotational semantics is given as follows.

Definition 4.16 (Denotational semantics of a unit)
We define $[\![\cdots]\!]_{\mathcal{D}}: Unit \rightarrow \bar{P}$. For a unit $U \in Unit$, with $U = < \ldots, C_n \Leftarrow < \ldots, s_n >>$, we set

$$[\![U]\!]_{\mathcal{D}} = \mathcal{D}_S[\![s_n]\!](\nu(\varnothing, C_n))(p_0) \| p_{St}.$$

The execution of a unit always starts with the creation of an object of class C_n and the execution of its body. Therefore, the meaning of a unit U is given by the parallel composition of the denotational meaning of the body of this first object together with the standard process p_{St}.

4.3 Semantic correctness of $[\![\cdots]\!]_{\mathcal{D}}$

Analogously to section 3.3, we can establish a similar correctness result for the denotational semantics of POOL with respect to the operational model. In other words, we can again define a suitable abstraction operator *abstr* and prove that

$$[\![U]\!]_{\mathcal{O}} = abstr([\![U]\!]_{\mathcal{D}}),$$

for every $U \in Unit$. We refer the reader to Rutten (1988), where this is proved in full.

5. References

G. Agha, *Actors: A Model of Concurrent Computation in Distributed Systems,* MIT Press, 1986.

P. America, *POOL-T: a parallel object-oriented language,* in "Object-Oriented Concurrent Programming" (A. Yonezawa and M. Tokoro, eds), MIT Press, 1987a, pp. 199-220.

P. America, *Inheritance and subtyping in a parallel object-oriented language,* in "ECOOP '87: European Conference on Object-Oriented Programming", Paris, June 15-17, 1987b, Springer Lecture Notes in Computer Science 276, pp. 234-242.

P. America, *Definition of POOL2, a parallel object-oriented language,* ESPRIT Project 415 Document 364, Philips Research Laboratories, Eindhoven, 1988a.

P. America, *Rationale for the design of POOL2,* ESPRIT Project 415 Document 393,

Philips Research Laboratories, Eindhoven, 1988b.

P. America, *Issues in the design of a parallel object-oriented language,* ESPRIT Project 415 Document 452, Philips Research Laboratories, Eindhoven, 1988c.

P. America and J.W. de Bakker, *Designing equivalent semantic models for process creation,* Theoretical Computer Science 60, 1988, pp. 109-176.

P. America, J.W. de Bakker, J.N. Kok and J.J.M.M. Rutten, *Operational semantics of a parallel object-oriented language,* in: "Conference Record of the 13th Symposium on Principles of Programming Languages, St Petersburg, Florida," 1986a, pp. 194-208.

P. America, J.W. de Bakker, J.N. Kok and J.J.M.M. Rutten, *A denotational semantics of a parallel object-oriented language,* Technical Report (CS-R8626), Centre for Mathematics and Computer Science, Amsterdam, 1986b. (To appear in: Information and Computation.)

P. America and J.J.M.M. Rutten, *Solving reflexive domain equations in a category of complete metric spaces,* in: Proceedings of the Third Workshop on Mathematical Foundations of Programming Language Semantics (M. Main, A. Melton, M. Mislove, D. Schmidt, eds), Lecture Notes in Computer Science 298, Springer-Verlag, 1988, pp. 254-288. (To appear in the Journal of Computer and System Sciences.)

ANSI, *Reference manual for the Ada programming language,* ANSI/MIL-STD 1815 A, United States Department of Defense, Washington D. C., 1983.

J.W. de Bakker, J.A. Bergstra, J.W. Klop and J.-J.Ch. Meyer, *Linear time and branching time semantics for recursion with merge,* Theoretical Computer Science 34, 1984, pp. 135-156.

J.W. de Bakker, J.N. Kok, J.-J.Ch. Meyer, E.-R. Olderog and J.I. Zucker, *Contrasting themes in the semantics of imperative concurrency,* in: Current Trends in Concurrency (J.W. de Bakker, W.P. de Roever and G. Rozenberg, eds), Lecture Notes in Computer Science 224, Springer-Verlag, 1986, pp. 51-121.

J.W. de Bakker and J.I. Zucker, *Processes and the denotational semantics of concurrency,* Information and Control 54, 1982, pp. 70-120.

A. de Bruin, *Experiments with continuation semantics: Jumps, backtracking, dynamic networks,* Ph. D. thesis, Free University of Amsterdam, 1986.

J. Dugundji, *Topology,* Allyn and Bacon, Boston, 1966.

E. Engelking, *General topology,* Polish Scientific Publishers, 1977.

M.J.C. Gordon, *The denotational description of programming languages,* Springer-Verlag, 1979.

A. Goldberg and D. Robson, *Smalltalk-80: The Language and its Implementation,* Addison-Wesley, 1983.

M. Hennessy and G.D. Plotkin, *Full abstraction for a simple parallel programming language,* in: Proceedings 8th MFCS (J. Bečvář ed.), Lecture Notes in Computer Science 74, Springer-Verlag, 1979, pp. 108-120.

J.N. Kok and J.J.M.M. Rutten, *Contractions in comparing concurrency semantics,* in: Proceedings 15th ICALP, Tampere, Lecture Notes in Computer Science 317, Springer-Verlag, 1988, pp. 317-332. (To appear in Theoretical Computer Science.)

B. Meyer, *Object-Oriented Software Construction,* Prentice-Hall, 1988.

E. Michael, *Topologies on spaces of subsets,* Trans. AMS 71, 1951, pp.152-182.

E.A.M. Odijk, *The* DOOM *system and its applications: a survey of ESPRIT 415 subproject A,* in: "Parallel Architectures and Languages Europe, Volume I" (J.W. de Bakker, A.J. Nijman, and P.C. Treleaven, eds), Lecture Notes in Computer Science 258, Springer-Verlag, 1987, pp. 461-479.

G.D. Plotkin, *A structural approach to operational semantics,* Report DAIMI FN-19, Comp. Sci. Dept., Aarhus Univ. 1981.

G.D. Plotkin, *An operational semantics for CSP,* in: Formal Description of Programming Concepts II (D. Bjørner ed.), North-Holland, Amsterdam, 1983, pp. 199-223.

J.J.M.M. Rutten, *Semantic correctness for a parallel object-oriented language,* Technical Report CS-R8843, Centre for Mathematics and Computer Science, Amsterdam, 1988. (To appear in SIAM Journal of Computation.)

B. Stroustrup, *The C++ Programming Language,* Addison-Wesley, 1986.

Appendix: Mathematical definitions

Definition A.1 (Metric space)
A *metric space* is a pair (M,d) with a non-empty set M and a mapping $d:M\times M\to[0,1]$ (a *metric* or *distance*) that satisfies the following properties:
(a) $\forall x,y\in M\,[d(x,y)=0 \Leftrightarrow x=y]$
(b) $\forall x,y\in M\,[d(x,y)=d(y,x)]$
(c) $\forall x,y,z\in M\,[d(x,y)\leqslant d(x,z)+d(z,y)]$.
We call (M,d) an *ultra-metric space* if the following stronger version of property (c) is satisfied:
(c′) $\forall x,y,z\in M\,[d(x,y)\leqslant\max\{d(x,z),d(z,y)\}]$.
Note that we consider only metric spaces with bounded diameters: the distance between two points never exceeds 1.

EXAMPLES A.1.1
(a) Let A be an arbitrary set. The *discrete* metric d_A on A is defined as follows. Let $x,y\in A$, then

$$d_A(x,y)=\begin{cases}0 & \text{if } x=y\\ 1 & \text{if } x\neq y.\end{cases}$$

(b) Let A be an alphabet, and let $A^\infty=A^*\cup A^\omega$ denote the set of all finite and infinite words over A. Let, for $x\in A^\infty$, $x[n]$ denote the prefix of x of length n, in case $length(x)\geqslant n$, and x otherwise. We put

$$d(x,y)=2^{-sup\{n:x[n]=y[n]\}},$$

with the convention that $2^{-\infty}=0$. Then (A^∞,d) is a metric space.

Definition A.2
Let (M,d) be a metric space, let $(x_i)_i$ be a sequence in M.
(a) We say that $(x_i)_i$ is a *Cauchy sequence* whenever we have
$\forall\epsilon>0\;\exists N\in\mathbb{N}\;\forall n,m>N\;[d(x_n,x_m)<\epsilon]$.

(b) Let $x \in M$. We say that $(x_i)_i$ *converges to* x and call x the *limit* of $(x_i)_i$ whenever we have
$\forall \epsilon > 0\ \exists N \in \mathbb{N}\ \forall n > N\ [d(x,x_n) < \epsilon]$.
Such a sequence we call *convergent*. Notation: $\lim_{i\to\infty} x_i = x$.

(c) The metric space (M,d) is called *complete* whenever each Cauchy sequence converges to an element of M.

Definition A.3

Let $(M_1,d_1),(M_2,d_2)$ be metric spaces.

(a) We say that (M_1,d_1) and (M_2,d_2) are *isometric* if there exists a bijection $f: M_1 \to M_2$ such that
$\forall x,y \in M_1\ [d_2(f(x),f(y)) = d_1(x,y)]$. We then write $M_1 \cong M_2$. When f is not a bijection (but only an injection), we call it an *isometric embedding*.

(b) Let $f: M_1 \to M_2$ be a function. We call f *continuous* whenever for each sequence $(x_i)_i$ with limit x in M_1 we have that $\lim_{i\to\infty} f(x_i) = f(x)$.

(c) Let $A \geqslant 0$. With $M_1 \to^A M_2$ we denote the set of functions f from M_1 to M_2 that satisfy the following property:
$\forall x,y \in M_1\ [d_2(f(x),f(y)) \leqslant A \cdot d_1(x,y)]$.
Functions f in $M_1 \to^1 M_2$ we call *non-expansive*, functions f in $M_1 \to^\epsilon M_2$ with $0 \leqslant \epsilon < 1$ we call *contracting*. (For every $A \geqslant 0$ and $f \in M_1 \to^A M_2$ we have: f is continuous.)

Proposition A.4 (Banach's fixed-point theorem)

Let (M,d) be a complete metric space and $f: M \to M$ a contracting function. Then there exists an $x \in M$ such that the following holds:

(1) *$f(x) = x$ (x is a fixed point of f),*

(2) *$\forall y \in M\ [f(y) = y \Rightarrow y = x]$ (x is unique),*

(3) *$\forall x_0 \in M\ [\lim_{n\to\infty} f^{(n)}(x_0) = x]$, where $f^{(0)}(x_0) = x_0$ and $f^{(n+1)}(x_0) = f(f^{(n)}(x_0))$.*

Definition A.5 (Closed and compact subsets)

A subset X of a complete metric space (M,d) is called *closed* whenever each Cauchy sequence in X has a limit in X and is called *compact* whenever each sequence in X has a subsequence that converges to an element of X.

Definition A.6

Let $(M,d),(M_1,d_1), \ldots, (M_n,d_n)$ be metric spaces.

(a) With $M_1 \to M_2$ we denote the set of all continuous functions from M_1 to M_2. We define a metric d_F on $M_1 \to M_2$ as follows. For every $f_1, f_2 \in M_1 \to M_2$

$$d_F(f_1,f_2) = \sup_{x \in M_1} \{d_2(f_1(x),f_2(x))\}.$$

For $A \geqslant 0$ the set $M_1 \to^A M_2$ is a subset of $M_1 \to M_2$, and a metric on $M_1 \to^A M_2$ can be obtained by taking the restriction of the corresponding d_F.

(b) With $M_1 \bar{\cup} \cdots \bar{\cup} M_n$ we denote the *disjoint union* of $M_1, \ldots, M_n$, which can be defined as $\{1\} \times M_1 \cup \cdots \cup \{n\} \times M_n$. We define a metric d_U on $M_1 \bar{\cup} \cdots \bar{\cup} M_n$ as follows. For every $x,y \in M_1 \bar{\cup} \cdots \bar{\cup} M_n$

$$d_U(x,y) = \begin{cases} d_j(x,y) & \text{if } x,y \in \{j\} \times M_j,\ 1 \leqslant j \leqslant n \\ 1 & \text{otherwise.} \end{cases}$$

(c) We define a metric d_P on $M_1 \times \cdots \times M_n$ by putting for every $(x_1, \ldots, x_n)$,

$(y_1, \ldots, y_n) \in M_1 \times \cdots \times M_n$

$$d_P((x_1, \ldots, x_n), (y_1, \ldots, y_n)) = \max_i\{d_i(x_i, y_i)\}.$$

(d) Let $\mathcal{P}_{closed}(M) = \{X: X \subseteq M \wedge X \text{ is closed}\}$. We define a metric d_H on $\mathcal{P}_{closed}(M)$, called the *Hausdorff distance,* as follows. For every $X, Y \in \mathcal{P}_{closed}(M)$ with $X, Y \neq \varnothing$

$$d_H(X, Y) = \max\{\sup_{x \in X}\{d(x, Y)\}, \sup_{y \in Y}\{d(y, X)\}\},$$

where $d(x, Z) =^{def} \inf_{z \in Z}\{d(x, z)\}$ for every $Z \subseteq M$, $x \in M$. For $X \neq \varnothing$ we put

$$d_H(\varnothing, X) = d_H(X, \varnothing) = 1.$$

The following spaces

$$\mathcal{P}_{compact}(M) = \{X: X \subseteq M \wedge X \text{ is compact}\}$$

$$\mathcal{P}_{ncompact}(M) = \{X: X \subseteq M \wedge X \text{ is non-empty and compact}\}$$

are supplied with a metric by taking the respective restrictions of d_H.

(e) Let $c \in (0, 1]$. We define: $id_c(M, d) = (M, c \cdot d)$.

Proposition A.7

Let (M,d), $(M_1,d_1), \ldots, (M_n,d_n)$, d_F, d_U, d_P and d_H be as in definition A.6 and suppose that (M,d), $(M_1,d_1), \ldots, (M_n,d_n)$ are complete. We have that

(a) $(M_1 \rightarrow M_2, d_F)$, $(M_1 \rightarrow^A M_2, d_F)$,

(b) $(M_1 \cup \cdots \cup M_n, d_U)$,

(c) $(M_1 \times \cdots \times M_n, d_P)$,

(d) $(\mathcal{P}_{closed}(M), d_H)$, $(\mathcal{P}_{compact}(M), d_H)$ and $(\mathcal{P}_{ncompact}(M), d_H)$

are complete metric spaces. If (M,d) and (M_i,d_i) are all ultra-metric spaces these composed spaces are again ultra-metric. (Strictly speaking, for the completeness of $M_1 \rightarrow M_2$ and $M_1 \rightarrow^A M_2$ we do not need the completeness of M_1. The same holds for the ultra-metric property.)

The proofs of proposition A.7 (a), (b) and (c) are straightforward. Part (d) is more involved. It can be proved with the help of the following characterization of the completeness of the Hausdorff metric.

Proposition A.8

Let $(\mathcal{P}_{closed}(M), d_H)$ be as in definition A.6. Let $(X_i)_i$ be a Cauchy sequence in $\mathcal{P}_{closed}(M)$. We have:

$$\lim_{i \to \infty} X_i = \{\lim_{i \to \infty} x_i \mid x_i \in X_i, (x_i)_i \text{ a Cauchy sequence in } M\}.$$

The proof of proposition A.8 can be found in Dugundji (1966) and Engelking (1977). The completeness of the Hausdorff space containing compact sets is proved in Michael (1951).

Chapter 2

AADL: A Net-Based Specification Method for Computer Architecture Design

Werner Damm and *Gert Döhmen*

FB Informatik, Universität Oldenburg, Ammerländer Heerstr. 114-118, 2900 Oldenburg, West Germany

This paper presents a specification language for computer architecture design together with its formal semantics. AADL (an acronym for axiomatic architecture description language) allows a modular and concise specification of multiprocessor architectures at levels of abstraction ranging from compiler/operating system interfaces down to chip level. The concepts of AADL are carefully chosen to cover this range of abstraction levels, using as unifying concept modules offering services to their environment through ports. As special cases purely structural descriptions of circuits at gate level as well as behavioural specifications in an extension of CSP are feasible. We illustrate the specification method with examples taken from the design of a multiprocessor architecture.

The main part of the chapter develops a compositional semantics of AADL. The need for describing behaviour at chip level entailed the need to support shared-memory parallelism including non-procedural activation of atomic actions upon condition on the state of the architecture. A proper treatment of the complex interactions of these two concepts in conflict situations is only feasible using a semantics based on partial orders. We show how to develop a compositional semantics via a two-stage approach: a translation of AADL into one-safe Petri nets makes the underlying concurrency explicit; given a process (an acyclic conflict-free unfolding) of the net we derive as its semantics a mapping from its places to states of the architecture by associating state transformations (corresponding to atomic actions of the architecture) with transitions of the process.

1. Introduction

With the step to fifth-generation architectures with estimated performance requirements in the Gigalips range, computer architectures are bound to explore innovative design styles in order to fully exploit the potential processing power offered by VLSI technology. Techniques emerging out of current research projects on fifth-generation computer systems such as ESPRIT 415 show a clear identification of three major vehicles towards meeting these far-stretched performance requirements: the use of highly parallel, distributed architectures; the design of architectures tailored towards knowledge processing by e.g. directly supporting key concepts of AI languages; and finally the use of custom VLSI designs for dedicated, time-critical subsystems. The design of such architectures adds at least two dimensions of complexity to computer architecture design: the need to isolate in the design process the key features requiring dedicated hardware support out of high-level requirements stemming from the direct support of knowledge processing; and, second, coping with the complexity of distributed systems. The design space is thus extended in two dimensions:

(1) *Vertically*, creating the need to cope with a multiplicity of design levels ranging from high-level requirements down to VLSI design;

(2) *Horizontally*, distributing functionality over typically highly replicated, but non-synchronized, architectural components.

A contrasting theme to this increase in the complexity of the design process is the availability of **computer architecture design tools** managing this complexity. In a key lecture the head of a major European company's VLSI department recently pointed out that the breakthrough in productivity in chip designtime needed to meet market requirements can only be achieved on the basis of highly advanced CAD - tools covering architecture design in **all** its phases. It was also pointed out that already for conventional architectures using current VLSI technology and the available support tools, about 70% of design time was spent at system level. In contrast, almost all available VLSI design tools assume at least a register transfer level design specification.

A major reason for the lack of tools for these higher design levels is the high degree of creativity required to bridge the gap from starting requirements to chip-level description in a distributed world. Clearly this process is not amenable to automation, even using knowledged-based techniques. The inherently interactive nature of this design process calls for an environment allowing the designer to focus on the purely creative aspects, while providing him with tools which rigorously screen his necessarily bounded insight into a possible design solution against the full complexity of the real system. We view the introduction of **formal design methods** complemented by **verification tools** as a necessary step to cope with the added complexity of the architecture design process. Indeed, already for small scale distributed algorithms published solutions were later proven to be incorrect.

This chapter presents **AADL,** a specification language designed to cover all these abstraction levels in architecture design. It provides the flexibility and expressivity to support the complete design process down to interfaces of VLSI-design tools, covering such different abstraction levels as operating-system modules, communication protocols, instruction-set specifications, register transfer level descriptions and finally chip specifications within **one** common framework. As such, it subsumes specification languages for the soft, firm, and hard phases of the design.

The role of AADL in such a design process is twofold:

(1) Because of its axiomatic style, AADL allows to cast our intuitive understanding of what we want concealed and what should be visible at a given level into an unambiguous, formal specification. It extends the typical interface definitions listing parameters of routines and global variables with a concise specification of the dynamic behaviour of the services available. Whatever property a higher level routine requires, it must be formally specified or derivable from the specification. This rigorous discipline is the prerequisite for a **hierarchical** verification of designs, as further discussed below.

(2) Anyone involved in the design of multiprocessor systems is aware of the difficulties in analyzing and establishing the behaviour of implemented subsystems. Even with disciplined ways of process communication, as in CSP (Hoare, 1978), proving the correctness of distributed algorithms is a hard task. In architecture design, communication between concurrent processes is often of the shared-memory type, and at low levels not even semaphores need to be available. To directly prove that a sequence of asynchronously activated hardware actions passes a structured message from one node to another node would be an impossible task. But once we have structured our design and provided AADL specifications of its architectural layers, we can prove the

correctness of the design in a hierarchical fashion. Indeed, it is then sufficient to establish the equivalence of a layer and its imple- mentation using the primitives of the adjacent lower layer. Moreover, as will be shown in subsequent papers, proving the correctness of one implementation step can be split up into an **automated proof of liveness properties** (Lamport, 1985), a **modular proof of safety properties,** and a **consistency proof of data structures** using rewrite techniques. This constitutes a clear advantage over operational approaches using bisimulation equivalence.

To assess the impact of covering such a range of abstraction levels, it is worth considering particular examples. A good test case for such a specification language is its ability to serve as a firmware specification language efficiently applicable to a broad range of microarchitectures. Here such a model has to be sufficiently expressive to cope with all variations in microinstruction formats, timing schemes, and residual control. Of at least equal importance is the chip level: industrial designs will use off-the-shelf components in the construction of prototypes, for cost considerations, observation of standards, or other commercial reasons. Thus timing aspects as propagation delays as well as signaling schemes in inter-chip communication have to be expressible and verifiable in the design process.

It is particularly necessary to incorporate hardware and possibly firmware subsystems into the formal specification method which distinguishes a general specification method for distributed systems from AADL. In computer architecture design, characteristics of hardware components (as e.g. communication bandwidth or availability of dedicated VLSI components) may well influence higher-level design decisions. This entails both that a precise specification of the behaviour of hardware components has to be part of the design (which could well serve additionally as input to VLSI design tools) and that in general a pure top-down approach is not feasible. Instead, designing intermediate architectural levels in a hierarchic design becomes a challenging task of trading abstraction (in order to ease implementation and verification) for the introduction of hardware aspects essential for an efficient realization of the design.

In AADL, the orientation towards architecture design becomes apparent in the following characteristics:

(1) The fundamental notion of the "state" of a computer architecture is explicitly visible (in contrast to e.g. Milner (1980) and Klaeren (1986)).

(2) Like most ADLs, AADL allows mixing *structural* and *functional* specifications of the dynamic behaviour of an architecture by either specifying the information flow between (already defined) subsystems or explicitly specifying the state transformations possible in an architecture.

(3) In order to deal with design levels close to hardware (as e.g. the microarchitectural level, the register transfer level, or in the description of off-the-shelf components) AADL has been enriched by a number of constructs allowing e.g. the detailed modelling of resource binding to microoperations (Damm, *et al.*, 1986a) as well as a specification of timing characteristics of chips (Sichelschmidt, 1989).

(4) In architecture design, semantic models which do not allow us to distinguish between nondeterminism and concurrency (such as traces (Manna and Pnueli, 1981), branching time (Lamport, 1985) and state-based approaches) are inapplicable, because they enforce an ordering of events which will never be visible in the hardware (which in general provides true concurrency rather than e.g. an interleaved execution of atomic

actions as underlying linear-time temporal logic or trace theory). Similarly, we consider the notion of a global state in a distributed system at least to be debatable, since it forces us to order events in some global time scale which are physically unrelated. We will thus base the semantics of AADL on a **partial** order of events (as e.g. in Pinter and Wolper, (1984) and Degano *et al.* (1985, 1987a, 1987b, 1988a, 1988b, 1988c, 1989a, 1989b)), by using Petri nets (Reisig, 1985) as an intermediate step in defining its semantics.

The design of AADL is the result of extensive case studies carried out at all addressed system levels (including virtual machines for parallel execution of AI languages, subsystems of operating systems, microcode level, microprocessor-chips, and a hierarchical specification of a communication processor down to chip-level; see Damm and Döhmen (1985, 1986, 1987), Döhmen and den Haan (1987), Gageik (1988a), Gerstner (1989), den Haan and Bronnenberg (1987), Loogen (1987) and Peikenkamp (1988)).

These case studies, which were carried out partially in an industrial context, established the flexibility of AADL to cover all involved system levels within **one** conceptual framework. In particular it allows purely structural descriptions of circuits at gate level as well as behavioural specifications in an extension of CSP (Hoare, 1978) supporting modules. The language was carefully designed to cover the addressed range of system levels with a minimal number of concepts. Particular attention was paid to achieve modularity in this often asynchronous context of computer systems. Modules, offering services to their environment through ports, may specify protocols ensuring their proper usage in a carefully chosen variant of propositional temporal logic, which supports modular proof techniques. Services are specified in an extension of CSP providing additionally asynchronous communication, shared-memory parallelism between atomic actions of a module, and non-procedural activation of actions upon conditions of the state of the system. Atomic actions define indivisible state transformations in an axiomatic style, possibly extended by an invariant assumed to be true upon activation of the action. The structure of the state (together with functions manipulating components of the structure) are specified using algebraic specification techniques providing hierarchical and parameterized specifications.

The constructs of the specification language allow a fully modular specification of concurrent behaviour and thus reusability of system specifications. Because protocols regulating the interaction of the environment and the functionality of the offered services are rigorously expressed in the specification of the module, a formal verification of the conformity of the use of a module in a particular context, called **horizontal verification** , is feasible. Note that critical-path calculations carried out when embedding chips into one design can be seen as a particular instance of horizontal verification, ensuring a sufficient duration of the clock cycle for the information flow required to implement a given instruction.

While modularity harmonizes with the horizontal dimension of the design space, a **hierarchic** design style is the natural reflection of the vertical dimension of design. **Vertical verification** establishes the behavioural equivalence of specification and implementation restricted to observable states and thus presumes the possibility expressing design steps as formally verifiable relations between different specifications.

In developing AADL, the efficiency of tools supporting such a specification language has been a major concern. The **COMDES** project currently underway at the computer-architecture group of the University of Oldenburg will produce an environment for

AADL for testing the requirement specification, allowing multi-level simulation of hierarchical specifications, the analysis of system properties ranging from e.g. global protocols to such standard tasks as proving absence of deadlocks or livelocks, and, more general, supporting both horizontal and vertical verification by verification tools.

We now highlight the key concepts of the formal semantics of AADL, which constitues the heart of this chapter.

The need for describing behaviour at chip level entailed supporting shared-memory parallelism as well as non-procedural activation of atomic actions upon conditions on the state of the architecture. Being tailored towards architectural description on different abstraction levels, AADL assumes constructs for expressing parallelism and communication adapted to these levels.

(1) **Parallelism** in AADL is explicitly defined in the CSP-style control section but with the notable difference to CSP that concurrently enabled actions may have conflicts. In such cases only one arbitrarily chosen action will be executed and the other actions are suspended, thus serializing them in some non deterministic (fair) way.

Using the " <u>on</u> trigger <u>do</u> statement <u>od</u> " construct (within the control section) AADL allows us also to express non-procedural activation of atomic actions upon conditions on the state of the architecture. Several non conflicting actions triggered by their activation conditions will run in parallel when these are simultaneously true. Note that a trigger of an operation trying to access a shared resource may become false while being suspended (unless a suitable protocol is part of the specification, which ensures that this will not happen!).

(2) **Communication** between AADL modules is either implicit via shared variables or explicit by the use of linked (synchronous or asynchronous) ports. No built-in primitives protecting access to shared resources are assumed, because they have to be realized explicitly at some level of the design. Communication over synchronous ports allows us to conceal the concrete implementation of protocols on higher abstraction layers, while on asynchronous ports only the transport of messages assigned to such a port will be guaranteed and the protocols need to be defined explicitly.

To give an adequate semantics to such a complex language without introducing any assumptions about the absolute or relative speed of operations we take a three-step approach:

(1) First, we **translate** an AADL specification into an **one-save predicate/transition net,** which shows all parallelism which can be explicitly or implicitly derived from the specification.

(2) In the second step all possible executions (runs) of an AADL net will be reflected by the set of its "processes" (i.e. acyclic and conflict-free condition/event nets obtained by "unfolding" the original net).

(3) Given such a process of the AADL net we derive as its semantics a mapping from its places to states of the architecture by associating state transformations (corresponding to atomic actions of the architecture) with transitions of the process.

For these processes we have defined a notion of fairness which guarantees the execution of an action only if all its trigger conditions are observably true infinitely often. The precise definition is based on the concept of "strongly concurrent places" of a process introduced in Reisig (1985). We note that a **direct** use of nets would in general lead to a large increase in specification size and not support compositional specification methods.

This chapter is organized in five sections. In section 2 we will present AADL's view of the design process and give an introduction of the key concepts of AADL. Throughout this and the following section, we will use the specification of a simple communication protocol (which is part of a hierarchical design of the complex protocol used in the DOOM system (den Haan and Hopmans, 1988)). The kernel of this chapter, section 3, defines the translation of AADL constructs into one-safe Petri nets. The construction of nets will be illustrated with examples taken from the specification of the communication protocol. Section 4 presents a breef outline of AADL's net semantics by use of the communication-protocol example. A final section compares AADL with existing specification and verification methods.

2. Specifying computer architectures in AADL

While allowing specifications at different abstraction levels AADL supports a hierarchical design method. Design decisions become explicit as implementation steps which relate two views of the same architecture at different levels of abstraction. This *vertical* dimension of the design process can be illustrated by a directed, acyclic graph. Each node captures a view of a component of the evolving architecture at some stage in the design. The arcs represent implementation steps, which provide a realization of the functionality of (a module of) the higher level using the services offered at a lower level. Each implementation step will typically involve assumptions about lower design levels which either become validated as the design proceeds or may induce a backtracking to an earlier state in the design process to explore other realizations. This standard concept of a hierarchical design has been successfully employed in the OSI standards to structure the design of complex communication protocols, enforcing information hiding. Extending OSI terminology, we will refer to nodes in the graph as *architectural layers*.

The level of abstraction of an architectural layer is essentially defined by selecting a collection of atomic actions. These together with a control specification define the possible behaviour of the architectural layer: they characterize exactly the allowed state transformations and at the same time set the level of granularity visible at this level (note that in general such actions will be executed in parallel). We postpone a discussion of the exact nature of actions and their control mechanism until the end of this section but note that their (pre/post-style) specification will make use of (first-order) formulae, whose signature stems from abstract data types used throughout the specification. In particular we will use type definitions to formalize the structure of the underlying state space and functions defined in the data-type specification within the formulae mentioned above. These entities allow us to define the "building blocks" of an architectural layer, the main ingredients being: a definition of the used data types, a specification of the transformed storage structures, a specification of the dynamic behaviour and an interface specification whose relevance will be discussed below. Examples of such building blocks may vary in complexity from gates to chips and from microprocessors to modules of an operating system, depending on our chosen level of abstraction.

As a particular example of the specification of an architectural layer in this section we will consider a simple protocol for buffering messages in a loosely coupled multiprocessor system. The protocol is part of a hierarchical design of a more complex protocol (den Haan and Hopmans, 1988) employed in the DOOM system (Odijk, 1985). It is used to implement process communication for user processes stemming from objects of the object-oriented language POOL (America, 1988), which communicate via synchronous message passing according to a dynamic changing, non-hierarchic interconnection structure.

The processing elements (nodes) of the DOOM system are able by the use of multiprogramming to execute several processes which are either user-defined or operating-system processes. The user-defined processes represent the objects of the POOL program actually running on the system. Therefore these processes (distributed over several nodes) have to provide the basic communication primitives between POOL objects: they can perform Send and Receive operations. The Send operation indicates that a process wants to deliver a message to a destination process which may reside on the same node or on a different one. Send will terminate after the destination process has accepted this message (and stored its content) by performing its Receive operation. Processes can perform their Send operation independently from other processes: thus several Send operations may be active which state one and the same destination process (many to one communication). According to POOL their messages have to be accepted on a first-come first-served basis requiring a message queueing-mechanism.

The operating system processes will implement these communication primitives in terms of the communication primitives offered by a communication network. Within the AADL specification of the DOOM protocol we have incorporated these processes in so-called protocol handlers which together with the network constitute the communication medium for exchanging messages between user processes running on processing nodes. Each protocol-handler is coupled to exactly one processing-node - it embodies the services which can be used by this processing node to perform non-local communication.

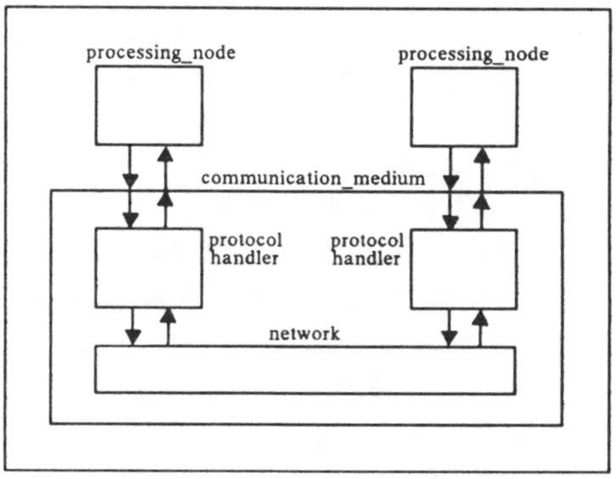

Figure 1: A global view of the DOOM-system

When a process on a node i sends a message to another process residing on a different node j, the protocol handlers assigned to nodes i and j have to communicate according to an operating system protocol. Several standardized communication protocols exist (such as ISO in Zimmermann, 1980) but for the DOOM system a new protocol has been designed to cope with limited memory sizes (den Haan and Hopmans, 1988). This so-called *optimal buffering protocol* is a combination of two basic protocols - *destination buffering protocol* and *distributed buffering protocol*. An AADL specification for all three protocols can be found in Gerstner (1989). In this chapter we will restrict ourselves to the most basic of these three protocols, using *destination buffering*. Within this protocol all messages will be stored at the destination - in our case inside the protocol handler. Therefore each protocol handler includes local queues to store (incoming) messages sent to processes present on the node attached to it.

The boxes in Figure 1 denote the building blocks for this particular view of the DOOM system. They describe the *horizontal* decomposition of DOOM at this particular level of abstraction and establish at the same time one architectural layer within the vertically ordered system of architectural layers. In general such a building block will offer its services via an interface. The interface designates (typed) ports for communication with the environment. Typically, services offered by a building block require the observation of protocols,[1] whose specification is part of the interface definition.

As shown in Figure 1, an architectural layer will (usually) consist of a combination of building blocks. In AADL specifications we use the term architecture both for building blocks and for their combinations and subarchitectures for the constituents of a combined architecture.

Linking subarchitectures by connecting their ports has a direct analogy in the physical connection of chips which then communicate asynchronously over these links, but it can also be used to specify synchronous or asynchronous communication on higher architectural layers (as will be illustrated in this chapter). In the first case it simply provides a unidirectional information flow. Clearly several protocols can be specified "on top" of this pure concept (e.g. by introducing acknowledge signals). We also allow CSP-style communication commands (Hoare, 1978), since at abstract levels a concept of synchronous communication over such links without establishing a particular protocol is desirable. Thus in such specifications the links represent communication channels.

We will now explain the AADL specification for the communication medium.

This is specified as architecture *destination_buffering_protocol* including as subarchitectures *N protocol_handlers* of type *protocol_services* and a *network* of type $FCN(N, msg)$.[2] The protocol handlers are specified by use of a so-called *range*. The expression $e \mid 1 \le i \le N$ (where typically e depends on i) abbreviates N copies of e with appropriate values of i. We enclose the index in angled brackets. When instantiating an architecture, specific local storage structures may be initialized (as in the example protocol_id) and ports may be renamed (discussed later).

Under the keyword interface those entities of an architecture are specified which are relevant for including it in an environment. Design parameters may be bound when instantiating an architecture within an environment (as e.g. $FCN(N, msg)$) or they allow for later adjustment by simulating the design with different choices of actual values. In our example specification we assume that the design parameter M is chosen high enough such that during a simulation the number of processes will not exceed it.

The interface definition also allows us to specify the behaviour of an architecture (its services) and the restrictions on how it can be used by (interact with) the environment (e.g. observation of protocols). This is specified in a special class of temporal formulae (see section 5). In Gerstner (1989) these formulae are included for all protocol specifications but we have omitted them here because the main intention of this chapter is the presentation of AADL's semantics.

[1] On the chip level it is thus possible to specify setup, hold, and enable/disable times for the ports involved.

[2] *FCN* denotes a fully connected network which is parameterized by the number of its interfaces and the *type* of messages which will be served by it.

```
architecture destination_buffering_protocol (N, M : design parameter) :
/* N = number of protocol-handlers,
   M = upper bound for processes served by one protocol-handler */
 interface
    parameter N, M : cardinal;
    sync  inport in_<i> : insignal | 1 ≤ i ≤ N;
          outport out_<i> : outsignal | 1 ≤ i ≤ N
 subarchitecture
    protocol_handler_<i> : protocol_services
       where    sig_in = in_<i>
            and sig_out = out_<i>
       init protocol_id = <i> | 1 ≤ i ≤ N;
    network : FCN(N,msg)
 link
    protocol_handler_<j>.p_out -> network.netin_<j>  | 1 ≤ j ≤ N;
    network.netout_<j> -> protocol_handler_<j>.p_in  | 1 ≤ j ≤ N
 type
    nodeno = 1..N;
    processno = 1..M;
    data = pending;
    insignal = (send_dem(processno,address,data), rec_dem(processno));
    outsignal = (send_ack(processno), rec_ack(processno,data));
    address = record /* form of the address of each process */
                 node : nodeno;
                 process : processno;
              end; /* record */
    message = record /* stored message at the receiver */
                 sender : address;
                 content : data;
              end; /* record */
    mess = (m_msg(message),ack); /to distinguish the messages */
    msg = (msg_con(address,mess)) /* delivered to and received from network */
end /* global architecture */
```

Figure 2: AADL specification for a communication medium

Two ports *in_<i>* and *out_<i>* constitute the interface to the processing nodes where *<i>* corresponds to the number of the linked nodes. Within the architecture *destination_buffering_protocol* these ports are identified with ports *sig_in* and *sig_out* (see architecture *protocol_services*) of the protocol handlers.

The link specifications in Figure 2 specify the connection of ports *p_out* and *p_in* of protocol handlers to ports specified within the network. They establish together with the renaming of ports the structure of the communication medium in Figure 1.

The type definitions of the architecture *destination buffering protocol* will formalize the structure of storage components. These type definitions will be used by the subarchitectures to define their local storage structures.

We will now consider in more detail the AADL specification of the architecture *protocol_services* used as the type of protocol handlers (each protocol handler is an incarnation of such an architecture).

In general, subarchitectures are only allowed to transform their (local) storage structures and their outports for communication. While a communication using shared storage structures could be specified by introducing an architecture with the desired components (a "memory module") and linking it to all "accessing" architectures, it is often desirable to abstract from the implementation of the parallel access to the memory module. To this end we allow shared storage structures to be declared when combining subarchitectures with the implicit meaning that they all can be granted exclusive accesss to these structures.

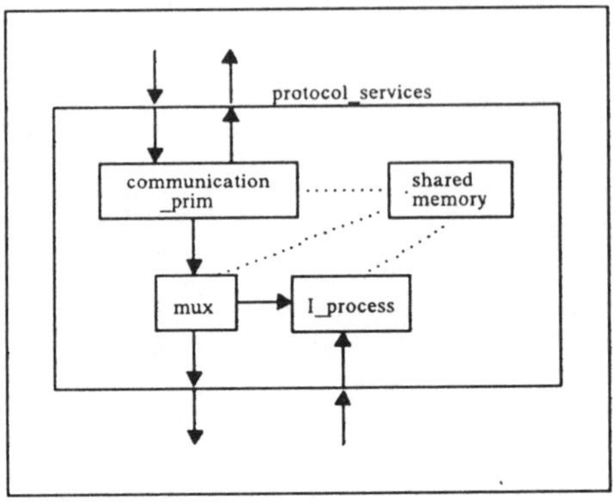

Figure 3: The structure of protocol handlers

Such *shared storage structures* are defined within the architecture *protocol_services* and can therefore be used by its subarchitectures *comm_prim*, *mux*, and *I_process*.

It is the task of the *comm_prim* subarchitecture to provide so-called *send_primitive* and *receive_primitive* services to the processes on the appropriate processing node. Upon activation of the *send primitive* by a *send_demand* message it will deliver the content of this message to the *mux* subarchitecture and wait until the *I_process* subarchitecture indicates, by setting the thus shared storage-structure *state*, that the acknowledge signal for a sent message has been arrived and thus the Send instruction on the processing node can terminate.

The storage structure *protocol_id* will be initialized with the number of the node to which the protocol handler is attached. The *mux* architecture will decide - by comparing the *node* field of the address given in a received message with *protocol_id* - whether this message must be delivered to the network for transporting it to (and storing it at) the destination protocol handler or - in the case of a "local" message - it can be stored (directly) on the same protocol handler because this is already the destination.

The *I_process* architecture has to handle incoming messages from the network as well as local messages from the *mux* architecture. It will store the messages in the shared storage structure *msg_buffer* which includes for each process (on the attached processing node) a queue to store the incoming messages. The number of elements in each of these queues will be count in the storage structure *bufcnt* which will initially consist of an array with zeros.

Message delivery from a queue in *msg_buffer* to the appropriate process will be done by the *receive_primitive* service of the *comm_prim*. Upon its activation by a *receive_demand* this service will get the next message from the queue and deliver it via a *rec_ack* message to the processing node. When the queue is empty (*bufcnt* =0) it will wait until this condition is violated.

```
architecture protocol_services :
 interface
    init protocol_id
    sync inport sig_in : insignal; /* from processes */
    sync outport sig_out : outsignal; /* to processes */
    sync inport p_in : msg; /* from the network */
    sync outport p_out : msg /* to the network */
 subarchitecture
    comm_prim : communication_prim; /* is used if a process wants to
                                        send or receive a message */
       where dem_in = sig_in and ack_out = sig_out; /* to arch. processes */

    mux : multiplexer; /* schedules the messages to the network or I_process */
       where remote_out = p_out;  /* connection to the network */

    I_process : I_process /* manages all messages from the network */
       where remote_in = p_in  /* accepts messages from the network */
 link
    comm_prim.msg_out -> mux.in;  /* to deliver the message to the network using the mux */
    mux.local_out -> I_process.local_in /* if the receiving process resides on the same node */
 shared storage
    protocol_id : nodeno;
    msg_buffer : array [1..M] of queue_of message;  /* each process has its own local queue */
    bufcnt : array [1..M] of  cardinal
       init makearray <i> : 0 | 1 ≤ i ≤ M end;   /* counts the number of messages */
    state = array [1..M] of (received, not_received)
       init makearray <i> : not_received | 1 ≤ i ≤ M end
end /* architecture protocol_services */
```

Figure 4: AADL specification for protocol handlers

AADL allows us to use abstract data types, specified in the algebraic specification language SRDL (Klaeren, 1986), for the definition of types. Such an abstract data type combines data structures which are structurally (recursively) defined over a set of constructors and functions which are constructively defined by case analysis on the possible constructors. It states explicitly in its export part which of the defined data structures and functions are visible outside. Access to the exported types is restricted to the set of exported functions defined for these types. Thus such an abstract data type represents a protection mechanism (Figure 5).

In our example specification the data structure *queue_of elem* is defined within the abstract data-type *QUEUE(elem : type).* *elem* is a type-parameter which determines the type of queue-elements. In the definition of *msg_buffer* (see architecture *protocol_services*) it is substituted by the actual type *message*. The nullary constructor *nil* which represents the empty queue and the constructor *put* which combines an existing queue with a new element define the structure of a *queue_of elem*. In Figure 5 we only show some of the functions for accessing such a queue. *dequeue* will take as argument a *queue_of elem* and results in a new *queue_of elem* shortened by the oldest content. *top* will also take a *queue_of elem* as argument but will result in the oldest element itself. *length* will simply compute the number of elements in the queue.

We will now consider in more detail the specification of the *send* and *receive_primitive* whose functionalities has been outlined above. They are defined within the architecture *communication_prim*.

```
data type QUEUE(elem : type) =
 export
    types queue_of elem
    functions all
 end /* export */
 types  queue_of elem = (nil, put(elem, queue_of elem))
 functions
    dequeue(q : queue_of elem) =  case q of
                                     put(e,nil) : nil;
                                     put(e,que) : put(e,dequeue(que));
                                     otherwise error
                                  esac : queue_of elem;
    top(q : queue_of elem) =   case q of
                                  put(e,nil) : e;
                                  put(e,que) : top(que);
                                  otherwise error
                               esac : elem;
    length(q : queue_of elem) =   case q of
                                     nil : 0;
                                     put(e,que) : length(que) + 1
                                  esac : cardinal
    . . . all further functions
end       /* data type QUEUE */
```

Figure 5: Example of an abstract data type

This architecture does not declare further subarchitectures but describes within its *behaviour* part the provided functionality. So-called *actions* define the (atomic) state transformations which can be performed. We will discuss them later in more detail. The activation of these actions is specified under the keyword *control*. This part of the specification defines the control flow between AADL actions and (synchronous) CSP-style input/output commands by using CSP control structures enriched by the construct " on ϕ do S od ". This additional control-structure models the fact that a process will wait for activating its statement S until its "trigger" condition ϕ becomes true.

As usual in CSP, sequentially ordered statements must be delimitated by a ";" sign and statements which can happen in parallel have to be bracketed by and delimitated by "||". The repetitive constructor rep ...per and the alternate constructor if ...fi allow commands which are guarded by a boolean condition as well as input or output guards. Separate alternative guarded commands within a repetitive or alternate construct have to be delimitated by the "[]" sign.

The control specification for the *communication_prim* consists of one par/rap including M (thus parallel running) repetitive commands which are specified using the range $1 \leq i \leq M$ (Figure 6). This ensures that processes on the processing node can use the send or receive primitives concurrently. Each repetitive statement includes a guarded command for the send and for the receive primitive. Since the receive primitive will be used as example in section 3 to explain the translation into AADL nets, we will concentrate on the second guarded command.

This alternative can be taken when a receive-demand message has been received over the synchronous inport *dem_in*. The process which has delivered this message to the protocol handler will include its own process number in the demandmessage and this number will be stored on the receiving side in the pattern variable *no*, which will then be used to

```
architecture communication_prim :

 interface
    sync inport dem_in : insignal; /* from processing_node */
    sync outport msg_out : msg; /* to the mux */
    sync outport ack_out : outsignal /* to processing_node */

 behaviour

    control
       par
          rep
             /* representing the send_primitive */
                dem_in ? send_dem(no : processno, dest : address, data : data) ->
                msg_out ! msg_con(dest, m_msg(makerecord ... end));
                on state[no] = received do
                   reset_state (no);
                   ack_out ! send_ack(no)
                od
             /* representing the receive_primitive */
             [] dem_in ? rec_dem(no : processno) ->
                on bufcnt[no] > 0 do
                   invariant length (msg_buffer[no]) ≠ 0;
                   msg_out ! msg_con(top(msg_buffer[no]).sender, ack);
                   ack_out ! rec_ack(no, top(msg_buffer[no]).content);
                   update_queue(no);
                   decrement_bufcnt(no)
                od
          per | 1 ≤ i ≤ M
       rap
    end /* control */

    . . . actions

end /* architecture communication_prim */
```

Figure 6: AADL specification for *communication_prim*

reference storage structures attached to this process. Note that the scope of such a pattern variable defined within an inputguard is restricted to the body of the guarded command. Thus each of the M guarded commands for the receive-primitive have their own variable *no*.

The receive primitive will wait until the condition $bufcnt[no] > 0$ is fulfilled and thus the queue for process *no* is non-empty. To approve the correct relation between the *bufcnt* and the *queue* we have included an *invariant* as a first statement in the body of the " on do od " which checks whether the length of the queue is unequal to zero. The four subsequently following statements will then

(1) Deliver an acknowledge signal to the *mux* which will be subsequently delivered to the sender process to indicate that its send-command can terminate;

(2) Deliver the next message content in the queue together with the identification of the process which has requested that message to the processing node;

(3) Activate the action *update_queue*; and

(4) Activate the action *decrement_bufcnt*.

We will now consider in more detail how actions are specified in AADL.

The key for introducing *abstraction* into architecture specifications is the *axiomatic* style of specifying atomic actions of an architecture used in AADL. In contrast to most

ADLs, the state transformation induced by activating an atomic action is not given operationally but, up to "syntactic sugar", by a pair of predicates: a state satisfying the precondition will be taken into one satisfying the second predicate, the postcondition. Note that nothing is said (thus specified) about how this state transformation is achieved. The above behavioural specifications show the "syntactic sugar" added to this pure axiomatic style to increase readability of more complex specifications. The "pure" specification is (automatically) constructed from a set of effects, which are in general evaluated in parallel.

When specifying pre- and postconditions we allow the user to specify design-dependent predicates and functions using a set of predefined primitives, which in particular include the canonical operations associated with AADL standard data types which are included in Damm *et al.* (1989). The specification of user-specific extensions is done in a purely functional style either locally within an action or globally for the current architecture (and its subarchitectures) in the abstract data-type specification.

```
action update_queue(const process : processno) :
   effect
      "take oldest message from corresponding msg_queue"
      post msg_buffer[process] = dequeue(msg_buffer[process]')
end /* action update_queue */

action decrement_bufcnt(const process : processno) :
   condition bufcnt[process] > 0
   effect
      "decrement corresponding bufcnt"
      post bufcnt[process] = bufcnt[process]' - 1
end /* action decrement_bufcnt */
```

Figure 7: Two actions for the *communication_prim*

The action *update_queue* will simply delete the message from the queue referenced by the parameter *process*. It will be activated within the receive primitive of the *communication_prim* with actual parameter *no*. Thus the queue which will be updated is attached to the process whose identification has been transferred within the receive-demand message. The state of this queue after the action *update_queue* has taken place is described as a postcondition of the effect. As stated earlier we also have to specify a precondition which must be satisfied by a state before the action will take place in order to require the validity of the postcondition after the action has terminated. But AADL allows to omit this precondition when - as in our case - it is identical to *true*. The effect of deleting an element from the queue is specified by applying the function *dequeue* defined in the abstract data-type QUEUE to *msg_buffer*[*process*]'. The '-sign refers to the "old" value of that storage structure. Thus the postcondition states that the current value of *msg_buffer*[*process*] (i.e. its value after the action has taken place) is equivalent to the result of applying *dequeue* to the "old" value of *msg_buffer*[*process*] (i.e. its value before the action has taken place).

The second action *decrement_bufcnt* will - in order to keep it consistent with the queues in *msg_buffer* - decrement the *bufcnt* at the place given as parameter *process*. Under the keyword *condition* a formula can be specified which has to be fulfilled whenever this action is activated.

Here we will point out that the pre/post-style specification of actions allows a readable specification for actions which are far more complex than those shown above. They can be split up into several effects specified as pre/post-conditions. Such effects can be clustered to so-called *evaluation states* which are evaluated in sequential order and in parallel within each evaluation state.

To complete the set of AADL specifications which are used as examples in section 3 we will now discuss the architecture *multiplexer* used as type of the *mux*-architecture within protocol services (Figure 8).

```
architecture multiplexer :

 interface
    sync inport in : msg;
    sync outport remote_out : msg;
    sync outport local_out : msg

 behaviour

    control
       rep
          in ? msg_con(a : address, ms : mess) ->
             case a.node of

                protocol_id : local_out ! msg_con(a,ms);
                   /* process resides on the same node */

                otherwise remote_out ! msg_con(a, ms);

             esac
       per
    end /* control */

end /* architecture multiplexer */
```

Figure 8: AADL specification for *mux*

This receives (from the *communication_prim*) over its inport *in* a message consisting of an address which will be stored in the local variable *a* and a message content stored in *ms*. By comparing the node field (see declaration of *address* in architecture *destination_buffering_protocol*) with the variable *protocol_id* (which contains the number of the node to which this protocol handler is attached) it will then decide whether the received message must be further delivered over the outport *local_out* to the *I_process* or over *remote_out* to the *network*. This functionality will be performed within a rep/per construct constituting an infinite loop.

We conclude this section by discussing the status of the trigger construct and the termination of actions.

While in synchronous systems the activation of an operation is controlled by a clock and/or the presence of some encoding, in general it will depend on (local or global) conditions on the state, which may be (asynchronously) set or reset as a result of executing other operations. As outlined in the above examples, such conditions can be handled implicitly by activating actions only at specific control points. But (especially for lower-level layers) the designer can also explicitly state such trigger conditions in the control section within the statement " on trigger do action od ". Combining several such statements with the *par*-constructor models that the respective actions await their trigger conditions and several of them will be executed in parallel when their triggers become true. Typically triggers will be specified by "almost" propositional formulae: think of interrupt requests becoming true, resources being freed, new messages arriving - all these are sample instances of conditions causing an action to be triggered. The qualifier "almost" refers to the fact that the tested storage structures might have a more complex type than just *bool* or *bitsequence*: any finite type will do. The critical property with respect to verification is the representability of situations which cause the accomplishment of a trigger within a Petri net. If the activation of actions can be modelled by "playing the token game", then the liveness properties expressible in our model can be verified automatically (by model-checking algorithms). But in several cases arcs labeled with conditions are needed to model conditional (and thus state-dependent) token flow.

The atomicity of actions entails, in particular, that we can only deal with terminating atomic actions, which sounds reasonable in theory but may be violated in "pathological" architectures (think of an uninterruptable memory-read operation with unbounded levels of indirect addressing). On the other hand, the termination will be exploited heavily in the design to specify liveness properties of lower design levels, where in particular one higher level action might be realized by a complex interaction of lower level atomic actions.

3. Representing AADL specifications by Petri nets

In this section we translate AADL specifications into (a special class of) Petri nets. Apart from their use as semantics of AADL these nets will also be used in CAD tools for the simulation and verification of AADL specifications. We start by describing the particular class of nets needed to define the semantics of AADL, which we refer to as AADL nets.

Briefly, AADL nets are one safe condition-event systems syntactically enriched by special arcs. Before we describe the process of generating such an AADL net, we explain the main points on which these nets differ from standard condition/event nets.

In AADL nets we will assume that the set of places is split into three disjoint classes:

(1) So called control places in the set *Con* will represent the flow of control as dictated by the AADL control specification;

(2) Semaphore places in the set *Sem* will be generated between concurrently executed actions which share resources;

(3) Trigger places in the set *Tri* represent conditions evaluated in a trigger command, causing non-procedural activation of its body. These places are labeled by the condition which they represent. The construction will ensure that the condition is true iff the place is marked.

To distinguish the different place classes in drawings we will represent control places by double circles and semaphore places by double-circles labeled *sem*.

In AADL nets there are two classes of arcs which point from places to transitions: *enabling arcs* and *consuming arcs* (Figures 9 and 10).

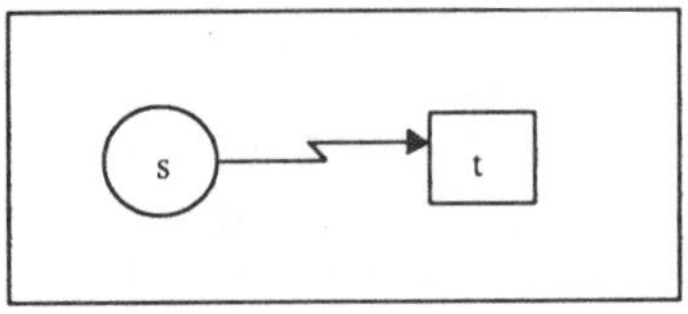

Figure 9: Enabling arc

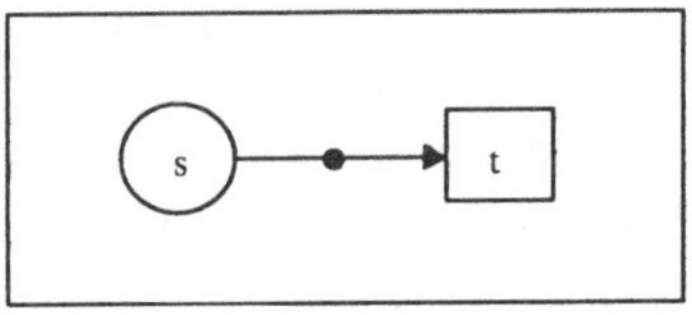

Figure 10: Consuming arc

The firing rule is extended to such arcs as follows. All places connected by an enabling arc with a specific transition have to carry a token (which will be represented by a black dot within the place) in order to allow the firing of that transition. Such a firing will not remove the token from a place (unless the place is also connected via a consuming arc - to be discussed below - to this transition).

In fact removal of tokens is only done via consuming arcs. Places which are exclusively connected by a consuming arc to a transition need not carry a token in order to allow the firing of that transition. But they may carry one which is then removed by the firing of that transition.

Combining the two different arcs (both pointing from one specific place to one specific transition) will constitute the normal Petri net arc whose firing necessitates the presence of a token in the place and which removes this token upon its firing. Control and semaphore places are always connected via combined arcs to transitions.

It is worth pointing out that these special arcs can be implemented in "normal" Petri nets. The enabling arcs can be represented by two normal Petri net arcs, one pointing from the place to the transition and the other pointing back from the transition to the place. But this construction is not correct with respect to conflicts: connecting transitions by enabling arcs to one and the same place does not introduce a conflict, whereas they would do so in the above-constructed Petri net. We can overcome this by duplicating the places involved and connecting each copy as explained above to only one of the transitions. All these copies have, of course, to be connected to several other transitions as for the original place (Figure 11).

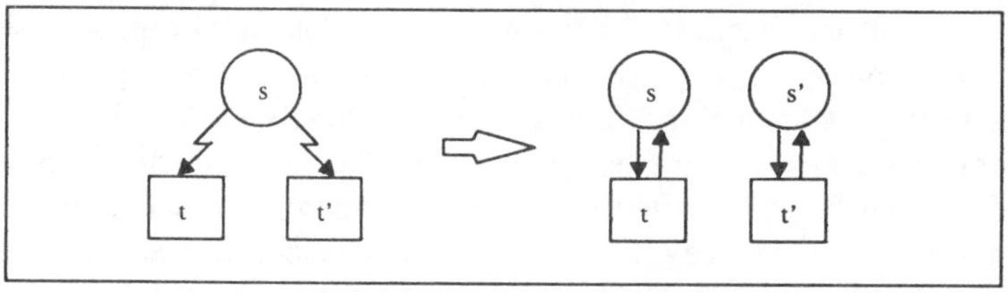

Figure 11: Representing enabling arcs by normal Petri nets

We have only one type of arc pointing from transitions to places. When they point to a *control* or *semaphor place* they have the same interpretation as in conventional Petri nets: after firing the transition they deliver a token to that place. Therefore they are called *delivering arcs*. Such an arc will be called *conditional* if it points to a trigger-place labeled with a non-trivial predicate (i.e. a predicate different from *true*) (Figure 12).

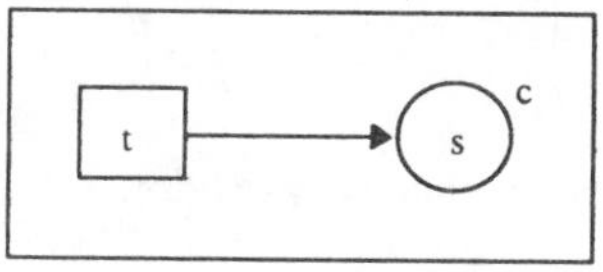

Figure 12: Delivering arc

Intuitively a conditional arc will only allow a token to be passed to its trigger place if the condition of that place is satisfied in the current state. Since this property cannot be decided on the schematic level, we introduce a firing-rule for conditional arcs, which "guesses" whether the condition is satisfied. The checking of the actual conditions will then be carried out in a further step after having generated the so-called "processes" which are Petri nets representing all possible unwindings of the original net (see section 4).

In Figure 13 we have given only one possible situation for the firing of t in which we assumed that c_5 is satisfied whereas c_7 is not. (Note that it is not relevant whether c_6 is true or not!) In fact the firing rule shown in the figure has only be introduced to strengthen the intuitive understanding of the semantics of AADL nets. In the formal development it will not be used.

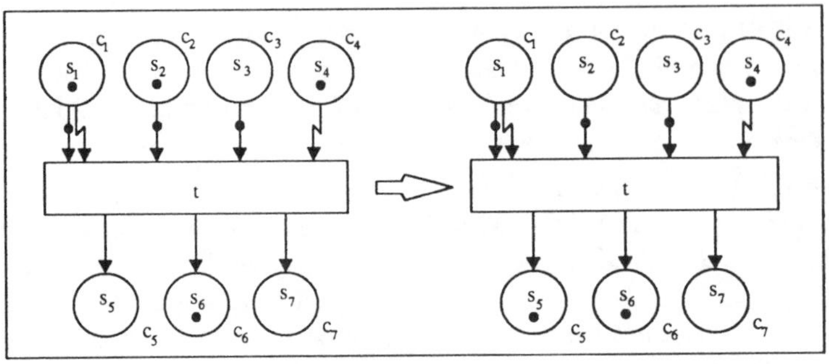

Figure 13: Firing rule

The firing rule for AADL nets also differs from that of normal condition/event Petri nets in contact situations. A transition in an AADL net can also fire in contact situations, i.e. when one or more of the places in the postset carries a token. Also in such situations the firing rule will guarantee the property that there is at most one token per place because it does not put a second token on such a place. This seemingly strange decision stems from the pragmatics associated with trigger places in AADL nets, which are associated with certain conditions on the state of the specified architecture. The nets will be constructed so that such a condition is true iff the corresponding place is marked. Thus a contact situation would merely represent the fact that the execution of an AADL action makes a condition true which was already valid in the state prior to the execution of this action. The construction of AADL nets will guarantee that contact situations only arise for trigger places.

To increase the readability of drawn nets we use the following two abbreviations:

(1) Combined enabling and consuming arcs will subsequently be referred to as "combined arc" and are drawn using the standard symbol for arcs in Petri nets;

(2) A self-loop involving a place s and a transition t will be represented by a bidirectional arc;

Definition 3.1 (AADL nets)

We define an AADL net as a structure

$$\Sigma = (S, T, F_{enb}, F_{cons}, F_{del}, \Gamma, \pi, M_0, s_0, s_e)$$

where

S and T are disjoint finite sets (they represent the places and transitions of the AADL net) and $S = Sem \uplus Con \uplus Tri$

$F_{enb} \subseteq S \times T$ and $F_{cons} \subseteq S \times T$ (representing the enabling and consuming arcs)

$F_{del} \subseteq T \times S$ (representing the delivering arcs)

$\Gamma : T \rightarrow CONT$ where $CONT$ is the set of transformations on the state-space underlying the AADL specification. The exact structure of $CONT$ is irrelevant for the development of AADL nets and is therefore not included in this chapter.

$\pi : Tri \rightarrow PRED$ where $PRED$ is the set of quantifier-free first-order formulas in a signature canonically determined by the underlying AADL specification[3]

$s_0, s_e \in Con$

$M_0 \subseteq S$ (representing the initially marked places) is such that $Sem \cup \{s_0\} \subseteq M_0$.

We denote the set of all AADL nets by N. □

Notation (pre-sets and post-sets)

For $x \in S \cup T$ we define

$$pre_{enb}(x) = \{y \in S \ / \ (y,x) \in F_{enb}\}$$

$$pre_{cons}(x) = \{y \in S \ / \ (y,x) \in F_{cons}\}$$

$$pre_{del}(x) = \{y \in T \ / \ (y,x) \in F_{del}\}$$

$$post_{enb}(x) = \{y \in T \ / \ (x,y) \in F_{enb}\}$$

$$post_{cons}(x) = \{y \in T \ / \ (x,y) \in F_{cons}\}$$

$$post_{del}(x) = \{y \in S \ / \ (x,y) \in F_{del}\}$$

We denote as *preset* (*postset*) the union of the above defined pre_{index} ($post_{index}$).

□

In what follows we define the net-generation process for AADL specifications. This is based mainly on the (CSP-style) control part of an AADL specification describing the activation of actions.

Most of the transitions in an AADL net directly reflect some action of the underlying AADL specification. The state transformation induced by such an action will be bound to its transition in the AADL net by the function Γ. But there are also some additional transitions called τ-transitions, which have no influence on the state space and in general no direct counterpart in the AADL specification. The τ-transitions simplify the modelling of the overall control flow induced by the control structure part of an AADL specification

[3] *PRED* includes the predicate *matched(expr, pattern)* which is *true* whenever *expr* and *pattern* fit together. As a second argument we also allow the value *dummy* for the case that the pattern is yet unknown. In this case the truth value of *matched(...)* cannot be determined.

by allowing us to consider only nets with a single start- and end-place; it can be shown that these transitions can be eliminated - in fact, our proof-methods will carry out the corresponding reductions in the associated case-graph automatically. We will refer to nets which consist only of a τ-transition with control-places in the *pre*- and *postset* by the term τ-nets.

We use composition operators for AADL's "control statements" with the aim of generating systematically AADL-net representations with finite net structure. Thus we aim for a calculus for constructing nets inductively by means of these composition operators allowing inductive proof techniques and giving rise to well-structured nets which are easier to analyse. More formally, we view the set of AADL nets as a carrier of an algebra whose operators are determined by the syntax of AADL control specifications.

We now proceed by considering the different AADL language constructs for specifying behaviour appearing in the control specification. We start with the most elementary ingredients of a command sequence,[4] which are nullary operators on the domain of AADL nets: skip, abort, and run-time assertions (Figure 14). Intuitively, *skip* defines the identity on the state space and *abort* causes the abortion of the computation by entering a special error state. Run-time assertions check the validity of an assertion c; if c evaluates to true, then the state is left unchanged and control is passed to the next statement, otherwise the computation is aborted. Thus the abortion statement could also be written as assertion $false$.

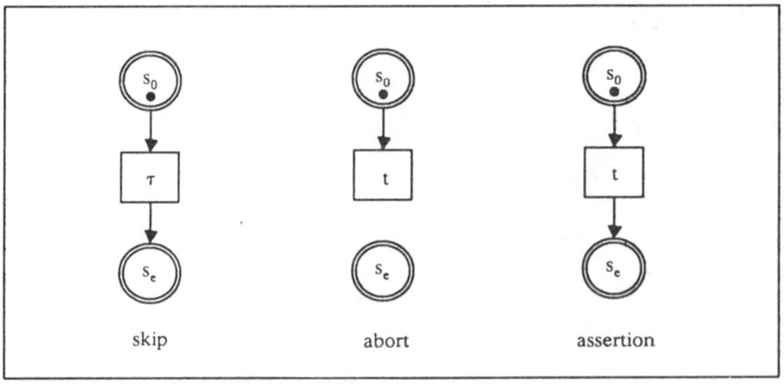

Figure 14: Elementary AADL nets

We will now define these AADL nets in a formal setting.

Definition 3.2 (AADL-net operators)

For the skip command we define the following AADL net Σ_{skip}.

$$\Sigma_{skip} = (S, T, F_{enb}, F_{cons}, F_{del}, \Gamma, \pi, M_0, s_0, s_e)$$

where the net components are given by

$$S = \{s_0, s_e\} = Con$$
$$T = \{\tau\}$$
$$F_{enb} = F_{cons} = \{(s_0, \tau)\}$$

[4] We denote as a "command sequence" either single commands which may contain further command sequences or several commands separated by the ";" sign.

$F_{del} = \{(\tau, s_e)\}$
$\Gamma(\tau) = id_{CONT}$
π is the empty function
$M_0 = \{s_0\}$.

For the abort command we define the following AADL net Σ_{abort}.

$\Sigma_{abort} = (S, T, F_{enb}, F_{cons}, F_{del}, \Gamma, \pi, M_0, s_0, s_e)$

where the net components are given by

$S = \{s_0, s_e\} = Con$
$T = \{t\}$
$F_{enb} = F_{cons} = \{(s_0, t)\}$
$F_{del} = \varnothing$
$\Gamma(t) = \lambda\, \sigma\, .\, error$
π is the empty function
$M_0 = \{s_0\}$.

For the assertion <u>invariant</u> c we define the following AADL net Σ_{invar}.

$\Sigma_{invar} = (S, T, F_{enb}, F_{cons}, F_{del}, \Gamma, \pi, M_0, s_0, s_e)$

where the net components are given by

$S = \{s_0, s_e\} = Con$
$T = \{t\}$
$F_{enb} = F_{cons} = \{(s_0, t)\}$
$F_{del} = \{(t, s_e)\}$
$\Gamma(t) = \lambda\, \sigma\, .\, c : \sigma \mid error$
π is the empty function
$M_0 = \{s_0\}$.

Example 3.1 (Net generation for the OS protocol)

In the rest of this chapter we will use parts of the AADL control programs written for the DOOM operating system protocol (see section 2) to illustrate the net-generation process. We will first concentrate on the control program of the architecture *communication prim*. In its second part - representing the *receive* primitive - we have the invariant $length(msg\_buffer[no]) \neq 0$ which is represented by the simple AADL net shown in Figure 15.

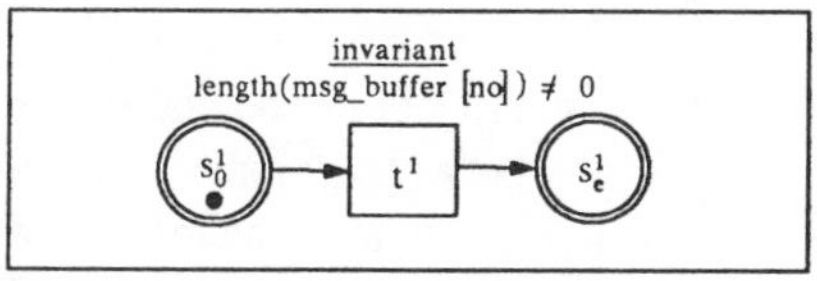

Figure 15: Net Σ_1 for an invariant in the OS protocol

In this illustration the state transformation containing the actual testing of the invariant is not visible. The start-place s_0^1 contains a token because it has to be in the initial marking M_0^1.

Another nullary net operator has to be defined for the action call. The AADL *action_call* defines an indivisible state transformation by invoking an axiomatically specified primitive action of an architecture. The question is, which places have to be in the pre- or postset of a transition t representing an action A?

To answer this question we will make some general comments about trigger places in AADL nets. Their main task is to state which transitions shall or shall not be able to fire. Thus a place with only outgoing consuming arcs is not usefull, because it has no influence on the firing/non-firing of transitions.

Control places (represented by a double circle in an AADL net) will be inductively joined together during the net-generation process to a formation reflecting the overall control-flow structure of the command sequence. All trigger-places are enriched with a formula (on the state space) which reflects (one part of) a (trigger-) condition involved in the activation of one or more actions. Thus given an AADL module one could compute the (finite) set of places *Tri* with formulae which constitute the trigger-places for the net representing this AADL module. Given one place $s \in Tri$ we then would have to connect it to a specific transition t (representing the action A) whenever A will potentially change one or more variables occurring in $\pi(s)$ (the formula attached to s).

Intuitively, the kind of connection between s and t depends on what we can expect as truth value for $\pi(s)$ after action A has been executed. In many cases this can be statically inferred on the basis of the AADL specification of action A.

We distinguish four cases:

(1) If A does not change the truth value of $\pi(s)$ - in particular, if A does not change free variables occurring in $\pi(s)$ - transition t and place s are not connected.

(2) If it can be statically inferred that A will falsify formula $\pi(s)$ we draw a consuming arc between s and t.

(3) If it can be statically inferred that A will validate formula $\pi(s)$ we draw a conditional arc between s and t.

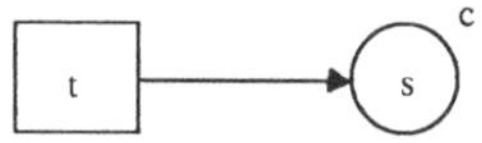

(4) If statically no assertions can be made about the validity of $\pi(s)$ after A has been executed we draw a conditional arc between t and s. Because in such a situation it is possible that A will falsify $\pi(s)$, we also have to introduce a consuming arc between A and s. Note that the conditional arc will "repair" (i.e. restore) an incorrectly removed token where A did not invalidate $\pi(s)$.

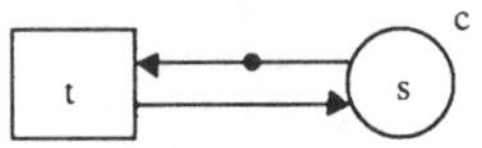

In the formal development we will construct the arcs between such trigger places and actions inductively in order to achieve our overall goal of defining the AADL nets and all further steps for the definition of the AADL semantics in a compositional way. To this end we will generate for each AADL net an auxiliary function *access*, which provides the "bookkeeping information" for the connection of trigger-places and actions.

Since this function only indicates for the storage structures referred by a net which actions read or write on them we can only distinguish the first and last of the four cases discussed above. Thus within the net semantics of AADL actions will be connected by consuming and conditional arcs to trigger-places s when they write - according to the function *access* - on a variable occurring free in $\pi(s)$.

Because of the AADL trigger command, this bookkeeping information has to be slightly more complex. In AADL, not only actions but also bodies of a trigger command claim all the resources needed for their execution before being executed. We thus choose as the range of the access function the critical sections of the net which are themselves complete AADL nets (rather than only transitions).

Definition 3.3 (Critical sections, *Store*, *access*)

For an AADL net Σ we let $Store(\Sigma)$ denote the set of storage structures referred to in Σ and $CS(\Sigma)$ the set of its critical sections which are subnets of Σ.

These functions are defined inductively. For the nets associated with the previously defined AADL commands we have:

$$Store(\Sigma) = \varnothing \quad \text{and} \quad CS(\Sigma) = \varnothing$$

The function $access_\Sigma$ associates with each storage structure α referred to in the transitions of Σ (thus $\alpha \in Store(\Sigma)$) the set of critical sections of Σ accessing α in either write or read mode:

$$access_\Sigma : Store(\Sigma) \to \{read, write\} \to CS(\Sigma) \qquad \square$$

Notation

For a net Σ we use the following auxiliary functions:

start (Σ) denotes the unique start-place of Σ;

end (Σ) denotes the unique exit-place of Σ;

entry (Σ) denotes the unique set of transitions having *start* (Σ) in their pre-set;

exit (Σ) denotes the unique set of transitions having *end* (Σ) in their post-set.

These functions will, for instance, be used when connecting places to critical sections.

□

We now resume our formal definition of the nets and auxiliary functions by considering an atomic action A. For an action A we define the net representation shown in Figure 16.

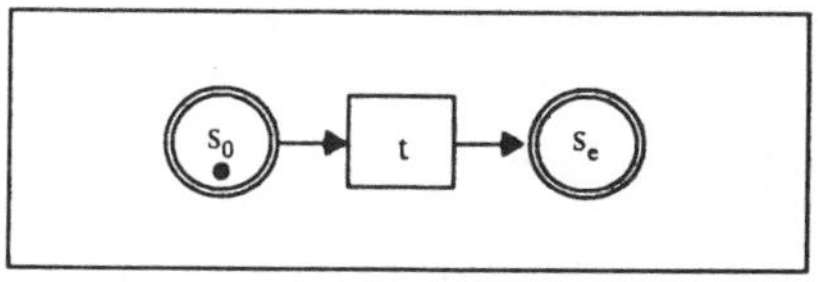

Figure 16: AADL net representing an action_call

This is formalized in the following definition which precedes that of net operators given before.

Definition 3.2 (AADL nets, continued)

$\Sigma_A = (S, T, F_{enb}, F_{cons}, F_{del}, \Gamma, \pi, M_0, s_0, s_e)$

where the net components are given by

$S = \{s_0, s_e\} = Con$

$T = \{t\}$

$F_{enb} = F_{cons} = \{(s_0, t)\}$

$F_{del} = \{(t, s_e)\}$

$\Gamma(t)$ can be canonically derived from the AADL specification of A (see Damm, 1984b)

π is the empty function

$M_0 = \{s_0\}$.

□

Definition 3.3 (Critical sections, *Store*, *access*, continued)

The set of critical sections of Σ_A consists of the singleton set containing Σ_A.

For the purpose of this chapter we assume that the set of storage elements accessed by an action A, $Store(A)$, and a mapping

$access_A : Store(A) \rightarrow \{read, write\}$

is given (see Damm, 1988). From this the corresponding functions for the associated AADL net can be derived canonically. □

Example 3.1 (Net generation for the OS protocol, continued)

Several actions are called within the control program of the architecture *communication_prim*. The nets for actions included in its second part are shown in Figure 17. We have provided each net with the name of the action represented by it.

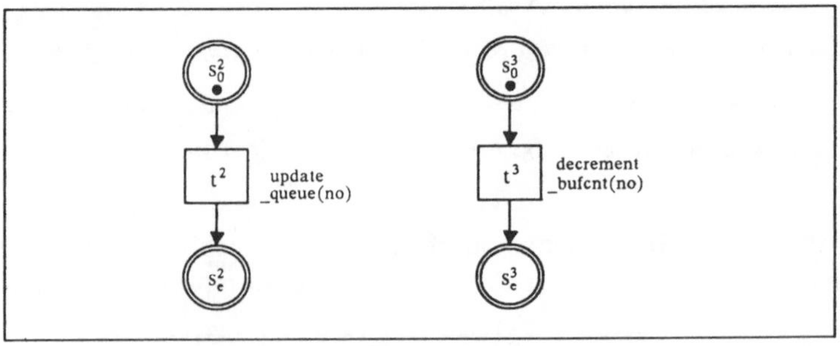

Figure 17: Nets Σ_2 and Σ_3 for actions in the OS protocol

□

The I/O-commands of AADL are derived from the CSP input and output commands. In AADL, I/O commands are only used for communication between modules. All processes within a module communicate via shared storage elements. A synchronous communication between modules can only take place in situations where an output command synchronizes with an appropriate input command. This situation is modelled in AADL nets by merging the corresponding transitions for input and output commands (located in different architectures) which read and write on linked ports.

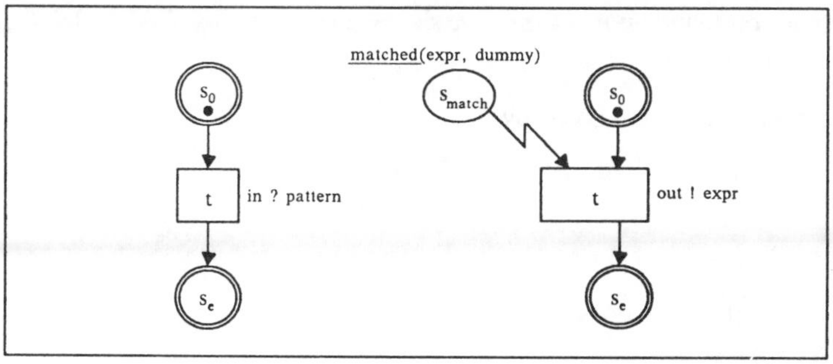

Figure 18: Net representation for input/output commands

This merging of transitions associated with I/O commands will be realized by the AADL net operator for the parallel composition of modules defined later in this chapter. In the case of one output command with more than one input command reading from the appropriate port we have to use several copies of the transition related to the output command with equal pre- and postsets. Each input transition will then be joined with one of these copies. To include the pattern matching we have to enrich the net for the sending subarchitecture "sender" by places representing the fact that "expression" and "pattern" for one pair of input and output commands match together. These "pattern-matching" places are then connected to the related (joined) transitions by an enabling arc.

All transitions in subarchitecture "sender" which potentially change the structure of "expression" will then be connected to this "pattern-matching" place in the way described before.

In the formal development we will provide each transition associated with an output command *port ! expr* with a trigger-place labeled by a predicate *matched(expr, dummy)*, where the actual pattern will be substituted for the placeholder when combining the nets of modules. Similarly, we will link - when combining this net with other nets - all transitions possibly affecting *expr* to this trigger-place.

Definition 3.2 (AADL net operators, continued)

For the input command *port ? pattern* we define the following AADL net Σ_{in}:

$$\Sigma_{in} = (S, T, F_{enb}, F_{cons}, F_{del}, \Gamma, \pi, M_0, s_0, s_e)$$

where the net components are given by

$$S = \{s_0, s_e\} = Con$$

$$T = \{t\}$$

$$F_{enb} = F_{cons} = \{(s_0, t)\}$$

$$F_{del} = \{(t, s_e)\}$$

$\Gamma(t) = \lambda\,\Theta\,.\,\lambda\,\sigma\,.\,\sigma\,[x/\Theta x\ /\ x \in free\,(pattern)]$ where Θ is of type substitution (i.e. a mapping from variables occurring in the pattern to values in a suitable semantic domain D).

π is the empty function

$M_0 = \{s_0\}$.

For the output command *port* ! *expr* we define the following AADL net Σ_{out}:

$\Sigma_{out} = (\ S, T, F_{enb}, F_{cons}, F_{del}, \Gamma, \pi, M_0, s_0, s_e\ )$

where the net components are given by

$S = \{s_0, s_e, s_{match}\}$ and $s_0, s_e \in Con$, $s_{match} \in Tri$

$T = \{t\}$

$F_{enb} = \{(s_0, t), (s_{match}, t)\}$

$F_{cons} = \{(s_0, t)\}$

$F_{del} = \{(t, s_e)\}$

$\Gamma(t) = \lambda\,\sigma\,.\,\sigma = id_{CONT}$

$\pi(s_{match}) \equiv matched\,(expr, dummy)$

$M_0 = \{s_0\}$.

□

Definition 3.3 (Critical sections, *Store*, *access*, continued)

The sets of critical sections $CS(\Sigma_{in})$, $CS(\Sigma_{out})$ consist of the singleton sets containing Σ_{in}, Σ_{out} respectively.

The storage structures referred to in the above-defined nets are:

$Store\,(\Sigma_{in})$ = the set of storage structures in *pattern*

$Store\,(\Sigma_{out})$ = the set of storage structures in *expr*

where an input command only writes on its storage structures whereas an output command reads on them. Thus

$access_{\Sigma_{in}}(\alpha)(read) = access_{\Sigma_{out}}(\alpha)(write) = \emptyset$

$access_{\Sigma_{in}}(\alpha)(write) = \Sigma_{in}$

$access_{\Sigma_{out}}(\alpha)(read) = \Sigma_{out}$

□

In order to be able to join appropriate in/output transitions we will again introduce a "bookkeeping-function", $comm_\Sigma$ which associates with each net a mapping from the visible ports to the transitions representing in/out commands on this port. For transitions representing input commands, this function will also provide the actual pattern to be substituted for the site holder.

Definition 3.4 (Communication capabilities)

The "local" state transformations associated with input and output commands will be "merged" when defining the net operator corresponding to a parallel composition of modules. Let $Ports\,(\Sigma)$ denote the set of ports referred to in Σ and $Pattern\,(\Sigma)$ denote its pattern. We associate with each net Σ its communication capabilities by $comm_\Sigma$ where

$$comm_\Sigma : Ports(\Sigma) \rightarrow \wp(T \times (Pattern(\Sigma) \cup \{out\}))$$

For the net Σ_{in} defined as above we have

$$Ports(\Sigma_{in}) = \{port\}$$

$$comm_{\Sigma_{in}}(port) = \{(t, pattern)\}$$

For the net Σ_{out} we have

$$Ports(\Sigma_{out}) = \{port\}$$

$$comm_{\Sigma_{out}}(port) = \{(t, out)\}$$

For the previously considered commands we have $Ports(\Sigma) = \emptyset$.

□

Example 3.1 (Net generation for the OS protocol)

One input and two output commands occur in the second part of the control program for architecture communication_prim. Their nets together with its communication capabilities $comm_\Sigma$ are shown in Figure 19.

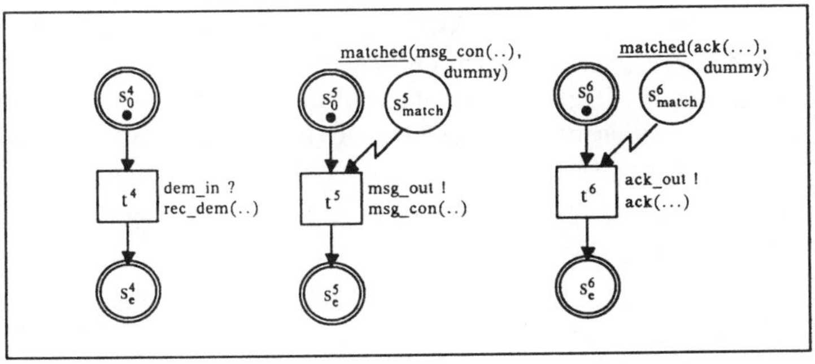

Figure 19: Nets Σ_4, Σ_5, Σ_6 ;
input and output commands in the OS protocol

The input command *dem_in ? rec_dem*(*no* :*processno*) and the output command *ack_out* ! *ack*(*no*, *top*(*msg_buffer*[*no*]).*content*) have according to the linking of their ports *dem_in* and *ack_out*, to synchronize with appropriate output resp. input commands in the architecture *processes* whereas the output command *msg_out* ! *msg_con*(...) has to sychronize with an input command in the architecture *multiplexer*.

The net operator used to construct a net for the combination of different (sub)architectures will use the functions $comm_{\Sigma_i}$ and $comm_{\Sigma_j}$ to find which commands read and write on linked ports and will combine the appropriate transitions. For the net Σ_5 shown above we have $comm_{\Sigma_5}(msg\_out) = \{(t^5, out)\}$.

□

We will now explain the net operators for the compound structures *sequence*, *trigger−command*, *alt−command*, *rep−command*, *par−command*, *case−command*, *procedure call*, and the *combination of subarchitectures* in this order.

Except for the last, all these commands take one ore more substructures (which can vary from simple skip/abort statements, single action calls or sequences of action calls up to compound structures) to build a new structure. The compositional net-generation process is based on this property and takes one or more already constructed nets and combines these with a new net which represents the compound structure. In the formal development we will only define the corresponding operators on nets.

We will first extract a number of operations on net components, which are independent of the particular operator. These operations will be used to identify places and adapt all net components according to this identification when nets are combined with a net operator.

Place identification will be performed by the operation $IDEN_S$ which takes as a first argument a set of sets, where each set contains places which have to be identified, and as a second argument a set of places in which these identifications will take place. The operations $IDEN_F$, $IDEN_\pi$, and $IDEN_M$, when called with the same set of sets as the first argument as $IDEN_S$ will then adapt the arcs, the formulae according to π, and the initial marking M_0 to the identified places.

There are three cases in which such place identifications will be performed:

(1) trigger places in the set *Tri* have in general to be identified when they represent the same formula (according to π). The only exception to this rule occurs for places s, s' when nets are combined with the *PAR* operator and non-conflicting transitions t, t' have s, s' in their pre_{enb} set respectively. The operation *EQUI* defines the decomposition of places into maximal sets in which all elements represent the same formula. This class decomposition can then be used as the first argument for the operations $IDEN_X$ ($X \in \{S, T, \pi, M\}$) to perform the identification for trigger places.

(2) Control places in the set *Con* have to be identified to reveal the intended behaviour of the net for a compound structure.

(3) Semaphor places in the set *Sem* will be identified when they synchronize each pair of critical sections within a set of critical sections.

Definition 3.5 (Glueing of places)

In the following definitions we assume that S, T are the sets of places respectively transitions of an AADL net Σ. For reasons of representation we assume further that the elements of S are sets which record from which elementary places (singleton sets) they have been built up through place identifications. The place-sets of the up to now constructed nets can be canonically altered into such sets by representing elements s through $\{s\}$. With $Set_1, \ldots, Set_k$ we denote the places of S that shall be identified. Thus the Set_i's are disjoint subsets of S.

We define the set $IDEN_S(\{Set_1, \ldots, Set_k\}, S)$ by condensing the places contained in a Set_i to a single new place named new_i.

$$IDEN_S(\{Set_1, \ldots, Set_k\}, S) = (S \setminus \bigcup_{1 \le i \le k} Set_k) \cup \{new_i = \bigcup_{s \in Set_i} s \;/\; 1 \le i \le k\}$$

Let $F \subseteq S \times T \cup T \times S$. We define a new relation $IDEN_F(\{Set_1, \ldots, Set_k\}, F)$ which constitutes an arc between a place new_i in the condensed set and a transition t whenever such an arc is present in the original relation F between one element of Set_i and t.

$$IDEN_F(\{Set_1,\ldots,Set_k\}, F) \subseteq IDEN_S(\{Set_1,\ldots,Set_k\}, S) \times T \cup T \times IDEN_S(\{Set_1,\ldots,Set_k\}, S)$$

$$IDEN_F(\{Set_1,\ldots,Set_k\}, F) = (F \setminus \{(s,t),(t,s) \,/\, s \in \bigcup_{1\le i\le k} Set_i\})$$
$$\cup \{(new_i, t) \,/\, \exists s \in S, t \in T, i \in \{1,\ldots,k\} : (s,t) \in F \wedge s \in Set_i\}$$
$$\cup \{(t, new_i) \,/\, \exists s \in S, t \in T, i \in \{1,\ldots,k\} : (t,s) \in F \wedge s \in Set_i\}$$

Let $\pi : S \rightarrow PRED$ and let $Set_1,\ldots,Set_k \subseteq S$ such that $\pi(s_1) \equiv \pi(s_2)$ for $s_1, s_2 \in Set_i$. We define the function $IDEN_\pi(\{Set_1,\ldots,Set_k\}, \pi)$ which maps condensed places to predicates and which can be canonically derived from the function π:

$$IDEN_\pi(\{Set_1,\ldots,Set_k\}, \pi) : \{new_1,\ldots,new_n\} \rightarrow PRED$$

where $IDEN_\pi(\{Set_1,\ldots,Set_k\}, \pi)(new_i) = \pi(s)$ for some $s \in Set_i$

Let $M \subseteq S$ and let $Set_1,\ldots,Set_k$ such that $Set_i \cap M = \emptyset$ or $Set_i \subseteq M$. We define the new initial marking $IDEN_M(\{Set_1,\ldots,Set_k\}, M)$ where the places in the sets Set_i are replaced by the single place s_{Set_i}:

$$IDEN_M(\{Set_1,\ldots,Set_k\}, M) \subseteq IDEN_S(\{Set_1,\ldots,Set_k\}, S)$$
$$IDEN_M(\{Set_1,\ldots,Set_k\}, M) = \{new_i \,/\, Set_i \subseteq M\} \cup (M \setminus \bigcup_{1\le i\le k} Set_i)$$

Let $\pi : S \rightarrow PRED$ and let $F, F' \subseteq S \times T$ denote two sets of arcs pointing from places to transitions. The elements of the set $EQUI(S, \pi, F, F')$ are themselves sets of (trigger) places which shall be identified because they represent the same formula. The relations F, F' will denote respectively the enabling and consuming arcs, which are used to determine places which are exclusively connected by enabling arcs to different transitions (and thus do not cause a conflict between these transitions):

$$EQUI(S, \pi, F, F') = \{Set_1,\ldots,Set_k\}$$

where $Set_1,\ldots,Set_k$ are maximal sets such that

$$\forall s, s' \in Set_i : (\pi(s) \equiv \pi(s')$$
$$\wedge \forall t, t' : (t \ne t' \wedge (s,t),(s',t') \in F) \Rightarrow (s,t) \in F' \vee (s',t) \in F').$$

□

Without loss of generality we assume in what follows that the sets of transitions and places occurring in the nets Σ_i are disjoint. Furthermore we assume that the places are themselves represented by sets. As pointed out above, this restriction can be satisfied by a simple conversion on the places.

Extension of the auxiliary functions to compound nets is defined below. Up to the trigger command the critical section of a compound net is always defined as the union of the critical sections of its constituents. Similarly, *access* and *comm* are extended canonically to compound structures.

Definition 3.3 (Critical sections, *Store*, *access*, continued)

For any operator *op* different from *TRIG* (which constructs the net for the " on ϕ do ... od ") we have

$$CS(op(\Sigma_1,\ldots,\Sigma_n)) = \bigcup_{i\in\{1,\ldots,n\}} CS(\Sigma_i)$$

For any operator *op* we have

$$Store\,(op\,(\Sigma_1,\ldots,\Sigma_n)) = \bigcup_{i\in\{1,..,n\}} Store\,(\Sigma_i)$$

$$access_{op\,(\Sigma_1,\ldots,\Sigma_n)} = \bigcup_{i\in\{1,..,n\}} access_{\Sigma_i}$$

□

Let us now continue our discussion regarding the connection of trigger-places to transitions. As pointed out earlier, we will introduce the corresponding arcs inductively. Thus, whenever we combine nets $\Sigma_1,\ldots,\Sigma_n$ with some operator op we have to combine the trigger places in Σ_j with the transitions in Σ_i affecting the validity of these places. To this end we will introduce operators $CONN_{exit}^{trigger}$ and $CONN_{entry}^{trigger}$ on nets, which define these arcs.

Definition 3.6 (Connection of trigger places)

To define the conditional and consuming arcs induced by connecting trigger places to exit resp. entry points in critical sections we define the auxiliary operations $CONN_{exit}^{trigger}$ and $CONN_{entry}^{trigger}$.

Let $\Sigma \in N$, S be a finite set, and $\pi : S \to PRED$:

$$CONN_{exit}^{trigger}(\Sigma, S, \pi) = \{(t, s) \,/\, s \in S \wedge \exists\, cs \in CS(\Sigma)\, \exists\, \alpha \in free(\pi(s)) : cs \in (access_{\Sigma}(\alpha)(write)) \wedge t \in exit(cs)\}$$

$$CONN_{entry}^{trigger}(\Sigma, S, \pi) = \{(s, t) \,/\, s \in S \wedge \exists\, cs \in CS(\Sigma)\, \exists\, \alpha \in free(\pi(s)) : cs \in (access_{\Sigma}(\alpha)(write)) \wedge t \in entry(cs)\}$$

□

We will now resume the construction of AADL nets by defining the net representation for a sequence of commands. To generate the net for two adjacent structures $constr_1\,;constr_2$ we have only to identify the end-place of $constr_1$ with the start-place of $constr_2$, identify trigger-places representing the same condition, and connect critical sections with trigger-places whose condition may be changed by the critical section (Figure 20).

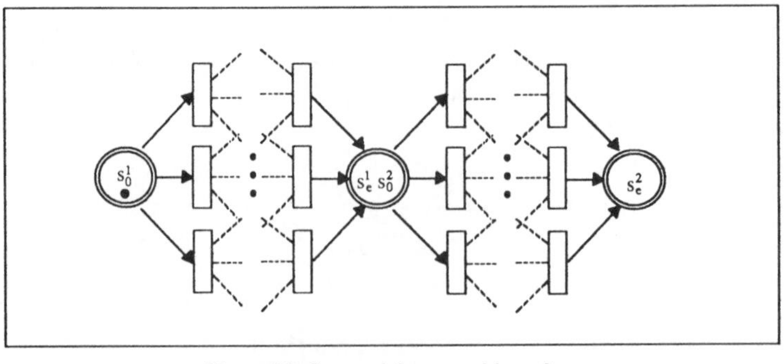

Figure 20: Sequential composition of nets

Definition 3.2 (AADL net operators, continued)

For the sequential composition of two command sequences com_1, com_2 we define the following net operator SEQ:

$SEQ : N \times N \rightarrow N$

Let two AADL nets Σ_1, Σ_2 be given with:

$$\Sigma_i = (S^i, T^i, F^i_{enb}, F^i_{cons}, F^i_{del}, \Gamma^i, \pi^i, M^i_0, s^i_0, s^i_e)$$

We use the abbreviation *glue* for the following set of places which have to be identified:

$$glue = EQUI(Tri^1 \cup Tri^2, \pi^1 \cup \pi^2, F^1_{enb} \cup F^2_{enb}, cons) \cup \{\{s^1_e, s^2_0\}\}$$

$$\text{with } cons = F^1_{cons} \cup F^2_{cons} \cup CONN^{trigger}_{entry}(\Sigma_1, Tri^2, \pi^2) \cup CONN^{trigger}_{entry}(\Sigma_2, Tri^1, \pi^1)$$

We define the net

$$SEQ(\Sigma_1, \Sigma_2) = (\hat{S}, \hat{T}, \hat{F}_{enb}, \hat{F}_{cons}, \hat{F}_{del}, \hat{\Gamma}, \hat{\pi}, \hat{M}_0, \hat{s}_0, \hat{s}_e)$$

where the net components are given by:

$$\hat{S} = IDEN_S(glue, S^1 \cup S^2)$$

$$\hat{T} = T^1 \cup T^2$$

$$\hat{F}_{enb} = IDEN_F(glue, F^1_{enb} \cup F^2_{enb})$$

$$\hat{F}_{cons} = IDEN_F(glue, cons)$$

$$\hat{F}_{del} = IDEN_F(glue, F^1_{del} \cup F^2_{del} \cup CONN^{trigger}_{exit}(\Sigma_1, Tri^2, \pi^2) \cup CONN^{trigger}_{exit}(\Sigma_2, Tri^1, \pi^1))$$

$$\hat{\Gamma} = \Gamma^1 \cup \Gamma^2$$

$$\hat{\pi} = IDEN_\pi(glue, \pi^1 \cup \pi^2)$$

$$\hat{M}_0 = IDEN_M(glue, M^1_0 \cup M^2_0 \setminus \{s^2_0\})$$

□

Example 3.1 (Net generation for the OS protocol, continued)

For the sequence of actions, invariants, and communication commands occurring as the body of the on ... do ... od construct in the second part of the control program the net shown in Figure 21 will be generated.

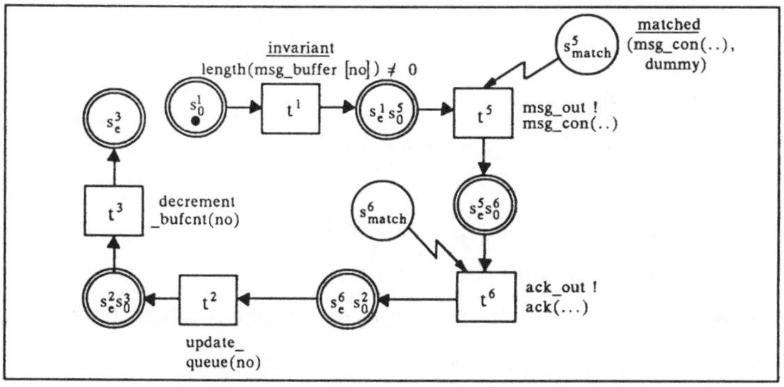

Figure 21: Net representing a sequence of commands in the OS protocol

Using the net operator *SEQ* this net can be constructed as

$$SEQ(SEQ(SEQ(SEQ(\Sigma_1, \Sigma_5), \Sigma_6), \Sigma_2), \Sigma_3)$$

where in each case the set *glue* contains as the only element $\{s_e^i, s_0^k\}$, where s_e^i is the end-place of the net given as the first argument and s_0^k is the start-place of the net given as the second. Thus the places s_e^i, s_0^k will be replaced by the place $\{s_e^i, s_0^k\}$ with connections to both nets.

□

For the trigger command <u>on</u> ϕ <u>do</u> command sequence <u>od</u> we have to connect the net representing the command sequence with a net consisting of places $s_1,\ldots,s_k$ for which $\phi \equiv \pi(s_1) \wedge \ldots \wedge \pi(s_k)$. We include enabling arcs from all places $s_1,\ldots,s_k$ to each start-transition of the net representing the command sequence (Figure 22).

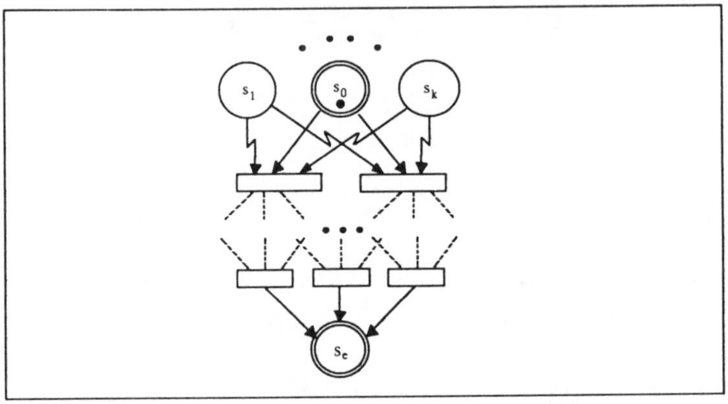

Figure 22: Net representation for the trigger command

In this way the entry transitions and therefore the whole command sequence of the trigger command can only fire when all places $s_1,\ldots,s_k$ carry a token, and consequently the trigger condition is *true*. Note that the glueing of nets will identify places representing the same formula and introduce new (consuming and conditional) arcs when a critical section writes on a (free) variable of the condition for a place.

Definition 3.2 (AADL net operators, continued)

For the trigger command we define the following AADL net operator *TRIG*:

$$TRIG : PRED \times N \rightarrow N$$

Let $\phi \equiv b_1 \wedge \ldots \wedge b_k$ and the net

$$\Sigma = (S, T, F_{enb}, F_{cons}, F_{del}, \Gamma, \pi, M_0, s_0, s_e)$$

be given.

Let $S_{trigger} = \{s_i \;/\; b_i \not\equiv true\}$ with $S_{trigger} \cap S = \emptyset$

and $\pi_{trigger} : S_{trigger} \rightarrow PRED$ with $\pi_{trigger}(s_i) = b_i$

We use the abbreviation *glue* for the following set of places which have to be identified:

$$glue = EQUI(Tri \cup S_{trigger}, \pi \cup \pi_{trigger}, enb, cons)$$

with $enb = F_{enb} \cup \{(s,t) \;/\; s \in S_{trigger} \wedge t \in entry(\Sigma)\}$

and $cons = F_{cons} \cup CONN_{entry}^{trigger}(\Sigma, S_{trigger}, \pi_{trigger})$.

We define the net

$$TRIG(\phi, \Sigma) = (\hat{S}, \hat{T}, \hat{F}_{enb}, \hat{F}_{cons}, \hat{F}_{del}, \hat{\Gamma}, \hat{\pi}, \hat{M}_0, \hat{s}_0, \hat{s}_e)$$

where the net components are given by:

$$\hat{S} = IDEN_S(glue, S \cup S_{trigger})$$

$$\hat{T} = T$$

$$\hat{F}_{enb} = IDEN_F(glue, enb)$$

$$\hat{F}_{cons} = IDEN_F(glue, cons)$$

$$\hat{F}_{del} = IDEN_F(glue, F_{del} \cup CONN_{exit}^{trigger}(\Sigma, S_{trigger}, \pi_{trigger}))$$

$$\hat{\Gamma} = \Gamma$$

$$\hat{\pi} = IDEN_\pi(glue, \pi \cup \pi_{trigger})$$

$$\hat{M}_0 = IDEN_M(glue, M_0 \cup initial_\Sigma(S_{trigger})).$$

The function $initial_\Sigma(x)$ denotes the subset of places in x whose conditions (with respect to π) are true according to the initialization of variables in AADL.

Definition 3.3 (Critical sections, *Store*, *access*, continued)

The AADL on ϕ do ... od construct includes a protection mechanism against external transitions having a read/write or write/write conflict with an internal transition. Therefore the whole trigger command builds a critical section and for the corresponding net we have

$$CS(TRIG(\phi, \Sigma)) = \{TRIG(\phi, \Sigma)\}$$

□

Example 3.1 (Net generation for the OS protocol, continued)

The net operator for the trigger command will generate a new place s_1 for the trigger condition $bufcnt[no] > 0$. This place has to be connected via an enabling arc to the *entry* transition t^1 of the generated command sequence. Since the variable $bufcnt[no]$ will be overwritten within the action $decrement\_bufcnt(no)$ the function $access_\Sigma(bufcnt[no])(write)$ contains the net for this action. Therefore the *entry* and *exit* transitions of this net which in both cases is the transition t^3 will be connected through the functions $CONN_{entry}^{trigger}$ and $CONN_{exit}^{trigger}$ via a consuming and conditional arc to s_1 (Figure 23).

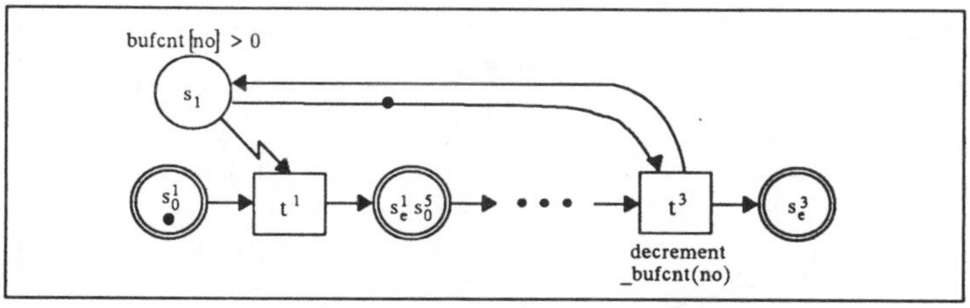

Figure 23: Net representation for the trigger command in the OS protocol

□

The next compound structures we will consider are the *alt* command and the *rep* command. For these structures we have to combine the nets for the I/O commands in the guards as well as the different command sequences for several guarded commands.

If an I/O guard is present for a particular guarded command we identify the terminate place of the net for this I/O command with the start place of the net for the command sequence and define the start place of the I/O command as the start place for this new net. If no I/O command is present in the guard we add a τ-transition in front of the command sequence (i.e. with an arc pointing from this τ-transition to the start place of the command sequence) with a new start place in its preset. The boolean condition in a guard will be represented by some places connected via enabling arcs to the I/O transition or τ-transition in front of the command sequence. The start place for the complete net will be obtained by identifying all start places of the nets above described which models the fact that only one guarded command will be executed.

For all further steps of the net construction we have to distinguish between *alt* and *rep* commands.

An *alt* command will terminate after the execution of one command sequence or lead to abortion when no guard is fulfilled. Thus we identify all terminate places (belonging to the different command sequences) to get the (unique) terminate place for the complete net. For the abortion case we introduce another τ-transition with an empty postset which is connected to the overall startplace by a consuming arc and has to be enabled by several places reflecting the case that all boolean guards are false. Figure 24 shows the net-representation for the command

<u>if</u>

$b_1 \wedge \ldots \wedge b_k \rightarrow sequence_1$

$[]\ c_1 \wedge \ldots \wedge c_m\ ;\ in\ ?\ pattern \rightarrow sequence_2$

<u>fi</u>

This will lead to abortion when $\neg\,(b_1 \wedge \ldots \wedge b_k)$ and $\neg\,(c_1 \wedge \ldots \wedge c_m)$ are both fulfilled.

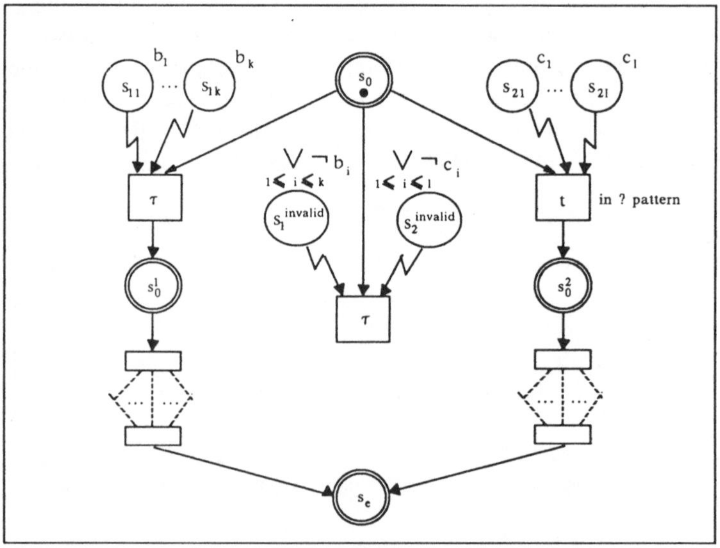

Figure 24: Net representation for the alt command

The net operator ALT_n defined below will construct the net for the structure if... fi where n denotes the number of guarded commands. It combines $2n$ constructed nets from which the first n have to represent the command sequences occurring within the guarded commands of the if... fi statement. All further nets have to represent the input/output command which occur as guards in the if... fi statement, or they are simple τ-nets when a guarded command has only a boolean guard.

Definition 3.2 (AADL net operators, continued)

For the *alt* command we define the following AADL net operator ALT_n.

$$ALT_n : N \times \ldots \times N \times PRED \times \ldots \times PRED \rightarrow N$$

Let for $i \in \{1,\ldots,2n\}$ the nets $\Sigma_i = (S^i, T^i, F^i_{enb}, F^i_{cons}, F^i_{del}, \Gamma^i, \pi^i, M^i_0, s^i_0, s^i_e)$ be given. The formulae $\phi_i \equiv c_{i1} \wedge \ldots \wedge c_{ik_i}$ shall denote the boolean conditions of the guards. We use the abbreviation *glue* for the following set of places which have to be identified:

$$glue = EQUI(trigger, \Pi, enb, cons) \cup \{\{s_0^{n+i} \,/\, 1 \le i \le n\}\} \cup \{\{s_e^i \,/\, 1 \le i \le n\}\} \cup \bigcup_{1 \le i \le n} \{\{s_0^i, s_e^{n+i}\}\}$$

with $trigger = \bigcup_{1 \le i \le 2n} Tri^i \cup \{s_{ij} \,/\, 1 \le i \le n \wedge 1 \le j \le k_i \wedge c_{ij} \not\equiv true\} \cup \{s_i^{invalid} \,/\, 1 \le i \le n\})$

and $\Pi : trigger \rightarrow PRED$ with $\Pi(s) = \begin{cases} \pi^i(s) & \text{for } s \in Tri^i \\ c_{ij} & \text{for } s = s_{ij} \\ \neg\, \phi_i & \text{for } s = s_i^{invalid} \end{cases}$

and $enb = \bigcup_{1 \le i \le 2n} F^i_{enb} \cup \{(s_{ij}, t) \,/\, 1 \le i \le n \wedge 1 \le j \le k_i \wedge t \in entry(\Sigma^{n+i})\} \cup \{(s_i^{invalid}, \tau) \,/\, 1 \le i \le n\} \cup \{(s_0^{n+i}, \tau) \,/\, 1 \le i \le n\}$

and $cons = \bigcup_{1 \le i \le 2n} F^i_{cons} \cup \bigcup_{1 \le i \le n} CONN^{trigger}_{entry}(\Sigma_i, trigger, \Pi)$

We define the net

$$ALT_n(\Sigma_1,\ldots,\Sigma_{2n}, \phi_1,\ldots, \phi_n) = (\hat{S}, \hat{T}, \hat{F}_{enb}, \hat{F}_{cons}, \hat{F}_{del}, \hat{\Gamma}, \hat{\pi}, \hat{M}_0, \hat{s}_0, \hat{s}_e)$$

where the net components are given by:

$$\hat{S} = IDEN_S(glue, \bigcup_{1 \le i \le 2n} S^i \cup \{s_{ij} \,/\, 1 \le i \le n \wedge 1 \le j \le k_i\} \cup \{s_i^{invalid} \,/\, 1 \le i \le n\})$$

$$\hat{T} = \bigcup_{1 \le i \le 2n} T^i \cup \{\tau\}$$

$$\hat{F}_{enb} = IDEN_F(glue, enb)$$

$$\hat{F}_{cons} = IDEN_F(glue, cons)$$

$$\hat{F}_{del} = IDEN_F(glue, \bigcup_{1 \le i \le 2n} F^i_{del} \cup \bigcup_{1 \le i \le n} CONN^{trigger}_{exit}(\Sigma_i, trigger, \Pi))$$

$$\hat{\Gamma}(x) = \begin{cases} \Gamma^i(x) & \text{for } x \in T^i \\ id_{CONT} & \text{for } x = \tau \end{cases}$$

$$\hat{\pi} = IDEN_\pi(glue, \Pi)$$

$$\hat{M}_0 = IDEN_M(glue, \bigcup_{1 \le i \le n} M_0^{n+i} \cup \bigcup_{1 \le i \le n} (M_0^i \setminus \{s_0^i\}) \cup initial_\Sigma(\{s_{ij} \mid 1 \le i \le n \wedge 1 \le j \le k_i\} \cup \{s_i^{invalid} \mid 1 \le i \le n\}))$$

□

A *rep* command can perform several of its internal command sequences and it terminates when all boolean guards evaluate to *false*. To obtain this behaviour we identify all terminate places together with the overall start place; thus several command sequences can take place in sequence. When all boolean guards are false we introduce an additional τ-transition which removes the token from the start place and delivers it to the unique terminate place in its postset (Figure 25).

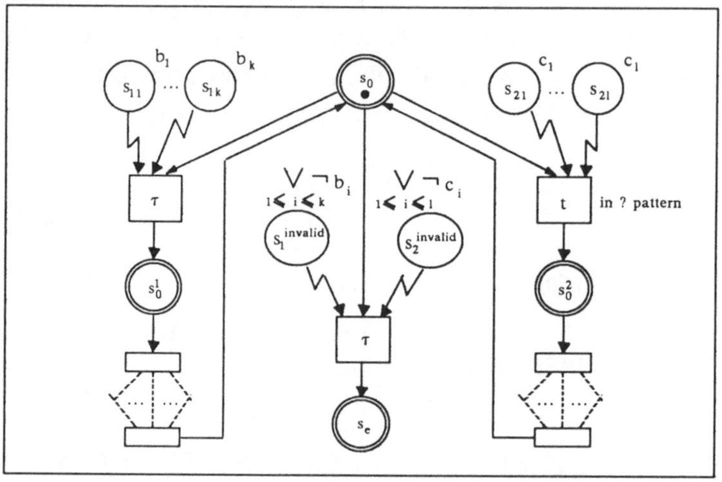

Figure 25: Net representation for the rep command

The net operator REP_n defined below will construct the net for the structure rep...per including n guarded commands. Like the ALT_n operator, the REP_n operator will also combine $2n$ nets where n of them either represent input/output guards or are simple τ-nets.

Definition 3.2 (AADL net operators, continued)

For the rep command we define the following AADL net operator REP_n:

$$REP_n : N \times \ldots \times N \times PRED \times \ldots \times PRED \rightarrow N$$

Let for $i \in \{1,\ldots,2n\}$ the nets $\Sigma_i = (S^i, T^i, F^i_{enb}, F^i_{cons}, F^i_{del}, \Gamma^i, \pi^i, M^i_0, s^i_0, s^i_e)$ be given. The formulae $\phi_i \equiv c_{i1} \wedge \ldots \wedge c_{ik_i}$ shall denote the boolean conditions of the guards. We use the abbreviation *glue* for the following set of places which have to be identified:

$$glue = EQUI(trigger, \Pi, enb, cons) \cup \{\{s_0^{n+i} \mid 1 \le i \le n\} \cup \{s_e^i \mid 1 \le i \le n\}\} \cup \bigcup_{1 \le i \le n} \{\{s_0^i, s_e^{n+i}\}\}$$

$$\text{with } trigger = \bigcup_{1 \le i \le 2n} Tri^i \cup \{s_{ij} \mid 1 \le i \le n \wedge 1 \le j \le k_i \wedge c_{ij} \not\equiv true\} \cup \{s_i^{invalid} \mid 1 \le i \le n\})$$

$$\text{and } \Pi : trigger \to PRED \text{ with } \Pi(s) = \begin{cases} \pi^i(s) & \text{for } s \in Tri^i \\ c_{ij} & \text{for } s = s_{ij} \\ \neg \phi_i & \text{for } s = s_i^{invalid} \end{cases}$$

$$\text{and } enb = \bigcup_{1 \le i \le 2n} F^i_{enb} \cup \{(s_{ij}, t) \,/\, 1 \le i \le n \wedge 1 \le j \le k_i \wedge t \in entry(\Sigma^{n+i})\}$$
$$\cup \{(s_i^{invalid}, \tau) \,/\, 1 \le i \le n\} \cup \{(s_0^{n+i}, \tau) \,/\, 1 \le i \le n\}$$

$$\text{and } cons = \bigcup_{1 \le i \le 2n} F^i_{cons} \cup \bigcup_{1 \le i \le n} CONN^{trigger}_{entry}(\Sigma_i, trigger, \Pi)$$

We define the net

$$REP_n(\Sigma_1,\ldots,\Sigma_{2n}, \phi_1,\ldots, \phi_n) = (\hat{S}, \hat{T}, \hat{F}_{enb}, \hat{F}_{cons}, \hat{F}_{del}, \hat{\Gamma}, \hat{\pi}, \hat{M}_0, \hat{s}_0, \hat{s}_e)$$

where the net components are given by:

$$\hat{S} = IDEN_S(glue, \bigcup_{1 \le i \le 2n} S^i \cup \{s_{ij} \,/\, 1 \le i \le n \wedge 1 \le j \le k_i\}$$
$$\cup \{s_i^{invalid} \,/\, 1 \le i \le n\} \cup \{\hat{s}_e\})$$

$$\hat{T} = \bigcup_{1 \le i \le 2n} T^i \cup \{\tau\}$$

$$\hat{F}_{enb} = IDEN_F(glue, enb)$$

$$\hat{F}_{cons} = IDEN_F(glue, cons)$$

$$\hat{F}_{del} = IDEN_F(glue, \bigcup_{1 \le i \le 2n} F^i_{del} \cup \bigcup_{1 \le i \le n} CONN^{trigger}_{exit}(\Sigma_i, trigger, \Pi)$$
$$\cup \{(\tau, \hat{s}_e)\})$$

$$\hat{\Gamma}(x) = \begin{cases} \Gamma^i(x) & \text{for } x \in T^i \\ id_{CONT} & \text{for } x = \tau \end{cases}$$

$$\hat{\pi} = IDEN_\pi(glue, \Pi)$$

$$\hat{M}_0 = IDEN_M(glue, \bigcup_{1 \le i \le n} M_0^{n+i} \cup \bigcup_{1 \le i \le n} (M_0^i \setminus \{s_0^i\})$$
$$\cup\, initial_\Sigma(\{s_{ij} \,/\, 1 \le i \le n \wedge 1 \le j \le k_i\} \cup \{s_i^{invalid} \,/\, 1 \le i \le n\}))$$

□

Example 3.1 (Net generation for the OS protocol)

In the OS example the generated net will be combined via a rep-statement to another net representing the send primitive. This rep-statement does not introduce additional trigger places because it contain only input/output guards. The nets for the input guards *dem_in ? send_dem(...)* and *dem_in ? rec_dem(...)* are sequentially combined with the nets for their respective bodies and their start places are identified together with the end places of the bodies to the new place s_0^4, s_0^{11} (Figure 26).

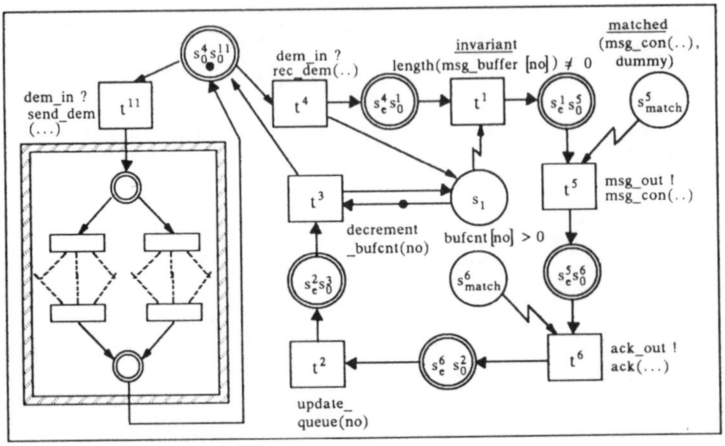

Figure 26: Net representation for a *rep* command of the OS protocol

□

The *par* command combines several command sequences $com_1,...,com_k$ to a new one constituting their parallel execution. Therefore its unique start place is connected to a τ-transition which will generate k copies of the incoming control token and deliver them to the start places $s_0^1,...,s_0^K$ of the net representations of $com_1,...,com_k$. All terminate places $s_e^1,...,s_e^k$ of $com_1,...,com_k$ will be in the preset of another τ-transition which has in its postset the unique terminate place for the *par* command. This models the fact that the complete *par* command will only terminate when all included command sequences $com_1,...,com_k$ have already terminated. Figure 27 shows the net for a *par* command with k = 2.

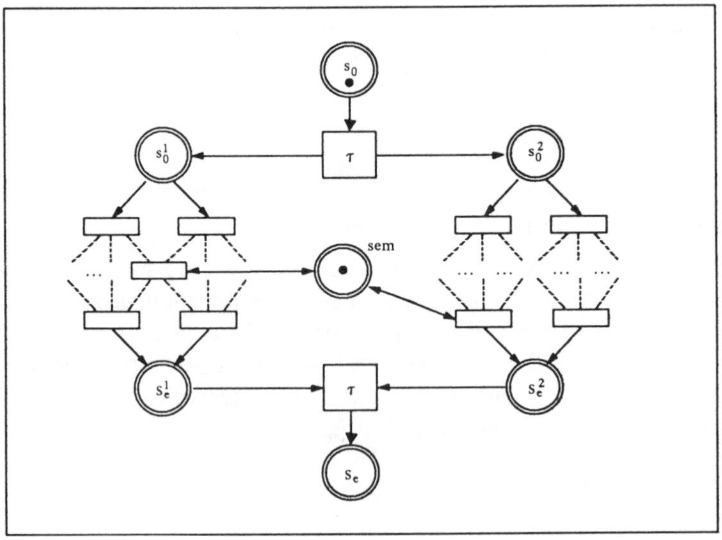

Figure 27: Net representation for the *par* command

But not all transitions in the different command sequences com_i and com_j are allowed to fire in parallel. There may be on the AADL level a read/write or write/write conflict on common variables. In this situation a new control place (also called a semaphore place) has to be introduced to solve this conflict in that these two transitions can only fire exclusively, i.e. the concurrent firing of these two transitions will be prohibited. In Figure 27 such a semaphor place between an internal transition of com_1 and an exit transition of com_2 is shown. Such additional semaphor places have also to be introduced between transitions in different architectures which have a conflict on a variable in shared storage.

In the case of a conflict with parts belonging to the internal command sequence of a trigger command we have to introduce the semaphor place in such a way that the complete command sequence is executed exclusively to the other conflicting part. Thus we introduce an enabling and a consuming arc from this semaphor place to the entry transitions of the net for the trigger command and let the backward arcs point from the exit transitions to it. Figure 28 shows the resulting net for the trigger command " on trigger-condition do sequence od " where "sequence" contains a statement which conflicts with another parallel activated action A with net representation t. In this situation the transition t (representing the action A) can fire only exclusively to the whole net representing "sequence".

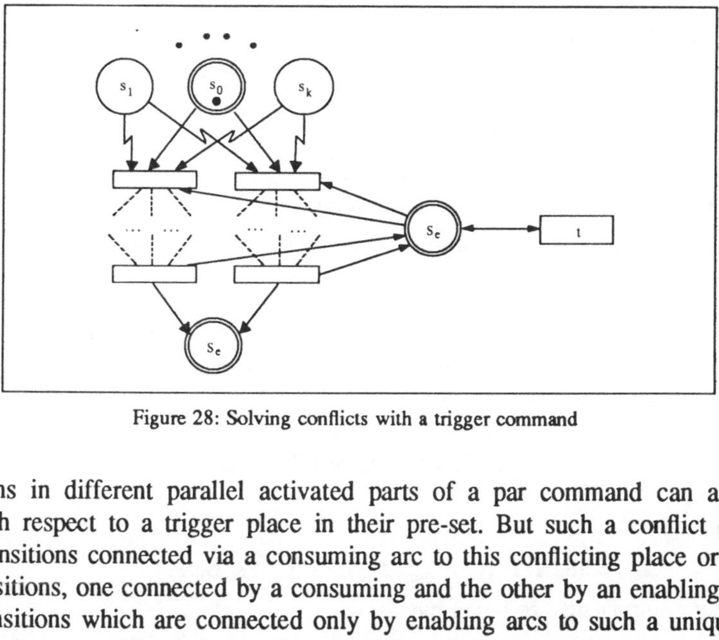

Figure 28: Solving conflicts with a trigger command

Transitions in different parallel activated parts of a par command can also have a conflict with respect to a trigger place in their pre-set. But such a conflict only arises between transitions connected via a consuming arc to this conflicting place or between a pair of transitions, one connected by a consuming and the other by an enabling arc to this place. Transitions which are connected only by enabling arcs to such a unique place in their preset do not conflict because the evaluation of the formula attached to this place does not change variables included in this formula, and the token residing on the place will not be removed when these transitions fire. To handle this situation within the processes generated for such an AADL net we generate the AADL nets in such a way that this situation will not arise. Whenever we find two transitions t_1, t_2 in different branches of a *par* command which have identifiable places s, s' in their presets pre_{enb} we will perform this identification only in the case that at least one of these transitions have s or s' in their pre_{cons} set.

Before we write down the fomal definition of these nets by defining the net operator PAR_n we will introduce some auxiliary functions.

Definition 3.7 (Creation and connection of semaphor places)

Let $\Sigma_i \in N$ for $1 \le i \le n$. We define the set $SEMA(\Sigma_1,\ldots,\Sigma_n)$ of semaphor places which will be used when $\Sigma_1,\ldots,\Sigma_n$ are combined in parallel to serialize conflicting critical sections belonging to different nets Σ_i, Σ_j. The semaphor places are named with the set of critical sections for which they are used.

$$SEMA(\Sigma_1,\ldots,\Sigma_n) = \{\{cs, cs'\} \,/\, \exists\, i,j : i \neq j \wedge \exists\, \alpha \in Store(\Sigma_i) \cap Store(\Sigma_j) : cs \in access_{\Sigma_i}(\alpha)(write) \wedge cs' \in (access_{\Sigma_j}(\alpha)(write) \cup access_{\Sigma_j}(\alpha)(read))\}$$

Let Sem be a set of semaphor places (each of them being represented by a set of critical sections). We define two functions $CONN^{semaphore}_{entry}$ and $CONN^{semaphore}_{exit}$ for the connection of these semaphor places to transitions of the critical sections. $CONN^{semaphore}_{entry}$ defines arcs pointing from semaphor places to transitions in the *entry* set of critical sections whereas $CONN^{semaphore}_{exit}$ defines arcs pointing in the opposite direction from transitions in the *exit* set to semaphor places:

$$CONN^{semaphore}_{entry}(Sem) = \{(\{cs_1,\ldots,cs_l\}, t) \,/\, \{cs_1,\ldots,cs_l\} \in Sem \wedge t \in \bigcup_{1 \le i \le l} entry(cs_i)\}$$

$$CONN^{semaphore}_{exit}(Sem) = \{(t, \{cs_1,\ldots,cs_l\}) \,/\, \{cs_1,\ldots,cs_l\} \in Sem \wedge t \in \bigcup_{1 \le i \le l} exit(cs_i)\}$$

□

Definition 3.2 (AADL net operators, continued)

For the *par* command we define the following AADL net operator PAR_n:

$$PAR_n : N \times \ldots \times N \to N$$

Let for $i \in \{1,..,n\}$ nets $\Sigma_i = (S^i, T^i, F^i_{enb}, F^i_{cons}, F^i_{del}, \Gamma^i, \pi^i, M^i_0, s^i_0, s^i_e)$ be given. We use the abbreviation *glue* for the following set of places which have to be identified:

$$glue = EQUI(\bigcup_{1 \le i \le n} Tri^i, \bigcup_{1 \le i \le n} \pi^i, \bigcup_{i \in \{1,..,n\}} F^i_{enb}, \bigcup_{1 \le i \le n} F^i_{cons}) \cup \bigcup_{1 \le i \le n} Sem^i \cup SEMA(\Sigma_1,\ldots,\Sigma_n)$$

We define the net

$$PAR_n(\Sigma_1,\ldots,\Sigma_n) = (\hat{S}, \hat{T}, \hat{F}_{enb}, \hat{F}_{cons}, \hat{F}_{del}, \hat{\Gamma}, \hat{\pi}, \hat{M}_0, \hat{s}_0, \hat{s}_e)$$

where the net components are given by:

$$\hat{S} = IDEN_S(glue, \bigcup_{1 \le i \le n} S^i \cup \{\hat{s}_0, \hat{s}_e\} \cup SEMA(\Sigma_1,\ldots,\Sigma_n))$$

$$\hat{T} = \bigcup_{1 \le i \le n} T^i \cup \{\tau_1, \tau_2\}$$

Let $enb = \bigcup_{i \in \{1,..,n\}} F^i_{enb} \cup CONN^{semaphore}_{entry}(\bigcup_{1 \le i \le n} Sem^i \cup SEMA(\Sigma_1,\ldots,\Sigma_n)) \cup \{(s^i_e, \tau_2) \,/\, i \in \{1,..,n\}\} \cup \{\hat{s}_0, \tau_1\}$

$$\hat{F}_{enb} = IDEN_F(glue, enb)$$

$$\text{Let } cons = \bigcup_{1 \le i \le n} F^i_{cons} \cup \bigcup_{1 \le i \le n} CONN^{trigger}_{entry}(\Sigma_i, \bigcup_{1 \le j \le n} Tri^j, \bigcup_{1 \le j \le n} \pi^j)$$
$$\cup\, CONN^{semaphore}_{entry}(\bigcup_{1 \le i \le n} Sem^i \cup SEMA(\Sigma_1,\ldots,\Sigma_n))$$
$$\cup\, \{(s^i_e,\tau_2) \mid i \in \{1,..,n\}\} \cup \{\hat{s}_0,\tau_1\}$$
$$\hat{F}_{cons} = IDEN_F(glue, cons)$$
$$\text{Let } cond = \bigcup_{1 \le i \le n} F^i_{del} \cup \bigcup_{1 \le i \le n} CONN^{trigger}_{exit}(\Sigma_i, \bigcup_{1 \le j \le n} Tri^j, \bigcup_{1 \le j \le n} \pi^j)$$
$$\cup\, CONN^{semaphore}_{exit}(\bigcup_{1 \le i \le n} Sem^i \cup SEMA(\Sigma_1,\ldots,\Sigma_n))$$
$$\cup\, \{(\tau_1, s^i_0) \mid i \in \{1,..,n\}\} \cup \{\tau_2, \hat{s}_e\}$$
$$\hat{F}_{del} = IDEN_F(glue, cond)$$
$$\hat{\Gamma}(t) = \begin{cases} \Gamma^i(t) & \text{for } t \in T^i \\ id_{CONT} & otherwise \end{cases}$$
$$\hat{\pi} = IDEN_\pi(glue, \bigcup_{i \in \{1,..,n\}} \pi^i)$$
$$\hat{M}_0 = IDEN_M(glue, \bigcup_{1 \le i \le n} (M^i_0 \setminus \bigcup_{i \in \{1,..,n\}} s^i_0)) \cup \{\hat{s}_0\}$$

□

Example 3.1 (Net generation for the OS protocol, continued)

The net operator for the *par* command will, according to the range $1 \le i \le M$, generate M nets whose structure is identical to the net generated up to now but which have different names for places and transitions. Figure 29 shows the net for $M = 2$. The net operator will also introduce a semaphor place labeled *sem* which solves the conflicts between actions in parallel activated trigger statements.

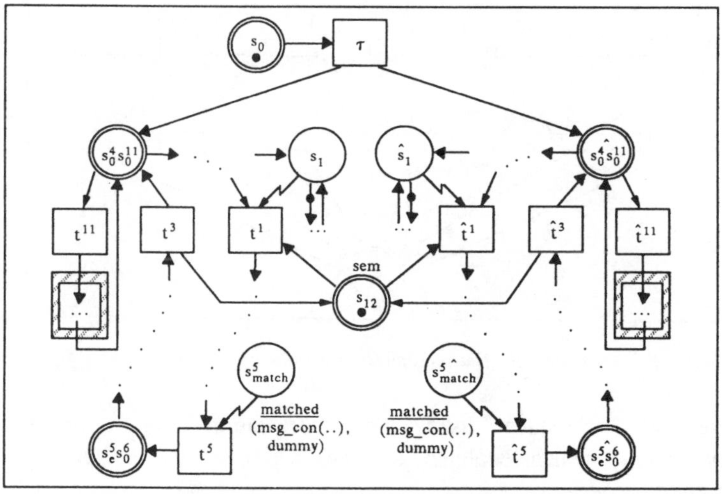

Figure 29: Net representation for a par command of the OS protocol

□

To construct the net representation for a *case* command

case *expr* of

$con_{1,1}, \ldots, con_{1,k_1}$: *sequence*$_1$;

.

.

.

$con_{n-1,1}, \ldots, con_{n-1,k_{n-1}}$: *sequence*$_{n-1}$

otherwise *sequence*$_n$

esac

we have to introduce places which indicate which of the pattern $con_{i,j}$ match the expression *expr* and include enabling arcs from these places to the entry transitions of the nets for the corresponding command sequences. For the "otherwise" case we have also to include places representing the fact that none of the pattern match the expression and connect these places with enabling arcs to the entry transitions of the net for *sequence*$_n$. Then we identify all start places for the command sequences to get the (unique) start place for the complete net; thus modelling one of the command sequences with a matching pattern will take place. The terminate places for all command sequences will also be identified to obtain the (unique) terminate place for the complete net.

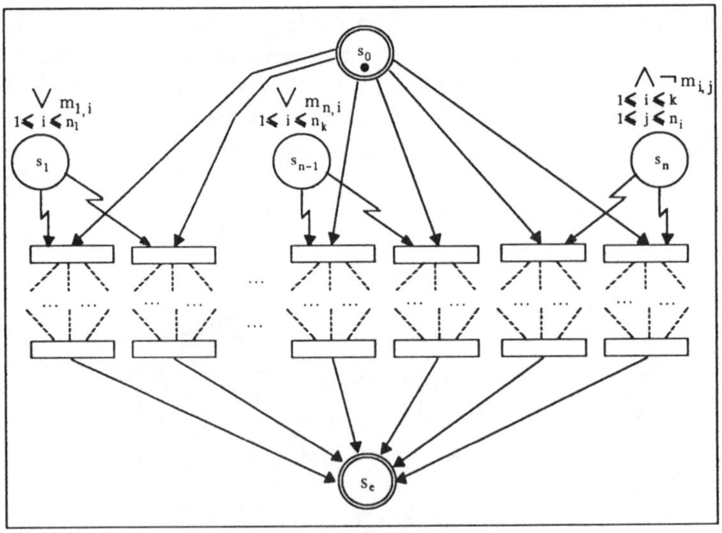

Figure 30: Net representation for the *case* command

In Figure 30 we have used the abbreviations $m_{i,j}$ for the formulae *matched*(*expr*, $con_{i,j}$) which evaluate to *true* whenever the actual expression *expr* matches the pattern $con_{i,j}$.

In this net construction process we have assumed that there is always an *otherwise* part present. A *case* command without *otherwise* can simply be transformed into one with *otherwise* by adding otherwise abort to it.

Definition 3.2 (AADL net operators, continued)

The net operator $CASE_n$ defined below will construct the net for a case command where n indicates the number of "cases":

$$CASE_n : N \times \ldots \times N \times PRED \times \ldots \times PRED \to N$$

Let for $i \in \{1,\ldots,n\}$ nets $\Sigma_i = (S^i, T^i, F^i_{enb}, F^i_{cons}, F^i_{del}, \Gamma^i, \pi^i, M^i_0, s^i_0, s^i_e)$ be given, and let ϕ_i indicate whether the i th case can be taken or not; thus

$$\phi_i \equiv matched(expr, con_{i,1}) \vee \ldots \vee matched(expr, con_{i,k_i}) \text{ for } 1 \leq i \leq n-1$$

$$\text{and } \phi_n \equiv \neg\, \phi_1 \wedge \ldots \wedge \neg\, \phi_{n-1}.$$

We use the abbreviation *glue* for the following set of places which have to be identified:

$$glue = EQUI(trigger, \Pi, enb, cons) \cup \{\{s^i_0 \,/\, 1 \leq i \leq n\}\} \cup \{\{s^i_e \,/\, 1 \leq i \leq n\}\}$$

$$\text{with } trigger = \bigcup_{1 \leq i \leq n} Tri^i \cup \{s_i \,/\, 1 \leq i \leq n \wedge \phi_i \not\equiv true\}$$

$$\text{and } \Pi : trigger \to PRED \text{ with } \Pi(s) = \begin{cases} \pi^i(s) & \text{for } s \in Tri^i \\ \phi_i & \text{for } s = s_i \end{cases}$$

$$\text{and } enb = \bigcup_{1 \leq i \leq n} F^i_{enb} \cup \{(s_i, t) \,/\, 1 \leq i \leq n \wedge t \in entry(\Sigma_i)\}$$

$$\text{and } cons = \bigcup_{1 \leq i \leq n} F^i_{cons} \cup \bigcup_{1 \leq i \leq n} CONN^{trigger}_{entry}(\Sigma_i, trigger, \Pi)$$

We define the net

$$CASE_n(\Sigma_1,\ldots,\Sigma_n, \phi_1,\ldots, \phi_n) = (\hat{S}, \hat{T}, \hat{F}_{enb}, \hat{F}_{cons}, \hat{F}_{del}, \hat{\Gamma}, \hat{\pi}, \hat{M}_0, \hat{s}_0, \hat{s}_e)$$

where the net components are given by:

$$\hat{S} = IDEN_S(glue, \bigcup_{1 \leq i \leq n} S^i \cup \{s_i \,/\, 1 \leq i \leq n\})$$

$$\hat{T} = \bigcup_{1 \leq i \leq n} T^i$$

$$\hat{F}_{enb} = IDEN_F(glue, enb)$$

$$\hat{F}_{cons} = IDEN_F(glue, cons)$$

$$\hat{F}_{del} = IDEN_F(glue, \bigcup_{1 \leq i \leq n} F^i_{del} \cup \bigcup_{1 \leq i \leq n} CONN^{trigger}_{exit}(\Sigma_i, trigger, \Pi))$$

$$\hat{\Gamma} = \Gamma$$

$$\hat{\pi} = IDEN_\pi(glue, \Pi)$$

$$\hat{M}_0 = IDEN_M(glue, \bigcup_{1 \leq i \leq n} M^i_0 \cup initial_\Sigma(\{s_i \,/\, 1 \leq i \leq n\}))$$

□

Example 3.1 (Net generation for the OS protocol, continued)

As an example of the *case* command we use the control program for the multiplexer of the OS protocol. This checks whether an input on the inport *in* stored in the variable *send_msg* has to be sent via the *local_out* outport for internal storing (when the addressed process resides on the same node) or via the *remote_out* outport for storing on another node (Figure 31).

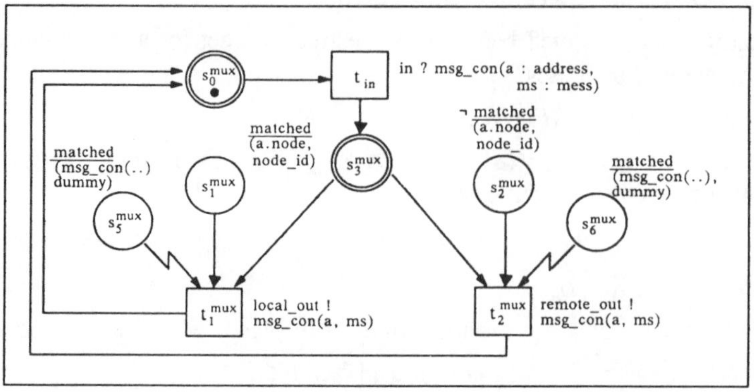

Figure 31: Net representation for a *case* command of the OS protocol

The set *Ports* for this net will contain the ports *in*, *local_out*, and *remote_out*. The function *comm* applied to the inport *in* results in the set $\{(t_{in}, msg\_con(a: address, ms: mess))\}$ which will be used later when t_{in} has to be glued to another transition representing an output command.

□

AADL allows in its *control* specification the definition and the call of procedures. Such a procedure can have three different kind of formal parameter:

(1) *port* parameters,

(2) *storage* parameters, and

(3) *const* parameters.

These will be substituted by ports, storage references and expressions as their respective actual parameters of procedure calls.

During the net-generation process a net template will be created for each procedure definition. In such a template the formal parameters are marked by a %-sign in front of them. Thus *%port* may occur in the set *Ports*(Σ), and *%location* in the set *Store*(Σ). The state transformation attached by Γ and the conditions attached by π may also depend on %-marked parameters.

For each call of a procedure a net will be generated which is a copy of the net template where the %-marked parameters have been substituted by their actual values. Note that all variables occurring in an expression substituted for a *const* parameter have to be included in the set *Store*(Σ).

For a procedure "proc" with *const*-parameter C of type *integer* which includes a trigger command <u>on</u> $C > 5$ <u>do</u> ... <u>od</u> the net template will contain a place s with an attached formula $\%C > 5$ (Figure 32).

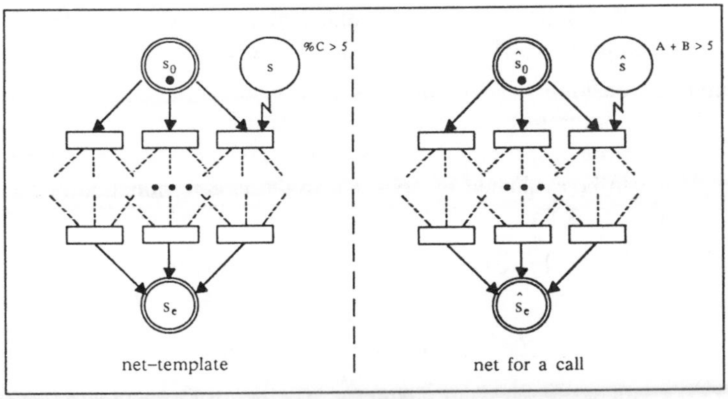

Figure 32: Net representations for procedure definitions and procedure calls

When "proc" is called with the actual parameter $A+B$ in the generated net the formula $A+B>5$ will be attached to $\hat{s}$ (the place derived from s).

The net-operator for the combination of independently specified modules (subarchitectures) is similar to that for the *par* command. The main difference is that subarchitectures can communicate over linked ports in a synchronous way (in addition to the communication over shared memory). To model this in the AADL net we introduce for each pair of transitions which read and write on linked ports a new transition originating from the glueing of the two original transitions. Thus such a combined transition can only fire when all places suitable for the firing of both transitions carry a token (Figure 33).

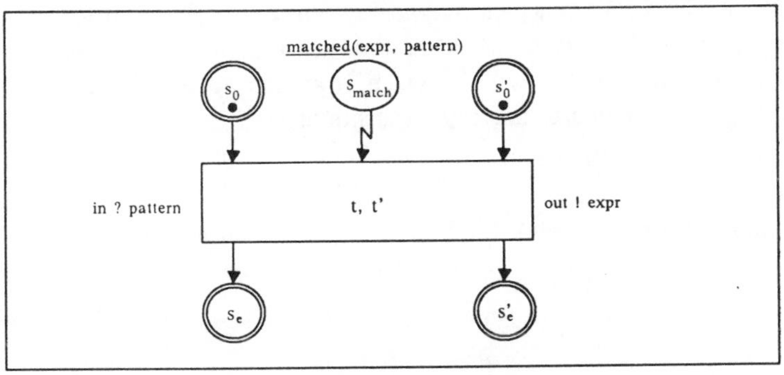

Figure 33: Joined transition for input/output

We define an auxiliary function *SYNCH* which constitutes the set of combined transitions and an auxiliary function *ADAPT* which performs the connection of arcs to these combined transitions. Another auxiliary function named *MATCH* will be used to substitute the "dummy" entry in the formula attached to the pattern-matching place in the preset of an output transition with the appropriate pattern. This pattern will be taken from the $comm_{\Sigma}$ function of the glued input transition.

Definition 3.8 (Identify transitions for linked input/output commands)

Let $\Sigma_i \in N$ for $1 \le i \le n$ and let T be the union of all transitions in the Σ_i's. Let *link* be a set of tuples (*outport*, *inport*) representing the connection of ports.

Each combined transition (representing a synchronous communication) will exist as a tuple (t, t') of an output transition t and an input transition t' in the set *SYNCH*(...). The transitions have to write resp. read on ports which are connected according to the *link* specification. This can be evaluated by considering the $comm_\Sigma$ function of the appropriate nets where the ports are defined:

$$SYNCH(\Sigma_1,\ldots,\Sigma_n, link) = \{(t, t') \mid t,t' \in T \wedge \exists\, (port, port') \in link : \\ port \in Ports(\Sigma_i) \wedge port' \in Ports(\Sigma_j) \\ \wedge (t, out) \in comm_{\Sigma_i}(port) \\ \wedge \exists\, pattern : (t', pattern) \in comm_{\Sigma_j}(port')\}$$

Let F be a set of arcs $F \subseteq S \times T \cup T \times S$ where S, T are disjoint sets (of places resp. transitions) and let *SYNCH* denote a set of combined transitions, i.e. tuples (t, t') with $t, t' \in T$. $ADAPT(F, SYNCH)$ denotes a new relation where an arc pointing to or from a transition occurring in a tuple $(t, t') \in SYNCH$ has been substituted by an arc pointing to or from that tuple. Thus

$$ADAPT(F, SYNCH) \subseteq (S \times (T \cup (T \times T))) \cup ((T \cup (T \times T)) \times S)$$

$$ADAPT(F, SYNCH) = \\ F \setminus \{(a, b) \mid \exists\, (x, y) \in SYNCH : x = a \vee y = a \vee x = b \vee y = b\} \\ \cup \{(a, b) \mid a = (x, y) \in SYNCH \wedge ((x, b) \in F \vee (y, b) \in F) \\ \vee b = (x, y) \in SYNCH \wedge ((a, x) \in F \vee (a, y) \in F)\}.$$

Let F, *SYNCH* as in the above definition and let $\pi : S \to PRED$. We define a function $MATCH(\ldots) : S \to PRED$ where the *dummy* entries occurring in formulae has been substituted by the concrete *pattern* when the attached output transition is combined with an input transition. The *pattern* will be taken from the value of the $comm_\Sigma$ function applied to the inport belonging to this input transition:

$$MATCH(\pi, SYNCH, F)(s) = \\ \begin{cases} matched(expr, pattern) & \text{for } \exists\, t,t' : (s, t) \in F \wedge (t, t') \in SYNCH \\ & \wedge\, \pi(s) = matched(expr, dummy) \\ & \wedge\, \exists\, port \in Ports(\Sigma) : (t', pattern) \in comm_\Sigma(port) \\ \pi(s) & otherwise \end{cases}$$

□

Definition 3.2 (AADL net operators, continued)

The operator $COMB_n$ combines n AADL nets which each represent different AADL (sub)architectures to a net representing their parallel execution:

$$COMB_n : N \times \ldots \times N \times link \to N$$

where *link* denotes the set of all possible linkings of ports where a linking is represented by a set of tuples (*outport*, *inport*).

Let for $i \in \{1,..,n\}$ the nets $\Sigma_i = (S^i, T^i, F^i_{enb}, F^i_{cons}, F^i_{del}, \Gamma^i, \pi^i, M^i_0, s^i_0, s^i_e)$ be given. We use the abbreviation *glue* for the following set of places which have to be identified:

$$glue = EQUI(\bigcup_{1 \le i \le n} Tri^i, \bigcup_{1 \le i \le n} \pi^i, enb, cons) \cup \bigcup_{1 \le i \le n} Sem^i \cup SEMA(\Sigma_1,\ldots,\Sigma_n)$$

with

$$enb = ADAPT(\bigcup_{i \in \{1,..,n\}} F^i_{enb} \cup CONN^{semaphore}_{entry}(\bigcup_{1 \le i \le n} Sem^i \cup SEMA(\Sigma_1,\ldots,\Sigma_n)) \cup \{(s^i_e, \tau_2) / i \in \{1,..,n\}\} \cup \{\hat{s}_0, \tau_1\}, SYNCH(\Sigma_1,\ldots,\Sigma_n, L))$$

and

$$cons = ADAPT(\bigcup_{1 \le i \le n} F^i_{cons} \cup \bigcup_{1 \le i \le n} CONN^{trigger}_{entry}(\Sigma_i, \bigcup_{1 \le i \le n} Tri^i, \bigcup_{1 \le i \le n} \pi^i) \cup CONN^{semaphore}_{entry}(\bigcup_{1 \le i \le n} Sem^i \cup SEMA(\Sigma_1,\ldots,\Sigma_n)) \cup \{(s^i_e, \tau_2) / i \in \{1,..,n\}\} \cup \{\hat{s}_0, \tau_1\}, SYNCH(\Sigma_1,\ldots,\Sigma_n, L))$$

We define the net

$$COMB_n(\Sigma_1,\ldots,\Sigma_n, L) = (\hat{S}, \hat{T}, \hat{F}_{enb}, \hat{F}_{cons}, \hat{F}_{del}, \hat{\Gamma}, \hat{\pi}, \hat{M}_0, \hat{s}_0, \hat{s}_e)$$

where the net components are given by:

$$\hat{S} = IDEN_S(glue, \bigcup_{1 \le i \le n} S^i \cup \{\hat{s}_0, \hat{s}_e\} \cup SEMA(\Sigma_1,\ldots,\Sigma_n))$$

$$\hat{T} = (\bigcup_{1 \le i \le n} T^i \setminus \{t / \exists (x,y) \in SYNCH(\Sigma_1,\ldots,\Sigma_n, L) : x = t \vee y = t\}) \cup SYNCH(\bigcup_{1 \le i \le n} T^i, \bigcup_{1 \le i \le n} comm_{\Sigma_i}, L))$$

$$\hat{F}_{enb} = IDEN_F(glue, enb)$$

$$\hat{F}_{cons} = IDEN_F(glue, cons)$$

$$\hat{F}_{del} = IDEN_F(glue, ADAPT(\bigcup_{1 \le i \le n} F^i_{del} \cup \bigcup_{1 \le i \le n} CONN^{trigger}_{exit}(\Sigma_i, \bigcup_{1 \le i \le n} Tri^i, \bigcup_{1 \le i \le n} \pi^i) \cup CONN^{semaphore}_{exit}(\bigcup_{1 \le i \le n} Sem^i \cup SEMA(\Sigma_1,\ldots,\Sigma_n)) \cup \{(\tau_1, s^i_0) / i \in \{1,..,n\}\} \cup \{\tau_2, \hat{s}_e\}), SYNCH(\Sigma_1,\ldots,\Sigma_n, L)))$$

$$\hat{\Gamma}(t) = \begin{cases} \Gamma^i(t) & \text{for } t \in T^i \\ \Gamma^i(y)(\theta) & \text{for } t = (x,y) \in SYNCH(\Sigma_1,\ldots,\Sigma_n, L) \\ id_{CONT} & \text{otherwise} \end{cases}$$

where θ is the mapping which substitutes pattern variables by their corresponding (sub)expressions according to the pattern-matching.

$$\hat{\pi} = IDEN_\pi(glue, MATCH(\bigcup_{i \in \{1,..,n\}} \pi^i, SYNCH(\Sigma_1,\ldots,\Sigma_n, L), \hat{F}_{enb}))$$

$$\hat{M}_0 = IDEN_M(glue, \bigcup_{1 \leq i \leq n} (M_0^i \setminus \bigcup_{i \in \{1,..,n\}} s_0^i)) \cup \{\hat{s}_0\}$$

□

Example 3.1 (Net generation for the OS protocol, continued)

We will use the net generated for the *communication_prim* shown in Figure 29 and the net representing the *multiplexer* of the OS protocol shown in Figure 31 to illustrate the *COMB* net operator. In the architecture *protocol* the subarchitectures *comm_prim* and *mux* are defined as incarnations of these architecture types. The outport *msg_out* of the *comm_prim* architecture is linked - by means of a link definition - to the inport *in* of the *mux* architecture.

In the net shown as Figure 34 the transition t_{in} of the *mux* net has been duplicated and each representative has been glued to one of the t^9 transitions of the *comm_prim* net. The *dummy* entry of the formula matched (*msg_con*(...), *dummy*) has been substituted by the actual pattern *msg_con*(*a* : *address*, *ms* : *mess*).

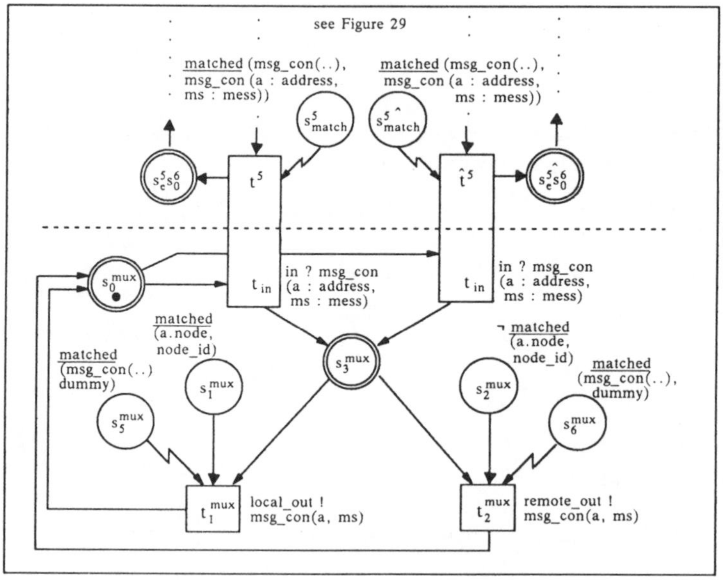

Figure 34: Net representation combining the *comm_prim* and the *mux*

□

4. An outline of further steps in AADL's net semantics

The AADL nets constructed in the previous section include all aspects of the underlying AADL specification which are relevant for tools based on AADL. They will be used to represent AADL specifications in the COMDES project which will provide tools such as a simulator and a verifier.

However these nets will also be used as a first step towards a formal semantics of AADL. In a second step we define so-called "processes" which are, intuitively, infinite unfoldings of (conventional) Petri nets. The identification of places and transitions in the unfolding to places and transitions in the original net will be given by a function named "H" which maps the components (places and transitions) of these nets onto the components of the underlying AADL nets. This function will in general not be injective; thus several representations of one and the same place or transition in an AADL net may occur in a process. Intuitively, a transition t of process P can be viewed as a time stamp, indicating that transition H(t) has fired at "time" t. Thus processes will be acyclic. The construction of processes will be such that two time stamps associated with one transition t will always be ordered.[5] The complete behaviour of an AADL net (and thus also of the original AADL specification) will be described by a (in general infinite) number of processes each of which represents one possible unwinding of the original net. Processes are conflict-free, i.e. each place has at most one transition in its postset. Moreover, the construction of processes also guarantees that the number of transitions in the preset of a place is limited by one. Different processes result from different choices taken in the (underlying) AADL net, because only one out of several conflicting transitions can fire.

In a further step we will then associate local states with the places of a process in such a way that the state transformations attached to the transitions of the AADL net are respected.

A forthcoming paper will define formally which processes belong to an AADL net and how states will be attached to the places of these processes. This is done in a modular way by constructing the processes out of finite subprocesses (so-called rules) with a fixed binding of places/transitions to the places/transitions of the AADL (sub)net. The set of rules belonging to an AADL specification can be constructed inductively over the structure of its control section. For each of the AADL net operators defined in the previous section we have to define which rules belong to it or - in the case of an net operator which combines already constructed nets - how they can be computed out of the rule sets constructed so far. Each process of a complete AADL net can then be successively constructed by applying a sequence of rules where the application of such a rule to a prefix of a process can be viewed as the identification of all places in the preset of that rule with appropriate end places (i.e. places without outgoing arcs) of the prefix.

To assign states to the places of finite processes we consider their representations by finite rule words. Inductively over the length of these rule words we define functions which map states associated with the start places of processes to states associated with the end places. In the formal development the extensions to infinite processes is carried out by defining a suitable partial order which allows us to view processes as elements of a complete partial order.

To obtain only an intuitive understanding of how processes appear we can construct processes together with the states belonging to the places of these processes by pushing state spaces through the AADL net rather than tokens. Each time such a state space passes a transition the transformation attached to that transition will take place and the formulae belonging to conditional arcs of that transition can be evaluated within this new state space thus restricting the flow of state spaces to those places whose formulae are fulfilled. The processes can then be defined by separately recording each single presence of a token (state space) in a place and firing of a transition together with the arcs actually used. In conflict situations the subprocesses constructed so far have to be duplicated, and

[5] I.e. there is an directed finite path from t_1 to t_2 in process P when H(t_1) = H(t_2).

each duplication will correspond to one of the possible choices for solving the conflict.

Another way is to generate processes and states in two steps. In the first step all potential processes will be "generated" without interpreting the formulae of places in the AADL net by having separate processes for all combinations of truth values for these places. The second step will then define the states for the places of a process in such a way that the formulae are fulfilled. It may be that no states can be attached to a process; therefore we have called the processes *potential*.

We will now explain a prefix of one process belonging to the net shown in Figure 35 which represents the *communication_prim* and the *multiplexer*.

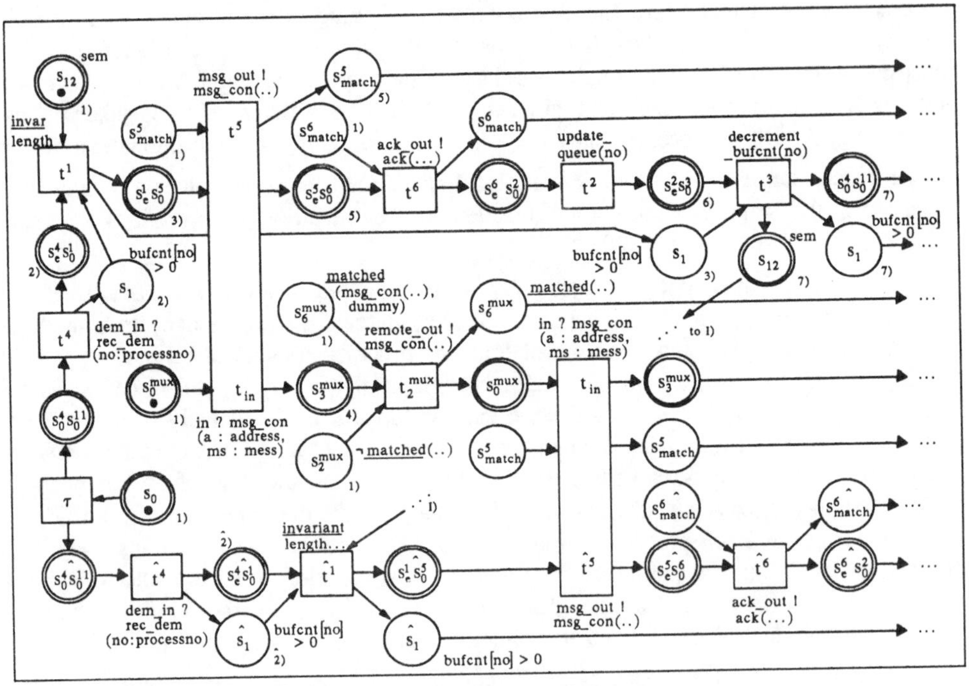

Figure 35: A process for an AADL net

In contrast to all nets previously shown we did not include the names for places and transitions in the graphical representation of this process but have marked them with the value of H applied to them; thus the names known in the underlying AADL net occur there. To increase the readability and comprehension of the process in Figure 35 we have added attributes like formulae (for places) and names of AADL statements (for transitions) which are not directly present in a process but which can be derived from the underlying AADL net by the use of H. This is also valid for the graphical subdivision of places into single and double circles which indicate whether the place in the underlying AADL net is a trigger place or a control/semaphor place.

The process whose prefix is shown in Figure 35 reflects the situation that the net for the *communication_prim* performs in parallel one run through its loops for receiving messages and that the net representing the multiplexer performs its loop twice to take over the accept messages from the *communication_prim* and deliver them via either the remote or the local outport. The part of the process which represents the unwinded loop of the multiplexer is depicted as a central line in Figure 35. It starts with a place bound to s_0^{mux} of the AADL net. The process parts representing the two unwound loops of the *communication_prim* are located in the upper and lower parts of the figure. The semaphor place s_{12} in the AADL net will ensure that the net sections between t^1, t^3 and $\hat{t}^1$, $\hat{t}^3$ can only be admitted exclusively.[6] In the process shown in Figure 35 the sequence related to t^1 up to t^3 (located in the upper part of the figure) is sequentially ordered before the sequence $\hat{t}^1$ up to $\hat{t}^3$ (located in the lower part) by means of the place between t^3 and $\hat{t}^1$ which is related to the semaphor place of the AADL net. The two transitions related to the communication transitions t^5 , t_{in} and $\hat{t}^5$, t_{in} of the AADL net are the only connection between the processes for the *multiplexer* and the *communication_prim*.

To determine the states which can be assigned to the places of a process we choose a starting state which has to fulfil the requirements according to initializations of storage structures. This starting place will be attached to all places with empty preset. The states for the subsequent places can then be computed by applying the state transformations of transitions in the underlying AADL net to states assigned to "earlier" places.

When more then one place is present in the postset of a transition t we have to duplicate states such that all these places will get the state resulting from the application of $\Gamma(H(t))$. On the other hand, it may also be the case that several places are in the preset of a transition. Then the "input-state" for this transition (used as an argument for $\Gamma(H(t))$) will be computed by joining the states attached to the pre-places. Such a join need only be applicable for states which are consistent in the sense that one and the same location has a new value in, at most, one state. The introduction of semaphor places (in AADL nets) will guarantee this property for processes reflecting the behaviour of an AADL specification. The joined state will then consist of the unique new values for altered state components and will leave all other state components unchanged.

We call the states attached to the places of a process *valid* when for all places s mapped (via H) to trigger places of the underlying AADL net the attached formulae $\pi(H(s))$ are true. Each structure of partially ordered states determined in the way above described will define one possible behaviour of an AADL specification under the condition that its states are valid. By choosing different starting states several state structures will belong to one process. The semantics of an AADL specification is defined as the set of all (valid) structures of partially ordered states derivable in the sense above described from a process of the AADL specification.

We will now illustrate the mechanism of state assignment to places at the example of the process in Figure 35. As a starting state we consider the state represented in Figure 36 attached to all places marked by 1) in Figure 35.

[6] $\hat{t}^3$ is not present in the part of the process we have shown in Figure 35. However, it follows as a second place after $\hat{t}^6$.

location	value	tag	location	value	tag
msg_buffer [1]	put(record ... end, put(record ... end, nil))	old	bufcnt [1]	2	old
msg_buffer [2]	put(record ... end, nil)	old	bufcnt [2]	1	old

Figure 36: One starting state for the example process

This state will be delivered from the place mapped onto s_0 to two further states $\{s_0^4, s_0^{11}\}$ and $\{\hat{s}_0^4, \hat{s}_0^{11}\}$ (the τ-transition does not change the state) and from there to the places marked with 2) and $\hat{2}$). While passing the transitions t^4 resp. $\hat{t}^4$ a new component *no* of type *processno* will be added to these states. In general these temporary locations will be initialized with process numbers given in the receive-demand message. For our example we assume that the locations *no* carry the values "1" and "2" for the states marked 2) resp. $\hat{2}$), which are shown in Figures 37(a) and (b).

location	value	tag	location	value	tag	location	value	tag
msg_buffer [1]	put(record ... end, put(record ... end, nil))	old	bufcnt [1]	2	old	no	1	new
msg_buffer [2]	put(record ... end, nil)	old	bufcnt [2]	1	old			

Figure 37(a)

location	value	tag	location	value	tag	location	value	tag
msg_buffer [1]	put(record ... end, put(record ... end, nil))	old	bufcnt [1]	2	old	no	2	new
msg_buffer [2]	put(record ... end, nil)	old	bufcnt [2]	1	old			

Figure 37(b)

The state transformation for $\hat{t}^1$ has to take place on the state space resulting from the join of the places marked with $\hat{2}$) and the semaphor place marked with 7). Thus we will first consider the states generated for the places in the upper part of Figure 35 up to the places marked with 7).

The input state for the transition t^1 can be composed by joining the starting state (see Figure 36) attached to the place marked with s_{12}, with the state of Figure 37(a). The resulting state, shown in Figure 38, is identical to the state in Figure 37(a) with the exception that the tag field of the location *no* has changed from *new* to *old*. It is attached to the places marked 3).

location	value	tag	location	value	tag	location	value	tag
msg_buffer [1]	put(record ... end, put(record ... end, nil))	old	bufcnt [1]	2	old	no	1	old
msg_buffer [2]	put(record ... end, nil)	old	bufcnt [2]	1	old			

Figure 38

The combined transition t^5, t_{in} will add two new locations *a* and *ms* to the state for the place marked 4) (see Figure 39). They are initialized with the values *top*(*msg_buffer*[*no*]).*sender* and *ack* according to the output command of t^5.

location	value	tag	location	value	tag	location	value	tag
msg_buffer [1]	put(record ... end, put(record ... end, nil))	old	bufcnt [1]	2	old	no	1	old
msg_buffer [2]	put(record ... end, nil)	old	bufcnt [2]	1	old			
a	top(msg_buffer[no]).sender	new	ms	ack	new			

Figure 39

Since in the *communication_prim* *a* and *ms* are not known we need not include these locations to the states for the places marked with 5). t^6 does not change this state, thus it is also input state for the transition t^2. This transition will overwrite the queue at location *msg_buffer*[1] with a new queue in which the last element has been deleted. The resulting state for the place marked with 6) is shown in Figure 40.

location	value	tag	location	value	tag	location	value	tag
msg_buffer [1]	put(record ... end, nil)	new	bufcnt [1]	2	old	no	1	old
msg_buffer [2]	put(record ... end, nil)	old	bufcnt [2]	1	old			

Figure 40

To construct the input state of t^3 we have to join the state in Figure 40 with that of Figure 38. The joined state shown in Figure 41 will have the value of Figure 40 for *msg_buffer*[1] because its tag is *new*.

location	value	tag	location	value	tag	location	value	tag
msg_buffer [1]	put(record ... end, nil)	old	bufcnt [1]	2	old	no	1	old
msg_buffer [2]	put(record ... end, nil)	old	bufcnt [2]	1	old			

Figure 41

The transition t^3 will set the *bufcnt*[1] location to the value "1" which results in the state of Figure 42 attached to the places marked 7).

location	value	tag	location	value	tag	location	value	tag
msg_buffer [1]	put(record ... end, nil)	old	bufcnt [1]	1	old	no	1	old
msg_buffer [2]	put(record ... end, nil)	old	bufcnt [2]	1	old			

Figure 42

We can now compute the input state for transition $\hat{t}^1$ as the join of this state with the state attached to the places marked $\hat{2}$). In this way the states for all places in the process can be built.

5. The place of AADL in the world of specification languages

In this final section we will discuss the merits of AADL as compared to existing specification methods. Since AADL covers such wide areas as hard, firm, and software design, we review separately the specification methods employed in these areas.

Software specification methods for distributed systems can be categorized according to their underlying semantic models. While first approaches tended to rely on a linear order of events (as in Manna's temporal logic, firing sequences of Petri nets, or trace theory) today there seems to be general agreement on the advantages of partial-order semantics (using e.g. event structures developed by Winskel (1986) or processes (Reisig, 1985)). Indeed, a partial-order semantics is now available for almost all typically employed specification methods, ranging from variants of CCS (Olderog, 1987; Degano *et al.*, 1985, 1987b, 1988a, 1988b, 1989a) to ACP (Gladbeek and Vaandrager, 1987) to CSP (Goltz and Loogen, 1985; Degano *et al.*, 1988c) to temporal logic (Pinter and Wolper, 1984; Reisig, 1987) to Petri nets (Reisig, 1985). The advantages of these approaches rely on their ability to express the concurrent execution of two causally unrelated events without forcing them into some hypothetical global time scale, which clearly need not exist in the world we are modelling (compare the notion of equipotential regions in VLSI designs (Seitz, 1980)). We conclude that the use of partial-order semantics is of major importance in order to adequately model levels in computer architecture design dealing with distributed software such as distributed operating systems and higher levels of communication protocols.

An equally important, though orthogonal, aspect addresses **modularity** of specification methods. Though modularization techniques are well understood in (sequential) software development, ways of combining concurrency and modularity in specification languages are currently about to be developed in various research projects. As an example, research in the DESCARTES project has arrived at a compositional specification method for state charts (and has also adressed compositional proof-techniques, see below; due to the orientation towards modelling of real-time systems, DESCARTES is based on a maximal parallelism semantics rather than a partial-order semantics). Again it must be emphasized that the use of modular specification methods is essential in assuring applicability in real-life designs.

Approaches taken towards **firmware** and **hardware specification** differ radically, depending on the intended use of the specification. For simulation and design automation applications, often operational specification languages like ISPS (Barbacci, 1984) or MIMOLA (Marwedel, 1984) are employed. Typically, VLSI design tools define their own specification language appropriate to the level of specification (register transfer, gate level, switch level) which they support. Attempts at standardization have produced VHDL (Shadad *et al.*, 1985) and EDIF (Marx *et al.*, 1987). While these languages cover a number of design levels, they are not adequate for higher levels of computer architecture design adressed in this chapter. Indeed, the challenge posed in the design of AADL was to use **one** specification language for levels ranging from virtual machines to the chip level. These design levels are characterized by the **interactive nature of design steps,** inducing as an additional requirement to the specification language the feasibility of verifying interactive design steps. We conclude that neither languages tailored towards a particular level of hardware description nor "broad-range" languages without support for design verification (such as DACAPO (Rammig, 1986)) meet this challenge.

Though the introduction of verification methods supporting AADL is beyond the scope of this chapter, it is instructive to briefly survey various approaches to the verification of distributed systems in order to appreciate concepts in AADL supporting design verification.

Embedding verification methods into computer architecture design is a far-reaching goal: not only do we have to address verification at the different system levels outlined earlier; we also have to attain for a manageable complexity of the verification process itself. We will thus have to discuss the various approaches taken towards verification with these two equally important aspects in mind. Clearly the degree of automation of verification procedures and the modularity of proof methods are of major importance. Given these constraints, we will only discuss proof systems at the software level, allowing us to reason about concurrency in a modular way or providing automated proof methods.

Recently compositional (and relatively complete) proof systems allowing us to establish **safety properties** (ensuring that "nothing bad will happen") of CSP-type languages have been developed (Zwiers, 1989). Most proof systems dealing with **liveness properties** (ensuring that "good things will happen") are based on temporal logic; **modular** proof techniques for a carefully chosen **propositional** temporal logic have been recently announced by Josko (1987a). Extensions allowing modular proofs of specifications in first-order temporal logic are not available. Clearly only **propositional** temporal properties can be verified automatically. Of particular interest are model-checking procedures for branching-time PTL because of their **linear** complexity (Clarke *et al.*, 1983). Though branching-time PTL does not support modular proof methods, a recent extension (Josko, 1987b) shows that the exponential-time complexity for model-checking of PTL formula based on linear time can be kept sufficiently small for typical applications.

Variants of PTL have also been employed for **hardware verification** by constructing a model out of a gate-level description of a circuit and using model checking to prove its consistency against a PTL specification of its behaviour (see e.g. Clarke and Mishra, 1985). These approaches suffer from two (unrelated) drawbacks. Note first, that even though model checking can be done in time linear to the size of the model, the model itself is exponential in the size of the circuit. (This problem can be partially overcome by using a higher-level description of the circuit if design tools are available to automatically generate the gate-level descripti- from of this representation.) The second drawback concerns the timing model underlying the construction of the model: either the construction assumes a common unit delay for all gates, or no assumptions at all about the relative speed of gates is made. To incorporate better timing models, extensions to interval temporal logic (Moszkowszki, 1983) or even higher-order predicate calculus (Gordon, 1985, Hanna, 1985) have been employed, at the cost of losing automated proof methods. This has been compensated in HOL by providing structuring mechanisms for application-dependent knowledge which can be injected naturally into the interactive proof process using e.g. the concepts of "tactics" (Gordon *et al.*, 1979).

Among the many approaches to **firmware verification** (see e.g. Crocker *et al.*, 1984; Gordon, 1983)) only the Microprogramming Logic developed in Damm (1988) provides compositional proof methods.

6. Acknowledgements

We thank the people from the DOOM Project at Philips Research Laboratories, in particular Eddy Odijk, Wim Bronnenberg, Peter den Haan, Jan Koen Annot, Rob van Twist, and Frans Hopmans for their support in the development of AADL. We also like to thank the members of the ESPRIT 415 Working Group on Semantics and Proof Techniques for many hours of fruitful discussions.

This work was partially funded by ESPRIT 415: Parallel Architectures and Languages for AIP - A VLSI-Directed Approach and by the DFG under grant No. Da 206/2-1.

7. References

Albert, I., Müller-Schloer, C. and Schwärtzel, H. (1986). CAD-Systeme für die industrielle Rechnerentwicklung. *Informatik-Spektrum*, 9, 14-28.

Aposporidis, E., Hoppe, F. and Lohnert F. (1987). *Design of the Multi-Level Simulator* ESPRIT 415, Doc. No. 027-87.

Barbacci, M.R. (1984). Structural and behavioural description of digital systems. In J. Tiberghien (Ed.), *New Computer Architectures, International Lecture Series in Computer Science*, 140-223.

Bardis, L. (1984). *Entwurf und Implementierung eines Interpreter-Generators für eine Familie von Mikroprogrammiersprachen*. Master's thesis, RWTH Aachen.

Beccard, R.-D. (1986). *Automatische und vollständige Generierung von Korrektheitsbeweisen für Mikroprogramme*. Master's thesis, RWTH Aachen.

Beccard, R., Damm, W., Döhmen, G. and Sichelschmidt, M. (1987). Two Techniques for Automating Firmware Design Verification. *Proc. 8th International Symposium on Computer Hardware Description Languages and their Applications*. North-Holland, Amsterdam, 249-266.

Bergstra, J.A., and Klop, J.W. (1986). Algebra of Communicating Processes. In J. W. de Bakker, M. Hazewinkel and J. K. Lenstra (Eds), *Proceedings of the CWI Symposium Mathematics and Computer Science*. North-Holland, Amsterdam.

Berthelot, G. and Terrat, R. (1982). Petri Nets Theory for the Correctness of Protocols. In C. Sunshine (Ed.) *Proceedings of the IFIP WG 6.1 Second International Workshop on Protocol Specification, Testing, and Verification*. North-Holland, Amsterdam.

Brown, J. S., Burton, R. R. and Bell, G. (1975). SOPHIE: a step forward creating a reactive learning environment. *Int. J. Man-Machine studies*, 7, 675-696.

Clarke, E.M., Emerson, E.A. and Sistla, A.P. (1983). Automatic verification of finite state concurrent systems using temporal logic specifications: a practical approach. *10th ACM Symp. Principles on Computer Programming Languages*, 117-126.

Clarke, E.M. and Mishra, B. (1985). Hierarchical verification of asynchronous circuits using temporal logic. *Theoretical Computer Science*, 38, 289-291.

Clarke, E.M., Emerson, E.A., and Sistla, A.P. (1986). Automatic Verification of Finite-State Concurrent Systems Using Temporal Logic Specifications. *ACM Transactions on Programming Languages and Systems*, 8(2), 244-263.

Crocker, H.K., Marcus, L. and Landauer, J.R. (1984). SDVS: A System for Verifying Microcode Correctness. *Proc. 17th Annual Workshop on Microprogramming*. IEEE Computer Society Press, 246-255.

Damm, W. (1984a). An Axiomatization of Low Level Parallelism in Micro-Architectures. *Proc. MICRO-17*. IEEE Computer Society Press, 314-323.

Damm, W. (1984b). Automatic Generation of Simulation Tools: A Case Study in the Design of a Retargetable Firmware Development System. In *Advances in Microprocessing and Microprogramming*, North-Holland, Copenhagen, 165-176.

Damm, W. (1985). Stepwise Design of Microprogrammed Computer Architectures. *Proc. 18th Annual Workshop on Microprogramming*, IEEE Computer Society Press, 3-9.

Damm, W. (1987). *Entwurf und Verifikation mikroprogrammierter Rechnerarchitekturen.* Informatik Fachberichte, 146, Springer-Verlag.

Damm, W. (1988). A Microprogramming Logic. *IEEE Transactions on Software-Engineering,* 14(5), 559-576.

Damm, W. and Döhmen, G. (1985). Verification of Microprogrammed Computer Architectures in the S*-system: A Case Study. *Proc. 18th Annual Workshop on Microprogramming,* IEEE Computer Society Press, 61-73.

Damm, W. and Döhmen, G. (1986). *The POOL Machine: A Top Level Specification for a Distributed Object Oriented Machine.* Internal Report, ESPRIT Project 415A.

Damm, W. and Döhmen, G. (1987). An Axiomatic Approach to the Specification of Distributed Computer Architectures. *Proc. Conference on Parallel Architectures and Languages Europe* (PARLE). Lecture Notes in Computer Science, 258, Springer-Verlag, 103-120.

Damm, W. and Döhmen, G. (1989). Specifying Distributed Computer Architectures in AADL. *Parallel Computing,* 9, North-Holland,Amsterdam, 193-211.

Damm, W., Döhmen, G., Merkel, K. and Sichelschmidt, M. (1986a). The AADL/S* Approach to Firmware Design Verification. *IEEE Software Magazine,* 3(4), 27-37.

Damm, W., Döhmen, G., Merkel, K. and Sichelschmidt, M. (1986b). The AADL/S* Approach to Firmware Design Verification. In J. W. de Bakker (Ed.), *Deliverable 2 of the ESPRIT 415 Working Group on Semantics and Proof Techniques,*

Damm, W., Döhmen, G. and den Haan, P. (1987). Using AADL to Specify Distributed Computer Architectures: A Case Study In J. W. de Bakker (Ed.), *Deliverable 3 of the ESPRIT 415 Working Group on Semantics and Proof Techniques.*

Damm, W., Döhmen, G., Josko, B. Korf, F. and Peikenkamp, T. (1989). *AADL Language Document.* Universität Oldenburg, internal report.

Dasgupta, S. (1982). Computer Design and Description Languages. *Advances in Computers,* 21, Academic Press, New York, 91-154.

Dasgupta, S. (1984). *The Design and Description of Computer Architectures.* John Wiley & Sons, New York.

Dasgupta, S. and Heinanen, J. (1985). On the Axiomatic Specification of Computer Architectures. *Proc. CHDL.*

Degano, P., De Nicola, R. and Montanari, U. (1985). Partial ordering derivations for CCS, Proc. 5th Int. Conf. Fundamentals of Computation Theory, Cottbus (DDR). Lecture Notes in Computer Science. Vol. 199, Springer-Verlag, 520-533.

Degano, P. and Marchetti, S. (1987a). Partial ordering models for concurrency can be defined operationally. *Int. Journal of Parallel Programming.* 16, 6, 451-478.

Degano, P., De Nicola, R. and Montanari, U. (1987b). CCS is an (augmented) contact-free C/E system. *Proc. Advanced School on Mathematical Models for the Semantics of Concurrency.* M. Venturini Zilli (Ed.), 1986. Lecture Notes in Computer Science, 280, Springer-Verlag, 144-168.

Degano, P., De Nicola, R. and Montanari, U. (1988a). A distributed operational semantics for CCS based on C/E systems. *Acta Informatica,* 26, 59-91.

Degano, P., De Nicola, R. and Montanari, U. (1988b). Partial Ordering Descriptions and Observations of Nondeterministic Concurrent Processes. *Proc. REX School/Workshop on Linear time, Branching Time and Partial Order in Logics and Models for Concurrency.* In J. W. de Bakker, W. de Rover and G. Rozenberg (Eds.). Lecture Notes in Computer Science, 354, Springer-Verlag, 438-466.

Degano, P., Gorrieri, R. and Machetti, S. (1988c). An exercise in concurrency: a CSP process as a Condition/Event system. *Advances on Petri Nets 1988.* G. Rozenberg (Ed.). Lecture Notes in Computer Science, 340, Springer- Verlag, 83-105.

Degano, P., De Nicola, R. and Montanari, U. (1989a). A partial ordering semantics for CCS. *Theoretical Computer Science,* to appear.

Degano, P., De Nicola, R. and Montanari, U. (1989b). On the Operational Semantics of Distributed Concurrent Systems. *Proc. IFIP 10.1 Workshop on Concepts and Characteristics of Declarative Systems.* R. T. Boute (Ed.), to appear.

Döhmen, G. (1985). *Verifikation eines Emulators: eine Fallstudie zur Verifikation mikroprogrammierter Rechnerarchitekturen*. Master's thesis, RWTH Aachen.

Döhmen, G. and den Haan, P. (1987). *The AADL Specification for the Intermediate Pool Machine*. ESPRIT 415 Document No. 326, Philips Research Labs, Eindhoven.

Gageik, T. (1988a). *Hierarchische Spezifikation eines Kommunikationsprozessors in AADL*. Master's thesis, RWTH Aachen.

Gageik, T. (1988b). *A Hierarchical Specification of the DOOM Communication Processor*. ESPRIT 415A, Philips Research Laboratories, Eindhoven.

Gerstner, V. (1989). *Anwendung der Temporalen Logik zur Verifikation hierarchischer Spezifikationen von Rechnersystemen*. Master's thesis, RWTH Aachen.

Glabeek, R.J. and Vaandrager, F. W. (1987). Petri net models for algebraic theories of concurrency (extended abstract). In *Proc. PARLE conference Eindhoven* 1987, Vol. II (Parallel Languages) (J.W. de Bakker, A.J. Nijman, P.C. Treleaven, (Eds.). Lecture Notes in Computer Science 259, Springer-Verlag, 224-242.

Goltz, U. and Loogen, R. (1985). *Toward a non-interleaving semantic model for nondeterministic concurrent processes*. Aachener Informatik Berichte, 87/15, RWTH Aachen.

Gordon, M. (1983). Proving a Computer Correct. *Technical Report* 42, University of Cambridge.

Gordon, M. (1985). HOL: A Machine Oriented Formulation of Higher Order Logic. *Technical Report*, 68, Computer Laboratory, University of Cambridge, Corn Exchange Street, Cambridge CB2 3QG, UK.

Gordon, M., Milner, R. and Wadsworth, C. (1979). *Edinburgh LCF*, VIII, Lecture Notes in Computer Science, 78, Springer-Verlag.

den Haan, P. and Bronnenberg, W. (1987). *Mapping POOL on DOOM*. ESPRIT 415 Document No. 303.

den Haan, P. and Hopmans, F. (1988). Efficient Message Passing in Parallel Systems with Limited Memory. *Proc. Conference on Distributed Processing*.

Hanna, F. K. and Daeche, N. (1985). Specification and Verification Using Higher Order Logic. In *Proc. 7th Int. Symp. on Computer Hardware Description Languages and Applications*, Tokyo, Japan, 418-443.

Hoare, C.A.R. (1978). Communicating Sequential Processes. *Communications ACM*, 21, 666-677.

Josko, B. (1987a). MCTL - An Extension of CTL for Modular Verification of Concurrent Systems. *Proc. Colloquium on Temporal Logic*, Manchester, UK.

Josko, B. (1987b). Modelcheking of CTL Formulae under Liveness Assumptions. *Proc. ICALP 87*, Lecture Notes in Computer Science, 267, 280 - 289.

Kitamura, Y., Hoshino, T., Kondo, T., Nakashima, T. and Sudo, T. (1986). Hardware Engines for Logic Simulation. In E. Hörbst (Ed.), *Logic Design and Simulation*, North-Holland, Amsterdam.

Klaeren, H. (1986). *An Introduction to Algebraic Specifications*. Springer-Verlag, Berlin.

Lamport, L. (1983). Specifying Concurrent Program Modules. *ACM Trans. Program. Lang. Systems*, 5, 190-222.

Lamport, L. (1985). Sometime is sometimes not never. *Proc. POPL '80*, 174-185.

Loogen, R. (1987). *Designing a Parallel Programmable Graph Reduction Machine with Distributed Memory*. Aachener Informatik Berichte, 87/11.

Maeder, C. (1987). *Ein Verifikationsbedingungsgenerator für die S*-Familie höherer Mikroprogrammiersprachen*. Master's thesis, RWTH Aachen.

Manna, Z., and Pnueli, A. (1981). Temporal Verification of Concurrent Programs: The Temporal Framework. In R.S. Boyer, J. Strother Moore (Eds), *The Correctness Problem in Computer Science, International Lecture Series in Computer Science*, 215-273.

Marwedel, P. (1984). A Retargetable Compiler for a High-Level Microprogramming Language. *17th Annual Workshop on Microprogramming*, IEEE Computer Society Press, 267-274.

Marx, E., Waters, H. and Switzer, H. (1987). *Use an interchance format to port component libraries*, Designer's Guide to EDIF - Part 1-4, EDN.

Milner, R. (1980). *A Calculus of Communicating Systems* Lecture Notes in Computer Science, 92, Springer-Verlag, Berlin.

Moszkowszki, B. (1983). A Temporal Logic for Multi-Level Reasoning About Hardware. In *Proc. 6th IFIP Int. Symp. on Computer Hardware Description Languages and their Applications*, Pittsburgh, Pennsylvania.

Odijk, E.A.M. (1985). The Philips Object-Oriented Parallel Computer. In J.V. Woods (Ed), *Fifth Generation Computer Architectures*, North-Holland, Amsteerdam.

Odijk, E.A.M., van Twist, R., Janssens, M., and Bronnenberg, W. (1987). The Architecture of DOOM. *Proc. of the ESPRIT Summer School on Future Parallel Computers*, Lecture Notes in Computer Science, Springer-Verlag.

Olderog, E.-R. (1985). Specification-oriented programming in TCSP. In K.R. Apt (Ed), *Logics and Models of Concurrent Systems*, NATO ASI Series, Series F: Computer and System Sciences, 13, Springer-Verlag.

Olderog, E.-R. (1987). Operational Petri Nets Semantics for CCSP. In G. Rozenberg (Ed.), *Advances in Petri Nets* 1987, Lecture Notes in Computer Science, 266, Springer-Verlag, 196-223.

Peikenkamp, T. (1988). *Systematische Entwicklung einer parallelen Prolog-Architektur*. Master's thesis, RWTH Aachen.

Pinter, S. S. and Wolper, P. (1984). A Temporal Logic for Reasoning about Partially Ordered Computations. In *Proc. 3rd ACM Symp. on Principles of Distributed Computing*, Vancouver, Canada, 28-37.

Rammig, F. J. (1986). Mixed Level Modelling and Simulation of VLSI Systems. In E. Hörbst (Ed.), *Logic Design and Simulation*, North-Holland, Amsterdam.

Reisig, W. (1985). *Petri Nets - An Introduction*. EATCS Monographs in Computer Science, 4, Springer-Verlag.

Reisig, W. (1987). *Towards a Temporal Logic for True Concurrency, Part I: Linear Time Propositional Logic*. Arbeitspapiere der GMD, 277.

Romberg, M. (1985). *Statische Analyse von höheren Mikroprogrammiersprachen*. Master's thesis, RWTH Aachen.

Seitz, C. L. (1980). System Timing. In C. Mead and L. Conway (Eds), *Introduction to VLSI Systems*, Addison-Wesley,Reading, Ma.

Shadad, M. and Lipsett, R. (1985). VHSIC hardware description language. *IEEE Computer*, 18(2), 94-102.

Sichelschmidt, I. (1989). *Systematischer Entwurf von Bitslice-Architekturen in AADL*. Master's thesis ,to appear.

Warren, D. H. D. (1983). An Abstract Prolog Instruction Set. *SRI Technical Report*, SRI International, Monto Park, CA.

Winskel, G. (1987). Event Structures. In W. Brauer, W. Reisig, G. Rozenberg (Eds), *Petri Nets: Applications and Relationships to Other Models of Concurrency*, Advances in Petri Nets 1986, Part II, Proceedings of an Advanced Course, Bad Honnef, Lecture Notes in Computer Science, 255, Springer-Verlag, 325-392

Zimmermann, H. (1980). OSI Reference Model - The ISO Model of Architecture for Open Systems Interconnection. *IEEE Trans. Commun.*, 28, 425-432.

Zwiers, J. (1989). *Compositionality, Concurrency and Partial Correctness: Proof Theories for Networks of Processes and Their Relationship*, Lecture Notes in Computer Science, 321, Springer-Verlag.

Chapter 3

Deriving a Parallel Evaluation Model for Lazy Functional Languages Using Abstract Interpretation

Geoffrey L. Burn

GEC Hirst Research Centre, East Lane, Wembley, Middlesex HA9 7PP, United Kingdom

Functional languages have the Church–Rosser property. The languages are therefore implicitly parallel, making them suitable for implementation on parallel architectures. However, the Church–Rosser property is only a correctness result modulo termination. We therefore develop a model for the parallel implementation of lazy functional languages which preserves their denotational properties. The model does not need a special scheduling strategy for the parallel tasks, and never does more work than it needs to in order to get a result from the program. In these senses, and from how it is defined, it is a natural extension of lazy evaluation to the parallel world.

In order to determine the information needed by the model, we develop and apply a framework for the abstract interpretation of functional programs. The application of the framework determines the definedness of a function in terms of the definedness of its arguments. This can then be used to determine evaluation transformers, which indicate how much evaluation of an argument expression can be done, given that a certain amount of evaluation is allowed of a function application. We prove that the evaluation transformers and the evaluation model satisfy a condition relating the operational and denotational semantics, in order to show that the model is correct and has the desired properties.

Finally, we give an indication of how this model can be supported in parallel architectures.

1. Introduction

Functional languages have their semantic foundations in the λ-calculus. The λ-calculus with β-reduction has the Church–Rosser property. Informally this property says that the same answer is received from reducing an expression, no matter in what order the redexes are reduced, as long as the reduction sequence terminates. This property of functional languages has made many people investigate them as being suitable for use on parallel machines, for if it does not matter in what order the redexes are reduced, then they may as well all be done in parallel. Parallelism is *implicit* in that it is a property of the mechanism which executes programs, relieving the programmer of worrying about writing parallel programs.

The only problem with the above suggestion is that the Church–Rosser property states a result modulo termination, that is, the answer is correct provided the reduction sequence terminates. It can be proved that the reduction strategy which always chooses to reduce the left-most outer-most redex in an expression terminates whenever any reduction strategy will, and this strategy gives the answers one would intuitively expect from programs. *Lazy evaluation* uses left-most outer-most reduction, reducing expressions as far as *head normal form (HNF)*. The problem with lazy evaluation for a parallel machine is that it is overly pessimistic about which expressions are going to be needed – it only knows that the left-most outer-most redex is needed – hardly a parallel reduction strategy! Since lazy evaluation gives the desired semantics of programs, our problem is to define a parallel reduction strategy which gives the same answer as lazy evaluation.

Another way of looking at lazy evaluation is to note that it never initiates a non-terminating computation unless the semantics of the original expression to be evaluated was undefined, that is, bottom. Our problem then reduces to ensuring that we do not initiate a computation unless its non-termination would imply that the semantics of the overall expression was bottom. We will call this our *semantic criterion.* Note that this precludes the evaluation of expressions whose values are not needed, even if it could be determined that their evaluation would terminate. A *safe* evaluation strategy is one which obeys the semantic criterion.

The purpose of this chapter is to define a parallel evaluation strategy and prove that it satisfies the semantic criterion. It is basically a summary of Burn (1987a), with some extra insights and pointers to further developments since that work was published. It must be noted that although this chapter is structured by first motivating the evaluation model and then proving it correct, the development was more in the other order; the evaluation model arose largely through an investigation of the semantics and the study of abstract interpretation. Having developed the model, it seems to be the natural parallel equivalent of lazy evaluation.

This chapter is structured as follows. Section 2 develops the parallel model in an intuitive manner. We argue that an *evaluation transformer* should be associated with each argument to each function. The evaluation transformer indicates how much evaluation can be done to an argument expression, given the amount of evaluation allowed of the function application. Parallelism occurs when this is non-zero and a parallel task can be created to evaluate the expression.

In developing the evaluation transformer model in section 2, we argue informally about how much evaluation a function needs to perform on its arguments. This needs to be proved, and the evaluation transformer model must be proved to satisfy the semantic criterion. We do this in three steps, in sections 3 to 5.

Section 3 develops a framework for the *abstract interpretation* of functional languages. Abstract interpretation is a method of finding out properties of programs without running them, by giving different, or abstract, interpretations to the constructs of the language. The section begins by introducing the way the framework will be developed by using the "rule of signs" in arithmetic expressions as an example. For the rest of the chapter we use the typed λ-calculus. It must be finitely typed in order to define the appropriate abstraction and concretization maps and to ensure the termination of the analysis. After some mathematical preliminaries, the framework is developed. At the end of the development we have two theorems which allow us to make inferences about programs. All that has to supplied in order to use the framework are finite lattices for abstract domains for the base types which capture the property of interest, continuous abstraction maps for the base types, and abstract interpretations of the constants of the language which satisfy a given constant criterion (Definition 3.2).

In section 4 we motivate and define some abstract domains which capture the property in which we are interested in order to obtain the information required for the evaluation transformer model of computation, namely the definedness of functions.

Section 5 interprets the correctness theorem of abstract interpretation with the particular interpretation of section 4 in order to prove that the parallel reduction model satisfies the semantic criterion. Some of the uniqueness of this work is that it was the first to give a formal proof of the correctness of a model which changed the evaluation order but maintained a formally defined safety criterion. Previous arguments had been only intuitive.

In section 6 we show how the evaluation model is being used in work on parallel architectures for functional languages within Subproject B of ESPRIT 415. The subject matter of this chapter is compared with related work in section 7.

2. The evaluation model

The evaluation model must describe where parallel reduction can take place, and how much evaluation of expressions is allowed. We motivate an evaluation model, based on evaluation transformers, which is a natural extension of lazy evaluation.

2.1 Evaluators

We know that in some function applications, the argument will need more reduction than just to HNF. The function *length* calculates the length of its argument list. The length of an empty list, [], is zero, whilst the length of a list whose head is x and tail xs is one more than the length of xs. This is expressed by the program:

$$\begin{aligned} &length\ [\,] = 0 \\ &length\ (x{:}xs) = 1 + length\ xs \end{aligned}$$

To evaluate an application of *length*, the whole of the argument list will need to be traversed, but none of the values of elements of the list will be needed. The function

$$\begin{aligned} &sumlist\ [\,] = 0 \\ &sumlist\ (x{:}xs) = x + sumlist\ xs \end{aligned}$$

needs to traverse the whole of its argument list and also obtain the values of the elements of the list. We will call the process of recursively evaluating the second argument of *cons* until we reach *nil* (if we do, which will only happen if the list is finite), creating the *structure* of the list. There is a similar idea for all recursively defined types, such as integer binary trees which have the Miranda (Turner, 1986)[1] type definition:

$$tree ::= NIL\_TREE \mid NODE\ \ num\ \ tree\ \ tree$$

where the second and third arguments to the *NODE* constructor are recursively evaluated. Basically, evaluating the structure of an expression is unfolding the recursive part of the data type definition. For simplicity of exposition, we will restrict our discussion to lists in the rest of the chapter.

We will say that we can evaluate an expression using a particular *evaluator*, and call an evaluator which evaluates expressions to HNF ξ_1, an evaluator which evaluates the structure of a list ξ_2, and an evaluator which evaluates the structure of a list and every element of the list to HNF ξ_3. For completeness, the evaluator ξ_0 does no evaluation. The relationship between the evaluators is

$$\xi_3 > \xi_2 > \xi_1 > \xi_0$$

where the relationship > is read as *stronger than*, because the first evaluator does more evaluation than the second.

[1] Miranda is a trademark of Research Software Ltd.

Note that although ξ_2 and ξ_3 are defined in terms of evaluating the whole structure of a list, they could be implemented so that they evaluated the list in chunks; when a chunk is consumed to a certain extent, the evaluation of the list can be reawakened to evaluate another chunk.

When an expression is being evaluated by ξ_2 or ξ_3, each *cons* cell needs to be made available as it is produced. Once an expression has been reduced to HNF, no more evaluation can be done to the cell which is created in heap, but only to the subexpressions. Each of the base functions *head*, *tail* and *null* only require their argument to be reduced to HNF (although *tail* can pass on an evaluator to the tail of the list). Therefore processes requiring the value of an expression need only be locked out whilst the expression is being evaluated to HNF. Also, from the discussion above defining the evaluators, it should be obvious that ξ_2 can be defined in terms of evaluating an expression to HNF and, if the result is a *cons*, recursively evaluating the second argument to the *cons* with ξ_2.

2.2 Evaluation transformers

Not only do some functions require more evaluation of their argument than to HNF, but the amount of evaluation of an argument may depend on the amount required of the application. Consider, for example, the function *append* defined by

$$\begin{aligned} &append\ []\ ys = ys \\ &append\ (x{:}xs)\ ys = x{:}(append\ xs\ ys) \end{aligned}$$

Normally the first argument to *append* is evaluated to HNF and no evaluation is done on the second argument because only a result in HNF is required. However, if one was to require that an application of *append* was to deliver the structure of a list, such as in the application *length* (*append* $E_1\ E_2$), then clearly it can only do this if the structure of both of its arguments are created.

For each argument of a function, therefore, we have to determine an *evaluation transformer*. An evaluation transformer for an argument is a mapping which says which evaluator may be used for evaluating the argument of a function, given the evaluator for an application of the function. For example, the evaluation transformers for *append* are given in Table 1. $APPEND_1$ and $APPEND_2$ are the evaluation transformers for the first and second argument of *append* respectively.

Table 1
Evaluation transformers for *append*

E	$APPEND_1(E)$	$APPEND_2(E)$
ξ_0	ξ_0	ξ_0
ξ_1	ξ_1	ξ_0
ξ_2	ξ_2	ξ_2
ξ_3	ξ_3	ξ_3

If an application of *append* is being evaluated with the evaluator ξ_2, then the first argument can be evaluated with the evaluator $APPEND_1(\xi_2)$ which, from the table, is ξ_2. Similarly, the second argument can be evaluated with ξ_2. Note that it is not always the case that evaluation transformers are nearly the identity.

2.3 The parallel model

Each function has a set of evaluation transformers associated with it, one for each formal parameter of the function. When a process is created to evaluate an expression, it has an evaluator associated with it, indicating how much evaluation of the expression is to be done to the expression. Each expression is evaluated using left-most outer-most reduction. At each reduction step, processes can be created to evaluate the arguments to the function in the application being reduced. The amount of evaluation allowed for each argument is found by applying the evaluation transformer of the function for that argument to the evaluator being used for the expression. Compiled code can be generated for this process (Burn, 1988b). Clearly no process is created if the amount of evaluation is ξ_0.

3. A framework for the abstract interpretation of functional languages

Abstract interpretation is a method for determining semantically correct information from a static analysis of the program text. We first introduce the main ideas of abstract interpretation by the way of an extended example. Following this, we give the language, a typed λ-calculus, to be used in this work, and a semantics which is parameterized by interpretations. The user of the framework is required to give three things. Finite lattices must be given for each base type, and a strict, continuous abstraction map from the standard domain to the abstract domain of each base type must be provided. Finally, abstract interpretations of the functional constants satisfying the constant criterion (Definition 3.2) must be given. Given this information, section 3.4 proceeds in a number of steps towards proving a correctness theorem relating the standard and abstract interpretations of a program.

This work can be seen as a generalization of the theory of Burn *et al.* (1986) to situations where we have more complex abstract domains than the two point domain for the abstract interpretations of base types.

3.1 An introduction to abstract interpretation

We are all familiar in everyday life with the idea that often we do not require the exact answer to a question – a distance of order of magnitude of ten kilometres can be cycled, whereas a distance of order of magnitude one hundred kilometres may require some automated form of transport. To answer the question "Do I ride my bicycle or do I go by train?", one needs only to know an approximation (order of magnitude) of the distance.

In a similar manner, we are taught at school that to tell whether a number is odd or even, all we need to do is see if the least significant digit is odd or even – a task which requires significantly less computational effort than dividing the whole number by two (unless we are dealing with a single-digit number!).

What is the key concept lying behind the answering of these and similar questions? The idea is that there is some property in which we are interested, and about which we can find information without having the exact answer or doing the whole calculation.

As a more complex example of abstract interpretation which shows most of the essential features we will use later, we introduce the "rule of signs", which is familiar from school mathematics. Our presentation is modelled on Hankin (1986). Let us consider the following abstract syntax of a language of arithmetic expressions:

$$Exp ::= c_n$$

$$|Exp + Exp$$

$$|Exp \times Exp$$

There is one constant, c_n for each integer n. A normal way to interpret such a language is to first interpret the set of constants $\{c_n\}$ as the integers, which we will denote by $\mathbf{Z}^{st}$, so that the constant c_n is interpreted to be the integer n. The symbols + and $\times$ are then interpreted as integer addition and multiplication respectively. These induce a standard interpretation function which we will denote by E^{st}:

$$E^{st} : Exp \rightarrow \mathbf{Z}^{st}$$

$$E^{st} \ [[c_n]] = n$$

$$E^{st} \ [[Exp_1 + Exp_2]] = E^{st} \ [[Exp_1]] \underline{+} E^{st} \ [[Exp_2]]$$

$$E^{st} \ [[Exp_1 \times Exp_2]] = E^{st} \ [[Exp_1]] \underline{\times} E^{st} \ [[Exp_2]]$$

where we have put a bar under the + and the $\times$ to help us remember that these are the real addition and multiplication functions.

If the property of interest is "Is the value of the expression positive or negative or zero?", we could use the standard interpretation of our language to determine the answer by doing the calculation and then seeing whether it was indeed positive or negative or zero. For example, for the expression

$$c_{29} \times c_{-33} \times c_{64}$$

we could calculate the answer to be

$$E^{st} \ [[c_{29}]] \underline{\times} E^{st} \ [[c_{-33}]] \underline{\times} E^{st} \ [[c_{64}]]$$

which is

$$29 \underline{\times} -33 \underline{\times} 64 = -61248$$

and then see that the answer is negative. However, we all know a simple way of doing this, for we know that, for example, multiplying a positive number by a negative number always gives a negative number. The way we normally answer the question about the sign of the the answer is to do the "calculation"

$$(+) \times (-) \times (+) = (-)$$

where (+) represents the property of being positive, and similarly (-) the property of being negative, and then say that the answer to the real calculation would have been negative.

What have we done? We have said that the important thing about the constant c_n was not its magnitude but its sign, and provided an abstract interpretation, which we will denote by E^{ab}, that says

$$E^{ab} \ [[c_n]] = sign\,(E^{st} \ [[c_n]])$$

where

$$sign\,(n) = \begin{cases} (+) \text{ if } n>0 \\ (0) \text{ if } n=0 \\ (-) \text{ if } n<0 \end{cases}$$

We also have the rule of signs, where we will write the interpretations of + and × under the rule of signs as $\overline{+}$ and $\overline{\times}$ respectively:

$$\begin{array}{ll}
(+)\,\overline{\times}\,(+) = (+) & (0)\,\overline{\times}\,(+) = (0) \\
(+)\,\overline{\times}\,(-) = (-) & (+)\,\overline{\times}\,(0) = (0) \\
(-)\,\overline{\times}\,(+) = (-) & (0)\,\overline{\times}\,(-) = (0) \\
(-)\,\overline{\times}\,(-) = (+) & (-)\,\overline{\times}\,(0) = (0) \\
(0)\,\overline{\times}\,(0) = (0) &
\end{array}$$

The rule of signs gives $\overline{\times}$ as an abstract interpretation of ×.

For the abstract interpretation, $\overline{+}$, of +, some of the rules are obvious: for example,

$$\begin{array}{ll}
(+)\,\overline{+}\,(+) = (+) & (0)\,\overline{+}\,(+) = (+) \\
(-)\,\overline{+}\,(-) = (-) & (0)\,\overline{+}\,(-) = (-) \\
(+)\,\overline{+}\,(0) = (+) & (0)\,\overline{+}\,(0) = (0) \\
(-)\,\overline{+}\,(0) = (-) &
\end{array}$$

When we have one of the expressions:

$$(+)\,\overline{+}\,(-) \text{ or } (-)\,\overline{+}\,(+)$$

then we can no longer say what the result is, because the sign of the result depends on the magnitude of the two values, and we have abstracted away that information. We thus introduce the value $\top$ (pronounced "top") to represent the idea that we do not know what the sign of the calculation is. Another way of representing this would be to use the set {(−),(0),(+)}, but we prefer this way because then we do not have to introduce sets into the abstract interpretation. The rules for $\top$ are:

$$\begin{array}{ll}
(-)\,\overline{\times}\,\top = \top & (-)\,\overline{+}\,\top = \top \\
(0)\,\overline{\times}\,\top = (0) & (0)\,\overline{+}\,\top = \top \\
(+)\,\overline{\times}\,\top = \top & (+)\,\overline{+}\,\top = \top
\end{array}$$

and the other six equations obtained by changing the order of the arguments to the operators and retaining the same answers.

For completeness, we will introduce the value $\perp$ (pronounced "bottom") to represent the undefined integer, even though in our language we will not be able to write an expression which has this as its standard semantics. We have thus extended our domain $\mathbf{Z}^{st}$ to $\mathbf{Z}^{st}_{\perp}$, where

$$\mathbf{Z}^{st}_{\perp} = \mathbf{Z}^{st} \cup \{\perp\}$$

and where we give the definedness ordering, ≤, on the domain

$$z_1 \leq z_2 \text{ if and only if } z_1 = \perp \text{ or } z_1 = z_2.$$

$\mathbf{Z}^{st}_{\perp}$ is an example of a *flat* domain because all of the elements from $\mathbf{Z}^{st}$ are on an equal level of definedness. We can draw this in a diagram as:

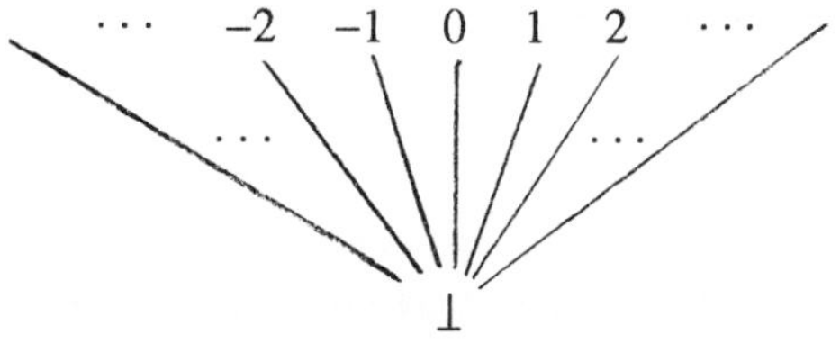

If $\perp$ appears as one of the arguments to $\underline{+}$ or $\underline{\times}$, then we must say what the answer is. We choose *strict* interpretations of these functions, so that the answer to an expression which has $\perp$ as either of the arguments must be $\perp$.

To model the bottom element in the domain $\mathbf{Z}_{\perp}^{st}$, we introduce $\perp$ into the elements in our abstract domain. For both $\overline{+}$ and $\overline{\times}$, $\perp$ in either of the argument positions gives $\perp$.

We now have an abstract domain, which we will call $\mathbf{Z}^{ab}$

$$\mathbf{Z}^{ab} = \{\perp,(-),0,(+),\top\}$$

where we define the ordering on the domain so that $\mathbf{Z}^{ab}$ is a complete lattice:

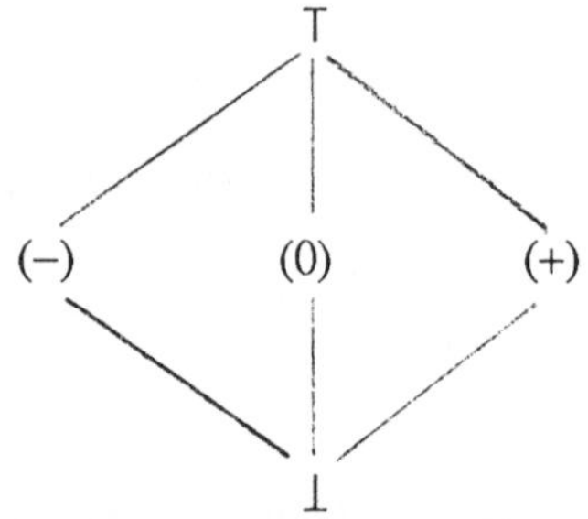

In the same way that we defined a standard interpretation for our language, we can provide an abstract interpretation, the semantic function being called E^{ab}:

$$E^{ab} : Exp \rightarrow \mathbf{Z}^{ab}$$

$$E^{ab}\ [[c_n]] = sign\,(E^{st}\ [[c_n]])$$

$$E^{ab}\ [[Exp_1 + Exp_2]] = E^{ab}\ [[Exp_1]] \overline{+} E^{ab}\ [[Exp_2]]$$

$$E^{ab}\ [[Exp_1 \times Exp_2]] = E^{ab}\ [[Exp_1]] \overline{\times} E^{ab}\ [[Exp_2]]$$

Note that the form of the abstract interpretation is exactly the same as that of the standard interpretation; all that has changed is the interpretation of the constants c_n, + and $\times$.

We now have two interpretations:

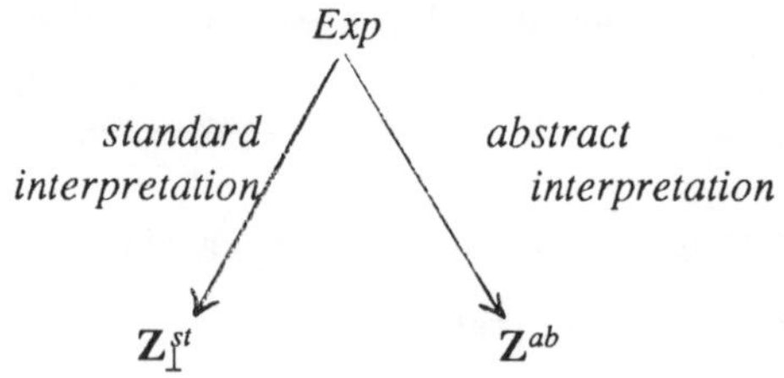

How can we say that if we get the answer (+) in the abstract interpretation, that the answer in the standard interpretation was really positive? That is, we must find a notion of correctness and prove that the abstract interpretation is correct. We begin by noting that the symbol (+) "represents" any positive integer. To capture this notion, we define a *concretization* map:

$$Conc : \mathbf{Z}^{ab} \rightarrow \mathbf{P}(\mathbf{Z}_{\perp}^{st})$$

where $\mathbf{P}(X)$ is the powerset of X. It returns an element in the powerset because each element in $\mathbf{Z}^{ab}$ represents (possibly) many elements of $\mathbf{Z}_{\perp}^{st}$.

Rather than define this map directly, we will do so in a manner which is similar to the way we will define such maps in section 3. We can define an abstraction map:

$$abs : \mathbf{Z}_{\bot}^{st} \rightarrow \mathbf{Z}^{ab}$$

which relates the standard interpretation and the abstract interpretation of the constants. In this case, the abstraction map is just the *sign* map defined earlier, augmented with the rule

$$sign(\bot) = \bot$$

to cope with the fact that we now are dealing with $\mathbf{Z}_{\bot}^{st}$ rather than just $\mathbf{Z}^{st}$.

We can now define a map

$$Abs : \mathbf{P}(\mathbf{Z}_{\bot}^{st}) \rightarrow \mathbf{Z}^{ab}$$

which will allow us to find the abstract interpretation of sets of elements. When we have a set of elements, we have the possibility of having elements of differing sign in the same set. Suppose we had the set $\{-3,4\}$ which we wanted to abstract. Then we could apply the abstraction map *abs* to each element in the set to obtain the set $\{(-),(+)\}$. We added the point $\top$ to represent the fact that we were not sure what the sign of a result of a computation was. Here we can give it another reading, where it says that it represents sets of elements which have more than one sign in them. Because of the ordering we introduced on our domain, we can obtain this result by taking the least upper bound of the sets of elements we get by abstracting each element in the set. (Note that $\bigsqcup\{(-),(+)\}$ is $\top$.) Thus we define *Abs* by

$$Abs(S) = \bigsqcup\{abs(n) \mid n \in S\}.$$

Finally we are able to define the concretization map. For $z \in \mathbf{Z}^{ab}$,

$$Conc(z) = \bigcup\{T \mid Abs(T) \leq z\}$$

The concretization map collects together all of the elements which abstract to something at most as defined as z. If we calculate what this means for each of the elements of $\mathbf{Z}^{ab}$, then we find that:

$$Conc(\bot) = \{\bot\}$$

$$Conc((-)) = \{n \mid n<0\} \cup \{\bot\}$$

$$Conc((0)) = \{0\} \cup \{\bot\}$$

$$Conc((+)) = \{n \mid n>0\} \cup \{\bot\}$$

$$Conc(\top) = \mathbf{Z}_{\bot}^{st}$$

and so see that indeed concretization captures our notion of an element "representing" a set of values.

We can now state what we mean by correctness. For any evaluation

$$z_1 \ \underline{op} \ z_2 => z_3$$

where z_1, $z_2 \in \mathbf{Z}^{ab}$ and $\underline{op}$ is either $\overline{+}$ or $\overline{\times}$, then we have that for all $n_1 \in Conc(z_1)$, $n_2 \in Conc(z_2)$,

$$n_1 \ \underline{op} \ n_2 \in Conc(z_3)$$

where $\underline{op}$ is $\underline{+}$ if $\underline{op}$ was $\overline{+}$, and $\underline{\times}$ otherwise. It can be shown that the abstract interpretation we have defined satisfies this property.

As an example of this, let us return to the previous example and ask what the sign of the expression:

$$c_{29} \times c_{-33} \times c_{64}$$

is. Our previous calculation showed that the real answer was −61248 and so the answer is negative. Doing the calculation in the abstract domain we obtain:

$$E^{ab}\ [[c_{29}]]\ \overline{\times}\ E^{ab}\ [[c_{-33}]]\ \overline{\times}\ E^{ab}\ [[c_{64}]]$$

which is

$$(+)\ \overline{\times}\ (-)\ \overline{\times}\ (+) = (-)$$

From this we conclude that the answer calculated in the standard interpretation is negative. If we concretize (−), we obtain the set of negative integers (plus $\perp$), and so we are able to conclude (because of the correctness of our abstract interpretation) that the result really was negative.

There is another feature of abstract interpretation that can be shown with this example. We note that the abstract interpretation does not give exact answers. For example,

$$\begin{aligned} E^{ab}\ [[c_{-10} + c_{11}]] &= E^{ab}\ [[c_{-10}]]\ \overline{+}\ E^{ab}\ [[c_{11}]] \\ &= (-)\ \overline{+}\ (+) \\ &= \top \end{aligned}$$

whereas the sign of the real answer

$$sign\,(E^{st}\ [[c_{-10} + c_{11}]]) = (+)$$

is (+), and so the abstract interpretation loses information, but in a safe way; the abstract interpretation says that it does not know what the sign of the answer is, but does not wrongly conclude that it is negative (or some other wrong answer).

Those familiar with universal algebra will notice that we almost have that *sign* is a homomorphism. We have the following diagram:

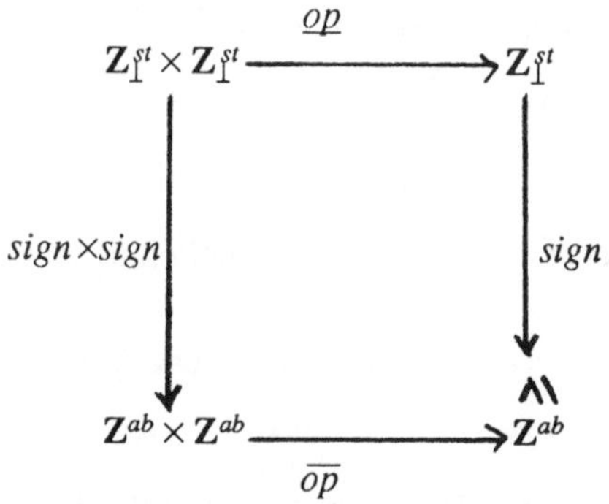

where in the bottom right-hand corner we have ≤ rather than equality. Our abstraction map, *sign*, is then a *semi-homomorphism*. This is the general case for abstraction maps when we are working in the world of domains rather than just sets.

We can now summarize the key features of abstract interpretation. Given a set of symbols, we must give them an interpretation. Thus, if we have a language, we must give an interpretation of the language. Usually the symbols are chosen with one particular interpretation in mind. However, sometimes there are questions one wishes to ask which are hard to answer using the standard interpretation of the language; in fact, the questions we will ask about the definedness of functions are not recursive. It is sometimes possible to give an interpretation of the language which answers the questions we want to ask, but requiring significantly less work to do so. Such an interpretation is called an abstract interpretation. The example we have given here is to ask what the sign of the result of a calculation is. For an abstract interpretation to be of any use, it must be correct, in that anything we conclude from it must really be true. Finally, answers given by abstract interpretations are not exact, but they are safe, that is, any conclusion we draw from the abstract interpretation will be weaker than a conclusion we could obtain from the standard interpretation.

3.2 The language

We use the typed λ-calculus for the development of the framework for abstract interpretation. Finite typing of the language means that computable abstract interpretations can be given for the language. In this section we introduce both the abstract syntax of the language and the idea of interpretations of the language which give different semantics to the language. Having more than one interpretation for a language is fundamental in the work of abstract interpretation. The presentation of this section is after the style of Abramsky (1985).

3.2.1 Syntax

Given a set of base types $\{A_1, A_2, \cdots\}$, we define type expressions $\sigma, \tau, \cdots$ by

$$\sigma ::= A_i \mid \sigma \to \sigma$$ [2]

The language has a set of typed constants, denoted by $\{c_\sigma\}$, and we will choose for our typed constants the following:

integers e.g. 0,5

booleans i.e. *true*, *false*

Alist - lists of elements of type A, i.e. elements of the recursive type $A \cong 1 + A \times Alist$

arithmetic functions e.g. $+, -, \times$

boolean functions e.g. **and** , **or**

a conditional for each type σ denoted by $\text{if}_{bool \to \sigma \to \sigma \to \sigma}$ (or just *if*)

list processing functions i.e. *hd*, *tl*, *cons* and *case*

For each type σ, we will assume an infinite supply of typed variables $Var_\sigma = \{x^\sigma, \cdots\}$. The terms in the language *Exp* then consist of typed terms $e : \sigma$ formed according to the following rules:

[2] Note that we have no type variables in the syntax of our type expressions, and so we are using a mono-typed λ-calculus and not a polymorphically typed λ-calculus.

(1) $x^\sigma : \sigma$ variables

(2) $c_\sigma : \sigma$ constants

(3) $\dfrac{e : \tau}{\lambda x^\sigma . e : \sigma \to \tau}$ λ-abstractions

(4) $\dfrac{e_1 : \sigma \to \tau \quad e_2 : \sigma}{e_1 \, e_2 : \tau}$ application

(5) $\dfrac{e : \sigma \to \sigma}{fix(e) : \sigma}$ fixed points

(Note that fix is part of the syntax and is not a constant.)

3.2.2 Interpretations

So far we have only given the syntactic constructions of our language. We need to give interpretations for our language. An interpretation, I, is given by

$$I = (\{D_A^I\}, \{c_\sigma^I\})$$

that is, interpretations for the base types and interpretations for each of the constants. For each base type A, we require that D_A^I must be a bounded-complete, ω-algebraic cpo (Scott, 1981).

This is extended to the interpretation of the type $\sigma \to \tau$ by defining $D_{\sigma \to \tau}^I$ to be the domain of continuous maps $D_\sigma^I \to D_\tau^I$ (Scott, 1981). Each c_σ^I is given interpretation in D_σ^I.

The interpretation of base types and constants induces a semantic function

$$E^I : Exp \to Env^I \to \bigcup D_\sigma^I$$

where $Env^I = \{Env_\sigma^I\}$ and $Env_\sigma^I = Var_\sigma \to D_\sigma^I$.

$$E^I \, [[x^\sigma]] \, \rho^I = \rho^I(x^\sigma)$$

$$E^I \, [[c_\sigma]] \, \rho^I = c_\sigma^I$$

$$E^I \, [[\lambda x^\sigma . e]] \, \rho^I = \lambda y^{D_\sigma^I} . E^I \, [[e]] \, \rho^I [y / x^\sigma]$$

$$E^I \, [[e_1 \, e_2]] \, \rho^I = (E^I \, [[e_1]] \, \rho^I) \, (E^I \, [[e_2]] \, \rho^I)$$

$$E^I \, [[fix \ e]] \, \rho^I = fix(E^I \, [[e]] \, \rho^I)$$

Note that abstraction, application and fix are interpreted the same way in all interpretations.

Throughout the rest of the chapter we will have a *standard* interpretation $(\{D_A^{st}\}, \{c_\sigma^{st}\})$ where we have the usual flat domains for items like integers and booleans. The standard interpretation for *Alist* is obtained by solving the isomorphism

$$Alist \cong 1 + A \times Alist$$

over the category of domains (Smyth and Plotkin, 1982) to obtain

$$D_{Alist}^{st} = D_A^{st} * .nil \cup D_A^{st} * . \bot_{D_{Alist}^{st}} \cup D_A^{st \, \omega}$$

Here * is the Kleene star, denoting a finite sequence (possibly empty) of elements from the set which is starred, and so $D_A^{st}*.nil$ are finite lists of elements of D_A^{st} (i.e. integers or booleans etc.), and $D_A^{st}*.\bot_{D_{Alist}^{st}}$ are lists which have a finite number of elements from D_A^{st} and then have an undefined tail. The set of infinite lists is denoted by $D_A^{st\,\omega}$

It is useful to have some terminology to refer to various types of lists.

Definition 3.1

A list, L, is

(1) *finite* if $L \in D_A^{st}*.nil$;

(2) *partial* if $L \in D_A^{st}.D_A^{st}*.\bot_{D_{Alist}^{st}}$;

(3) *infinite* if $L \in D_A^{st\,\omega}$.

□

Note that although the bottom list is normally called a partial list, we have separated it out because in section 4 we will need to consider the set containing only the bottom list and the set containing all other partial lists. Thus, for our purposes, a partial list has at least one element of D_A^{st} in it, that is, it can be written as $cons\,(e_1,e_2)$ for some e_1 and e_2.

We will call the induced semantic function E^{st}, and we will always use the environment ρ^{st} for the standard interpretation.

For the standard interpretation of constants we will have the strict versions of all of the arithmetic and boolean functions. The conditional has the following interpretation:

$$(E^{st}\ [[\text{if}_{bool\to\sigma\to\sigma\to\sigma}]]\ \rho^{st})\ \bot_{D_{bool}^{st}}\ x\ y = \bot_{D_\sigma^{st}}$$

$$(E^{st}\ [[\text{if}_{bool\to\sigma\to\sigma\to\sigma}]]\ \rho^{st})\ true\ \ x\ y = x$$

$$(E^{st}\ [[\text{if}_{bool\to\sigma\to\sigma\to\sigma}]]\ \rho^{st})\ false\ \ x\ y = y$$

The standard semantics of the *case* function is given by:

$$E^{st}\ [[case\ \ s\ f\ \ L]]\ \rho^{st} = E^{st}\ [[if\,L{=}nil\ then\ s\ else\ f\ \ (hd\ L)\ (tl\ L))]]\ \rho^{st}$$

It is meant to be a translation of the more user-friendly pattern-matching style of writing programs, being a case on the structure of the list. Thus

$$\begin{aligned}&sumlist\ [\,] = 0\\ &sumlist\ x{:}xs = x + sumlist\ xs\end{aligned}$$

is translated into our language as:

$$sumlist = fix\,(\lambda f^{Alist\to int}.\lambda L_1^{Alist}.case\ \ 0\ (\lambda x^A.\lambda L_2^{Alist}.x{+}(f\ \ L_2)\,L_1))$$

where this means that the name *sumlist* stands for the expression on the right-hand side of the equality symbol. This shorthand way of referring to expressions in the language will be used throughout the rest of this chapter.

For *abstract* interpretations we will allow any finite lattices, D_A^{ab} for each base type A, and the properties of finiteness and completeness are preserved by the interpretation of the type structure. In the examples of the use of the framework in this chapter, we will use in particular two abstract domains, namely the two-point domain and the four-point chain domain. We will induce the interpretations of the constants as abstractions of their standard interpretation. The induced semantic function will be called E^{ab} and we will always denote the environment used in the abstract interpretation by ρ^{ab}.

Note that in our abstract interpretation we have only parameterized out the interpretation of the base types and the constants. This is because we only need to change the interpretations of these items to answer the questions about evaluation strategies that we wish to ask. A framework for the abstract interpretation of the pure λ-calculus is provided in Mycroft and Jones (1985), where the meaning of λ-abstraction and application are also part of the interpretation.

3.3 Domains, powerdomains, functions and algebraic relationships[3]

Because we will be developing a framework for abstract interpretation which is semantically well founded, we will of necessity have to delve into the world of domain theory in which the semantics of programming languages exists. It is possible to understand the technical details of this chapter using only basic concepts from domain theory (Scott 1981, 1982), category theory (Arbib and Manes, 1975) and powerdomains (Plotkin, 1976; Smyth, 1978). The main results that we use can be summarized as a set of algebraic rules, which we will now develop. The proofs of the basic facts cited below are either directly in the literature, or obtainable by minor modifications therefrom; see (Plotkin, 1976; Hennessy and Plotkin, 1979).

We shall be working over the category of domains described in Scott (1981, 1982). The objects of this category are the bounded-complete ω-algebraic cpo's, and the morphisms are the continuous functions between domains. The composition of morphisms $f:D \to E$, $g:E \to F$ is written thus:

$$g \circ f : D \to F.$$

The identity morphism on D is written id_D. Given domains D and E, the domain $D \to E$ is formed by taking all continuous functions from D to E, with the pointwise ordering:

$$f \leq g \text{ iff for all } x \in D, f(x) \leq g(x)$$

Given a domain D, then **P**D, the *Hoare* (*lower* or *"partial" correctness*) *powerdomain* is formed by taking as elements all non-empty Scott-closed[4] subsets of D, ordered by subset inclusion. A subset $X \subseteq D$ is *Scott-closed* if

(1)If $Y \subseteq X$ and Y is directed, then $\bigsqcup Y \in X$.

(2)If $y \leq x \in X$ then $y \in X$.

The least Scott-closed set containing X is written X°.

Another useful concept is that of *"left"-closure*; a set $X \subseteq D$ is left-closed if it satisfies (2) above. The left-closure of a set X is written $\mathbf{LC}(X) = \{y \mid \text{there exists } x \in X, y \leq x\}$.

[3] This section is lifted almost verbatim from some material in Burn *et al.* (1986a), and we are indebted to Samson Abramsky for his original presentation of it.

[4] This terminology is due to the fact that these are the closed sets with respect to the Scott topology (cf. Gierz *et al.*, 1980).

Note that for elements of the Hoare powerdomain, the subset inclusion ordering is equivalent to the well-known Egli-Milner ordering:

$$X \subseteq Y \text{ iff for all } x \in X \text{, there exists } y \in Y, x \le y$$
$$\text{and for all } y \in Y \text{, there exists } x \in X, x \le y$$

We shall also apply **P** to morphisms. If $f : D \to E$, then $\mathbf{P}f : \mathbf{P}D \to \mathbf{P}E$ is defined thus:

$$(\mathbf{P}f)(X) = \{f(x) \mid x \in X\}^{\circ}$$

The main properties of **P** are:

(P1) If D is a domain, $\mathbf{P}D$ is a domain.
(P2) If $f : D \to E$, $\mathbf{P}f : \mathbf{P}D \to \mathbf{P}E$ is a continuous function.
(P3) $\mathbf{P}(f \circ g) = (\mathbf{P}f) \circ (\mathbf{P}g)$
(P4) $\mathbf{P}id_D = id_{\mathbf{P}D}$.

This says that **P** is a *functor* from the category of domains to itself. A further property of **P** is that it is *locally monotonic* and *continuous*. This means that if $\{f_i\}$ is a chain of functions in $A \to B$, then for all i, $\mathbf{P}f_i \le \mathbf{P}f_{i+1}$, and $\mathbf{P}(\bigsqcup f_i) = \bigsqcup \mathbf{P}f_i$. Whenever we write **P** from now on we will mean the Hoare powerdomain functor.

Why are we using the Hoare powerdomain construction? The Hoare powerdomain naturally captures the idea of sets of elements with a certain level of definedness which is what is needed for our applications. It is also pleasant to work with from a technical point of view.

We shall need to use some additional constructions associated with the powerdomain functor. First, for each domain D we have a map

$$\{\!|.|\!\}_D : D \to \mathbf{P}D$$

defined by:

$$\{\!|d|\!\}_D = \mathbf{LC}(\{d\}).$$

This satisfies the following properties:

(P5) $\{\!|.|\!\}_D$ is continuous.
(P6) For $f : D \to E$, $\mathbf{P}f \circ \{\!|.|\!\}_D = \{\!|.|\!\}_E \circ f$.

This says that $\{\!|.|\!\}$ is a *natural transformation* from **I**, the identity functor on the category of domains, to **P**.

Second, for each domain D we define

$$\biguplus_D : \mathbf{PP}D \to \mathbf{P}D$$

by

$$\biguplus_D(\Theta) = \{x \mid \text{for some } X \in \Theta, x \in X\} = \bigcup \Theta^5$$

This satisfies:

[5] The last equality says that $\biguplus$ is just the same as the ordinary set-theoretic union in the case of the

(P7) $\biguplus_D$ is continuous.
(P8) for $f : D \rightarrow E$, $\biguplus_E \circ \mathbf{PP}f = \mathbf{P}f \circ \biguplus_D$.

This says that $\biguplus$ is a natural transformation from $\mathbf{P}^2$ to $\mathbf{P}$.

Now ($\mathbf{P}$, $\{\!|.|\!\}$, $\biguplus$) forms a *monad* or *triple*. We shall not use this fact, but we will use the following additional observation. Suppose D is a domain which is a complete lattice. Then the least upper bound operation, viewed as a function

$$\bigsqcup : \mathbf{P}D \rightarrow D$$

satisfies:

(P9) $\bigsqcup$ is continuous
(P10) $\bigsqcup \circ \{\!|.|\!\}_D = id_D$
(P11) $\bigsqcup \circ \mathbf{P}(\bigsqcup) = \bigsqcup \circ \biguplus_D$.

This says that $\bigsqcup : \mathbf{P}D \rightarrow D$ is an *algebra* of the monad ($\mathbf{P}$, $\{\!|.|\!\}$, $\biguplus$). We will use (P9) and (P10) in the sequel.

Henceforth, we shall omit the subscripts from instances of $\{\!|.|\!\}$, $\biguplus$ where they are clear from the context. The facts we shall be assuming about the constructions introduced above are summarized in (P1) – (P11). By using "function-level reasoning", we are able to give simple, algebraic proofs of many results.

3.4 The framework

The framework is developed in a number of stages. In section 3.4.1 we motivate and define a relationship between the standard and the abstract interpretations which captures our intuition that the abstract interpretation gives correct information. The main thrust of the section is then to show that the abstract interpretation defined in section 3.2.2 satisfies this condition, given appropriate abstract domains and abstraction functions for the base types and abstract interpretations for the functional constants. Also in the first section, we motivate the definition of a number of abstraction and concretization maps that are needed for the development of the theory. We formally define these maps and prove they are well behaved in the second section. Some more useful forms of the definition of the abstraction maps are given in the third section. Properties such as strictness and bottom-reflexivity are often useful to have, and it is shown that these properties are inherited from the abstraction maps on the base types. We defined abstraction and concretization maps in such a way that they are adjoined functions. This is proved to be true in the fifth section, and in the following section we prove two propositions which are useful in proving a safety relation between the abstract interpretation and standard interpretation which will allow us to prove the correctness of the abstract interpretation. The final two theorems give practical tests for finding out information which is true either in all contexts or in some particular context, respectively.

Hoare powerdomain. This is not true in general for other powerdomain constructions.

3.4.1 Motivation for the definition of abstraction and concretization maps

In section 3.2.2 we introduced the idea of interpretations. We were particularly interested in providing a computable abstract interpretation with which we could do calculations and make assertions about computations in the standard interpretation. Suppose $f : \sigma \rightarrow \tau$ and that we have the abstract interpretation of f:

$$D^{ab}_{\sigma} \xrightarrow{E^{ab}\,[[f\,]]\,\rho^{ab}} D^{ab}_{\tau}$$

and wish to make assertions about a calculation using the standard interpretation:

$$D^{st}_{\sigma} \xrightarrow{E^{st}\,[[f\,]]\rho^{st}} D^{st}_{\tau}$$

Given that

$$(E^{ab}\,[[f\,]]\,\rho^{ab})\,\bar{s} = \bar{t}$$

what do we wish to conclude? A reasonable statement would be that for all s "represented by" $\bar{s}$, the value $\bar{t}$ "represents" the calculation $(E^{st}\,[[f\,]]\,\rho^{st})\,s$.

If we call the process of going from $\bar{s}$ to the set of items that $\bar{s}$ "represents" *concretization*, and assume that for each type σ that we have a map $Conc_{\sigma}$ which does this, then we can state the above condition formally.

Definition 3.2

An abstract interpretation is *correct* if $(E^{ab}\,[[f\,]]\,\rho^{ab})\,\bar{s} = \bar{t}$ implies that for all $s \in Conc_{\sigma}(\bar{s})$, $(E^{st}\,[[f\,]]\,\rho^{st})\,s \in Conc_{\tau}(\bar{t})$.

□

We shall see in section 3.4.8 that the correctness of an abstract interpretation is implied by the following *safety diagram*, which is essentially an adaptation to the world of the Hoare powerdomain of diagrams appearing elsewhere (for example, Cousot and Cousot, 1979; Mycroft, 1981; Mycroft and Nielson, 1983):

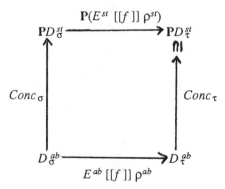

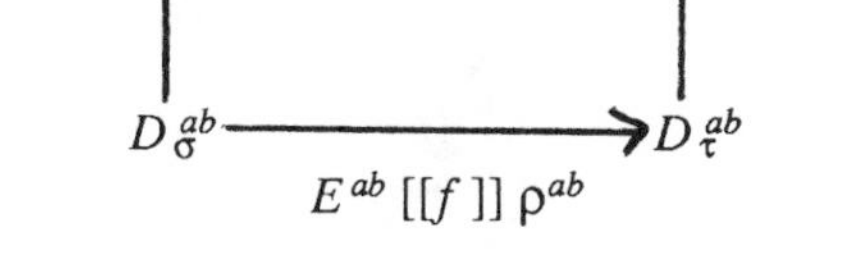

i.e. $Conc_{\tau} \circ (E^{ab}\,[[f\,]]\,\rho^{ab}) \supseteq \mathbf{P}(E^{st}\,[[f\,]]\,\rho^{st}) \circ Conc_{\sigma}$

The use of $\supseteq$ in the above diagram captures the notion of safety, for it implies that the result obtained in a calculation in the abstract interpretation represents a superset of the possible results in the standard interpretation.

So far we have been assuming that we have a concretization map $Conc_\sigma$ for each type σ; we now turn our attention to how we can define such concretization maps. Initially we look at the question the opposite way around. For each type σ, there are possibly many items in D_σ^{st} which have equal levels of definedness. As an example, consider $\lambda x^{D_{int}^{st}}.x+1$ and $\lambda x^{D_{int}^{st}}.x+2$ which are in $D_{int\to int}^{st}$ and both of which are defined everywhere except at $\bot_{D_{int}^{st}}$. It would be useful to be able to define a map

$$Abs_\sigma : \mathbf{P}D_\sigma^{st} \to D_\sigma^{ab}$$

which mapped sets of items of equal definedness to the same element in the abstract domain.[6]

A natural way of defining maps is to define them inductively over the type structure. Suppose therefore that Abs_σ, Abs_τ and $Conc_\sigma$ and $Conc_\tau$ have been defined and that we wish to define

$$Abs_{\sigma\to\tau} : \mathbf{P}(D_\sigma^{st} \to D_\tau^{st}) \to (D_\sigma^{ab} \to D_\tau^{ab})$$

$$Conc_{\sigma\to\tau} : (D_\sigma^{ab} \to D_\tau^{ab}) \to \mathbf{P}(D_\sigma^{st} \to D_\tau^{st})$$

Given a set $S \in \mathbf{P}(D_\sigma^{st} \to D_\tau^{st})$, remember that Abs_σ says that the maximum level of definedness of the elements of S is a particular value in the abstract domain. Thus we need to define a map

$$abs_{\sigma\to\tau} : D_{\sigma\to\tau}^{st} \to D_{\sigma\to\tau}^{ab}$$

so that we can test the level of definedness of each element of S and then choose the maximum one of these for the value of $Abs_{\sigma\to\tau}(S)$.

Given an $f \in D_\sigma^{st} \to D_\tau^{st}$:

$$D_\sigma^{st} \xrightarrow{\quad f \quad} D_\tau^{st}$$

how do we define

$$D_\sigma^{ab} \xrightarrow{\quad abs_{\sigma\to\tau}(f) \quad} D_\tau^{ab}\,?$$

We know that $abs_{\sigma\to\tau}(f)$ will be applied to $\bar{s} \in D_\sigma^{ab}$, and that $\bar{s}$ "represents" all values in $Conc_\sigma(\bar{s})$. Furthermore, concretization returns a set of values, that is, an element of $\mathbf{P}D_\sigma^{st}$. So we have the following situation:

[6] We note that Abs_σ is a map which takes an element of the Hoare powerdomain and so a more correct intuition is that $Abs_\sigma(S)$ represents the most defined elements in a (left-closed) set S.

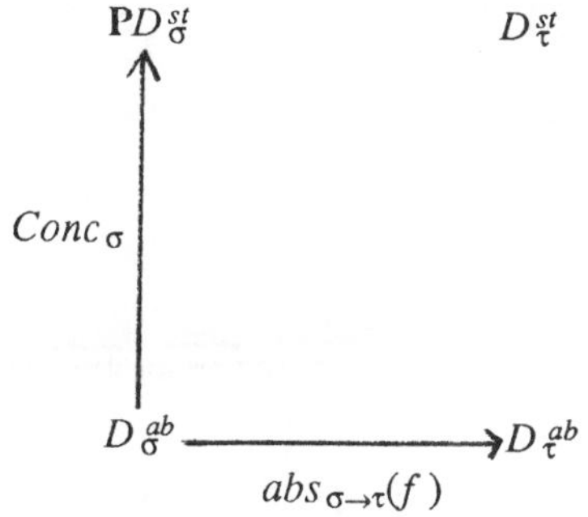

We wish to say that $f \in D^{st}_{\sigma} \to D^{st}_{\tau}$ is "at most as defined as" something, by saying that $(abs_{\sigma\to\tau}(f))\,\bar{s} = \bar{t}$ where $\bar{t}$ represents the most defined values that f can take for values represented by $\bar{s}$. This implies that we must apply f to all of the elements s in $Conc_{\sigma}(\bar{s})$ and we can do this by applying **P** to f to obtain the diagram:

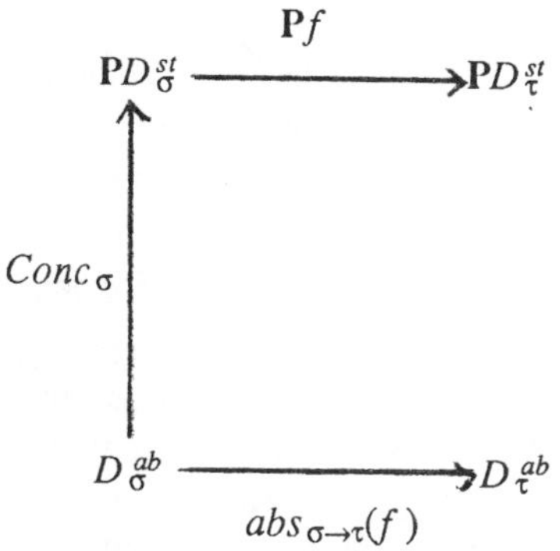

All that we need to find now is a map from $\mathbf{P}D^{st}_{\tau}$ to D^{ab}_{τ}, which maps a set of values down to the element in the abstract domain that represents that set, and we already have such a map in Abs_{τ}. Thus we can complete the diagram for the definition of $abs_{\sigma\to\tau}(f)$:

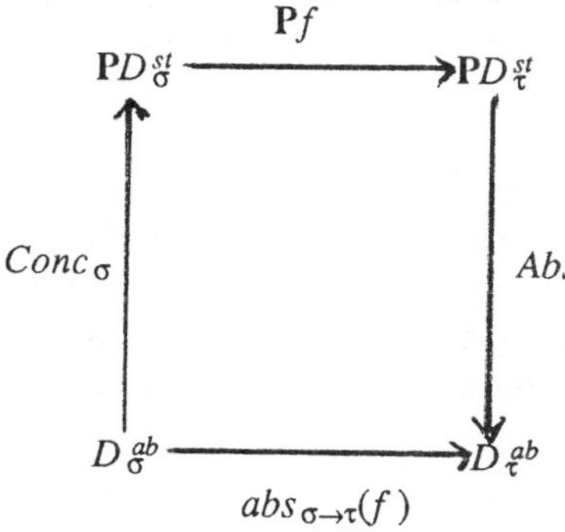

and write it out as a formula:

$$abs_{\sigma\to\tau}(f) = Abs_{\tau} \circ \mathbf{P}f \circ Conc_{\sigma}$$

We have so far said that Abs_{σ} picks out a value which represents the most defined elements in a set of items, and now we have a map, abs_{σ}, which works out the definedness level of a single element. Thus we can find out the definedness of a set of items by applying

abs_σ to each element in the set. Furthermore, since we have insisted our abstract domains are finite, complete lattices, we can take the least upper bound of the set of results from applying abs_σ to a set of values in the standard interpretation to model the idea of choosing the maximum value. Thus a reasonable definition of Abs_σ is

$$Abs_\sigma = \bigsqcup \circ \mathbf{P}abs_\sigma$$

The least upper bound in the definition is capturing two intuitions. First, an upper bound is necessitated by the fact that we are developing a safety analysis, and second, having the least upper bound means that we have the best safe representation of the value.

We will also define $Conc_\sigma$ so that Abs_σ and $Conc_\sigma$ are adjoined functions for each type σ. Adjointness is a very important mathematical property (Gierz *et al.*, 1980), and can be interpreted in this context to mean that the abstract domain models the standard domain as closely as possible.

Furthermore, if we can prove

$$E^{ab}\,[[e]]\,\rho^{ab} \geq abs_\sigma(E^{st}\,[[e]]\,\rho^{st}) \qquad (\S)$$

for all σ and all $e{:}\sigma$, and the maps Abs_σ and $Conc_\sigma$ are adjoined functions, then we can prove the correctness of abstract interpretation. (See the progression of the argument from Theorem 3.22 to Theorem 3.24.)

It is shown in Abramsky (1985) that the definition of abs_σ we have motivated above is the "best" possible abstraction map in that it loses least information while still satisfying (§).

One final point worth noting is that we have a dual reading of the elements of the abstract domain. First they can be seen as the abstraction of one particular element of the standard interpretation (using abs_σ) and second as saying the elements of a set of items from the standard interpretation are at most as defined as a certain value. Concretization captures the second reading by returning the set of all values which abstract to something less than (or equal to) the element which we are concretizing.

3.4.2 Formal definition of the abstraction and concretization maps

At the base types we presume that we are given abstract domains D_A^{ab}, for each base type A, which are finite lattices, and strict, continuous abstraction maps

$$abs_A : D_A^{st} \to D_A^{ab}$$

where these make the distinctions on the base types that the user wishes to make. The abstract domains need to be complete lattices because we will need to take least upper bounds, and they should be finite so that the testing of equality of functions when taking least fixed points is an effective procedure. Strictness of the abstraction maps is required so that concretization is well defined and for the proof of Proposition 3.20. We can then define:

Definition 3.3

$$Abs_\sigma : \mathbf{P}D_\sigma^{st} \to D_\sigma^{ab}$$

$$Abs_\sigma = \bigsqcup \circ \mathbf{P}abs_\sigma$$

□

Definition 3.4

$$Conc_{\sigma} : D_{\sigma}^{ab} \rightarrow \mathbf{P}D_{\sigma}^{st}$$

$$Conc_{\sigma}(\overline{s}) = \biguplus\{T \mid Abs_s(T) \leq \overline{s}\}^7$$

□

Definition 3.5

$$abs_{\sigma\rightarrow\tau} : D_{\sigma\rightarrow\tau}^{st} \rightarrow D_{\sigma\rightarrow\tau}^{ab}$$

$$abs_{\sigma\rightarrow\tau}(f) = Abs_{\tau} \circ \mathbf{P}f \circ Conc_{\sigma}$$

□

In the definition of Abs_{σ}, $\biguplus$ is used as the abstract domain element must represent all of the elements in the set being abstracted, a notion which is captured using $\biguplus$.

We must of course show that these maps are well defined and continuous, but first a definition and a subsidiary fact.

Definition 3.6

A function $f \in D \rightarrow E$ is *strict* if $f(\bot_D) = \bot_E$.

□

Fact 3.7

If $f \in D_{\sigma}^{l} \rightarrow D_{\tau}^{l}$ is strict and D_{τ}^{l} is a complete lattice, then $\biguplus \circ \mathbf{P}f$ is strict (Burn, 1987a, Lemma 2.2.7).

□

Lemma 3.8

If for each base type A, we are given a strict, continuous abstraction map $abs_A : D_A^{st} \rightarrow D_A^{ab}$, then for all types σ

(1) abs_{σ} is continuous.
(2) Abs_{σ} is continuous.
(3) abs_{σ} and Abs_{σ} are strict.
(4) $Conc_{\sigma}$ is well defined and continuous.

Proof

We prove this by induction on the type structure.

(1) This is true of the base types by our condition of the continuity of the abstraction maps on base types.

(2) On base types we have that this is true since $\biguplus$ is continuous, $\mathbf{P}f$ is continuous if f is (P2), and the composition of continuous functions is continuous.

(3) abs_A is strict by the condition of the lemma and thus Abs_A is strict by Lemma 3.8.

[7] Note how we have defined $Conc_A$ so that it will be an upper adjoint to Abs_A (Gierz *et al.*, 1980).

(4) We have to prove that $Conc_A$ is well defined and monotonic, for its source is a finite domain and hence is continuous if it is monotonic.

To prove well definedness, we must show that $\{T \mid Abs_A(T) \leq \bar{a}\}$ is a non-empty Scott-closed subset of $\mathbf{PP}D_A^{st}$. Since we have that Abs_A is strict (part (3) of induction), we have that the set $\{T \mid Abs_A(T) \leq \bar{a}\}$ is non-empty. Denoting $\{T \mid Abs_A(T) \leq \bar{a}\}$ by Θ, to show that Θ is Scott-closed we need to show that *(a)* Θ is left-closed and that *(b)* Θ is closed under least upper bounds of directed sets. The first is true since if $Y \leq X \in \Theta$, then $Abs_A(Y) \leq Abs_A(X) \leq \bar{a}$ and so $Y \in \Theta$. The second is true for if $\Delta \subseteq \Theta$ is a directed set, then $Abs_A(\bigsqcup \Delta) = \bigsqcup\{Abs_A(X) \mid X \in \Delta\}$ and since $Abs_A(X) \leq \bar{a}$ for all $X \in \Delta$, $\bigsqcup\{Abs_A(X) \mid X \in \Delta\} \leq \bar{a}$.

To show monotonicity of $Conc_A$, let $s_1, s_2 \in D_A^{ab}$, $s_1 \leq s_2$. Then

$$Conc_A(s_1) = \biguplus\{T \mid Abs_A(T) \leq s_1\} \text{ and } Conc_A(s_2) = \biguplus\{T \mid Abs_A(T) \leq s_2\}.$$

Clearly, $\{T \mid Abs_A(T) \leq s_1\} \subseteq \{T \mid Abs_A(T) \leq s_2\}$ since $s_1 \leq s_2$ and so $Conc_A(s_1) \leq Conc_A(s_2)$. Thus $Conc_A$ is monotonic and hence continuous.

Assuming (1) to (4) are true for types σ and τ we prove them for type $\sigma \to \tau$.

(1) $abs_\sigma(f) = Abs_\tau \circ \mathbf{P}f \circ Conc_\sigma$ and is thus continuous because by the induction hypothesis it is the composition of continuous functions.

(2) Follows as for the base case.

(3) $abs_{\sigma\to\tau}(\bot_{D^{st}_{\sigma\to\tau}})\, \bar{s} = (Abs_\tau \circ \mathbf{P}(\bot_{D^{st}_{\sigma\to\tau}}) \circ Conc_\sigma)\,(\bar{s})$

$$= \biguplus(\mathbf{P}(abs_\tau \circ \bot_{D^{st}_{\sigma\to\tau}}) \circ Conc_\sigma)\,(\bar{s})$$

$$= \biguplus(\mathbf{P}(abs_\tau \circ \bot_{D^{st}_{\sigma\to\tau}}))\ \{s \mid s \in Conc_\sigma(\bar{s})\})$$

$$= \biguplus\{abs_\tau(\bot_{D^{st}_{\sigma\to\tau}}(s)) \mid s \in Conc_\sigma(\bar{s})\}^\circ$$

$$= \biguplus\{abs_\tau(\bot_{D^{st}_\tau})\}^\circ$$

$$= \biguplus\{\bot_{D^{ab}_\tau}\}^\circ \qquad \text{by induction hypothesis (3)}$$

$$= \bot_{D^{ab}_\tau} \qquad \text{(P10)}$$

The result holds for $Abs_{\sigma\to\tau}$ by Lemma 3.8.

(4) Follows as for the base case.

□

In the proof of Lemma 3.8 we have made use of all of the properties of the abstraction maps and abstract domains for base types which we have insisted upon. First, continuity is needed for the abstraction maps on the base types so that all of the maps we use are continuous, which is needed for proving the safety of the framework. The strictness of the abstraction maps on base types, which is preserved by the abstraction maps on higher types, is needed to prove the well-definedness of the concretization maps. To guarantee the existence of least upper bounds for the definition of the abstraction maps, we need the property that the abstract domains are complete lattices. Finally, finiteness of the abstract domains is needed not only so that we will develop an effective analysis, but because we were able to use the fact that we needed only to prove that the concretization maps were monotonic for them to be continuous. Abramsky (1985) has shown that if the abstract domains are any complete lattices (including infinite ones), then the concretization maps which are induced from the abstraction maps are not in general continuous. If the abstraction maps also map finite elements (Scott, 1981) to finite elements, then the concretization maps will be continuous (Abramsky, 1985). Since our abstract domains are finite, this condition trivially holds.

3.4.3 Two useful forms of the definition of the abstraction map

We present two alternative forms for the abstraction map $abs_{\sigma\to\tau}$ when τ is a function space.

Fact 3.9

Suppose $f \in D^{st}_{\sigma_1} \to \cdots \to D^{st}_{\sigma_n} \to D^{st}_{\tau}$. Then

$$abs_{\sigma_1\to\cdots\to\sigma_n\to\tau}(f) = \lambda\overline{x_1}^{D^{ab}_{\sigma_1}} \cdots \lambda\overline{x_n}^{D^{ab}_{\sigma_n}}.\bigsqcup\{abs_\tau(f\ x_1\ \cdots\ x_n) \mid \operatorname*{and}_{i=1}^{n} abs_{\sigma_i}(x_i)\leq\overline{x_i}\}^{\circ}$$

(Burn, 1987a, Proposition 2.3.1).

□

Fact 3.10

Suppose $f \in D^{st}_{\sigma_1} \to \cdots \to D^{st}_{\sigma_n} \to D^{st}_{\tau}$. Then

$$abs_{\sigma_1\to\cdots\to\sigma_n\to\tau}(f) = \lambda\overline{x_1}^{D^{ab}_{\sigma_1}} \cdots \lambda\overline{x_n}^{D^{ab}_{\sigma_n}}.\bigsqcup\{abs_\tau(f\ x_1\ \cdots\ x_n) \mid \operatorname*{and}_{i=0}^{n} x_i \in Conc_{\sigma_i}(\overline{x_i})\}^{\circ}$$

(Burn, 1987a, Proposition 2.3.3).

□

3.4.4 Properties of abstraction and concretization maps of higher types

Many useful properties of abstraction maps of the base types are carried over to the abstraction maps for the higher types. We record here three such properties which are useful in the ensuing development.

Fact 3.11

If abs_A is strict for all base types A, then abs_σ and Abs_σ are strict for all types σ (Burn, 1987a, Lemma 3.4.2.8 (*iii*)).

□

Definition 3.12

A function $f \in D \to E$ is *⊥-reflecting* if $f(d) = \bot_E \Rightarrow d = \bot_D$.

□

Fact 3.13

If $f \in D^l_\sigma \to D^l_\tau$ is ⊥-reflecting and D^l_τ is a complete lattice, then $\bigsqcup \circ \mathbf{P}f$ is ⊥-reflecting (Burn, 1987a, Lemma 2.4.3).

□

Fact 3.14

If for each base type A abs_A is $\perp$-reflecting, then abs_σ and Abs_σ are $\perp$-reflecting for each type σ (Burn, 1987a, Lemma 2.4.4).

□

While ontoness is not required for the technical development of this thesis, if we have onto abstraction functions on the base types, then there are no useless elements in the abstract domains. The fact that this can often be shown to be true for higher types means that there are no useless elements in the abstract domains for higher types either.

Fact 3.15

If $f \in D^l_\sigma \to D^l_\tau$ is onto and D^l_τ is a complete lattice, then $\biguplus \circ \mathbf{P}f$ is onto (Burn, 1987a, Lemma 2.4.5).

□

Fact 3.16

If abs_A is onto for each base type, and for each base type A we can define a continuous function $abs_A^{-1} : D_A^{ab} \to D_A^{st}$ which is a right inverse of abs_A, that is, $abs_A \circ abs_A^{-1} = id_{D_A^{ab}}$, then for all types σ:

(1)There is a continuous function $abs_\sigma^{-1} : D_\sigma^{ab} \to D_\sigma^{st}$ which is a right inverse of abs_σ;

(2)abs_σ and Abs_σ are onto; and

(3)$Abs_\sigma \circ Conc_\sigma = id_{D_\sigma^{ab}}$

(Burn, 1987a, Lemma 2.4.6).

□

The following fact is often useful in applications of this framework.

Fact 3.17

If abs_A is strict and bottom-reflexive for each base type A, then for all types σ, $Conc_\sigma(\perp_{D_\sigma^{ab}}) = \{\perp_{D_\sigma^{st}}\}$ (Burn, 1987, Lemma 2.4.7).

□

3.4.5 Adjointness of Abs_σ and $Conc_\sigma$

Proposition 3.18

Abs_σ and $Conc_\sigma$ are a pair of adjoined functions, i.e.

(1) $Conc_\sigma \circ Abs_\sigma \geq id_{\mathbf{P}D_\sigma^{st}}$

(2) $Abs_\sigma \circ Conc_\sigma \leq id_{D_\sigma^{ab}}$

Furthermore, if Abs_σ is onto for all σ, then

(3) $Abs_\sigma \circ Conc_\sigma = id_{D_\sigma^{ab}}$

Proof

(1)Let $S \in \mathbf{P}D_{\sigma}^{st}$

$$Conc_{\sigma}(Abs_{\sigma}(S)) = \biguplus\{T \mid Abs_{\sigma}(T) \leq Abs_{\sigma}(S)\}$$

and $Abs_{\sigma}(S) \leq Abs_{\sigma}(S)$, so $S \in \{T \mid Abs_{\sigma}(T) \leq Abs_{\sigma}(S)\}$. Hence the result follows since $\geq$ is just $\supseteq$ in the Hoare powerdomain.

(2) $Abs_{\sigma}(Conc_{\sigma}(\bar{a})) = Abs_{\sigma}(\biguplus\{T \mid Abs_{\sigma}(T) \leq \bar{a}\})$

$= \bigsqcup(\mathbf{P}abs_{\sigma}(\biguplus\{T \mid Abs_{\sigma}(T) \leq \bar{a}\}))$

$= \bigsqcup(\biguplus(\mathbf{P}\ \mathbf{P}abs_{\sigma}(\{T \mid Abs_{\sigma}(T) \leq \bar{a}\})))$ (P8)

$= \bigsqcup(\biguplus(\{\mathbf{P}abs_{\sigma}(T) \mid Abs_{\sigma}(T) \leq \bar{a}\}^{\circ}))$ definition of **P** on morphisms

$= \bigsqcup(\bigcup\{\mathbf{P}abs_{\sigma}(T) \mid Abs_{\sigma}(T) \leq \bar{a}\})^{\circ}$

by a simple adaptation of a result in (Plotkin, 1976, p. 477)

Let $S = \bigcup\{\mathbf{P}abs_{\sigma}(T) \mid Abs_{\sigma}(T) \leq \bar{a}\}$. For each element $\bar{s}' \in S$, $\bar{s}' \leq \bar{s}$. Hence $\bar{s}$ is an upper bound of the set of elements of S, and so $\bigsqcup S \leq \bar{s}$. It is not necessarily equal because abs_{σ} may not be onto, so $\bar{s}$ may not be in S.

(3)Fact 3.16 (3).

□

3.4.6 Semi-homomorphic property of abs_{σ} and fix

For each type σ we have that abs_{σ} is a semi-homomorphism of function application, that is, if $f \in D_{\sigma\to\tau}^{st}$ then

$$abs_{\sigma\to\tau}(f) \circ abs_{\sigma} \geq abs_{\tau} \circ f$$

or, in terms of elements, if $s \in D_{\sigma}^{st}$ then

$$abs_{\sigma\to\tau}(f)\ (abs_{\sigma}(s)) \geq abs_{\tau}(f\ (s))$$

We will need this to prove Theorem 3.22. It can be seen to be intuitively true by studying the definition of $abs_{\sigma\to\tau}(f)(abs_{\sigma}(s))$:

$$abs_{\sigma\to\tau}(f)\ (abs_{\sigma}(s)) = \bigsqcup\{abs_{\tau}(f\ s') \mid abs_{\sigma}(s') \leq abs_{\sigma}(s)\}^{\circ} \qquad \text{Fact 3.9}$$

We see that $abs_{\sigma\to\tau}(f)\ (abs_{\sigma}(s))$ applies f to all the values in D_{σ}^{st} which abstract to something less than or equal to what s abstracts to, some of which may give a more defined answer, and hence may be abstracted to a greater value than $f\ (s)$ would.

Proposition 3.19

For all types σ, abs_{σ} is a semi-homomorphism of function application.

Proof

$abs_{\sigma\to\tau}(f) \circ abs_{\sigma} = Abs_{\tau} \circ \mathbf{P}f \circ Conc_{\sigma} \circ abs_{\sigma}$

$= \bigsqcup \circ \mathbf{P}abs_{\tau} \circ \mathbf{P}f \circ Conc_{\sigma} \circ abs_{\sigma}$ definition of $Abs_{\sigma\to\tau}$

$= \bigsqcup \circ \mathbf{P}abs_{\tau} \circ \mathbf{P}f \circ Conc_{\sigma} \circ \bigsqcup \circ \{\!|.|\!\} \circ abs_{\sigma}$ (P10)

$= \bigsqcup \circ \mathbf{P}abs_{\tau} \circ \mathbf{P}f \circ Conc_{\sigma} \circ \bigsqcup \circ \mathbf{P}abs_{\sigma} \circ \{\!|.|\!\}$ (P6)

$$= \biguplus \circ \mathbf{P}abs_\tau \circ \mathbf{P}f \circ Conc_\sigma \circ Abs_\sigma \circ \{\!|.|\!\} \qquad \text{definition of } Abs_\sigma$$
$$\geq \biguplus \circ \mathbf{P}abs_\tau \circ \mathbf{P}f \circ \{\!|.|\!\} \quad \text{Proposition 3.18 (1)}$$
$$= \biguplus \circ \mathbf{P}(abs_\tau \circ f) \circ \{\!|.|\!\} \quad \text{(P3)}$$
$$= \biguplus \circ \{\!|.|\!\} \circ abs_\tau \circ f \qquad \text{(P6)}$$
$$= abs_\tau \circ f \qquad \text{(P10)}$$

□

As a consequence of the semi-homomorphic property of abstraction, and the fact that the abstraction maps are continuous, we have that *fix* is a semi-homomorphism of abstraction, which is also needed in the proof of Theorem 3.22.

Proposition 3.20

fix is a semi-homomorphism of abstraction, that is, $fix \circ abs_{\sigma\to\sigma} \geq abs_\sigma \circ fix$.

Proof

Let $f \in D^{st}_{\sigma\to\sigma}$, and let h_i be the approximations to $fix(abs_{\sigma\to\sigma}(f))$ and f_i be the approximations to $fix(f)$. Then $h_0 = \perp_{D^{ab}_\sigma} = abs_\sigma(\perp_{D^{st}_\sigma})$ (since we have insisted that the abstraction maps on base types are strict, and by Lemma 3.8 (3) the abstraction maps for all types are strict) $= abs_\sigma(f_0)$. Assume that $h_k \geq abs_\sigma(f_k)$ for all $k \leq i$. Then

$$h_{i+1} = (abs_{\sigma\to\sigma}(f))(h_i)$$
$$\geq (abs_{\sigma\to\sigma}(f))(abs_\sigma(f_i)) \quad \text{induction hypothesis and monotonicity of } abs_{\sigma\to\sigma}$$
$$\geq abs_\sigma(f(f_i)) \qquad \text{Proposition 3.19}$$
$$= abs_\sigma(f_{i+1})$$

So $h_i \geq abs_\sigma(f_i)$ for all i. Taking the least upper bounds of both sides we obtain

$$fix(abs_{\sigma\to\sigma}(f)) = \bigsqcup\{h_i\}$$
$$\geq \bigsqcup\{abs_\sigma(f_i)\}) \qquad \text{by the above induction}$$
$$= abs_\sigma(\bigsqcup\{f_i\}) \qquad \text{since } abs_\sigma \text{ is continuous and } \{f_i\} \text{ is directed}$$
$$= abs_\sigma(fix(f))$$

□

3.4.7 A result relating the abstract and standard interpretations

Definition 3.21

The abstract interpretation of a constant c_σ *satisfies the constant criterion* if

$$E^{ab}\,[[c_\sigma]]\,\rho^{ab} \geq abs_\sigma(E^{st}\,[[c_\sigma]]\,\rho^{st}).$$

The following result is crucial for proving the correctness of the framework for abstract interpretation (cf. Nielson, 1984, Theorem 3.4.3:14).

Theorem 3.22

Suppose that the abstract interpretations of all constants satisfy the constant safety criterion. Then for all $\rho^{st} \in Env^{st}$, $\rho^{ab} \in Env^{ab}$ such that for all x^{τ}, $\rho^{ab}(x^{\tau}) \geq abs_{\tau}(\rho^{st}(x^{\tau}))$, we have for all $e : \sigma$:

$$Eab\,[[e]]\,\rho^{ab} \geq abs_{\sigma}(E^{st}\,[[e]]\,\rho^{st})$$

Proof

We prove this by structural induction over the terms in our language (see section 3.2.1).

(1) $E^{ab}\,[[x^{\sigma}]]\,\rho^{ab} = \rho^{ab}(x^{\sigma})$

$$\geq abs_{\sigma}(\rho^{st}(x^{\sigma})) \qquad \text{condition of Theorem}$$

$$= abs_{\sigma}(E^{st}\,[[x^{\sigma}]]\,\rho^{st})$$

(2) $E^{ab}\,[[c_{\sigma}]]\,\rho^{ab} \geq abs_{\sigma}(E^{st}\,[[c_{\sigma}]]\,\rho^{st})$ by condition of Theorem

(3)Let $\bar{s} \in D^{ab}_{\sigma}$. Then

$$(E^{ab}\,[[\lambda x^{\sigma}.e]]\,\rho^{ab})\,\bar{s} = (\lambda \bar{y}^{D^{ab}_{\sigma}}.E^{ab}\,[[e]]\,\rho^{ab}[\bar{y}/x^{\sigma}])\,\bar{s}$$

$$= E^{ab}\,[[e]]\,\rho^{ab}[\bar{s}/x^{\sigma}]$$

and

$$(abs_{\sigma\to\tau}(E^{st}\,[[\lambda x^{\sigma}.e]]\,\rho^{st}))\,\bar{s}$$

$$= (\lambda \bar{s}^{D^{ab}_{\sigma}}.\bigsqcup\{abs_{\tau}((E^{st}\,[[\lambda x^{\sigma}.e]]\,\rho^{st})\,s) \mid abs_{\sigma}(s) \leq \bar{s}\}^{\circ})\,\bar{s}$$

$$= \bigsqcup\{abs_{\tau}((\lambda y^{D^{st}_{\sigma}}.E^{st}\,[[e]]\,\rho^{st}[y/x^{\sigma}])\,s) \mid abs_{\sigma}(s) \leq \bar{s}\}^{\circ}$$

$$= \bigsqcup\{abs_{\tau}(E^{st}\,[[e]]\,\rho^{st}[s/x^{\sigma}]) \mid abs_{\sigma}(s) \leq \bar{s}\}^{\circ}$$

Now $\rho^{ab}[\bar{s}/x^{\sigma}]$ and $\rho^{st}[s/x^{\sigma}]$ still satisfy the conditions on the environment since $abs_{\sigma}(s) \leq \bar{s}$, and so by the induction hypothesis, every element in the set $\{abs_{\tau}(E^{st}\,[[e]]\,\rho^{st}[s/x^{\sigma}]) \mid abs_{\sigma}(s) \leq \bar{s}\}$ approximates $E^{ab}\,[[e]]\,\rho^{ab}[\bar{s}/x^{\sigma}]$ and hence the required result holds (by the definition of the *least* upper bound).

(4) $E^{ab}\,[[e_1\,e_2]]\,\rho^{ab} = E^{ab}\,[[e_1]]\,\rho^{ab}\,E^{ab}\,[[e_2]]\,\rho^{ab}$

$$\geq abs_{\sigma\to\tau}(E^{st}\,[[e_1]]\,\rho^{st})(abs_{\sigma}(E^{st}\,[[e_2]]\,\rho^{st})) \qquad \text{induction hypothesis}$$

$$\geq abs_{\tau}(E^{st}\,[[e_1]]\,\rho^{st}\,E^{st}\,[[e_2]]\,\rho^{st}) \qquad \text{Proposition 3.19}$$

$$= abs_{\tau}(E^{st}\,[[e_1\,e_2]]\,\rho^{st})$$

(5) $E^{ab}\,[[fix\;e]]\,\rho^{ab} = fix\,(E^{ab}\,[[e]]\,\rho^{ab})$

$$\geq fix\,(abs_{\sigma\to\sigma}(E^{st}\,[[e]]\,\rho^{st})) \qquad \text{induction hypothesis}$$

$$\geq abs_{\sigma}(fix\,(E^{st}\,[[e]]\,\rho^{st})) \qquad \text{Proposition 3.20}$$

$$= abs_{\sigma}(E^{st}\,[[fix\;e]]\,\rho^{st})$$

□

3.4.8 A proof of the correctness of the abstract interpretation framework

Theorem 3.23

The safety diagram of section 3.4.1 holds. That is, for environments satisfying the conditions of Theorem 3.22, if $f : \sigma \to \tau$ then

$$Conc_{\tau} \circ (E^{ab} [[f]] \rho^{ab}) \sqsupseteq \mathbf{P}(E^{st} [[f]] \rho^{st}) \circ Conc_{\sigma}$$

Proof

$$Conc_{\tau} \circ (E^{ab} [[f]] \rho^{ab}) \sqsupseteq Conc_{\tau} \circ abs_{\sigma\to\tau}(E^{st} [[f]] \rho^{st})$$

Theorem 3.22 and monotonicity of $Conc_{\tau}$

$$\sqsupseteq Conc_{\tau} \circ Abs_{\tau} \circ \mathbf{P}(E^{st} [[f]] \rho^{st}) \circ Conc_{\sigma}$$

definition of $abs_{\sigma\to\tau}$

$$\sqsupseteq \mathbf{P}(E^{st} [[f]] \rho^{st}) \circ Conc_{\sigma} \quad \text{Proposition 3.18 (1)}$$

□

Theorem 3.24 (Correctness theorem for abstract interpretation)

The abstract interpretation we have developed is correct. That is, given $f : \sigma \to \tau$, environments satisfying the conditions of Theorem 3.22, and interpretations of constants satisfying the constant criterion, we have that if $\overline{s} \in D_{\sigma}^{ab}$ and $(E^{ab} [[f]] \rho^{ab})(\overline{s}) = \overline{t}$ then for all $s \in Conc_{\sigma}(\overline{s})$, $(E^{st} [[f]] \rho^{st})(s) \in Conc_{\tau}(\overline{t})$.

Proof

This is a direct corollary of Theorem 3.23.

$$Conc_{\tau}(\overline{t}) = Conc_{\tau}((E^{ab} [[f]] \rho^{ab})(\overline{s})) \quad \text{by hypothesis}$$

$$\sqsupseteq \mathbf{P}(E^{st} [[f]] \rho^{st})(Conc_{\sigma}(\overline{s})) \quad \text{Theorem 3.23}$$

$$= \{(E^{st} [[f]] \rho^{st})(s) \mid s \in Conc_{\sigma}(\overline{s})\}^{\circ} \quad \text{definition of } \mathbf{P} \text{ on morphisms}$$

and hence the result.

□

3.4.9 Context-free and context-sensitive issues

In the world of first-order functions and strictness analysis, the information about arguments to functions is true in all applications of a function. When we move from the domain of first-order functions to higher-order functions, or to using more complex analyses than strictness analysis, we no longer have that the information about a function is constant in all applications of that function. In the case of a higher-order function, for instance, the information can vary according to the information about a functional parameter. Consider the function

$$g = \lambda f^{A \to A}.\lambda x^{A}.f(x)$$

which has abstract interpretation

$$\lambda f^{D_A^{ab} \to D_A^{ab}}.\lambda x^{D_A^{ab}}.f(x).$$

Clearly any information in an application of g is going to depend on the information given by its first argument in an application.

In our application of the theory in section 5, we will give each argument of a function an evaluation transformer. From the above example it may be desirable to try to carry around information which said, for example, that if a function was given as a parameter a function which was strict in its argument, then the other function was strict in another of its parameters. This would mean that definedness information would have to be available at run-time, and that some of the interpretation of the abstract interpretation would also have to occur at run-time, and we would rather try to avoid the problems this causes.

An attempt to solve this problem was made in Burn *et al.* (1986), where it was suggested that application nodes be labelled with information rather than the arguments to functions, and so the abstract interpretation could take into account the contextual information of the function application. Thus, in an application

$$g\ h\ e$$

of the above function g, we could take into account the information about h in determining information about the second parameter to g in this application. It is shown in Hankin *et al.* (1986) that, in the case of strictness analysis, this gives more information than if we had have just labelled the arguments to functions with strictness information. We term such information *context-sensitive*.

However, the evaluation of functional programs dynamically creates function applications which were not present in the program text, and so could not be analysed statically using abstract interpretation. For example, the expression

$$(\textit{if condition then } f_1 \textit{ else } f_2)\ e$$

will create the application $f_1\ e$ or $f_2\ e$ depending on the truth of the *condition*. As a first approximation to the solution of the problem of finding out information about such applications, we can determine the strictness information about the arguments to a function which is true in any application, and so is *context-free* information. Clearly context-sensitive information will be stronger than context-free information for applications that appear explicitly in the program.

We will give an example in section 5.2 where the information available from the context-sensitive theorem is greater than that available from the context-free theorem.

Theorem 3.25 (Context-free information theorem)

If $f : \sigma_1 \to \cdots \sigma_n \to \tau$ and

$$(E^{ab}\,[[f\,]]\,\rho^{ab})\ \top_{D^{ab}_{\sigma_1}} \cdots \top_{D^{ab}_{\sigma_{i-1}}}\ \overline{s_i}\ \top_{D^{ab}_{\sigma_{i+1}}} \cdots \top_{D^{ab}_{\sigma_n}} = \overline{t}$$

then for all $e_j : \sigma_j,\ j \neq i$, for all $s_i \in Conc_{\sigma_i}(\overline{s_i})$, we have

$$E^{st}\,[[f\,]]\,\rho^{st}\,E^{st}\,[[e_1]]\,\rho^{st} \cdots E^{st}\,[[e_{i-1}]]\,\rho^{st}\,s_i\,E^{st}\,[[e_{i+1}]]\,\rho^{st} \cdots E^{st}\,[[e_n]]\,\rho^{st} \in Conc_\tau(\overline{t})$$

Proof

$$\overline{t} = (E^{ab}\,[[f\,]]\,\rho^{ab})\ \top_{D^{ab}_{\sigma_1}} \cdots \top_{D^{ab}_{\sigma_{i-1}}}\ \overline{s_i}\ \top_{D^{ab}_{\sigma_{i+1}}} \cdots \top_{D^{ab}_{\sigma_n}}$$

$$\geq E^{ab}\,[[f\,]]\,\rho^{ab}\,E^{ab}\,[[e_1]]\,\rho^{ab} \cdots E^{ab}\,[[e_{i-1}]]\,\rho^{ab}\,\overline{s_i}\,E^{ab}\,[[e_{i+1}]]\,\rho^{ab} \cdots E^{ab}\,[[e_n]]\,\rho^{ab}$$

since $\top_{D^{ab}_{\sigma_i}} \geq E^{ab}\,[[e_j]]\,\rho^{ab}$ for all $j \neq i$.

$$= (\lambda \overline{x}^{D^{ab}_{\sigma_i}}.E^{ab}\,[[f\,]]\,\rho^{ab}\,E^{ab}\,[[e_1]]\,\rho^{ab}\,\cdots\,E^{ab}\,[[e_{i-1}]]\,\rho^{ab}\,\overline{x}$$

$$E^{ab}\,[[e_{i+1}]]\,\rho^{ab}\,\cdots\,E^{ab}\,[[e_n]]\,\rho^{ab})\,\overline{s_i}$$

where $\overline{x}^{D^{ab}_{\sigma_i}}$ is a new variable

$$= (\lambda \overline{x}^{D^{ab}_{\sigma_i}}.E^{ab}\,[[f\,]]\,\rho^{ab}[\overline{x}/x^{\sigma_i}]\,E^{ab}\,[[e_1]]\,\rho^{ab}[\overline{x}/x^{\sigma_i}]\,\cdots\,E^{ab}\,[[e_{i-1}]]\,\rho^{ab}[\overline{x}/x^{\sigma_i}]$$

$$E^{ab}\,[[x^{\sigma}]]\,\rho^{ab}[\overline{x}/x^{\sigma_i}]\,E^{ab}\,[[e_{i+1}]]\,\rho^{ab}[\overline{x}/x^{\sigma_i}]\,\cdots\,E^{ab}\,[[e_n]]\,\rho^{ab}[\overline{x}/x^{\sigma_i}])\,\overline{s_i}$$

$$= (\lambda \overline{x}^{D^{ab}_{\sigma_i}}.E^{ab}\,[[f\ e_1\,\cdots\,e_{i-1}\,x^{\sigma_i}\,e_{i+1}\,\cdots\,e_n]]\,\rho^{ab}[\overline{x}/x^{\sigma_i}])\,\overline{s_i}$$

$$= (E^{ab}\,[[\lambda x^{\sigma_i}.f\ e_1\,\cdots\,e_{i-1}\,x^{\sigma_i}\,e_{i+1}\,\cdots\,e_n]]\,\rho^{ab})\,\overline{s_i}$$

$\Rightarrow$for all $s_i \in Conc_{\sigma_i}(\overline{s_i})$,

$(E^{st}\,[[\lambda x^{\sigma_i}.f\ e_1\,\cdots\,e_{i-1}\,x^{\sigma_i}\,e_{i+1}\,\cdots\,e_n]]\,\rho^{st})\,(s_i) \in Conc_{\tau}(\overline{t})$

by a slight adaptation of Theorem 3.24, possible since $Conc_{\sigma_i}$ is continuous

i.e. $(\lambda x^{D^{st}_{\sigma_i}}.E^{st}\,[[f\ e_1\,\cdots\,e_{i-1}\,x^{\sigma_i}\,e_{i+1}\,\cdots\,e_n]]\,\rho^{st})\,(s_i) \in Conc_{\tau}(\overline{t})$

i.e. $(\lambda x^{D^{st}_{\sigma_i}}.E^{st}\,[[f\,]]\,\rho^{st}\,E^{st}\,[[e_1]]\,\rho^{st}\,\cdots\,E^{st}\,[[e_{i-1}]]\,\rho^{st}\,x^{\sigma_i}\,E^{st}\,[[e_{i+1}]]\,\rho^{st}$

$\cdots\,E^{st}\,[[e_n]]\,\rho^{st})\,(s_i) \in Conc_{\tau}(\overline{t})$

i.e. $E^{st}\,[[f\,]]\,\rho^{st}\,E^{st}\,[[e_1]]\,\rho^{st}\,\cdots\,E^{st}\,[[e_{i-1}]]\,\rho^{st}\,s_i\,E^{st}\,[[e_{i+1}]]\,\rho^{st}\,\cdots\,E^{st}\,[[e_n]]\,\rho^{st}$

$\in Conc_{\tau}(\overline{t})$

□

Theorem 3.26 (Context-sensitive information theorem)

Given $f : \sigma_1 \rightarrow \cdots \rightarrow \sigma_n \rightarrow \tau$ and an application $f\ e_1\,\cdots\,e_n : \tau$, if

$E^{ab}\,[[f\,]]\,\rho^{ab}\,E^{ab}\,[[e_1]]\,\rho^{ab}\,\cdots\,E^{ab}\,[[e_{i-1}]]\,\rho^{ab}\,\overline{s_i}\,E^{ab}\,[[e_{i+1}]]\,\rho^{ab}\,\cdots\,E^{ab}\,[[e_n]]\,\rho^{ab} = \overline{t}$

then for all $s_i \in Conc_{\sigma_i}(\overline{s_i})$

$E^{st}\,[[f\,]]\,\rho^{st}\,E^{st}\,[[e_1]]\,\rho^{st}\,\cdots\,E^{st}\,[[e_{i-1}]]\,\rho^{st}\,s_i\,E^{st}\,[[e_{i+1}]]\,\rho^{st}\,\cdots\,E^{st}\,[[e_n]]\,\rho^{st} \in Conc_{\tau}(\overline{t})$

Proof

The proof of this theorem follows exactly as in the proof of Theorem 3.25, except that the first two lines are replaced by the following:

$\overline{t} = E^{ab}\,[[f\,]]\,\rho^{ab}\,E^{ab}\,[[e_1]]\,\rho^{ab}\,\cdots\,E^{ab}\,[[e_{i-1}]]\,\rho^{ab}\,\overline{s_i}\,E^{ab}\,[[e_{i+1}]]\,\rho^{ab}\,\cdots\,E^{ab}\,[[e_n]]\,\rho^{ab}$

i.e. we have equality instead of the inequality on the second line of the other proof.

□

3.4.10 The undual duality

Those familiar with category theory may have noticed something most tantalizing while reading through this chapter. In section 3.4.1 we made a fundamental decision about what we meant by the correctness of an abstract interpretation, and said that it was correct if the result in the abstract interpretation represented all of the possible results in the standard interpretation. This meant that a result in the abstract interpretation may represent considerably more values than were really possible in the standard interpretation. A related decision was the choosing of the Hoare powerdomain and the least upper bound operator in defining the abstraction maps for higher types.

The point is that most of these items have a dual; the dual to making sure that the result represents all possible values is to ensure that it represents a subset of the values; the dual to the least upper bound is the greatest lower bound; in some ways the Smyth powerdomain (Smyth, 1978) is a dual to the Hoare powerdomain.

Working in a monotone framework, Abramsky (1985) was able to develop a termination analysis which was a dual of the strictness analysis he presents. Because all of the abstract domains are finite, the interpretation is computable even though the abstraction maps are not continuous. However, it was not possible to raise the termination analysis to a continuous world, and the sets resulting from the obvious induced concretization map are not, in general, elements of the Smyth powerdomain.

We can get some intuition about why this is true by considering the following example. For each base type A, we define D_A^{ab} to be the two-point domain $2 = \{0,1\}$ with $0 \leq 1$, and define

$$abs_A : D_A^{st} \rightarrow D_A^{ab}$$

by

$$abs_A(a) = \begin{cases} 0 \text{ if } a = \perp_{D_A^{st}} \\ 1 \text{ otherwise} \end{cases}$$

The concretization map we have given for safety interpretations (Definition 3.4) gives the following interpretations to the values in the two-point domain:

$$Conc_A(0) = \{\perp_{D_A^{st}}\}$$

$$Conc_A(1) = D_A^{st}$$

which says intuitively that 0 represents the idea of definite undefinedness and 1 represents the possibility that something may be defined.

Another way to interpret this domain is to let 1 represent the idea of definite definedness and 0 represent the possibility that something may be undefined, defining:

$$Conc'_A(0) = D_A^{st}$$

$$Conc'_A(1) = D_A^{st} - \{\perp_{D_A^{st}}\}$$

But here is the problem – the set which we have given for the concretization of 1 is not a member of the Smyth powerdomain! To handle analyses such as these, a special powerdomain has been developed (Mycroft and Nielson, 1983; Nielson, 1984), but has only been applied to a first-order framework.

4. A definedness abstract interpretation for determining evaluation transformers

We now develop an abstract interpretation for the base types of our language, which can be inserted into the framework of the previous section and used to determine evaluation transformers. Abstract interpretations that satisfy the constant criterion (Definition 3.2) are given for the functional constants in the language. We then give the abstract interpretations of some example functions. In the final section, we are able state that Theorems 3.25 and 3.26 hold for this application because the abstract interpretations we give for the base types and constants and the abstraction maps for the base types satisfy the necessary conditions.

As a notational convention, we will denote the abstract interpretation of a function, f, by placing a bar over the name of the function, thus $\bar{f}$.

4.1 Abstraction of base domains

Choosing an abstract domain and abstraction functions which capture the properties of interest seems to be one of the hardest tasks in abstract interpretation. We have two intuitions about the way abstract domains can be defined for the base types in our application. First, since we are looking for information about the definedness of functions, we consider the abstract domains that arise from looking at the definedness structure of the domains which are the standard interpretation of the base types. However, since we really want to use the abstract interpretation to change evaluation mechanisms by allowing some arguments to functions to be evaluated, we need to choose abstract domains which model the behaviour of evaluators. It turns out that both intuitions lead to the same abstract domains, namely the two-point domain of Mycroft (1981) for flat base domains and the four-point chain domain of Wadler (1987) for list data types.

4.1.1 Defining abstract domains and abstraction maps from the definedness structure of the standard interpretation

Let us first consider the case of a flat domain such as the standard interpretation of integers and booleans. Here there are two levels of definedness – either something is undefined (i.e. bottom), or it is totally defined. Thus, to capture the definedness information for such domains, we can define a simple abstract domain and abstraction map. Denoting the type by A, we have that D_A^{st} is a flat domain, and we can define $D_A^{ab} = 2$, where $2 \doteq \{0,1\}$, with $0 \leq 1$. Then we define

$$abs_A : D_A^{st} \to D_A^{ab}$$

$$abs_A(a) = \begin{cases} 0 \text{ if } a = \bot_{D_A^{st}} \\ 1 \text{ otherwise} \end{cases}$$

We have chosen *Alists*, that is, lists of elements of type A as our prototypical example of a domain which is an infinite sum of products. Initially, we will simplify the discussion by restricting ourselves to the case where the standard interpretation of A is a flat domain so that, for example, we are considering list of integers or lists of booleans. The type of *Alist* is given by the recursive type equation

$$Alist \cong 1 + A \times Alist$$

(where 1 is the one-point domain, + is disjoint sum and × is cartesian product) and the standard interpretation, as we mentioned in section 1.5.2, is obtained by solving this over the category of domains (Smyth and Plotkin, 1982) to give

$$D^{st}_{Alist} = D^{st}_{A}{}^{*}.nil \cup D^{st}_{A}{}^{*}.\bot_{D^{st}_{Alist}} \cup D^{st}_{A}{}^{\omega}.$$

How might we go about defining an abstract domain which captures the definedness of elements of D^{st}_{Alist}? At first we may think of using the fact, since we are for the moment assuming that the elements of the list are from a flat domain, that for each element of the list we have two levels of definedness – either the element is bottom or it is not – and so we could represent the strictness information for a list as a list of 0's and 1's. The theoretical development of section 3 required that we have a finite, complete lattice as the abstract domain for any base type, so clearly we cannot have an abstract domain which contains a list of 0's and 1's for every list in the standard domain and, in any case, such an abstract domain would be useless because we could never do all of the calculations required! A way to obtain finiteness of the domain would be to choose some n and have only lists of length at most n in the abstract domain. However, this is only ever going to give us information about the behaviours of a function on the first n elements of a list. Furthermore, the abstract domain would have 2^n elements in it, and so it would be computationally very expensive to find out any information about functions using it.

The main problem with the above abstract domain is that it treats the elements of a list in a way which is not typical of how we use lists in programs; the first n elements of the list are treated differently from the rest of the elements of the list, whereas lists are used most naturally in the case that we wish to treat all of the elements in a uniform way.

If we ignore infinite lists for a moment, then we note that we can divide up the standard domain for lists into four natural subsets:

(1)The set containing only $\bot_{D^{st}_{Alist}}$, i.e. $\{\bot_{D^{st}_{Alist}}\}$;

(2)The set containing all of the partial lists plus $\bot_{D^{st}_{Alist}}$, i.e. $D^{st}_{A}{}^{*}.\bot_{D^{st}_{Alist}}$;

(3)The set containing finite lists with at least one bottom element, the partial lists and $\bot_{D^{st}_{Alist}}$, i.e. $D^{st}_{A}{}^{*}.\bot_{D^{st}_{Alist}} \cup D^{st}_{A}{}^{*}.\bot_{D^{st}_{A}}.D^{st}_{A}{}^{*}.nil$; and

(4)The set containing all lists, i.e. D^{st}_{Alist}.

In going from one subset to the next, we are adding elements which are more defined in some way; in going from (1) to (2), we have added lists which have at least one element in them, but still have an undefined tail after a finite number of elements from D^{st}_{A}, and the extra elements added in (3) represent becoming more defined by replacing the undefined tail by *nil*, and the final addition in (4) adds all of the finite lists which have no bottom elements.

We can define an abstract domain and abstraction map which captures these various levels of definedness. Let us use the four distinct elements 0, 1, 2 and 3,[8] ordered by $0 \le 1 \le 2 \le 3$, as our abstract domain D^{ab}_{Alist}, and define

$$abs_{Alist} : (D^{st}_{Alist} - D^{st}_{A}{}^{\omega}) \rightarrow D^{ab}_{Alist}$$

$$abs_{Alist}(L) = \begin{cases} 0 \text{ if } L = \bot_{D^{st}_{Alist}} \\ 1 \text{ if } L \in D^{st}_{A}.D^{st}_{A}{}^{*}.\bot_{D^{st}_{Alist}} \\ 2 \text{ if } L \in D^{st}_{A}.\bot_{D^{st}_{A}}.D^{st}_{A}{}^{*}.nil \\ 3 \text{ if } L \in (D^{st}_{A} - \{\bot_{D^{st}_{A}}\})^{*}.nil \end{cases}$$

Moving from one level in the abstract interpretation to the next corresponds to being an element in the standard interpretation of *Alist* which is in one of the sets (1) to (4) above but not in any proper subset of that set.

We can add infinite lists into the above discussion by noting that we need to have a continuous abstraction map for each base type. Since all of the approximations to an infinite list (i.e. partial lists) are abstracted to 1, we must have that the abstraction of any infinite list is also 1 by the definition of continuity. Thus we finish the definition of the abstraction map for *Alist*:

$$abs_{Alist} : D^{st}_{Alist} \rightarrow D^{ab}_{Alist}$$

$$abs_{Alist}(L) = \begin{cases} 0 \text{ if } L = \perp_{D^{st}_{Alist}} \\ 1 \text{ if } L \in D^{st}_A . D^{st}_A {}^* . \perp_{D^{st}_{Alist}} \cup D^{st\,\omega}_A \\ 2 \text{ if } L \in D^{st}_A . \perp_{D^{st}_A} . D^{st}_A {}^* . nil \\ 3 \text{ if } L \in (D^{st}_A - \{\perp_{D^{st}_A}\})^* . nil \end{cases}$$

It is worth noting that with this domain we can see the dual reading of the elements in the abstract domain which was introduced in section 2.1. From the point of view of the map abs_{Alist}, an element in the abstract domain represents a single list. However, if one was to take the view of the map $Conc_{Alist}$, then the elements 0 to 3 represent respectively the sets (1) to (4) above.

4.1.2 Defining abstract domains and abstraction maps from the sensible levels of evaluation

The abstract domains derived from the definedness levels are useful because they capture the way that the evaluators we have chosen behave. For example, the evaluator ξ_1 will fail to terminate if and only if the expression being evaluated denotes an undefined value, that is, the value represented by the bottom of the appropriate abstract domain (0 for atomic base types and lists). In a similar manner, because ξ_2 evaluates the structure of a list, it will fail to terminate precisely in the case that the list is not finite, that is, if an expression denotes any value represented by 1. Finally, ξ_3 will also fail to terminate if the expression denotes a list which is either not finite or has any undefined elements in it, that is, it fails to terminate on any expression denoting an element represented by 2. For this reason, we will say that the evaluator ξ_1 *corresponds* to the bottom of the appropriate abstract domain, that ξ_2 *corresponds* to 1 and that ξ_3 *corresponds* to 2.

4.1.3 Formal definition of the abstract domains

In the previous two sections we have attacked the problem of finding abstract domains and abstraction functions for the base types from two natural intuitions and found that they pointed to the same abstract domains and abstraction maps for the various interpretations of base types. We thus formally make these definitions in this section.

[8] The elements 0, 1, 2 and 3 correspond respectively to $\perp$, ∞, $\perp\varepsilon$ and $\top\varepsilon$ of Wadler (1987).

If A is a base type whose standard interpretation is a flat domain, then we define D_A^{ab}:

Definition 4.1

$D_A^{ab} = 2$, where $2 = \{0,1\}$ with 0 and 1 distinct elements and $0 \leq 1$.

□

We define the abstraction map:

Definition 4.2

$$abs_A : D_A^{st} \rightarrow D_A^{ab}$$

$$abs_A(a) = \begin{cases} 0 \text{ if } a = \bot_{D_A^{st}} \\ 1 \text{ otherwise} \end{cases}$$

□

For the type $Alist$, we define the abstract domain, where we lift the restriction that D_A^{st} has to be a flat domain, but we will still use the two-point domain for the abstract interpretation of elements of the list:

Definition 4.3

$D_{Alist}^{ab} = \{0,1,2,3\}$, where 0, 1, 2 and 3 are all distinct and are ordered by $0 \leq 1 \leq 2 \leq 3$.

□

We define the abstraction map:

Definition 4.4

$$abs_{Alist} : D_{Alist}^{st} \rightarrow D_{Alist}^{ab}$$

$$abs_{Alist}(L) = \begin{cases} 0 \text{ if } L = \bot_{D_{Alist}^{st}} \\ 1 \text{ if } L \in D_A^{st}.D_A^{st}*.\bot_{D_{Alist}^{st}} \cup D_A^{st\,\omega} \\ 2 \text{ if } L \in D_A^{st}*.\bot_{D_A^{st}}.D_A^{st}*.nil \\ 3 \text{ if } L \in (D_A^{st} - \{\bot_{D_A^{st}}\})*.nil \end{cases}$$

□

4.1.4 Some useful facts

Since the abstract domains for the base types are finite lattices and the abstraction maps for the base types are strict and continuous, as required by the theory of section 3, we have the following facts. They are useful in the ensuing development.

Fact 4.5

For all types σ, abs_σ is continuous (Lemma 3.8 (1)).

□

Fact 4.6

For all types σ, abs_σ is strict (Lemma 3.8 (3)).

□

Fact 4.7

For all types σ, abs_σ is bottom-reflexive (Fact 3.14).

□

Lemma 4.8

For all types σ, abs_σ is onto.

Proof

From Fact 3.16 we have to provide a continuous function $abs_A^{-1} : D_A^{ab} \to D_A^{st}$ which is a right inverse of abs_A for each base type A, and then the result follows. For $D_A^{ab} = 2$ we can make the following definition:

$$abs_A^{-1}(0) = \bot_{D_A^{st}}$$

$$abs_A^{-1}(1) = a \in D_A^{st}, a \neq \bot_{D_A^{st}}$$

For D_{Alist}^{ab}, a suitable $abs_{Alist}^{-1} : D_{Alist}^{ab} \to D_{Alist}^{st}$ is:

$$abs_{Alist}^{-1}(\bot_L) = \bot_{D_{Alist}^{st}}$$

$$abs_{Alist}^{-1}(I) = \bot_{D_A^{st}}.\bot_{D_{Alist}^{st}}$$

$$abs_{Alist}^{-1}(F) = \bot_{D_A^{st}}.nil$$

$$abs_{Alist}^{-1}(\top_L) = a.nil \qquad a \in D_A^{st}, a \neq \bot_{D_A^{st}}$$

Clearly abs_A^{-1} and abs_{Alist}^{-1} are continuous and have the required inverse property.

□

Fact 4.9

For all σ, $Conc_\sigma(\bot_{D_\sigma^{ab}}) = \{\bot_{D_\sigma^{st}}\}$ (Fact 3.17).

□

4.2 Abstract interpretation of constants

The theory of section 3 requires abstract interpretations of constants which satisfy

$$E^{ab}\ [[c_\sigma]]\ \rho^{ab} \geq abs_\sigma(E^{st}\ [[c_\sigma]]\ \rho^{st})$$

for all constants c_σ. Definitions of abstract interpretations for the constants satisfying this condition are given in section 4.2.1. They were derived by applying the abstraction map of the appropriate type to the standard semantics of the constants and, where necessary, using the semi-homomorphic property of abs_σ. The derivations are given in section 4.2.2. A similar method was used in Nielson (1986b).

4.2.1 Definition of the abstract interpretations of the constants

The function $test_\sigma$, which is clearly continuous, is used in giving the abstract interpretation of the conditional.

Definition 4.10

$$test_\sigma : 2 \rightarrow D_\sigma^{ab} \rightarrow D_\sigma^{ab}$$

$$test_\sigma(0,s) = \bot_{D_\sigma^{ab}}$$

$$test_\sigma(1,s) = s$$

□

This satisfies the reduction rule given in Fact 4.15.

We are now able to define the abstract interpretations of the constant functions in the language.

Definition 4.11

(1) $E^{ab}\,[[f\,]]\,\rho^{ab} = \lambda x_1^2.\lambda x_2^2.x_1$ **and** x_2

if f is a strict, binary arithmetic or logical operator.

(2) $E^{ab}\,[[\text{if}_{bool\rightarrow\sigma\rightarrow\sigma\rightarrow\sigma}]]\,\rho^{ab} = \lambda x^2.\lambda y^{D_\sigma^{ab}}.\lambda z^{D_\sigma^{ab}}.test_\sigma(x, \bigsqcup\{y,z\})$

where $\bigsqcup$ for function spaces is calculated pointwise, i.e. $(\bigsqcup\{f,g\})\,x = \bigsqcup\{f(x), g(x)\}$.

(3) $(E^{ab}\,[[hd]]\,\rho^{ab})\,\overline{L} = \overline{hd}\;\overline{L} = \begin{cases} 0 \text{ if } \overline{L}=0 \\ 1 \text{ otherwise} \end{cases}$

(4) $(E^{ab}\,[[tl]]\,\rho^{ab})\,\overline{L} = \overline{tl}\;\overline{L} = \begin{cases} 0 \text{ if } \overline{L}=0 \\ 1 \text{ if } \overline{L}=1 \\ 3 \text{ otherwise} \end{cases}$

(5) $(E^{ab}\,[[cons]]\,\rho^{ab})\,\overline{a}\;\overline{L} = \overline{cons}\;\overline{a}\;\overline{L} = \begin{cases} 1 \text{ if } \overline{L}=0 \textbf{ or } \overline{L}=1 \\ 2 \text{ if } \overline{L}=2 \textbf{ or } (\overline{a}=0 \textbf{ and } \overline{L}=3) \\ 3 \text{ if } \overline{a}=1 \textbf{ and } \overline{L}=3 \end{cases}$

(6) $(E^{ab}\,[[case]]\,\rho^{ab})\,\overline{s}\;\overline{f}\;\overline{L} = \overline{case}\;\overline{s}\;\overline{f}\;\overline{L} = \begin{cases} \bot_{D_\sigma^{ab}} & \text{if } \overline{L}=0 \\ \overline{f}\;1\;1 & \text{if } \overline{L}=1 \\ (\overline{f}\;1\;2)\bigsqcup(\overline{f}\;0\;3) & \text{if } \overline{L}=2 \\ \overline{s}\bigsqcup(\overline{f}\;1\;3) & \text{if } \overline{L}=3 \end{cases}$

□

There are some simplification rules for expressions involving applications of the abstract interpretations of *hd*, *tl* and *cons*. To give them, we will first state the standard definitions of two terms.

Definition 4.12

A function $f \in D_{\sigma_1}^I \rightarrow \cdots \rightarrow D_{\sigma_{n+1}}^I$, where each $D_{\sigma_i}^I$ is a complete lattice, is *multiplicative* in its ith argument if

$$f\;s_1\;\cdots\;s_{i-1}\,(s_i \sqcap s'_i)\,s_{i+1}\;\cdots\;s_n = (f\;s_1\;\cdots\;s_i\;\cdots\;s_n) \sqcap (f\;s_1\;\cdots\;s'_i\;\cdots\;s_n)$$

□

Definition 4.13

A function $f \in D^I_{\sigma_1} \rightarrow \cdots \rightarrow D^I_{\sigma_{n+1}}$, where each $D^I_{\sigma_i}$ is a complete lattice, is *additive* in its ith argument if

$$f\ s_1\ \cdots\ s_{i-1}\ (s_i \bigsqcup s'_i)\ s_{i+1}\ \cdots\ s_n = (f\ s_1\ \cdots\ s_i\ \cdots\ s_n) \bigsqcup (f\ s_1\ \cdots\ s'_i\ \cdots s_n)$$

□

Fact 4.14

Both $\overline{hd}$ and $\overline{tl}$ are multiplicative and additive and *cons* is multiplicative and additive in both of its arguments (Burn, 1987a, Propositions 3.2.5 and 3.2.6).

□

Fact 4.15:

If $\overline{e_1} \in D^{ab}_{bool}$ (=2), $\overline{e_2} \in D^{ab}_{\sigma\rightarrow\tau}$ and $\overline{e_3} \in D^{ab}_{\sigma}$, then

$$(\overline{\text{if}_{\sigma\rightarrow\tau}}(\overline{e_1},\overline{e_2}))\ \overline{e_3} = \overline{\text{if}_\tau}(\overline{e_1},\overline{e_2}\ \overline{e_3})$$

(Burn, 1987a, Lemma 3.2.2.2).

4.2.2 Derivation of the abstract interpretation of the constant functions

Except for *case*, we have equality between the abstract interpretations we have given for the constants and the abstraction of their standard semantics, which is a stronger result than that required by the constant criterion. Each abstract interpretation is obtained by applying the abstraction map of the appropriate type to the standard semantics of the constant. In the derivation for *case*, we must make some safe approximations.

4.2.2.1 Abstract interpretation of strict functions

Let A be a base type with abstract interpretation the two-point domain. If we denote A by A^1 and $A \rightarrow A^n$ by A^{n+1}, then if $f : A^{n+1}$ is such that for all i

$$(E^{st}\ [[f\,]]\ \rho^{st})\ a_1\ \cdots\ a_{i-1}\ \bot_{D_A^{st}}\ a_{i+1}\ \cdots\ a_n = \bot_{D_A^{st}}$$

i.e. f is strict in each of its parameters, and

$$E^{st}\ [[f\ a_1\ \cdots\ a_n]]\ \rho^{st} = \bot_{D_A^{st}} \Rightarrow E^{st}\ [[a_i]]\ \rho^{st} = \bot_{D_A^{st}}$$

for some i, i.e. a generalization of $\bot$-reflexivity, then define the abstract interpretation of f by:

Definition 4.16

$$E^{ab}\ [[f\,]]\ \rho^{ab} = \lambda x_1^2 \cdots \lambda x_n^2.x_1 \textbf{ and } \cdots \textbf{ and } x_n.$$

□

Thus functions like '+' and '×' have abstract interpretation $\lambda x^2.\lambda y^2.x \textbf{ and } y$.

Lemma 4.17

Given such an f,

$$E^{ab}\ [[f\,]]\ \rho^{ab} = abs_{A^{n+1}}(E^{st}\ [[f\,]]\ \rho^{st})$$

Proof

We prove this by induction with the base case being $n = 2$. In this proof we will denote the standard interpretation of f by f^{st}.

$$(abs_{A\to A}(f^{st}))\ 0 = \bigsqcup\{abs_A(f^{st}\ x)\,|\,x\in Conc_A(0)\}^\circ \qquad \text{Fact 3.10}$$

$$= \bigsqcup\{abs_A(f^{st}\ \bot_{D_A^{st}})\}^\circ \qquad \text{Fact 4.9}$$

$$= \bigsqcup\{0\}^\circ \qquad \text{since } f^{st} \text{ and } abs_A \text{ are strict}$$

$$= 0 \qquad \text{(P10)}$$

$$(abs_{A\to A}(f^{st}))\ 1 = \{abs_A(f^{st}\ x)\,|\,x\in Conc_A(1)\}^\circ \qquad \text{Fact 3.10}$$

$$= \bigsqcup\{abs_A(f^{st}\ a)\,|\,a\in D_A^{st}\}^\circ$$

$$= \bigsqcup\{0,1\}^\circ \qquad \text{since } f^{st} \text{ is strict and not } \bot_{D_{A\to A}^{st}}$$

$$= 1$$

Therefore, by extensionality, $abs_{A\to A}(f^{st}) = \lambda x^2.x$. In the induction step, we assume the result for all $n \le k$.

$$(abs_{A^{k+1}}(f^{st}))\ 0 = \bigsqcup\{abs_{A^k}(f^{st}\ x)\,|\,x\in Conc_A(0)\}^\circ \qquad \text{Fact 3.10}$$

$$= \bigsqcup\{abs_{A^k}(f^{st}\ \bot_{D_A^{st}})\}^\circ \qquad \text{Fact 4.9}$$

$$= \bigsqcup\{abs_{A^k}(\lambda x_1^{D_A^{st}} \cdots \lambda x_{k-1}^{D_A^{st}}.\bot_{D_A^{st}})\}^\circ \qquad \text{since } f^{st} \text{ is strict}$$

$$= \lambda x_1^2 \cdots \lambda x_{k-1}^2.0 \qquad \text{since } abs_{A^k} \text{ is strict}$$

$$(abs_{A^{k+1}}(f^{st}))\ 1 = \bigsqcup\{abs_{A^k}(f^{st}\ x)\,|\,x\in Conc_A(1)\}^\circ \qquad \text{Fact 3.10}$$

$$= \bigsqcup\{abs_{A^k}(f^{st}\ a)\,|\,a\in D_A^{st}\}^\circ$$

$$= \bigsqcup\{abs_{A^k}(f^{st}\ a)\,|\,a\neq\bot_{D_A^{st}}, a\in D_A^{st}\}^\circ \qquad \text{since } f^{st} \text{ is monotonic}$$

$$= \bigsqcup\{\lambda x_1^2 \cdots \lambda x_{k-1}^2.x_1 \textbf{ and } \cdots x_{k-1}\}^\circ$$

by induction hypothesis for $(f^{st}\ a)$ satisfies

the condition of the Lemma

$$= \lambda x_1^2 \cdots \lambda x_{k-1}^2.x_1 \textbf{ and } \cdots \textbf{ and } x_{k-1} \qquad \text{(P10)}$$

Hence, $abs_{A^{k+1}}(f^{st}) = \lambda x_1^2 \cdots \lambda x_k^2.x_1 \textbf{ and } \cdots \textbf{ and } x_k$.

□

4.2.2.2 Abstract interpretation of the conditional

Lemma 4.18

$$E^{ab}\,[[\text{if}_{bool\to\sigma\to\sigma\to\sigma}]]\,\rho^{ab} = abs_{bool\to\sigma\to\sigma\to\sigma}(E^{st}\,[[\text{if}_{bool\to\sigma\to\sigma\to\sigma}]]\,\rho^{st})$$

Proof

In this proof we will denote the standard semantics of $\text{if}_{bool\to\sigma\to\sigma\to\sigma}$ by if^{st}.

$$abs_{bool\to\sigma\to\sigma\to\sigma}(\text{if}^{st})$$

$$= \lambda\overline{x}^2.\lambda\overline{y}^{D_\sigma^{ab}}.\lambda\overline{z}^{D_\sigma^{ab}}.\{abs_\sigma(\text{if}^{st}(x,y,z))\,|\,abs_A(x)\leq\overline{x}, abs_\sigma(y)\leq\overline{y}, abs_\sigma(z)\leq\overline{z}\}^\circ$$

Fact 3.4.3-1

$$(abs_{bool\to\sigma\to\sigma\to\sigma}(\text{if}^{st}))\ 0$$

$$= \lambda\overline{y}^{D_\sigma^{ab}}.\lambda\overline{z}^{D_\sigma^{ab}}.\biguplus\{abs_\sigma(\text{if}^{st}(\bot_{D_{bool}^{st}},y,z))\,|\,abs_\sigma(y)\leq\overline{y}, abs_\sigma(z)\leq\overline{z}\}^\circ$$

since abs_A is $\bot$-reflexive

$$= \lambda\overline{y}^{D_\sigma^{ab}}.\lambda\overline{z}^{D_\sigma^{ab}}.\biguplus\{abs_\sigma(\bot_{D_\sigma^{st}})\}^\circ \quad \text{by the standard semantics of the conditional}$$

$$= \lambda\overline{y}^{D_\sigma^{ab}}.\lambda\overline{z}^{D_\sigma^{ab}}.\biguplus\{\bot_{D_\sigma^{ab}}\}^\circ \qquad \text{since } abs_\sigma \text{ is strict}$$

$$= \lambda\overline{y}^{D_\sigma^{ab}}.\lambda\overline{z}^{D_\sigma^{ab}}.\bot_{D_\sigma^{ab}} \qquad \text{(P10)}$$

$$(abs_{bool\to\sigma\to\sigma\to\sigma}(\text{if}^{st}))\ 1$$

$$= \lambda\overline{y}^{D_\sigma^{ab}}.\lambda\overline{z}^{D_\sigma^{ab}}.\biguplus\{abs_\sigma(\text{if}^{st}(x,y,z))\,|\,x\in D_{bool}^{st}, abs_\sigma(y)\leq\overline{y}, abs_\sigma(z)\leq\overline{z}\}^\circ$$

$$= \lambda\overline{y}^{D_\sigma^{ab}}.\lambda\overline{z}^{D_\sigma^{ab}}.\biguplus\{abs_\sigma(\bot_{D_\sigma^{st}}), abs_\sigma(y), abs_\sigma(z)\,|\,abs_\sigma(y)\leq\overline{y}, abs_\sigma(z)\leq\overline{z}\}^\circ$$

by the standard semantics of the conditional

$$= \lambda\overline{y}^{D_\sigma^{ab}}.\lambda\overline{z}^{D_\sigma^{ab}}.\biguplus\{\overline{y},\overline{z}\}^\circ \qquad (\S)$$

by monotonicity of abs_σ and since abs_σ is onto (Lemma 4.8)

$$= \lambda\overline{y}^{D_\sigma^{ab}}.\lambda\overline{z}^{D_\sigma^{ab}}.\bigsqcup\{\overline{y},\overline{z}\}$$

since $\biguplus X^\circ = \bigsqcup X$ for finite, complete lattices (Abramsky, 1985)

and so we have the result by extensionality.

□

Note that we have equality in the step marked by (§), where we would have to replace this by $\leq$ if the abstraction map for the type σ was not onto.

In the case that $\sigma = A$, we have that

$$E^{ab}\,[[\text{if}_{bool\to A\to A\to A}]]\ \rho^{ab} = \lambda\overline{x}^2.\lambda\overline{y}^2.\lambda\overline{z}^2.\overline{\text{if}_A}(\overline{x},\bigsqcup\{\overline{y},\overline{z}\})$$

$$= \lambda\overline{x}^2.\lambda\overline{y}^2.\lambda\overline{z}^2.\overline{x}\ \textbf{and}\ (\overline{y}\ \textbf{or}\ \overline{z})$$

and so this abstract interpretation of the conditional can be seen as a generalization of the interpretation given in Mycroft (1981).

4.2.2.3 Abstract interpretation of *hd*

Lemma 4.19

$$E^{ab}\,[[hd]]\,\rho^{ab} = abs_{Alist\to A}(E^{st}\;[[hd]]\,\rho^{st})$$

Proof

In this proof we will denote the standard semantics of *hd* by hd^{st}.

$$(abs_{Alist\to A}(hd^{st}))\,\bar{L} = \biguplus\{abs_A(hd^{st}(L))\,|\,L\in Conc_{Alist}(\bar{L})\}^{\circ} \quad \text{Fact 3.10}$$

(1)If $\bar{L}=0$, then the only L in $Conc_{Alist}(0)$ is $\bot_{D^{st}_{Alist}}$ (Fact 4.9) and so we obtain $\bot_{D^{ab}_{A}}$ for the above as both hd^{st} and abs_A are strict.

(2)If $\bar{L}$ is any other element of D^{ab}_{Alist}, then the concretization of $\bar{L}$ contains lists, L, with defined heads, and $abs_A(hd^{st}(L))$ for these will be 1 and hence the result.

□

If we were to use the two-point domain for the abstract interpretation of the type *Alist*, then it can easily be shown that $abs_{Alist\to A}(hd^{st}) = \lambda x^2.x$.

4.2.2.4 Abstract interpretation of *tl*

Lemma 4.20

$$E^{ab}\,[[tl]]\,\rho^{ab} = abs_{Alist\to Alist}(E^{st}\;[[tl]]\,\rho^{st})$$

Proof

In this proof we will denote the standard semantics of *tl* by tl^{st}.

$$(abs_{Alist\to Alist}(tl^{st}))\,\bar{L} = .\biguplus\{abs_{Alist}(tl^{st}(L))\,|\,L\in Conc_{Alist}(\bar{L})\}^{\circ} \quad \text{Fact 3.10}$$

(1)If $\bar{L}$ is 0, then as $Conc_{Alist}$ is strict (Fact 4.9), and tl^{st} and abs_{Alist} are strict, we have the result.

(2)If $\bar{L}$ is 1, then L is in the concretization of $\bar{L}$ if and only if L is the bottom list or partial or infinite. Taking the tail of such a list returns one of the bottom list, a partial list or an infinite list, and the least upper bound of the abstraction of these things is 1.

(3)If $\bar{L}$ is 2 or 3, then the concretization of $\bar{L}$ contains, besides other things, all the finite lists. Taking the tail of a list which has only an undefined head returns a list with no bottom elements, and so we can get 3 for both 2 (finite lists with bottom elements) and 3. We obtain the result since we take the least upper bound.

□

If we were to use the two-point domain for the abstract interpretation of the type *Alist*, then it can easily be shown that $abs_{Alist\to Alist}(tl^{st}) = \lambda x^2.x$.

4.2.2.5 Abstract interpretation of *cons*

Lemma 4.21

$$E^{ab}\,[[cons]]\,\rho^{ab} = abs_{A\to Alist\to Alist}(E^{st}\;[[cons]]\,\rho^{st})$$

Proof

We denote the standard semantics of *cons* by $cons^{st}$ in the following proof.

$$abs_{A\to Alist\to Alist}(cons^{st})\ \bar{a}\ \bar{L} =$$

$$\bigsqcup\{abs_{Alist}(cons^{st}\ a\ L) \mid a \in Conc_A(\bar{a}), L \in Conc_{Alist}(\bar{L})\}^{\circ} \qquad \text{Fact 3.10}$$

We give two examples of the calculation for two pairs of arguments from the table. The others follow in a similar manner.

$$(1)\ (abs_{A\to Alist\to Alist}(cons^{st}))\ 0\ 0 = \bigsqcup\{abs_{Alist}(cons^{st}(\bot_{D_A^{st}}, \bot_{D_{Alist}^{st}}))\}^{\circ}$$

Fact 4.9

$$= \bigsqcup\{1\}^{\circ}$$

$$= 1 \qquad \text{(P10)}$$

$$(2)\ (abs_{A\to Alist\to Alist}(cons^{st}))\ 1\ 2$$

$$= \bigsqcup\{abs_{Alist}(cons^{st}\ a\ L) \mid a \in D_A^{st}, L \in Conc_{Alist}(2)\}^{\circ}$$

The most defined result of the above formula is going to be when we have a total element for the first argument to the $cons^{st}$ and an element from $D_A^{st}*.\bot_{D_A^{st}}.D_A^{st}*.nil$ for the second element, in which case $cons^{st}\ a\ L$ is a finite list with bottom elements and so the formula collapses to 2, as in the table. The other six cases follow in a similar manner.

□

If we wish to use the two-point domain for the abstract interpretation of the type *Alist*, then it can easily be shown that $abs_{A\to Alist\to Alist}(cons^{st}) = \lambda x^2.\lambda y^{D_{Alist}^{st}}.1$.

4.2.2.6 Abstract interpretation of the case statement

Lemma 4.22

$$E^{ab}[[case]]\ \rho^{ab} \geq abs_{\sigma\to(A\to Alist\to\sigma)\to Alist\to\sigma}(E^{st}\ [[case]]\ \rho^{st})$$

Proof

We denote the standard interpretation of the case statement by $case^{st}$ in the following proof.

$$(abs_{\sigma\to(A\to Alist\to\sigma)\to Alist\to\sigma}(case^{st}))\ \bar{s}\ \bar{f}\ \bar{L}$$

$$= \bigsqcup\{abs_{\sigma}(case^{st}\ s\ f\ L) \mid abs_{\sigma}(s) \leq \bar{s}, abs_{A\to Alist\to\sigma}(f) \leq \bar{f}, abs_{Alist}(L) \leq \bar{L}\}^{\circ} \qquad (\S)$$

Fact 3.9

We will give two examples for $\bar{L}$.

(1)If $\bar{L} = 0$, then $L = \bot_{D_{Alist}^{st}}$ in (§) by Fact 4.9, and $case^{st}\ s\ f\ \bot_{D_{Alist}^{st}} = \bot_{D_{\sigma}^{st}}$. The result then follows from the strictness of abs_{σ}.

(2)If $\bar{L} = 1$, then we have that $L \in D_A^{st}*.\bot_{D_{Alist}^{st}} \cup D_A^{st\,\omega}$ and so $case^{st}\ s\ f\ L = f\,(hd\,(L), tl\,(L))$. We have that $a = hd(L)$ can be any element in D_A^{st}, and that $L' = tl\,(L)$ is in the same set as L. Hence (§) becomes

$$\biguplus\{abs_\sigma(f\ a\ L') \mid abs_{A\to Alist\to\sigma}(f) \le \bar{f}, abs_A(a) \le 1, abs_{Alist}(L') \le 1\}^\circ$$

There is no way to simplify this other than by expanding out $abs_\sigma(f\ a\ L')$ and replacing $=$ by $\le$ by the semi-homomorphic property of abstraction (Proposition 3.19) to obtain

$$\begin{aligned}
&\biguplus\{abs_\sigma(f\ a\ L') \mid abs_{A\to Alist\to\sigma}(f) \le \bar{f}, abs_A(a) \le 1, abs_{Alist}(L') \le 1\}^\circ\\
&\quad \le \biguplus\{(abs_{A\to Alist\to\sigma}(f))\ (abs_A(a))\ (abs_{Alist}(L'))\\
&\qquad\quad \mid abs_{A\to Alist\to\sigma}(f) \le \bar{f}, abs_A(a) \le 1, abs_{Alist}(L') \le 1\}^\circ\\
&\quad = \biguplus\{\bar{f}\ 1\ 1\}^\circ\\
&\quad = \bar{f}\ 1\ 1 \qquad \text{(P10)}
\end{aligned}$$

The other two cases follow in a similar manner. We note that the inequality is produced in both of the other two cases for the same reason as the above. Finally, $\bar{s}$ only appears in the case that $\bar{L}$ is 3 as *nil* is a total list and so only appears in the concretization of 3.

□

This is the only constant we consider for which we will not be able to obtain equality between the abstract interpretation and the abstraction of the standard interpretation (except for the conditional if the abstraction maps of the base domains are not onto). This is because *case* is not only a higher-order function, but the functional argument is applied to (parts of) one of the other arguments, and so our requirement about safety means we end up with the inequality.

If we were to use the two-point domain for the abstract interpretation of *Alist*, then it can easily be shown that

$$(abs_{\sigma\to(A\to Alist\to\sigma)\to Alist\to\sigma}(E^{st}\ [[case]]\ \rho^{st})) \le g$$

where

$$g\ \bar{s}\ \bar{f}\ \bar{L} = \begin{cases} \bot_{D_\sigma^{ab}} & \text{if } \bar{L}=0 \\ \bar{s} \sqcup (\bar{f}\ 1\ 1) & \text{otherwise} \end{cases}$$

4.3 Some example abstract interpretations

We give the abstract interpretation for some standard functions. Note that *map* is a higher-order function.

length [] = 0
length (*x*:*xs*) = 1 + *length xs*

sumlist [] = 0
sumlist (*x*:*xs*) = *x* + *sumlist xs*

append [] *ys* = *ys*
append (*x*:*xs*) *ys* = *x*:(*append xs ys*)

$$reverse\ [\,] = [\,]$$
$$reverse\ (x{:}xs) = append\ (reverse\ xs)\ (x{:}[\,])$$

$$map\ f\ [\,] = [\,]$$
$$map\ f\ x{:}xs = (f\ x){:}(map\ f\ xs)$$

Wadler (1987) and Burn (1987a) show how to derive the abstract interpretation of a function using the parameterized semantics given in section 3.2.2 and using this interpretation. Here we content ourselves with giving the results for our examples. Table 2 gives the abstract interpretation of *sumlist*, *length* and *head*.

Table 2
Abstract interpretation of *sumlist*, *length*, and *hd*

$\overline{xs}$	$\overline{sumlist}(\overline{xs})$	$\overline{length}(\overline{xs})$	$\overline{hd}(\overline{xs})$
0	0	0	0
1	0	0	1
2	0	1	1
3	1	1	1

The abstract interpretation of *reverse* and *tl* are given in Table 3.

Table 3
Abstract interpretation of *reverse* and *tl*

$\overline{xs}$	$\overline{reverse}(\overline{xs})$	$\overline{tl}(\overline{xs})$
0	0	0
1	0	1
2	2	3
3	3	3

Table 4 gives the values of $\overline{append}\ \overline{xs}\ \overline{ys}$.

Table 4
Abstract interpretation of *append*

$\overline{ys} \backslash \overline{xs}$	0	1	2	3
0	0	1	1	1
1	0	1	1	1
2	0	1	2	2
3	0	1	2	3

Remembering that we are working in a (mono-)typed framework, Table 5 gives the values of $\overline{map}\ \overline{f}\ \overline{xs}$ for a *map* of type $(int \rightarrow int) \rightarrow list\ int \rightarrow list\ int$.

It can seen that these abstract interpretations capture our intuitions about the definedness of functions. For example, the function *sumlist* is undefined (has value 0 in the abstract domain) whenever the argument is not a finite list with no undefined elements in it (has the value 2 in the abstract domain). The only slightly curious result is the value of $\overline{map}\ (\lambda x^2.0)\ 3$ which is 3 rather than 2 (recalling that $\lambda x^2.0$ represents the bottom function

Table 5
Abstract interpretation of *map*

$\overline{xs} \backslash \overline{f}$	$\lambda\overline{x}^2.0$	$\lambda\overline{x}^2.x$	$\lambda\overline{x}^2.1$
0	0	0	0
1	1	1	1
2	2	2	3
3	3	3	3

and applying the bottom function to each element of a finite list returns a finite list all of whose elements are bottom). The value 3 is correct because when *map* is applied to the empty list, which has 3 as its abstract interpretation (as it is a finite list with no bottom elements in it!), then it returns the empty list. As the abstract interpretation has to capture all possible results of an application of *map*, then the result in this case has to be 3.

4.4 Two theorems

Since the abstract domains and abstraction maps for the base types satisfy the conditions of the framework, and the abstract interpretations of the constants satisfy the constant criterion, we have the following two theorems for this abstract interpretation. They follow directly from Theorems 3.25 and 3.26, and so are presented without proof. In section 5 they are used to give two theorems for determining evaluation transformers and proving the evaluation transformer model correct.

Theorem 4.23 (Context-free definedness theorem)

If $f : \sigma_1 \rightarrow \cdots \sigma_n \rightarrow \tau$ and

$$(E^{ab}\, [[f\,]]\, \rho^{ab})\ \top_{D^{ab}_{\sigma_1}} \cdots \top_{D^{ab}_{\sigma_{i-1}}}\ \overline{s_i}\ \top_{D^{ab}_{\sigma_{i+1}}} \cdots \top_{D^{ab}_{\sigma_n}} = \overline{t}$$

then for all $e_j : \sigma_j,\ j \neq i$, for all $s_i \in Conc_{\sigma_i}(\overline{s_i})$, we have

$$E^{st}\, [[f\,]]\, \rho^{st}\, E^{st}\, [[e_1]]\, \rho^{st} \cdots E^{st}\, [[e_{i-1}]]\, \rho^{st}\, s_i\, E^{st}\, [[e_{i+1}]]\, \rho^{st} \cdots E^{st}\, [[e_n]]\, \rho^{st} \in Conc_\tau(\overline{t})$$

□

We note that the concept of the information being true in any context is captured by putting $\top_{D^{ab}_{\sigma_j}}$ for the jth argument, $j \neq i$ where we are testing the ith argument. This is because all the elements of the standard domain abstract to something which is less than or equal to the top of the abstract domain.

Theorem 4.24 (Context-sensitive definedness theorem)

Given $f : \sigma_1 \rightarrow \cdots \rightarrow \sigma_n \rightarrow \tau$ and an application $f\ e_1 \cdots e_n : \tau$, if

$$E^{ab}\, [[f\,]]\, \rho^{ab}\, E^{ab}\, [[e_1]]\, \rho^{ab} \cdots E^{ab}\, [[e_{i-1}]]\, \rho^{ab}\, \overline{s_i}\, E^{ab}\, [[e_{i+1}]]\, \rho^{ab} \cdots E^{ab}\, [[e_n]]\, \rho^{ab} = \overline{t}$$

then for all $s_i \in Conc_{\sigma_i}(\overline{s_i})$

$$E^{st}\, [[f\,]]\, \rho^{st}\, E^{st}\, [[e_1]]\, \rho^{st} \cdots E^{st}\, [[e_{i-1}]]\, \rho^{st}\, s_i\, E^{st}\, [[e_{i+1}]]\, \rho^{st} \cdots E^{st}\, [[e_n]]\, \rho^{st} \in Conc_\tau(\overline{t})$$

□

5. Evaluation transformers

Having developed an abstract interpretation which captures the idea of evaluators, we are now able to apply the correctness result of the abstract interpretation framework in order to be able to determine evaluation transformers. As a result of the discussion in section 3.4.9, we will give theorems for determining both context-free and context-sensitive evaluation transformers. We will show, by means of an example, that the latter can sometimes give more information.

5.1 Context-free evaluation transformers

Theorem 5.1

Suppose that f is a function of type $\sigma_1 \rightarrow \cdots \sigma_n \rightarrow \tau$, and that $\overline{f}$ is the abstract interpretation of f. If

$$\overline{f}\ \top_{D_{\sigma_1}} \cdots \top_{D_{\sigma_{i-1}}}\ \overline{s_i}\ \top_{D_{\sigma_{i+1}}} \cdots \top_{D_{\sigma_n}} \leq \overline{t}$$

then when the evaluator corresponding to $\overline{t}$ is allowed by the semantic criterion to evaluate an application of f, the evaluator corresponding to $\overline{s_i}$ is allowed to be used for the evaluation of the ith argument to f.

Proof

Given any application $f\ e_1 \cdots e_n$ there are two cases.

(1)Suppose $E^{st}\ [[e_i]]\ \rho^{st} \in Conc_{\sigma_i}(\overline{s_i})$. Then the evaluation of e_i may initiate a non-terminating computation. However, in this case, we are assured by Theorem 4.23 that

$$E^{st}\ [[f\ e_1 \cdots e_n]]\ \rho^{st} \in Conc_\tau(\overline{t}).$$

Since ξ is was allowed to evaluate the expression by the semantic criterion, we have that the original expression must have had bottom as its semantics because ξ fails to terminate on any elements in $Conc_\tau(\overline{t})$. Thus it is safe to initiate a non-terminating computation when evaluating the ith argument.

(2)If $E^{st}\ [[e_i]]\ \rho^{st} \notin Conc_{\sigma_i}(\overline{s_i})$ then, since we have chosen an evaluator which terminates when evaluating all expressions denoting not in $Conc_{\sigma_i}(\overline{s_i})$, no divergent computation will be initiated in evaluating e_i and so the evaluation strategy satisfies the semantic criterion.

□

If the maximum $\overline{s_i}$ satisfying the criterion is chosen, then this will give the maximum amount of evaluation allowed of the ith argument. Lesser amounts of evaluation are also permissible. In the examples, we will find the maximum allowable evaluator.

A context-free evaluation transformer must be determined for each argument to a function. For each possible evaluator of an application of a function, the transformer must give an evaluator. The evaluator ξ_0 means that it is not safe to do any evaluation of an expression. If it is not safe to do any evaluation of a function application, then it is not safe to do any evaluation of an argument.[9] Thus all evaluation transformers will give ξ_0 at ξ_0.

[9] This is true by our definition of safety. However, if one was to have a looser definition of safety which just ensured that no non-terminating computation was initiated unless the semantics of the original expression was undefined, then the evaluation of such an expression may terminate and so it would be perfectly safe to evaluate it. However, this potentially wastes machine resources for we may not need

Examples of determining the evaluation transformers for functions are now given. The function *reverse* has a list as its result and therefore an application of *reverse* may appear in the context of being evaluated by any of the evaluators ξ_0 to ξ_3. From the above discussion the evaluation transformer will be ξ_0 at ξ_0. We will denote the evaluation transformer for the ith argument of a function f by F_i, that is, the name of the function in upper case letters, subscripted by the argument number. This notation has been borrowed from Hughes (1985). Thus we have determined that

$$REVERSE_1(\xi_0) = \xi_0$$

We must determine the values for the other possible evaluators.

The evaluator ξ_1 corresponds to the point 0 and so we put in the value 0 on the right-hand side of the above test and determine the maximum $\bar{s}$ such that

$$\overline{reverse}\ \bar{s} \leq 0$$

From the abstract interpretation of *reverse* in Table 3 we find that the maximum value is 1 which corresponds to ξ_2, and so

$$REVERSE_1(\xi_1) = \xi_2$$

We can see that this is intuitively true by noting that ξ_1 is asking for an expression to be evaluated to head normal form and that *reverse* must traverse the entire list before it can create the first *cons* cell, so the list must be finite if it is to be able to give a result in head normal form.

Corresponding to the evaluator ξ_2 we have the point 1, and from the abstract interpretation we see the maximum point satisfying the condition is again 1, and thus the evaluation transformer is ξ_2 at ξ_2. Note that in this case we have that $\overline{reverse}$ 1 is 0, which is strictly less defined than 1. This says that it is impossible for *reverse* to return a list which is partial or infinite.

Finally, the point 2 corresponds to the evaluator ξ_3, and the abstract interpretation says that the maximum $\bar{s}$ satisfying the criterion is 2, and so ξ_3 is a safe evaluator for the argument in this case. We interpret this as saying that for an application of *reverse* to return a finite list with no bottom elements, then it must be given a finite list with no bottom elements as an argument. The evaluation transformer for *reverse* is given in Table 7.

For functions such as *length* and *sumlist*, which have results which come from flat domains like integers and booleans, there is only ever one sensible evaluator for an application which does any work, namely ξ_1, and so we have only to determine the evaluation transformer at that point. The evaluation transformers of these functions are given in Table 6. When determining the evaluation transformers for a function which returns a function as its result, if the function eventually grounds to a type whose abstract interpretation is a flat domain, then the evaluation transformer only needs to be determined at ξ_1. Otherwise, the function eventually grounds to an element of type *Alist* and so the evaluation transformer must be determined at each of the points ξ_1 to ξ_3.[10]

the value of the expression. Moreover, our abstract interpretation is not able to give us this information. However, see Mycroft and Nielson (1983) and Abramsky (1985).

[10] This is in contrast with Burn (1987a, 1987b), where it is said that, since such a function returns a functional result, it can only ever be evaluated with ξ_1. Whilst this is correct if the entire expression to be evaluated is just an application of the function, it is not true in general, for such a function can be applied as part of a reduction sequence being evaluated with evaluator ξ_2 or ξ_3, where there are enough

As an example of the use of Theorem 5.1 for a function of more than one argument, we find the evaluation transformer for the first argument of *append* when a safe evaluator for the application is ξ_2. Using the above test, we find the maximum $\bar{s}$ such that

$$\overline{append}\ \bar{s}\ 3 \leq 1$$

noting that 3 is the top of the abstract domain for lists, and that 1 corresponds to the evaluator ξ_2. From the abstract interpretation of *append* given in Table 4, we find that the maximum value of $\bar{s}$ is 1, and thus

$$APPEND_1(\xi_2) = \xi_2.$$

The rest of the evaluation transformer for the first argument and the evaluation transformer for the second argument can be determined in a similar manner, and are given in Table 8.

The evaluation transformers for *map* are given in Table 9.

Table 6
Evaluation transformers for *sumlist*, *length* and *hd*

E	$SUMLIST_1(E)$	$LENGTH_1(E)$	$HD_1(E)$
ξ_0	ξ_0	ξ_0	ξ_0
ξ_1	ξ_3	ξ_2	ξ_1

Table 7
Evaluation transformers for *reverse* and *tl*

E	$REVERSE_1(E)$	$TL_1(E)$
ξ_0	ξ_0	ξ_0
ξ_1	ξ_2	ξ_1
ξ_2	ξ_2	ξ_2
ξ_3	ξ_3	ξ_2

Table 8
Evaluation transformers for *append*

E	$APPEND_1(E)$	$APPEND_2(E)$
ξ_0	ξ_0	ξ_0
ξ_1	ξ_1	ξ_0
ξ_2	ξ_2	ξ_2
ξ_3	ξ_3	ξ_3

5.2 Context-sensitive evaluation transformers

Theorem 5.2 (Context-sensitive evaluation transformer theorem)

arguments left to proceed with the reduction sequence after applying the function. We discovered this when defining the parallel abstract machine in Burn (1988b).

Table 9
Evaluation transformers for *map*

E	$MAP_1(E)$	$MAP_2(E)$
ξ_0	ξ_0	ξ_0
ξ_1	ξ_0	ξ_1
ξ_2	ξ_0	ξ_2
ξ_3	ξ_0	ξ_2

Suppose that $f : \sigma_1 \rightarrow \cdots \rightarrow \sigma_n \rightarrow \tau$ and that ξ is a safe evaluator for an application $f\ e_1 \cdots e_n$. If

$$E^{ab}\ [[f]]\ \rho^{ab}\ E^{ab}\ [[e_1]]\ \rho^{ab}\ \cdots\ E^{ab}\ [[e_{i-1}]]\ \rho^{ab}\ \overline{s_i}\ E^{ab}\ [[e_{i+1}]]\ \rho^{ab}\ \cdots\ E^{ab}\ [[e_n]]\ \rho^{ab} \leq \overline{t}$$

then when the evaluator corresponding to $\overline{t}$ is allowed by the semantic criterion to evaluate an application of f, the evaluator corresponding to $\overline{s_i}$ is allowed to be used for the evaluation of the ith argument to f.

Proof

The proof follows exactly as in the proof of Theorem 5.2 except that we appeal to Theorem 4.24 instead of Theorem 4.23.

□

If there is no such $\overline{s_i}$ then it is not safe to do any evaluation of the expression e_i.

The reason for having context-sensitive theorems is that they give more information than context-free ones in the case that more complex domains than the two-point domain are used for the abstract interpretation of base types, or higher-order functions where a functional argument is applied to an expression in the body of the function are used. As an example of the use of this theorem, we will use an application of the function *map*:

$$map\ f\ [\,] = [\,]$$
$$map\ f\ x{:}xs = (f\ x) : (map\ f\ xs)$$

The abstract interpretation, $\overline{map}$, of *map* is given in Table 10, which is just a copy of Table 5.

Table 10
Abstract interpretation of *map*

$\overline{xs}$ $\overline{f}$	$\lambda\overline{x}^2.0$	$\lambda\overline{x}^2.x$	$\lambda\overline{x}^2.1$
0	0	0	0
1	1	1	1
2	2	2	3
3	3	3	3

We will determine the context-sensitive evaluation transformer for the second argument to *map* in the application

$$map\ plus1\ e$$

where *plus*1 is the strict function

$$plus\ 1\ n = n+1$$

and so

$$E^{ab}\ [[plus\ 1]]\ \rho^{ab} = \lambda x^2.x.$$

If the evaluator for the application is ξ_0, then it is not safe to do any evaluation of the second argument, and so the evaluation transformer is ξ_0 at ξ_0.

The evaluator ξ_1 corresponds to 0, and so from the theorem we must find an $\bar{L}$ such that

$$E^{ab}\ [[map]]\ \rho^{ab}\ E^{ab}\ [[plus\ 1]]\ \rho^{ab}\ \bar{L} \leq 0$$

that is,

$$\overline{map}\ (\lambda x^2.x)\ \bar{L} \leq 0$$

From Table 10 we find that the maximum such $\bar{L}$ is 0, which corresponds to ξ_1.

For ξ_2 we must find the maximum $\bar{L}$ such that

$$\overline{map}\ (\lambda x^2.x)\ \bar{L} \leq 1$$

to find the value of the evaluation transformer at ξ_2. The most defined $\bar{L}$ for which this is the case is 1, which corresponds to ξ_2.

Finally, ξ_3 corresponds to 2 and so we must find the most defined $\bar{L}$ such that

$$\overline{map}\ (\lambda x^2.x)\ \bar{L} \leq 2.$$

Here 2 is the maximum element, which corresponds to ξ_3. Thus the evaluation transformer for the second argument to *map* in this application is as follows.

Table 11
A Context-sensitive evaluation transformer for *map*

E	$MAP_2(E)$
ξ_0	ξ_0
ξ_1	ξ_1
ξ_2	ξ_2
ξ_3	ξ_3

If one compares this with the context-free evaluation transformer for the second argument of *map* given in Table 9, then we can see that a stronger evaluator is allowed (ξ_3 instead of ξ_2) when ξ_3 is a safe evaluator for the application. This is because the test for the context-free evaluation transformer had to use $\lambda x^2.1$ in the test of the second argument, and a function which is defined everywhere and a strict function only differ in the way they behave in terms of the definedness of the result on finite lists with bottom elements in them.

6. Implementing the evaluation transformer model of parallel reduction

We designed a parallel reduction model because we wished to explore the implementation of lazy functional languages on parallel architectures. The COBWEB-1 (Hankin *et al.*, 1985) architecture was chosen for study whilst we were working on the model (Karia, 1987). Our first results from abstract interpretation were used to generate parallel SKI-combinator code (Hankin *et al.*, 1986) for the COBWEB machine, which were used in the experiments.

About the time that the study of COBWEB-1 was finished, we had also completed the development of the parallel reduction model. Whilst we learnt a lot from studying a particular concrete architecture, we found that focusing our attention on one particular architecture, and especially one which used SKI-reduction, was limiting our vision. Therefore, we designed an abstract, distributed memory architecture which supported the evaluation transformer model (Bevan *et al.*, 1989). This paper described the data structures needed in a machine, the concept of a task in such a machine, how graphs should be stored, and the communication and synchronization needed by the model. Since the paper was originally written, we have developed the distributed memory architecture in a more systematic way, starting with an infinite machine which supported the evaluation model, and restricting it in a series of steps (Burn, 1988a).

We believe that a fast parallel machine will be made from a number of fast sequential ones. Two fast abstract machines for the sequential implementation of functional languages are the G-machine (Johnsson, 1987; Augustsson, 1987; Burn *et al.*, 1988) and Tim (Fairbairn and Wray, 1987). As we are more familiar with the G-machine, and it has been shown in Burn *et al.* (1988) that the two machines are interconvertible, we have chosen to develop our parallel machine by incorporating the evaluation transformer model of computation into a parallel G-machine, using the results of Burn (1988a). So far we have specified and simulated the shared memory version of the machine (Burn, 1988b).

A more complete overview of the project of which this work forms a part can be found in Burn (1989a).

7. Relationship to other work

Mycroft (1981) was the first to apply abstract interpretation to functional languages, where he developed a framework for abstract interpretation of first-order functional languages over base types with flat domains as standard interpretations of the types.

There are five other higher-order frameworks that we are aware of. We mention first the theory presented in Burn *et al.* (1985) and Hankin *et al.* (1986), to which this work is the closest, being basically a generalization of it to allow abstract domains which are more complex than the two-point domain.

Two other frameworks (Maurer, 1985; Mycroft and Jones, 1985) define abstract domains which model the standard interpretation of the type

$$D \cong A + D \to D$$

although we note that Maurer (1985) also has products and lifting in the above equation. This is in direct contrast to our philosophy of using the type structure of the language in a strong way to allow us to have an abstract interpretation that is computable and as accurate as possible. It is notable that the framework of Maurer (1985) is only designed to cope with strictness analysis.

A further point worth noting is that in our framework we have parameterized only the interpretation of the types and the constants, for this is what we need for our applications. However, in Mycroft and Jones (1985) the meanings of λ-abstraction and application are also parameterized, so making a more general framework. The work is based on logical relations (Plotkin, 1980) rather than domain theory.

In Hudak and Young (1985) the abstract interpretation really is a non-standard semantics, returning for each function a set of variables in which it is strict. The first-order case is equivalent to the first-order case of our work in that it explicitly calculates the set of variables in which a function is strict rather than calculating its characteristic function. To extend the work to higher-order functions, they introduce *strictness ladders*, where the ith element in the strictness ladder seems to give strictness information about the first i arguments given that the function has been applied to i arguments. Their main problem is that they are dealing in a pseudo-untyped framework. Since it is impossible to get finite answers for functions with non-finite type, the framework could probably be reworked to take into account the type information and thus eliminate strictness ladders.

The final higher-order framework is due to Abramsky (1985) and is based on logical relations rather than domain-theoretic ideas. Two dual analyses, *safety* and *liveness*, are developed in a monotone framework. In particular, they are applied to developing respectively a strictness and a termination analysis. Furthermore, conditions are proved which show when the analysis can be raised to the world of continuous functions.

Nielson (1984, 1986, 1988a,b) has given the most complete framework for the abstract interpretation of denotational definitions. Giving an interpretation of a language can be viewed as a two-step process, first translating the language into some standard "meta-language" (for example, the λ-calculus with constants), and then giving an interpretation of the meta-language. In Nielson (1984), which is overviewed in Nielson (1986), a meta-language is presented which is powerful enough to give the denotational definition of most programming languages. It cannot, however, express the denotation of languages with storable procedures.

The outstanding feature of the meta-language is that it has a two-level type system, with the intuition that the top-level types represent the type of compile-time objects and run-time objects have bottom-level types. In using the framework, it is the interpretation of the bottom-level types that is changed, while the interpretation of the top-level types is fixed in all interpretations.

To apply the framework to our problem of testing the definedness of functions expressed in the λ-calculus with constants, we note that we wish to change the interpretation of all of the base types in the language, and so these would be made into bottom-level types. Their interpretation would then be allowed to change.

Due to a technical restriction on the constants allowed in the framework of Nielson (1984, 1986), namely that they be *contravariantly pure*, Nielson's original work was not able to give an abstract interpretation to our entire language. A type is contravariantly pure if there is a bottom-level type as the first argument to the function space constructor. Thus, all our higher-order constants like the conditional could not be treated in the framework. This situation has since been remedied in Nielson (1988a,b), where the restriction of contravariant purity has been weakened. In the first paper, the resulting theory is applied to proving the strictness result of Burn *et al.* (1986), as well as the results in Mycroft and Jones (1985).

More recently, other techniques have been developed for finding out information similar to that available from the abstract interpretation given in section 4 of this chapter. Wadler and Hughes (1987) build on the work of Hughes (1985) to give a backwards analysis technique based on the mathematical concept of a projection (an idempotent function which is at most as defined as the identity function). The results it gives are related to evaluation transformers, but they are not the same, and higher-order functions cannot be dealt with. At the moment, the relationship between the two pieces of work is unclear, but Burn (1989b) proves a relationship between a certain class of projections and a certain class of abstract interpretation.

The information we need for determining evaluation transformers is related to the question of how much information must be put into a function in order to produce a certain amount from the function. Dybjer (1987) gives an analysis which takes the information that is required as output of a function and determines its inverse image. Again it is restricted to first-order functions.

Other authors are using some of the implementation ideas mentioned in section 6. Their work can be traced through the references in that section.

8. Conclusion

Functional languages are interesting candidates for parallel evaluation because, having the Church–Rosser property, redexes may be reduced in any order, and hence in parallel, whilst still obtaining the same answer from a program, modulo termination. This implicit parallelism, in the implementation, could free the programmer from the complex problem of trying to write a complex program consisting of a number of communicating processes.

The problem is to know which redexes to reduce in a program. Using the intuition of lazy evaluation, that no infinite process is started unless the result of the program is undefined, we developed a parallel reduction model which also had this property. For an implementation, this means that the fairness of the scheduling strategy for tasks is not an issue; if the program terminated when evaluated lazily, then it will also terminate when evaluated in parallel with this reduction model, no matter what scheduling strategy is chosen. As a corollary of this, if the program produces an answer, there will be no infinite processes left in the machine when the answer has been produced. It also means that we are able to use fast sequential abstract machines as a basis for the parallel implementation, for within the evaluation of an expression, the next redex is deterministic. Furthermore, such a model means that there is never any useless work done; only expressions whose values are needed at some time in the running of the program are evaluated. All these lead us to hope that a fast parallel implementation will be possible.

The parallel model needs to know how much evaluation can be done to an argument expression in a function application, so that the argument expression can be evaluated in parallel with the application. This is semantic information. As we were developing a model for implicit parallelism, it must be determinable by a compiler. We developed a framework for abstract interpretation of functional languages, and then a particular abstract interpretation which gave us definedness information about functions. Using the abstract interpretation, and a result relating the operational and denotational semantics of functional programs, we were able to obtain the information required by the evaluation model.

Thus, a parallel implementation of a lazy functional language is possible, where the parallel model is a natural extension of lazy evaluation, and where the parallelism information can be extracted by a compiler. In a final section we gave pointers to papers which discuss the realization of this model in parallel architectures.

9. Acknowledgements

The work in the main body of this chapter was part of the author's PhD thesis. Chris Hankin was the supervisor, and we spent many long hours discussing ideas and problems together. We were fortunate in having the expert knowledge about domain theory of Samson Abramsky available to us. At the GEC Hirst Research Centre, David Bevan was also very helpful in discussing the ideas. Work on the architectures side has been done with a number of other colleagues at Hirst. Rajiv Karia was responsible for the COBWEB work, and was involved in the early architectural work. John Robson worked on the Spineless G-machine. Latterly, David Lester has been applying his skills to the project. We have benefited greatly from our discussions with Simon Peyton Jones. We have also been fortunate in being able to discuss ideas with other partners in the ESPRIT project, notably Werner Damm from the University of Oldenburg and the CSELT group.

This work was partially funded by ESPRIT 415: Parallel Architectures and Languages for AIP - A VLSI-Directed Approach.

10. References

Abramsky, S., *Abstract Interpretation, Logical Relations and Kan Extensions*, Draft Manuscript, Imperial College, University of London, October, 1985.

Arbib and Manes, *Arrows, Structures and Functors: The Categorical Imperative*, Academic Press, New York and London, 1975.

Augustsson, L., *Compiling Lazy Functional Languages, Part II*, PhD Thesis, Department of Computer Sciences, Chalmers University of Technology, 1987.

Bevan, D.I., Burn, G.L., Karia, R.J., and Robson, J.D., Design Principles of a Distributed Memory Architecture for Parallel Graph Reduction, To be published in *The Computer Journal*, 1989.

Burn, G.L., *Abstract Interpretation and the Parallel Evaluation of Functional Languages*, PhD Thesis, Department of Computing, Imperial College of Science and Technology, University of London, 1987.

Burn, G.L., Evaluation Transformers - A Model for the Parallel Evaluation of Functional Languages (Extended Abstract), in Kahn, G., (ed.), *Proceedings of the Third International Conference on Functional Programming Languages and Computer Architecture*, Portland, Oregon, USA, 14-16 Sept., 1987, Springer Verlag LNCS vol. 274, pp. 446-470.

Burn, G.L., Developing a Distributed Memory Architecture for Parallel Graph Reduction, To be published in *Proceedings of CONPAR 88*, UMIST, 12-16 September 1988, Cambridge University Press.

Burn, G.L., A Shared Memory Parallel G-machine Based on the Evalaution Transformer Model of Computation, Draft manuscript, distributed at *Workshop on the Implementation of Lazy Functional Languages*, Aspenas, Sweden, 5-8 September, 1988.

Burn, G.L., Overview of a Parallel Reduction Machine Project II, *Proceedings of PARLE 89*, Eindhoven, The Netherlands, 12-16 June, 1989, Springer-Verlag LNCS 365, pp. 385-396.

Burn, G.L., A Relationship Between Abstract Interpretation and Projection Analysis, *Draft Manuscript*, June, 1989.

Burn, G.L., Hankin, C.L., and Abramsky, S., Strictness Analysis for Higher-Order Functions, *Science of Computer Programming*, *7*, November 1986, pp.249-278.

Burn, G.L., Peyton Jones, S.L., and Robson, J.D., The Spineless G-Machine, *Proceedings of the 1988 ACM Conference on Lisp and Functional Programming*, 25-27 July, 1988, Snowbird, Utah, pp. 244-258.

Cousot, P., and Cousot, R., Systematic Design of Program Analysis Frameworks, *Conference Record of the 6th ACM Symposium on Principles of Programming Languages*, pp. 269-282, 1979.

Dybjer, P., Inverse Image Analysis, *Proceedings of the 14th ICALP*, July, 1987, Karlsruhe, Germany, Springer-Verlag LNCS 267, pp. 21-30.

Fairbairn, J., and Wray, S., TIM: A Simple, Lazy Abstract Machine To Execute Supercombinators, in Kahn, G., (ed.), *Proceedings of the Third International Conference on Functional Languages and Computer Architecture*, Portland, Oregon, USA, 14-16 September, 1987, Springer-Verlag LNCS 274, pp. 34-45.

Gierz, G., Hofmann, K.H., Keimel, K., Lawson, J.D., Mislove, M. and Scott, D.S., *A Compendium of Continuous Lattices*, Springer-Verlag, 1980.

Hankin, C.L., *Personal Communication*

Hankin, C.L., Burn, G.L., and Peyton Jones, S.L., A Safe Approach to Parallel Combinator Reduction (Extended Abstract), *Proceedings ESOP 86 (European Symposium on Programming)*, Saarbrucken, Federal Republic of

Germany, March 1986, Robinet, B., and Wilhelm, R. (eds.), Springer-Verlag LNCS 213, pp. 99-110.

Hankin, C.L., Osmon, P.E., and Shute, M.J., COBWEB: A Combinator Reduction Architecture, in : *Proceedings of IFIP "International Conference on Functional Programming Languages and Computer Architecture,* Nancy, France, 16-19 September, 1985, Jouannaud, J.-P. (ed.), Springer-Verlag LNCS 201, pp. 99-112.

Hennessy, M., and Plotkin, G.D., Full Abstraction for a Simple Parallel Programming Language, *Proceedings MFCS '79,* Becvar, J. (ed.), Springer-Verlag LNCS 74, 1979.

Hudak, P., and Young, J., *A Set-Theoretic Characterisation of Function Strictness in the Lambda Calculus,* Research Report YALEU/DCS/RR-391, Department of Computer Science, Yale University, 1985, Also presented at the *Workshop on Abstract Interpretation,* University of Kent at Canterbury, August, 1985.

Hughes, R.J.M., Strictness Detection in Non-Flat Domains *Workshop on Programs as Data Objects,* DIKU, Denmark, 17-19 October, 1985, Ganzinger, H., and Jones, N.D., (eds.) Springer-Verlag LNCS 217, pp. 112-135.

Johnsson, T., *Compiling Lazy Functional Languages,* PhD Thesis, Department of Computer Sciences, Chalmers University of Technology, 1987.

Karia, R.J., *An Investigation of Combinator Reduction on Multiprocessor Architectures,* PhD Thesis, University of London, 1987.

Maurer, D., Strictness Computation Using Special λ-Expressions, *Workshop on Programs as Data Objects,* DIKU, Denmark, 17-19 October, 1985, Ganzinger, H., and Jones, N.D., (eds.) Springer-Verlag LNCS 217, pp. 136-155.

Mycroft, A., *Abstract Interpretation and Optimising Transformations for Applicative Programs,* PhD. Thesis, University of Edinburgh, 1981.

Mycroft, A., and Jones, N.D., A new framework for abstract interpretation, *Workshop on Programs as Data Objects,* Copenhagen, Denmark, October 17-19, 1985, Ganzinger, H., and Jones, N.D., (eds.) Springer-Verlag LNCS 217, pp. 156-171.

Mycroft, A., and Nielson, F., Strong Abstract Interpretation Using Power Domains (Extended Abstract) *Proc. 10th International Colloquium on Automata, Languages and Programming:* Springer-Verlag LNCS 154, Diaz, J. (ed.), Barcelona, Spain, 18-22 July, 1983, 536-547.

Nielson, F., *Abstract Interpretation Using Domain Theory,* PhD Thesis, University of Edinburgh, 1984.

Nielson, F., Abstract Interpretation of Denotational Definitions, *Proceedings STACS 1986,* Springer-Verlag LNCS vol. 210.

Nielson, F., Strictness Analysis and Denotational Abstract Interpretation, *Information and Computation, 76,* 1, January 1988, pp. 29-92.

Nielson, F., *Two-Level Semantics and Abstract Interpretation,* Report ID-TR:1988-33, Instituttet for Datateknik, Danmarks Tekniske Hojskole, Bygning 344, DK-2800 Lyngby, Denmark.

Plotkin, G.D., A Powerdomain Construction, *SIAM J. Comput. 5* 3 (Sept. 1976) 452-487.

Plotkin, G.D., Lambda definability in the full type hierarchy, in Seldin, J.P., Hindley, J.R., *To H.B. Curry: Essays on combinatory logic, lambda-calculus and formalism,* Academic Press, 1980.

Scott, D., *Lectures on a Mathematical Theory of Computation,* Tech. Monograph PRG-19, Oxford Univ. Computing Lab., Programming Research Group, 1981.

Scott, D., Domains for Denotational Semantics, *Automata, Languages and Programming, Proceedings of the 10th International Colloquium,* Nielsen M, and Schmidt, E.M., (eds.), Springer-Verlag LNCS 140, 1982, 577-613.

Smyth, M.B., Power Domains, *Journal of Computer and System Sciences 16,* 1978, 23-36.

Smyth, M.B., and Plotkin, G.D., The category-theoretic solution of recursive domain equations, *SIAM J. Comput. 11* 4 (1982), pp.761-783.

Turner, D.A., An Overview of Miranda,[11] *SIGPLAN NOTICES,* December 1986.

Wadler, P., *Strictness Analysis on Non-Flat Domains (by Abstract Interpretation over Finite Domains),* in Abramsky, S., and Hankin, C., (eds), *Abstract Interpretation of Declarative Languages,* Ellis Horwood, 1987. (Originally distributed on the FP mailboard November, 1985.)

[11] Miranda is a trademark of Research Software Ltd.

Wadler, P., and Hughes, R.J.M., Projections for Strictness Analysis, in Kahn, G., (ed.), *Proceedings of the Third International Conference on Functional Languages and Computer Architecture,* Portland, Oregon, USA, 14-16 September, 1987, Springer-Verlag LNCS 274, pp. 385-407.

Chapter 4

Using Resolution for a Sound and Efficient Integration of Logic and Functional Programming

P.G. Bosco, C. Cecchi, C. Moiso
CSELT, via Reiss Romoli 274, 10148 Torino, Italy
E. Giovannetti
Università di Torino, Corso Svizzera 185, 10149 Torino, Italy
and
C. Palamidessi
Università di Pisa, Corso Italia 40, 56100 Pisa, Italy

1. Introduction: the reasons for the integration and our global approach

Logic programming and functional programming are the two most popular styles of declarative programming, and there has been some debate in the past on their respective advantages and disadvantages. It is not surprising that attempts to resolve this discussion by combining the two paradigms and thus the advantages of both (without their drawbacks) were developed relatively quickly. For a survey see Bellia and Levi (1986).

Logic programming is characterized by two essential features: non-determinism, i.e. search-based computation, and logical variable, i.e. unification. The bidirectionality of unification, in contrast with the unidirectionality of pattern-matching, allows procedure invertibility and partially determined data structures, and thus a more compact and flexible programming style. The central role of search (or *don't know* non-determinism) in logic programming languages is connected with their being halfway between theorem provers and standard programming languages, which makes them particularly adequate for artificial intelligence applications, or as executable specification languages.

Since its introduction with Lisp, functional programming has always been characterized by the notion of higher-order function, which is a clean and powerful abstraction and structuring tool. Higher-order function definitions can implement generic procedures that take procedures as parameters ("abstraction"); functions being passed as actual parameters to higher-order functions are able to act as local definitions with static scoping ("structuring"), due to the well-known equivalence between *let*-construct and functional application. Modern functional languages are, moreover, characterized by the presence of a polymorphic typing system, whose introduction with ML successfully achieved the goal of combining the (static) checking capability of strong typing with the flexibility of the untyped languages. Even more sophisticated type systems have been invented, which also can encompass in one formal framework and therefore in one type-checking algorithm those composition mechanisms for programming in the large, such as (parametric) modules and abstract data types, which had formerly to be distinct and superimposed on the underlying language. From a user point of view, this development, exemplified in the module constructs of Standard ML, is analogous to the history, from

Pascal to Ada, of modern imperative languages. Unlike the latter, functional languages share with logic languages the formal simplicity (function application as the only control construct) that derives from being immediately based on a well-established mathematical theory, in this case lambda-calculus.

Our approach to integration is based on two levels. The upper level, or user interface, represented by the experimental language IDEAL (Bosco and Giovannetti, 1986), is a sort of extension of a Miranda-like functional language with logical operators (where the absence of negation prevents the occurrence of Curry's paradox) or, equivalently, a higher-order extension of a Horn-clause logic language. This level is still subject to evolution, as it should eventually contain all the desirable features for this kind of language for different fields of applications. Some theoretical aspects still have to be deepened, in particular concerning a satisfactory definition and semantic characterization of the programming problems we want to be able to solve. The lower level is a Prolog-like language augmented with directed equality, which is represented at the present stage of research by K-LEAF (Bosco *et al.*, 1987b), an evolution and refinement of the language LEAF (Barbuti *et al.*, 1986). It is a rather well-assessed language, with a clear and original declarative semantics, and a sound and complete operational semantics, namely flattening plus outermost SLD-resolution.

The upper level is mapped into this intermediate language by means of a transformation which removes the higher-order features by compiling it into first-order clauses (through a meta-interpretation).

2. An IDEAL integrated language by examples

This section attempts to motivate the use of a powerful integrated logic plus functional language through a non-naive example, i.e. specification/implementation of a simple logic simulator which can also be used as a kernel fault-finder. The reader familiar with LISP (or ML) and Prolog should be able to understand without a formal introduction to the language (which is presented in section 4).

2.1 A simple logic simulator written in IDEAL

A logic simulator is a tool used to test the behaviour of logic circuits. It reproduces an abstract evolution of the circuit state: the continous range of wire voltage is discretized (into 0 and 1, or High, Low and Unknown) and gates are modeled by functions on the chosen discrete domains. The simple logic simulator we have developed in IDEAL is an event-driven simulator (i.e. the state of the circuit is computed only when an event that may change it happens), where the voltage is discretized into two values (0 and 1).

It is based on functions working on streams of pairs (events): the first element of an event denotes the time when it occurred, while the second represents the state of a wire ($0 or $1). A stream describes the history of a wire:
the stream d(t0,$1):(t1,$0):(t2,$1):..., where ti<ti+1, denotes a wire that has state $1 from t0 to t1, state $0 from t1 to t2, etc.

The simulated circuit is mapped into an IDEAL function of type:

stream(event)#....#stream(event) → stream(event)#....#stream(event)
m times n times

where m and n are the number of inputs and outputs of the circuit, respectively. The value of the function in correspondence to a m-tuple of streams denoting the histories of the input wires is the n-tuple of streams denoting the histories of the output wires.

The construction of such a function is based on the composition, according to the topology of the circuit, of functions simulating the behaviours of gates in the circuit. A gate is simulated by an IDEAL function from stream(s) of events to one stream of events. The function corresponding to a gate G processes an event in an input stream in two phases: the first computes the new state of the output wire of G (i.e. the second component of a new event inserted into the output stream), according to the boolean function associated with the gate, while the second phase computes the time when the new value is delivered (i.e. the first component of the event), according to the delay time associated with the gate. Therefore the higher-order features present in IDEAL are used to parameterize a (function representing a) gate with respect to the computed boolean function, along with the delay time. In fact, basic logic components (e.g. andgates, orgates, etc.) are defined as instances of general schemes (e.g. 2-input gates) which in turn are higher-order functions taking a boolean function as input and returning a mapping on streams as output (see the definitions of *gate1* and *gate2* below). The following function definitions correspond to *halfadder* and *fulladder* circuits.

```
sum_of((S,C)) = S.            % pair selectors

carry_of((S,C)) = C.

halfadder(X, Y) = let sum  = xorgate(X, Y),      % halfadder
                      carry = andgate(X, Y)
                  in (sum, carry).

fulladder(X, Y, C) = let aux1 = halfadder(X, Y),       % fulladder
                         aux2 = halfadder(sum_of(aux1), C),
                         carry = orgate(carry_of(aux1), carry_of(aux2))
                     in (sum_of(aux2), carry).
```

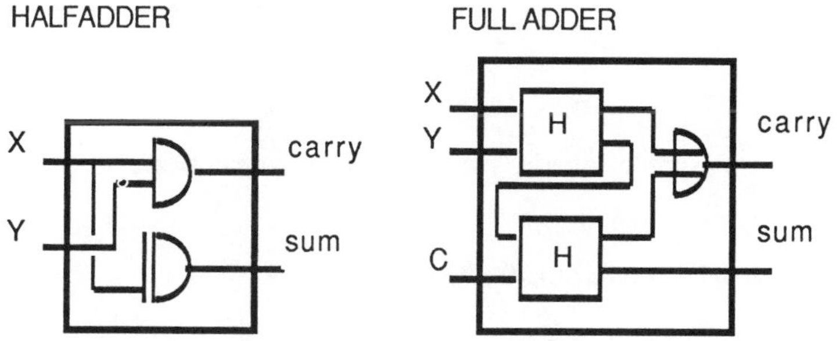

Note that there is a one-to-one correspondence between either the functional description of circuits or their graphic representation and the IDEAL functions used for their simulation.

Moreover, as suggested by many researchers in the field of hardware specification/ description languages which have adopted a higher-order functional framework for their languages, recursion can be exploited to synthetically describe circuits with a regular structure, and, thus, in our case, to define the functions simulating them. The following definition shows the IDEAL function, defined by recursion on the number of bits, simulating the behaviour of a n-bit adder:

```
adder@0@([X0],[Y0]) =
                        let h = halfadder(X0,Y0)
                        in ([sum_of(h)],carry_of(h) ).

adder@s(N)@([Xn|X],[Yn|Y]) =
                        let add = adder@N@(X,Y),
                            fulladd = fulladder(Xn,Yn,carry_of(add))
                        in ([sum_of(fulladd) | sum_of(add)],carry_of(fulladd) ).
```

whose type is:

int → list(stream(event)) # list(stream(event)) → list(stream(event)) # stream(event)

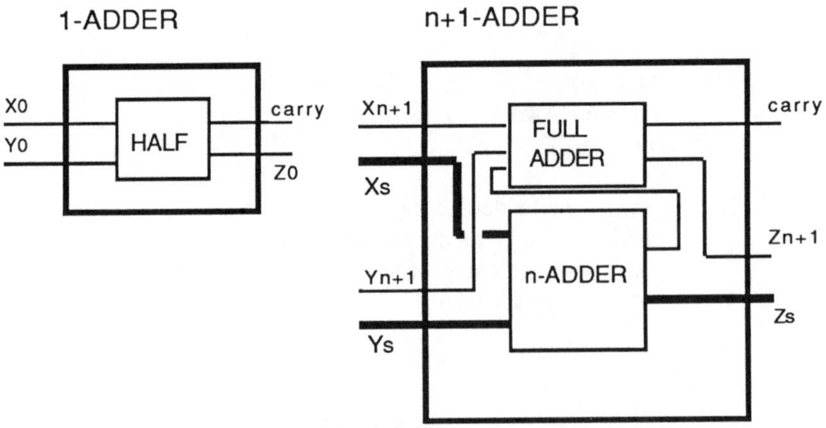

The following are simple queries to show how streams are processed by logic components.

?- andgate(d(0,$0):d(2,$1):lnil, d(0,$0):d(3,$1):lnil) = R.

R = d(0,$0):d(2,$0):d(4,$0):d(5,$1):lnil

?- fulladder(d(0,$0):lnil,d(0,$0):d(1,$1):lnil, d(0,$0):d(2,$1):lnil) = (S,C).

S = d(0, $0):d(2, $0):d(3,$0):lnil
C = d(0, $0):d(2, $0):d(4,$0):d(5, $1):lnil

When cyclic circuits, i.e. with feed-back as in flip-flops, are simulated, the special event *stop* is inserted at the end of the input streams; in this way it is possible to recognize the end of the simulation. This section is completed with the full description of the developed logic simulator.

Type definitions

```
stream(X) ::= lnil;   X:stream(X).  % Stream declaration.
value ::= $0 ; $1.                  % Boolean values.
event::= d(int, value) ; stop.      % Events are bool. values, paired to time values.
```

Boolean functions

```
bnot@$0 = $1.
bnot@$1 = $0.   % not
band@$0 = λx.$0.
band@$1 = λx.x.% and
bor@$0 = λx.x.
bor@$1 = λx.$1.% or
...
```

The following functions are the actual basic logic components corresponding to basic logic gates, through which the functions simulating the circuits are built; they are instantiations of the generic gates, *sgate1* and *sgate2*, with one and two inputs, respectively.

```
notgate(In) = sgate1(In, bnot, 2).
andgate(In1,In2) = sgate2(In1, In2, band, 2).
...
```

The simulated generic gates initialize an actual simulated gate with its actual boolean function (F) and delay (D); moreover, the states of the input and output wire are initialized to $0.

```
sgate1(In, F, D) = d(0,$0):kdelay(gate1@F@In, D).
sgate2(In1,In2,F,D)= d(0,$0):kdelay(gate2@F@($0,$0)@(In1,In2),D).
```

The function *kdelay* adds a time delay D to the time fields of all the events of an input stream.

```
kdelay(stop:In, D) = stop:lnil.
kdelay(lnil, D) = lnil.
kdelay(d(T,V):In, D) = d(T+D, V):kdelay(In, D).
```

The behaviour of a generic 1-input gate is simulated by *gate1* whose first argument is the computed boolean function, while the second is the stream denoting the history of the input wire.

```
gate1@F@stop:L = stop:lnil.
gate1@F@lnil = lnil.
gate1@F@d(T,V):In = d(T,F@V):gate1@F@In.
```

The behaviour of a generic 2-input gate is simulated by *gate2* whose first argument is the computed boolean function, the second is the pair (*ov1,ov2*) of the input wires states, while the last is the pair of the streams denoting the history of the two input wires. Informally, let *d(t1,v1)* and *d(t2,v2)* be the first elements of the two input streams:

(1) If *t1=t2* then the new state of the output wire is *F@v1@v2* and the state of the input wires is updated to *v1* and *v2*, respectively;
(2) If *t1<t2* then the new state of the output wire is *F@v1@ov2* and the state of the first input is updated to *v1*;
(3) The case *t1>t2* is symmetric to the previous one;

```
gate2@F@(OV1,OV2)@(stop:L, In2) = stop:lnil :- non_stop(In1).
gate2@F@(OV1,OV2)@(In1, stop:L) = stop:lnil.
gate2@F@(OV1,OV2)@(lnil, In2) = gate22(In2, F, OV1) :- non_end(In2).    % End of strea
gate2@F@(OV1,OV2)@(In1, lnil)  = gate21(In1, F, OV2) :- non_stop(In1).  % End of strea
gate2@F@(OV1,OV2)@(d(T1,V1):In1, d(T2,V2):In2) =
    if T1=T2 then
            d(T1, F@V1@V2):gate2@F@(V1,V2)@(In1, In2)                    % (1)
    else if T1<T2 then
            d(T1,F@V1@OV2):gate2@F@(V1,OV2)@(In1,d(T2,V2):In2)   % (2)
    else
            d(T2,F@V2@OV1):gate2@F@(OV1,V2)@(d(T1,V1):In1,In2).  % (3)

non_end(d(T,V):L).
non_stop(lnil).
non_stop(L) :- non_end(L).
```

The function *gate21* (resp. *gate22*) simulates a generic 2-input gate with just the first (resp. second) active input.

```
gate21(stop:L, F, OV) = stop:lnil.
gate21(lnil, F, OV) = lnil.
gate21(d(T,V):In, F, OV) = d(T, F@V@OV):gate21(In, F, OV).
gate22(stop:L, F, OV) = stop:lnil.
gate22(lnil, F, OV) = lnil.
gate22(d(T,V):In, F, OV) = d(T, F@OV@V):gate22(In, F, OV).
```

2.2 Turning the logic simulator into a fault-finder.

Each logic component has an extra parameter that specifies its status *ok/faulty*. If the status of a component is *ok*, it behaves according to the specifications provided in the previous section. The *faulty* status is defined as a structured term, according to the following type declaration:

```
faults ::=      ok ;                % Basic faults; ok is no faults.
                up ;                % Short circuit: the output wire is always $1.
                down ;              % Broken wire: the output is always $0.

                andg(faults) ; ...  %Faults in basic components.

                half(faults,faults)              % Faults in a half adder
                full(faults,faults,faults)       % Faults in a full adder
                n_add(list(faults),faults)       % Faults in a n-adder.
```

Complex circuits have structured fault descriptors in order to hold together the status of all subcomponents; a fault descriptor of a circuit is essentially its parse tree, where the leaves of the tree report the status of the basic gates. The following are the definitions of possibly faulty components:

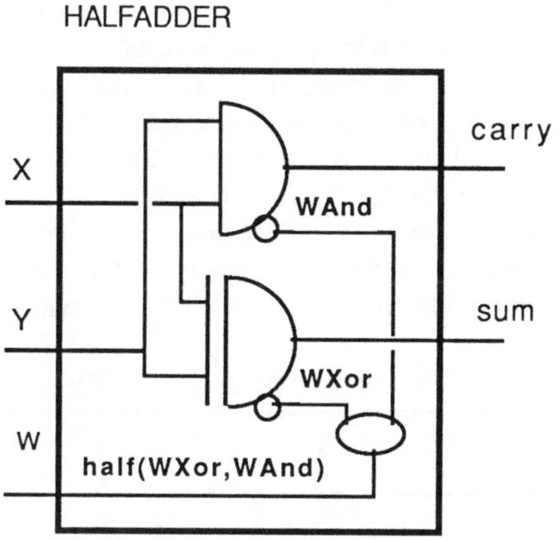


```
xorgate@ok@(X,Y) = sgate2(X, Y, bxor, 1),        % As before
xorgate@xorg(up)@(X,Y) = sgate2(X, Y, lx.$1, 1),
xorgate@xorg(down)@(X,Y) = sgate2(X, Y, lx.$0, 1):

            faults → stream # stream → stream.


halfadder@half(WXor,WAnd)@(X, Y) =
            ( xorgate@WXor@(X,Y),  andgate@Wand@(X,Y) )
```

```
fulladder@full(WH1, WH2, WOr)@(X,Y,C)=
        let half1 = halfadder@WH1@(X,Y),
            half2 = halfadder@WH2@(sum_of(half1), C),
            carry = orgate@WOr@(carry_of(half1), carry_of(half2))
        in (sum_of(half2),  carry).


adder@0@n_add([], WH)@([X0],[Y0])=
        let h = halfadder@WH@(X0,Y0)
        in ([sum_of(h)], carry_of(h) ),


adder@s(N)@n_add([WFull | WRest], WH)@([Xn| Xs],[Yn| Ys])=
        let nadd  = adder@N@n_add(WRest, WH)@(Xs, Ys),
            fulla  =  fulladder@WFull@( Xn , Yn, carry_of(nadd))
        in ([sum_of(fulla) | sum_of(nadd)] , carry_of(fulla) ) :

int → faults → list(stream) # list(stream) → list(stream) # stream.
```

The type of *adder@n* is an instance of the polytype *faults* → *IN* → *OUT* where *IN*, *OUT* stand for the type of the input and of the output of an n-adder, respectively. Any circuit representation *CR* has a type that is an instance of the above one. Therefore, for any circuit representation *CR*, the following is a well-typed IDEAL query: *?-CR@F@In=Out.*, where *F*, *In* and *Out* are expressions of the appropriate type. The simulation of a component is obtained by having *F* and *In* instantiated and *Out* unbound. Fault diagnosis is performed by letting *F* unbound and *In*, *Out* instantiated. Test-pattern generation requires *F* and *Out* specified and *In* unbound. The following table displays the various modes of activation of the above query and its interpretation for each of them. An instantiated expression is annotated with the symbol *+*; a *?* marks an uninstantiated one.

Instanciation Modes				Interpretations
?-CR@Fault@Inp=Out				
	+	+	?	Simulation
	?	+	+	Fault-finding
	+	?	+	Test-pattern Generation

The following query simulates the processing of a faulty 2-bit adder on the bit-strings [$0,$1] and [$1,$1]. The adder has two faults: the *carry* is *down* in both the half adder and the full adder.

```
?- ( [Z1, Z0],  C) = adder@s(0)@fault@([x1, x0], [y1, y0])
        where
x1 = d(0,$0):lnil,  x0 = d(0,$1):lnil,
y1 = d(0,$1):lnil,  y0 = d(0,$1):lnil,
fault = n_add([full(half(xorg(ok),andg(ok)),half(xorg(ok),andg(ok)),orgate(down))],
          half(xorg(ok),andg(down))).
```

```
C   = d(0,$0):d(2,$0:d(4,$0):d(6,$0):lnil,
Z1 = d(0,$0):d(2,$0):d(4,$1):lnil,
Z0 = d(0,$0):d(2,$0):lnil.
```

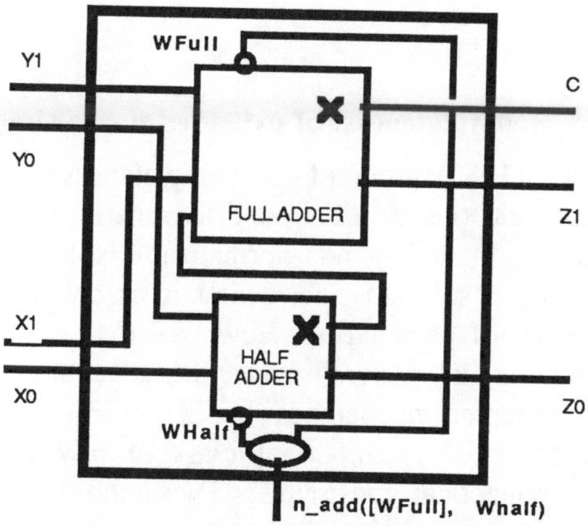

The next query is to diagnose the faults in a 2-adder whose observed behaviour is that of the previous query. The values of the circuit output-wires are taken from the previous simulation, whilst in a realistic application they would be obtained from the observation of a physical device.

```
?- adder@s(0)@What@ ([x1, x0], [y1, y0])= ( [z1, z0] , c)
                where x, x0, y1, y0, z1, z0, c: those of the previous query.
```

```
What =  n_add([full(half(xorg(ok),andg(ok)),
    half(xorg(ok),andg(ok)),
    orgate(ok))],
        half(xorg(ok),andg(down))).
```

```
What =  n_add([full(half(xorg(ok),andg(ok)),
    half(xorg(ok),andg(ok)),
    orgate(down))],
        half(xorg(ok),andg(down))).
...
```

3. The first-order language K-LEAF

In this section the first-order logic-plus-functional language Kernel LEAF, or K-LEAF, is presented; its operational semantics is merely SLD resolution, without the addition of any E-unification algorithm, following the technique used in Barbuti *et al* (1986) and Tamaki (1984) and in agreement with the results of Bosco *et al* (1988a): function nestings are flattened into conjunctions of atoms, so that functional dependencies are explicitly represented. The flattened form of a K-LEAF program can be considered as a program in an intermediate language on the same alphabet, which we will call flat LEAF (or Flat-LEAF).

3.1 The rationale

3.1.1 Completeness (and incompleteness) of extended narrowing

A consequence of Hullot's (1980) proof of the completeness of narrowing as equation-solving algorithm for canonical (i.e. confluent and terminating) equational systems is that termination only plays a role in finding non-normalizable solutions. Therefore, if one is only interested in normal-form solutions, narrowing is complete for (globally) confluent theories even in the absence of termination. However, if the system is not terminating, global confluence, which is in general undecidable, cannot be reduced to local confluence. Hence the completion methods based on rule superposition cannot be exploited. Nevertheless, there is an important class of rewrite systems where global confluence is ensured by syntactical constraints. Two conditions are sufficient: (1) *non-ambiguity*, i.e. there is no superposition between rules, and (2) *left-linearity*, i.e. in the left-hand sides (lhs) of a rule each variable only occurs once (see, for example, Klop, 1985)). These conditions are usually satisfied in the context of a Logic plus Functional (L+F) programming language, where the rules are function definitions in the ordinary deterministic sense. Narrowing is therefore complete for this kind of systems with respect to normalizable solutions, while non-terminating computations and infinite data structures are allowed.

To reduce the search space, essentially two refinements which do not cause loss of completeness have been proposed. One is the basic narrowing introduced by Hullot (1980) in the same paper, the other is the *normalizing* narrowing considered in Fay (1979) and Rety *et al.* (1985), where a reduction to normal form is performed after each narrowing step, thus leading, in general, to a remarkable shrinkage of the search space. In the case of non-terminating systems, this latter refinement cannot be applied, while the former, in general, causes loss of completeness. However, we conjecture that, if the non-terminating system is non-ambiguous and left-linear, completeness of basic narrowing (w.r.t. normalized solutions and equations between normalizable terms) is preserved.

In order to define an interpreter for an integrated L+F language we must consider conditional equations. A result in this direction can be found in Kaplan (1984), where *conditional narrowing* is proved complete for *canonical conditional systems* if, in addition, no *extra variables* (i.e. variables that do not occur in the lhs's of the rules) occur in the corresponding right-hand sides (rhs) or conditions. For confluent but possibly non-terminating systems completeness only holds, once again, with respect to normalized solutions, while for basic conditional narrowing we make the same conjecture as in the unconditional case.

If, on the other hand, extra variables are present in the conditions, global confluence is no longer sufficient to guarantee completeness w.r.t. normalizable solutions and, similarly, global canonicity is no longer sufficient for absolute completeness (Giovannetti and Moiso, 1988). The slightly stronger notion of *level-confluence* (Giovannetti and Moiso, 1988) can be profitably introduced: the rewriting relation $\rightarrow_R$ can be defined as the infinite union $\cup\{\rightarrow_i\}$ of the i-level rewriting relations for all i from 1 to ω, where the 1-level relation is that established by non-conditional rules, while level i+1 is the rewriting that can be performed with conditions being verified by means of i-level rewriting. Conditional narrowing is then complete only if confluence separately holds for each i-level rewriting relation $\rightarrow_i$ (level-confluence), and if, moreover, the termination property holds.

With level-confluent but non-terminating systems, conditional narrowing may fail to find even normalizable solutions, when the conditions for the application of some rewrite rule contain an existential equation that can only be satisfied by a non-normalizable solution for which the two sides of the equation are also non-normalizable. For example, given the system

$$f \rightarrow c(f)$$
$$g \rightarrow b \ :- \ x = c(x)$$

the normal-form solution b of the equation $\leftarrow g=z$ cannot be found, because in order to rewrite g into b one should solve the equation $x=c(x)$, whose solution f, which is not normalizable and instantiates the two sides of the equation to the non-normalizable terms f and $c(f)$, cannot be computed by narrowing.

The possibility of extra variables and non-termination should, however, be retained in the definition of a general L+F integrated language based on HCL-with-equality, and able to cope with infinite data structures.

On the other hand, no problem is raised by allowing non-equational literals: conditional narrowing can easily accommodate clauses where equalities and ordinary predicates are mixed together in any combination. Predicates have merely to be considered boolean functions. More precisely, a relational atom p must be read as a rewrite rule $p\rightarrow true$ when it is a clause head, as an equation $p=true$ when occurring in a clause body or in the goal (rules corresponding to trivial critical pairs between predicates and functions may have to be added). The pure logic component can thus be handled by the same computational mechanism as the functional component.

3.1.2 Theories with constructors, partial functions and "data"-Herbrand Universe

An important design choice is the restriction to *equational theories with constructors*, where the distinction is made between functions and data constructors. This allows us to characterize theories which essentially define *functional programs*, ruling out equations that could better be viewed as program properties. For example, if *nil* and *cons* are considered data constructors, the equations

append (nil,x) = x
append (cons(x,y),z) = cons(x,append (y,z)),

such that the left parts contain only one (outermost) function symbol are function definitions, while an equation like

append (append (x,y),z) = append (x,append (y,z))

would be considered a program property and would not be allowed as a program component.

If this distinction between functions and data constructors is present, the natural semantics is that only ground data terms, i.e. terms built from (constants and) constructors only, are (denote) individuals in the model for the language. If the application of a function f to an argument a gives rise to a non-terminating computation we do not want to consider $f(a)$, or any of the functional terms generated in the infinite rewriting sequence of $f(a)$, as the "value" of $f(a)$, therefore the possible loss of $f(a)$ as a solution of some equation corresponds to the intended semantics. This amounts to considering the Herbrand Universe as consisting of ground data terms only, with exclusion of all the functional terms. For example, the equation $?\text{-}\ f(a)=f(a)$ is no longer true in the model if the function f happens to be non-terminating, or non-defined, in a.

In this framework the fact that conditional narrowing may not be able to find some non-normalizable solutions, instead of being a drawback, becomes a perfectly adequate behaviour. On the contrary, the algorithm exhibits the opposite flaw: it still produces undesired "non-data" solutions or solutions that instantiate the two sides of the equation to non-data terms. For example, the goals $?\text{-}\ g(f(a))=g(z)$, $?\text{-}\ f(a)=f(x)$ would succeed by trivial syntactical unification. Therefore, if soundness with respect to the advocated semantics is to hold, the "final" step consisting in the syntactical unification between the two sides of the equation has to be allowed between data terms only, and forbidden between "true" functional terms.

This can be achieved by considering the equality symbol in the goal (and in the bodies of program clauses) as an ordinary predicate represented by a new symbol $\equiv$, whose definition is given by a clause $c_i \equiv c_i$ for each constant c_i, and a clause

$$d_i(x_1, ..., x_m) \equiv d_i(y_1, ..., y_m) \text{ :- } x_1 \equiv y_1, ..., x_m \equiv y_m$$

for each m-adic constructor d_i. These clauses, as already noted, should be respectively intended as

$$c_i \equiv c_i \rightarrow true \qquad \text{and}$$
$$d_i(x_1, ..., x_m) \equiv d_i(y_1, (x_m \equiv y_m) = true$$

Narrowing steps using these clauses are then able to simulate the desired restriction of the final syntactical-unification step of the algorithm.

If function definitions are constrained to be left-linear and with non-overlapping patterns, the language belongs to the the class called III_n in Bergstra and Klop's (1986) classification of rewriting systems. This class is characterized by (1) left-linearity, (2) (weak) non-ambiguity, and (3) the additional condition that the body literals have the form $t_i=e_i$ where the e_i are ground *unconditional normal forms*, i.e. are ground terms not unifiable with any of the lhs's of the heads. In our case, all the e_i simply coincide with the boolean constant *true*. III_n rewriting systems are level-confluent, and, moreover, every body equation, having the form $p=true$, or $(t1 \equiv t2)=true$, trivially satisfies the property that every solution instantiates the two sides of the equation to normalizable terms.

This allows us to conclude that basic conditional narrowing is complete with respect to normalized solutions, which (as noted above) are all the solutions we are interested in.

As a marginal comment, predicate definitions need not be non-overlapping, since they always have the constant *true* as implicit rhs's, and, therefore, the possible ambiguity is inessential. In rewriting system terminology, *weak* non-ambiguity still holds. A side-effect of this property is that the left-linearity constraint can also be dropped for predicates, provided that clauses of the form

$$p(x,x) \text{ :- } B_1, ..., B_n$$

are intended as

$$p(x,y) \text{ :- } x \equiv y,\ B_1,\dots,\ B_n.$$

The left-linearity constraint cannot be relaxed for functional heads, because it could introduce head superpositions, i.e. ambiguity.

Note, however, that the above transformation modifies the meaning of the clause, since what in the original version was syntactic unification becomes data-term unification in the new form.

The semantics we are trying to define has also to cope with the important role played by non-strict functions, i.e. those which may terminate even on inputs from non-terminating functions. They are typically selectors which operate on infinite data structures, as in the following example:

nats(n) =[n|nats(s(n))]
first-three([x,y,z | l]) =[x,y, z]

By composing the selector *first-three* with the generator *nats* we can write, for example, a term *first-three(nats(0))* whose value is a finite data structure, i.e. its normal form *[0, 1, 2]*. Now if the compositional character of meaning has to be preserved, also non-normalizable terms, like *nats(0)*, which may occur as subterms within normalizable expressions, have to be assigned a denotation, which is bound to be the class of all the partial results of the infinite computation along with the usual approximation ordering on them or, equivalently, the infinite data structure defined as the limit of this class (or, to be more precise, its least upper bound). This means that the Herbrand Universe has to be augmented with the indefinite constant $\bot$ (bottom) and with all the other "partial terms", i.e. data terms containing some occurrence of $\bot$, and then possibly completed into an algebraic cpo by adding all the missing lubs, i.e. the infinite objects.

In the model, $\equiv$ is strict equality, i.e. equality between total finite terms, while $=$ is non-strict equality, which may also hold on infinite (or partial) terms.

3.1.3 Flattening and resolution

Basic narrowing can be transformed into resolution if the program and the goal are previously flattened through the elimination of function nestings. Resolution of the flattened goal using the transformed program augmented with the clause $x=x$ is able to exactly mimic basic narrowing. In particular, SLD-resolution has been shown to be equivalent to a refined strategy of narrowing (Bosco *et al.*, 1988a), which eliminates redundant search and results in a considerable gain in efficiency with respect to ordinary narrowing.

In this correspondence (if no distinction is operated between non-strict and strict equalities) resolution with $x=x$ plays two quite different roles. In one of them it binds intermediate variables created by the flattening procedure and not present in the original goal. The binding may therefore be to any term, including functional terms possibly denoting infinite objects. The other case corresponds to the syntactic unification at the end of a narrowing chain. Therefore, soundness with respect to the semantics outlined above can only be achieved if variables are bound to data terms (i.e. terms not containing function symbols) only.

In other words, the equalities originally present in the bodies of the clauses or in the goal have to be dealt with quite differently from those which are introduced by the flattening procedure, between subterms and new intermediate variables; they should be marked so as to restrict resolution with $x=x$ to *data-term unification*. This corresponds exactly to the above-mentioned distinction between = and ≡. Resolution can remain unchanged, as was the case for narrowing, provided the original body and goal equations are written with the symbol ≡ and are only resolved with the above clauses for ≡.

Therefore, in our language the clause bodies can only contain strict equalities, where the new symbol simply becomes a particular kind of predicate, with its own defining clauses. SLD-resolution on flattened programs, equivalent to narrowing, is therefore also complete.

In conclusion, starting from a HCL-with-equality program, where equalities in the bodies and in the goal are interpreted as ≡, with the left-linearity and non-superposition constraints on functions, the narrowing-based goal-solving interpreter can be transformed into a resolution interpreter via the introduction of a flattening compilation phase wholly identical to that described in the earlier version of LEAF (Barbuti *et al.*, 1986).

After flattening, the goal will in general contain both strict equations, which are the original ones, and non-strict equations, which were generated by the flattening procedure. The heads of the program clauses, i.e. the rewrite rules, which may give rise to non-terminating computations, are, of course, non-strict, and therefore must use the symbol =.

3.1.4 Cpo semantics versus standard semantics

The model-theoretic semantics of our language is based on a notion of interpretation, outlined in section 3.1.2, somewhat different from the one customary in first-order logic, i.e. algebraic cpo's instead of unstructured sets. It should be noted that the relation corresponding to ordinary first-order-logic equality is basically ≡ . Non-strict equality when not coinciding with ≡, i.e. equality between infinite terms, is not even semidecidable. It could only be proved by means of inductive methods, but there is no general induction scheme able to derive all the equalities holding between infinite terms. This is not surprising because, even with respect to our new partial-order semantic, non-strict equality may be true in the term model, i.e. the Herbrand model, without being true in every model.

Take, for example, the function definitions

f(a) = c(f(a))
g(a) = c(g(a)).

In the Herbrand model, the denotations of both *f(a)* and *g(a)* are the infinite term *c(c(c(...)))*, which is the lub of the set of the partial results {⊥, c(⊥), c(c(⊥)), c(c(c(⊥))), ...}. Therefore, the non-strict equality *f(a)=g(a)* is true in that model. In an algebraic-cpo model, on the other hand, the denotations of the two terms do not need to be the same. Hence the above equation is not a logical consequence of the previous function definitions, but only an inductive consequence, i.e. a proposition which is true in the initial model. This corresponds to the fact that in the ordinary first-order-logic semantic *f(a)* and *g(a)* have two different denotations even in the Herbrand model, namely the two equivalence classes *{f(a), c(f(a)), c(c(f(a))),...}* and *{g(a), c(g(a)), c(c(g(a))),...}*, which in the partial-order semantic collapse into one, via the substitution of the elements *f(a)* and *g(a)* with ⊥.

The above argument also shows that in this new "functional-logic" semantics it is no longer true that if a set of clauses has a model, then it has a Herbrand model. For instance, there are algebraic-cpo models, but no Herbrand model, for the above set of clauses *{f(a) = c(f(a)), g(a)=c(g(a)), ?-f(a)=g(a)}*. The loss of this fundamental property, however, is not important, because in the programming language the occurrence of the two different equality symbols is not free but restricted to perfectly precise roles. For example, a non-strict equation like $f(a)=g(a)$ is not an acceptable goal. Therefore a non-Herbrand satisfiable set of clauses like that above could never appear. For acceptable sets of clauses, satisfiability always implies Herbrand satisfiability.

The advocated partial-order logic is, in conclusion, not so far from standard Horn clause logic with equality, restricted, of course, to superposition-free (i.e. non-ambiguous) left-linear systems. Every goal solution that can be found in the standard framework by a complete inference system, e.g. narrowing, is also valid - and can therefore be found - in the new logic, with the exception of equations like $f(x)=f(x)$ for f non-defined or non-terminating in x. On the other hand, every acceptable goal - and therefore every equality between total finite terms - which is true with respect to the new semantics (and thus derivable) is also true in the standard semantics.

Nevertheless, the two underlying viewpoints are quite different. The equivalence classes of terms which in the ordinary semantics are the elements of the initial model and so - via *confusion* and the addition of *junk*, to use Goguen's (1986b) terminology - of every model, in the new semantics, instead of being unstructured sets, contain the information on the dynamic structure of the computation, i.e. on the sequences of rewriting steps which are performed in building the equivalence.

The design decisions emerging from the above argument have led us to the definition of a logic+functional programming system which, while at the user interface level is the same as LEAF (Bärbuti *et al.*, 1986), i.e. basically Prolog with equality, is endowed with an operational and model-theoretic semantics which are deeply modified with respect to the earlier version, mainly due to the explicit introduction of the two kinds of equality. An elegant and rigorous completeness result can then be achieved, in contrast to most proposals of L+F-integrated languages. The proof was carried out directly on the flattening+SLD-resolution algorithm, without making reference to narrowing. This is also an indirect formal proof of the above informally argued properties of (conditional) narrowing.

3.2 Syntax of K-LEAF.

The *language alphabet* consists of:

(1) A set **C** of data constructor symbols, including a non-empty subset of 0-adic constructor symbols (data constant symbols),
(2) A set **F** of function symbols,
(3) A set **P** of predicate symbols,
(4) A set **V** of variable symbols,
(5) The special predicate symbols $=$, $\equiv$.

A *data term* is:

(i) A variable symbol, or
(ii) A data constructor application $c(d_1,\ldots,d_n)$, where c is an n-adic data constructor symbol and $d_1,\ldots,d_n$ are data terms.

We denote by **D(V)** the set of data terms, and by **D** the set of ground data terms.

A *term* is:

(i) A data term, or
(ii) A data constructor application $c(t1,\ldots,tn)$, where c is an n-adic data constructor symbol and $t_1,\ldots,t_n$ are terms, or

(iii) A function application $f(t_1,...,t_n)$, where f is an n-adic function symbol and $t_1,...,t_n$ are terms.

We denote by **T(V)** the set of terms, and by **T** the set of ground terms. Terms of the form (iii) will be called *functional terms.*

A <u>header atom</u> is:

(i) A *functional header* $f(d_1,...,d_n) = t$, where f is an n-adic function symbol, $d_1,...,d_n$ are data terms, and t is a term, or

(ii) A *relational header* $p(d_1,...,d_n)$, where p is an n-adic predicate symbol and $d_1,...,d_n$ are data terms.

The header atoms have to satisfy the following two conditions:

(1) Left-linearity: multiple occurrences of the same variable in $(d_1,...,d_n)$ are not allowed;

(2) In a functional header all the variables occurring in t must also occur in $(d_1,...,d_n)$.

A <u>body atom</u> is:

(i) A *strict equation,* that is, a formula of the form: $t_1 \equiv t_2$, where t_1 and t_2 are terms, or

(ii) A *relational atom* $p(t_1,...,t_n)$, where p is an n-adic predicate symbol and $t_1,...,t_n$ are terms.

For any atom or term A , $Var(A)$ denotes the set of variables occuring in A.

A <u>definite clause</u> is a formula of the form:

$$A \leftarrow B_1,..., B_n \qquad (n \geq 0)$$

where A is a header atom and $B_1,..., B_n$ are body atoms. If $n = 0$ then the clause A ← is called a *unit clause* and is denoted by A.

A <u>goal statement</u> is a formula of the form:

$$\leftarrow B_1,..., B_n \qquad (n \geq 0)$$

where $B_1,..., B_n$ are body atoms. If $n = 0$ then the goal is called *empty goal,* and is written ←.

A <u>program</u> W is a set of definite clauses $\{C_1,..., C_m\}$ such that:

for each pair of equational headers $f(d'_1,...,d'_n) = t'$ and $f(d''_1,...,d''_n) = t''$, $f(d'_1,...,d'_n)$ and $f(d''_1,...,d''_n)$ are not unifiable (superposition free).

Example 3.1

The following set of clauses is a correct K-LEAF program:

```
{ plus(0,x) = x.
plus(s(x),y) = s(plus(x,y)).
nat(x) = cons(x,nat(s(x))).
odd(cons(x,cons(y,z))) = cons(x,odd(z)).
sqrlist = cons(0,sqrlist1(0,odd(nat(s(0))))).
sqrlist1(x,cons(y,z)) = cons(plus(x,y),sqrlist1(plus(x,y),z)).
p(x,y,z) ← p1(x,y,z,sqrlist).
p1(x,y,z,w) ← sqr(z,w) ≡ plus(sqr(x,w),sqr(y,w)).
```

sqr(0,cons(x,y)) = x.
sqr(s(x),cons(y,z)) = sqr(x,z). }

The example defines some non-terminating functions, such as *nat* (the list of naturals), *sqrlist* (the list of squares), *odd* (the list of odd numbers); the relation p(x,y,z) denotes all the triples <x,y,z>, such that: $x^2+y^2=z^2$.

Some comments about the definition of the language are in order:

(1) K-LEAF is a first-order language based on Horn clauses with equality.

(2) There are two equality symbols = and ≡, with two different interpretations in the declarative semantics; they are both defined through a set of Horn clauses. Their intuitive meaning is the following:
   (a) =, which occurs only in the heads of K-LEAF programs, is a "definitional" equality, in the sense that it is used to define functions; it closely resembles to the *reducibility* symbol in Tamaki (1984), and the clauses with an equational header can be interpreted as conditional rewrite rules. The atom $f(d_1,\ldots,d_n)$ can be read as either "$f(d_1,\ldots,d_n)$ is equal to t" or "$f(d_1,\ldots,d_n)$ is reducible to t"
   (b) ≡ , which occurs only in the clause bodies or in the goals, is a "testing" equality: the atom $t_1 \equiv t_2$ tests whether the two terms t_1 and t_2 are equal, i.e. if they have the same finite "interpretation": using the terminology of rewriting systems, $t_1 \equiv t_2$ is true if t_1 *and* t_2 have the same (finite) normal form. This kind of equality is the most definite one which preserves continuity, while at the same time being computable.

(3) The presence of two kinds of equalities should not be surprising: for they are found in almost all the functional languages, though usually written by one and the same symbol. For example, in a definition such as

$$\text{fact(X) = if X=0 then 1 else n*fact(n-1)}$$

the first occurrence of = is the non-strict equality = of K-LEAF, while the second is actually K-LEAF's strict equality ≡ . Therefore, the undifferentiated user-syntax = is parsed as = if occurring in a clause head, as ≡ if occurring in a body or in a goal.

(4) The only restrictions on the definition of *clause* concern the header atoms: left-linearity is the only constraint on relational headers, while those on functional headers are:
   (a) The condition of being superposition free;
   (b) $var(t) \subseteq var(f(d_1,\ldots,d_n))$;
   (c) Left-linearity.

   They are necessary conditions to ensure that the interpretation of any functional symbol is actually a function : in the case of relational headers, because multiple occurrences of the same variable would introduce between subterms in predicates an implicit equality test, which, in order to preserve the continuity of the predicates and the functions definable in the language, should be realized through the predicate ≡. In the user syntax this constraint is discarded: a clause like $p(x,x) \leftarrow B_1,\ldots, B_n$ will be automatically transformed by the parser into $p(x,y) \leftarrow x{\equiv}y, B_1,\ldots, B_n$.

3.3 The flat LEAF

In this section we introduce the flat LEAF, a Horn-clause language defined on the same alphabet of K-LEAF, whose operational semantics is merely SLD-resolution, compositions of functions not being allowed. A procedure will be described which transforms every K-LEAF program into a (semantically equivalent) flat LEAF program (called flat form), by flattening functional compositions into conjunctions of functional atoms (i.e. atoms of the form $f(d_1,...,d_n)=x$), explicitly representing input-output dependencies; thus, the operational semantics of K-LEAF is provided by the composition of the flattening procedure with the operational semantics of flat LEAF; flat LEAF can be considered as an intermediate language for implementing K-LEAF, with all the well-known advantages of having a declarative intermediate language.

Some new constraints will be introduced in order to be able to define strategies for executing resolution on flattened K-LEAF programs; moreover, the same constraints will be found to be essential to guarantee consistency from a declarative point of view.

A *flat atom* is

(1) An equational atom $f(d_1,...,d_n) = d$, where $d_1,...,d_n$ and d are data terms, or
(2) A strict equation $d_1 \equiv d_2$, where d_1 and d_2 are data terms, or
(3) A relational atom $p(d_1,...,d_n)$, where $d_1,...,d_n$ are data terms.

In order to define the constraints on the clauses, the following definitions are introduced. If A is a (header or body) atom of the form $t_1 = t_2$ (*equational atom*), then $In(A)$ (input variables) is the set of all the variables occurring in t_1, while $Out(A)$ (output variables or produced variables) is the set of all the variables occurring in t_2. The atom $t_1 = t_2$ is the producer of all the variables in $Out(t_1 = t_2)$. If A is a relational atom or a strict equation then $In(A) = Var(A)$. If A_1, A_2 are equational atoms, then the producer-consumer relationship $\rightarrowtail$ is defined as follows: $A_1 \rightarrowtail A_2$ iff $Out(A_1) \cap In(A_2) \neq \emptyset$.

A definite flat clause is a clause $A \leftarrow B_1,...,B_n$ where $A, B_1,...,B_n$ are flat atoms, and, moreover, the following conditions hold:

(1) The relation $\rightarrowtail$ on the equational atoms of the body is acyclic, that is,

$$\exists\, B_{j1},..., B_{jk}\ (k \geq 1)\ B_{j1} \rightarrowtail ... \rightarrowtail B_{jk} \rightarrowtail B_{j1}$$

(or, equivalently, the transitive closure of $\rightarrowtail$ is an order relation).

(2) If B_i and B_j are equational body atoms, if $i \neq j$ then $Out(B_1) \cap Out(B_2) = \emptyset$ (no multiple productions).

(3) If A is a header, then:
(a) for every variable $x \in Out(A)$, either $x \in In(A)$ or there exists an equational body atom *with definite inputs* B_j such that $x \in Out(B_j)$. B_j *has definite inputs* iff for every variable $y \in In(B_j)$, either $y \in In(A)$ or, recursively, there exists a different equational body atom *with definite inputs* B_i such that $y \in Out(B_i)$.
(b) for every equational atom B_j in the body $Out(B_j) \cap In(A) = \emptyset$ (clauses do not introduce multiple productions).
(c) A must be left-linear (unification does not introduce multiple productions).

(4) For every equational body atom $t_1 = t_2$ there are no multiple occurrences of the same variable in t_2 (right linearity).

A *flat goal* is a goal $\leftarrow B_1,...,B_n$ where $B_1,...,B_n$ are flat atoms and conditions (1), (2) and (4) in the above definition hold (i.e. the relation $\rightarrowtail$ on the equational atoms is acyclic, there are no multiple productions, and there are no multiple occurrences of the same variable in the left part of equational atoms). If $n = 0$ then the goal is the called *empty goal*, and is written $\leftarrow$.

A few comments are in order. Constraints (1) and (2) are necessary to correctly define an outermost strategy of computation with flat programs, as we will show later. Constraint (3a) is necessary for the correctness of function definitions. Finally, constraints (3b), (3c) and (4) are needed to preserve conditions (1) and (2) during the computation.

A *flat program* is a set of definite flat clauses, which satisfy the condition of being superposition free; note that condition (2) is replaced (and implied) by (3c), in ensuring that the function symbols are interpreted as actual functions.

The flattening algorithm is the same as in the original version of LEAF (Barbuti *et al.*, 1986), with ≡ dealt with as an ordinary predicate. The result of the application of the flattening procedure to the program in Example 3.1 is the following set of flat clauses:

```
{ plus(0,x) = x.
  plus(s(x),y) = s(v)← plus(x,y) = v.
  nat(x) = cons(x,v)← nat(s(x)) = v.
  odd(cons(x,cons(y,z))) = cons(x,v)← odd(z) = v.
  sqrlist = cons(0,v1)← sqrlist1(0,v2)=v1, odd(v3)=v2, nat(s(0))=v3.
  sqrlist1(x,cons(y,z)) = cons(v1,v2)←plus(x,y) = v1,sqrlist1(v3,z)=v2,plus(x,y) =v3.
  p(x,y,z) ← p1(x,y,z,w), sqrlist = w.
  p1(x,y,z,w) ← sqr(z,w) = v1,v1 ≡ v2,sqr(x,w) = v3,sqr(y,w)= v4,plus(v3,v4) = v2.
  sqr(0,cons(x,y)) = x.
  sqr(s(x),cons(y,z)) = v ←sqr(x,z) = v. }
```

As the clauses of K-LEAF programs and goals trivially satisfy conditions (1)-(4), the following theorem holds. Let *C* be a K-LEAF clause (a definite clause or a goal). Then *flatc(C)* is a correct flat clause (i.e. it satisfies conditions (1)-(4) of the definition).

3.4 Clauses for equality and strict equality

Given a K-LEAF or a flat LEAF program *W*, there are two sets of clauses, *=(W)* and *≡(W)*, which define, in a Horn-clause style, the axioms for equality and strict equality.

The intended meaning of equations is the (algebraic) congruence relation induced by the clauses (with equational headers) of W, viewed as conditional equivalence axioms. We want this relation to be non-strict, that is, it must hold even if the arguments are both undefined or partially defined (with the same values in the defined component). Note that this condition implies the relation to be non-monotonic. This form of non-strictness allows us to handle functions which are (partially or totally) undefined, or functions whose output is infinite.

Example 3.2

W = { first-three(cons(x,cons(y,cons(z,cons(w,nil))))) = cons(x,cons(y,cons(z,nil))).
ints(N) = cons(N,ints(s(N))).
test(cons(x,cons(y,cons(z,nil)))). }.

first-three is a function which computes the first three elements of its list argument. It does not depend on the remaining part of the argument (w). *ints* is a function which computes an infinite list representing the integer sequence.

If we give to *first-three* a non-strict semantics with respect to w, then the goal

G : ← test(first-three(ints(zero)))

should succeed. Now, consider the flat form of W:

W′ = { first-three(cons(x,cons(y,cons(z,cons(w,nil)))))=cons(x,cons(y,cons(z,nil))).
ints(n) = cons(n,v) ← ints(s(n)) = v.
test(cons(x,cons(y,cons(z,nil)))). }.

and consider the flat form of G:

G′ :← ints(zero) = y, first-three(y) = x, test(x).

In order to solve G′ successfully (and finitely), equations such as *ints(zero) = y* (and the other it entails) also have to be satisfied by undefined or partially undefined argument values.

For the general case of (not necessarily flat) programs, consider the left part $f(t_1,\ldots,t_n)$ of an equational body atom, and assume that the program definition for f does not depend (is not strict) on the ith argument. By definition, if t_i is a functional term $g(u_1,\ldots,u_m)$ then the flattening algorithm introduces an equation of the form $g(u_1,\ldots,u_m) = x$ (*) (and replaces t_i by x in $f(t_1,\ldots,t_n)$). Therefore, we must allow equations such as (*) to be true also when x has an undefined value, since it represents the ith argument of f. This can be achieved by giving a uniform definition of $=(W)$ which forces every equation with a pure variable in the right part to be true for an undefined value of that variable. Note that a similar argument applies to the case where f is not strict only on a component of the ith argument.

Definition 3.1 (Additional clauses for equality)

Given a program W, $=(W)$ is the set of all the clauses of the form

$$f(x_1,\ldots,x_n) = \bot$$

where f is an n-adic function symbol of W, $x_1,\ldots,x_n$ are variable symbols, and $\bot$ is a special symbol, representing the undefined value, and considered as a non-reducible term (in other words, it is an additional data constant).

The clauses in $=(W)$ allow us to solve equations involving functional terms. Note that they can be applied if and only if the other member of the equation is a variable.

Moreover, note that this definition establishes that every function has a special data constant ($\perp$) as a default output value. In the following section we will see that $=(W)$ can equivalently be defined as the set containing only the equation x = x, if we extend the notion of unification by allowing the substitution of a variable with a functional term.

Unlike = , the relation ≡ is intended to model the strict (synctactic) equality over (standard) data terms. ≡ is introduced to provide an equality relation (for example, to test equality between function outputs), which does not affect the monotonic behaviour of the bodies of the clauses. This relation is defined by the standard axioms which define the equality on ground data terms as identity. The following definition gives the axioms as Horn clauses.

Definition 3.2 (Clauses for strict equality)
Given a program W, ≡(W) is the set of all the clauses of the form

(1) $c \equiv c$, for every 0-adic data constructor (data constant) symbol c of W, and
(2) $d(x_1,...,x_n) \equiv d(y_1,...,y_n) \leftarrow x_1 \equiv y_1 ,..., x_n \equiv y_n$, for every n-adic data constructor symbol d of W.

Note that this definition allows us to define ≡ as a strict relation. This would not be case if (2) were replaced by a clause of the form $d(x_1,...,x_n) \equiv d(x_1,...,x_n)$.

3.5 Declarative semantics

The declarative semantics can more naturally be defined both for K-LEAF and for its flat form, i.e. it can formally be given for a general language which is the union of the Kernel form and the flat form, where functional composition is allowed as in K-LEAF, and also non-strict equations in clause bodies and goals are allowed under the constraints of section 3.3, as in the flat form. These constraints, which mirror the original properties of K-LEAF programs, must be retained in the definition of a consistent model-theoretic semantics. In fact, the constraints on (non-strict) equality are an essential feature of the language.

As noted in section 3.1, the natural setting for assigning meanings to possibly partial functions is found in the concept of algebraic CPO.

Let us briefly summarize the related notions. Let X be a set and let ≤ be an *order relation* on X. A set D ⊆ X is a *directed set* iff for any $a, b \in D$ there exists $c \in D$ such that $a, b \leq c$. (X, ≤) is a Complete Partial Order (CPO) iff there exists a minimal element $\perp_X$ (bottom) and every directed set D ⊆ X has a least upper bound $\bigsqcup D \in X$. $a \in X$ is a *finite* (or *algebraic*) element iff for every directed set D, if $a \leq \bigsqcup D$, then $\exists\, d \in D$ $d \leq a$. Let X_0 be the set of algebraic elements of X, and, for $a \in X$, let $\hat{a}$ be the set $\{ b \in X_0 \mid b \leq a \}$. (X,≤) is an *algebraic* CPO iff for every $a \in X$ $\hat{a}$ is a directed set and $\bigsqcup \hat{a} = a$. If (X, ≤) and (Y, ≤) are CPO's, and f is a function from X to Y, then f is *continuous* iff for every directed set D ⊆ X $f(\bigsqcup D) = \bigsqcup_{d \in D} f(d)$. If (X, ≤) and (Y, ≤) are algebraic CPO's, then it is sufficient $f(\bigsqcup D) = \bigsqcup_{d \in D} f(d)$ holds for every directed algebraic set $D \subseteq X_0$. A simple algebraic CPO is the set $LL = \{ \perp_{LL}, true, false\}$, with the ordering $\perp_{LL} \leq true$ and $\perp_{LL} \leq false$ (three-valued boolean CPO). Note that all the elements of LL are algebraic. The formulae of the language receive - from interpretations - truth-values in this CPO: we have therefore a three-valued logic, with "undefined" besides *true* and *false*.

Definition.
Given a Kernel or flat LEAF program W, an *interpretation* for W consists of an algebraic CPO (X, ≤), and a meaning function $[\![\ ]\!]_X$ which assigns to every constructor or function symbol a continuous function on X (of the same arity), and to every predicate symbol a continuous function from X to LL. The meaning of ground terms and atoms (still denoted, for the sake of simplicity, by the symbol $[\![\ ]\!]_X$), is derived by imposing the structural compositionality, i.e.:

$$[\![f(t_1,\dots,t_n)]\!]_X = [\![f]\!]_X(\,[\![t_1]\!]_X,\dots,[\![t_n]\!]_X\,) \quad \text{for } f \in C \cup F \text{ and } t_1,\dots,t_n \in T$$
$$[\![p(t_1,\dots,t_n)]\!]_X = [\![p]\!]_X(\,[\![t_1]\!]_X,\dots,[\![t_n]\!]_X\,) \quad \text{for } p \in P \text{ and } t_1,\dots,t_n \in T$$

The interpretation of non-ground terms and atoms involves, as usual, the notion of *environment*, i.e. a function $\rho : V \to X$, where V is the set of variables.

$$[\![v]\!]_{X,\rho} = v\rho \quad \text{for } v \in V$$
$$[\![f(t_1,\dots,t_n)]\!]_{X,\rho} = [\![f]\!]_X(\,[\![t_1]\!]_{X,\rho},\dots,[\![t_n]\!]_{X,\rho}\,) \quad \text{for } f \in C \cup F,\ t_1,\dots,t_n \in T(V)$$
$$[\![p(t_1,\dots,t_n)]\!]_{X,\rho} = [\![p]\!]_X(\,[\![t_1]\!]_{X,\rho},\dots,[\![t_n]\!]_{X,\rho}\,) \quad \text{for } p \in P,\ t_1,\dots,t_n \in T(V)$$

The non-strict equality, i.e. the symbol =, is interpreted as the identity eq_X on the CPO (X, ≤), i.e.:

$$[\![t_1 = t_2]\!]_{X,\rho} = [\![t_1]\!]_{X,\rho}\ eq_X\ [\![t_2]\!]_{X,\rho} = \begin{cases} true & \text{if } [\![t_1]\!]_{X,\rho} \text{ and } [\![t_2]\!]_{X,\rho} \text{ are identical} \\ false & \text{otherwise} \end{cases}$$

Note that eq_X is non-strict and non-monotonic (and, therefore, non-continuous): for example, $\bot\ eq_X \bot = true$, while $\bot\ eq_X\ \xi = false$, for ξ different from $\bot$.

On the other hand, the symbol ≡ , having to represent a sort of semidecidable test of equality, must be given a continuous interpretation. Hence the largest set on which strict equality can be true is the set of algebraic maximal elements. Maximality ensures that equal elements cannot become distinct by adding more information. Algebraicity guarantees that the comparison can be done in a finite time (by exploring a finite amount of information). A possible solution is the assignment of a fixed interpretation of ≡ which satisfies this requirement, for example:

$$[\![t_1 \equiv t_2]\!]_{X,\rho} = \begin{cases} true \text{ if } [\![t_1]\!]_{X,\rho} \text{ and } [\![t_2]\!]_{X,\rho} \text{ are algebraic, maximal and identical} \\ false \text{ if } [\![t_1]\!]_{X,\rho} \text{ and } [\![t_2]\!]_{X,\rho} \text{ are algebraic and maximal, but non-identical} \\ \bot_{LL} \text{ otherwise} \end{cases}$$

Note that this interpretation is strict and continuous.

Alternatively, we can consider ≡ as an ordinary predicate (whose interpretations must be continuous by definition) and axiomatize its truth, by adding to the program the clauses:

$$d(x_1, \dots, x_m) \equiv d(y_1, \dots, y_m) \leftarrow x_1 \equiv y_1, \dots, x_m \equiv y_m \qquad (m \geq 0)$$

for each constructor symbol *d* (this alternative will be the one chosen for implementing K-LEAF). Note that the two ways of defining ≡ are equivalent, relatively to the set in which the value of strict-equality is *true*.

The meaning of non-atomic formulas is defined, as usual, by assigning the meanings, i.e. the truth-tables, of the boolean connectives, in our case conjunction and implication. If we denote by *and* and $\Leftarrow$ some suitable extensions of the corresponding classical operators to the three-valued logic, we have, of course,

$$[\![A \leftarrow B_1, ..., B_n]\!]_{X,\rho} = [\![A]\!]_{X,\rho} \Leftarrow [\![B_1, ..., B_n]\!]_{X,\rho}$$
$$[\![B_1, ..., B_n]\!]_{X,\rho} = [\![B_1]\!]_{X,\rho} \ \textit{and} \ ... \ \textit{and} \ [\![B_n]\!]_{X,\rho}$$

There are several possibilities. Our choice is the non-strict monotonic extension in the case of *and*, and a non-monotonic one in the case of $\Leftarrow$, so that for any conjunction of ground atoms $B_1, ..., B_n$, $[\![B_1, ..., B_n]\!]_X$ is true iff $[\![\leftarrow B_1, ..., B_n]\!]_X$ is not true (Giovannetti *et al.*, 1986). The truth value of a ground clause of the form $A \leftarrow B_1, ..., B_n$ is not true iff all the B_i 's are true and A is not true.

Definitions.

Let W be a set of Kernel or flat LEAF (program and goal) clauses. A *model* of W is any interpretation M = ((X, ≤), [[ ]]) such that, for every clause *cl* in W and for every environment ρ, $[\![cl]\!]_{X,\rho} = \textit{true}$.

W is *satisfiable* or *consistent* if it has a model, *unsatisfiable* or *inconsistent* if it has no models.

An atomic formula, or a conjunction of atomic formulae, G, is true in M iff for every environment ρ $[\![G]\!]_{X,\rho} = \textit{true}$.

An atomic formula, or a conjunction of atomic formulae, G, is *valid* with respect to W, or is a *logical consequence* of W, iff it is true in every model of W.

A special class of interpretations is represented by Herbrand interpretations, which are based on a purely syntactical domain, the Herbrand universe. In our case the Herbrand universe, as argued in section 3.1, is simply the set of the ground data terms, ground data partial terms and ground data infinite terms, i.e. the set of terms that can be built by means of the (constants and) constructors of the language and of the new constant ⊥, where infinite terms may be defined in the standard way as infinite (finite-branching) trees. The ordering is the usual approximation order, which correctly gives to the above set the structure of an algebraic CPO. The construction is quite standard (see, for example, Goguen *et al.*, 1977; Lloyd, 1984).

A *Herbrand model* for W is any Herbrand interpretation which is a model. In the following, HI will denote the set of Herbrand interpretations, while HM will denote the set of Herbrand models.

Let us point out the meaning of equality and strict equality on Herbrand interpretations. Equality is simply syntactic identity. To understand the meaning of strict equality, note that in the CPO (CU, ≤) maximal algebraic elements are the data terms which contain no occurrences of ⊥. Hence strict equality is the syntactic identity only on the subset of the Herbrand Universe which is isomorphic to the ordinary "data-term" Herbrand Universe.

Consider the set of functions from a poset (X, ≤) into a poset (Y, ≤). This set is naturally ordered by the following relation:

$$g \leq g' \quad \text{iff} \quad \forall x \in X \;\; g(x) \leq g'(x)$$

The minimal function (Ω) is, of course, the function which maps every element of X in the bottom element of Y ($\forall x \in X \;\; \Omega(x) = \bot_Y$). This functional ordering induces an ordering on Herbrand interpretations:

Definition (Ordering on Herbrand interpretations)
HI is ordered by the relation $\leq$ defined as follows:

$$\text{for } I, I' \in HI, \quad I \leq I' \;\text{ iff }\; \forall f \in F \,.\, \forall p \in P. \quad [\![f]\!]_I \leq [\![f]\!]_{I'} \text{ and } [\![p]\!]_I \leq [\![p]\!]_{I'}$$

The interpretation I_0, which maps in Ω every function and predicate symbol, is the minimal element of HI. Also (HI, $\leq$) is a CPO, as proved in Giovannetti *el al.* (1986).

Also in this kind of logics, Herbrand models can be proved to keep the special role they have in standard logic. Namely, if W is a set of Kernel or flat LEAF (program and goal) clauses, W has a model iff W has a Herbrand model. A ground atom or a conjunction of ground atoms A is a logical consequence of W iff A is true in all the Herbrand models of W.

If P is a Kernel or flat LEAF program, the lub of its Herbrand models is a Herbrand model, hence the minimal Herbrand model. A ground atom or a conjunction of ground atoms is true in all the Herbrand models iff it is true in the minimal Herbrand model. A theorem proved in Giovannetti *et al.* (1986) ensures the correctness of the flattening algorithm.

Theorem.
Let W be a K-LEAF program and let W′ be the flat program obtained by flattening W. Then W and W′ have exactly the same Herbrand models.

3.6 Equivalence results

A sequence of theorems, reported with their proofs in Giovannetti *et al.* (1986), establishes the soundness and completeness of the SLD-resolution of flattened goals on "compiled" programs (the "compiled" version of a program W consists of the set of flattened clauses *flat(W)*, the clauses in =(W), and ≡(W)), with respect to the declarative semantics described in the previous section.

3.6.1 Soundness theorem.

Let W be a K-LEAF program and ←G a K-LEAF goal. Assume that ←*flatb*(G) has a refutation with a computed answer substitution ρ. Then for each Herbrand model I of W, and for each ground substitution $\theta : Var(G\rho) \rightarrow D$ (i.e. the standard Herbrand Universe), $G\rho\theta$ is *true* in I.

3.6.2 Completeness theorem.

Let W be a "compiled" K-LEAF program, and $\leftarrow$ G a K-LEAF goal. If Gσ, with σ a finite ordinary substitution, is a logic consequence of W, then there is a SLD-refutation of $\leftarrow$*flatb*(G) with computed answer substitution σ' not less general than σ, i.e. such that for some substitution τ, $\sigma'/Var(G)\ \tau = \sigma$.

4. The IDEAL Language

4.1 The rationale behind IDEAL

A direct integration of the characterizing features of functional and logic programming, as they were stated in the introduction, would amount to (some kind of) lambda-calculus supplemented with unification, i.e. higher-order unification.

At first, a naive reductionistic approach could consist in axiomatizing the desired form of lambda-calculus in first-order logic, i.e. in viewing the functional language as an object language whose operational semantics (basically, the beta-convertibility relation) is described using first-order logic as a metalanguage; a suitable inference system for first-order logic could then be employed to perform reasoning in this theory.

Pure (untyped) lambda-calculus can be axiomatized as a confluent Horn equational theory, that is, a confluent conditional rewriting system; for this kind of system, oriented paramodulation, along with the functional reflexive axioms and resolution against $X=X$ (and ordinary SLD-resolution, if non-equational predicates are present) has been proved (Hoelldobler, 1988) to constitute a complete inference system for solving existential goals, i.e. existential equations. This inference rule, which is a sort of extended narrowing, would therefore automatically provide us with a general unification algorithm for untyped lambda-calculus, in the sense that it would allow us to solve equations between lambda-terms containing (existentially quantified) logical variables, w.r.t. the beta convertibility. The model-theoretic semantics of the higher-order language is simply given by the standard semantics of the first-order Horn theory, with a minimal Herbrand model on the Herbrand Universe consisting of the equivalence classes of terms (Jaffar et al., 1984, 1986a). The induced model of the lambda-calculus is then the trivial term model consisting of classes of beta convertibility. Note the well-known fact that lambda-variables (and more generally, open lambda-terms) are elements of this model, and cannot be eliminated by considering them as logical variables; the closed-term model of lambda-calculus is therefore not a model in this induced semantics, and logical variables of sort *lambda-term* are always to be considered as ranging over a semantical domain that includes, in addition to denotations for "function definitions" and possibly for primitive data, a countable set of elements corresponding to lambda-variables (and to open lambda-terms).

The same argument could be applied to a lambda-calculus with a polymorphic ML-like type assignment system, because the type system is a Horn theory, and the convertibility theory is the same as in the untyped case. As is well known, in the core system, where the type of every term is inferred from the types of its subterms, untyped lambda-terms acting as recursors, like the combinator Y, cannot be assigned a type, and every well-typed term is strongly normalizable, i.e. all successfully type-checked programs are terminating. However, the recursion operator can be consistently (in the sense of the type discipline) assigned a type by an independent axiom. It may therefore be viewed from the user as a polymorphic constant with its own primitive reduction rule. This skeletal functional language can then be enriched with pattern abstraction, and also with logic features such as conditional definitions with possibly existential variables in the conditions. Its axiomatization in a (many-sorted) first-order metalanguage will still be a Horn theory with equality, which could in principle be made confluent through suitable restrictions and formalization; for example, by directly incorporating a (normalizing) strategy into the theory itself.

This approach, though highly speculative, is nonetheless indicative of both the huge expressive power and the related extreme computational weakness that can result from merely combining the essential properties of logic and functional programming.

On the one hand, it would lead us quite outside the scope of the programming languages proper, rather into the domain of program synthesis and program transformation: a system like those outlined above would abstractly be able to instantiate existential logical variables to lambda-terms (possibly containing recursion operators) not present in the program, i.e. it would be able to synthetize (possibly recursive) procedures given, for example, the input/output behaviour.

On the other hand, there is, of course, no hope of obtaining this synthesis capability from a purely automatic and general inference system like those cited above: the algorithm would behave in much the same way as a blind enumerator of all the possible ML (or Pascal, for that matter) programs followed by an ML (or Pascal) interpreter that checks whether the input/output behaviour is the specified one! Such a task can only be performed interactively and by a system endowed with suitable search strategies. Moreover, if we want to reason about program equivalence and program transformation, the theory of beta-convertibility can become inadequate, since terms (programs) which are not convertible to each other may be equivalent in some desired meaningful sense (for example, they may build a same "infinite structure"). Stated differently, reasoning only on the syntactic term models of lambda-calculus, which is what is done by writing down in first-order logic the conversion rules, is no longer sufficient: the consideration of more "semantic" models becomes necessary (for example, Scott's domains), which amounts to introducing induction principles in the inference system.

However, the naive reduction to first-order logic can serve as a general framework where specific mechanisms for specific classes of problems can be developed and experimented, taking into account the fact that, as far as the interest is confined to program synthesis only, and does not include proofs of equivalence between programs, reasoning on the syntactic models of higher-order functional languages may be sufficient. The integrated logic-functional language IDEAL, considered as a programming system still in evolution, is based on this framework.

A different but related approach, followed in lambda-Prolog (Miller and Nadathur, 1986), and which can also be of interest for future developments of IDEAL, consists in allowing the logical variables to range only on the lambda-terms that are well typed in the simple Church-type system without recursion operators, so that - reasonably - the too general but fictitious program synthesis capability is given up. This is technically achieved by only permitting recursion in logical definitions (as in Prolog) and excluding functional recursion operators. In fact, lambda-Prolog is a logic language, built on a sound proof-theoretical basis, which shares with IDEAL the essential feature of being higher order, but differs from it in many other respects (for example, in obtaining program structuring by logical instead of functional means, i.e. intuitionistic implication instead of functional application).

The elimination of most of the abstract program-synthesis capability is also the basis for a realistic integration of logic and functional *programming*, where higher-order functions, i.e. general lambda-terms, can be applied to arguments and reduced, but cannot be synthetized from scratch. This means that existential logical variables can only be first-order or, if higher-order, can only be instantiated to functions whose definitions are contained (at least implicitly, in a sense to be specified later) in the program. The advantage of this purely functional usage of the higher order lies in that the main source of inefficiency in the first-order interpreter of the higher-order language, namely the textual substitution of arguments to lambda-variables, can be avoided by means of the old standard technique that consists in putting the actual arguments in memory locations or registers which can be statically referenced by the function code. This mechanism is particularly easy to implement for first-order languages - and easily extends to first-order *logic* languages: in fact, it is the basis for every reasonable Prolog implementation, the only difference being that actual values are not always put in memory before the procedure call, but can be written later by unification. It is not surprising, therefore, that the now well-established compilation technique for functional languages called lambda-lifting consists in transforming higher-order function definitions into first-order rewrite rules equivalent to the former w.r.t. reduction, i.e. w.r.t. purely functional computation. Stated in a more logical way, specialized lemmata for the function *apply* are derived from the axioms of the higher-order language and are then substituted for the original axiomatization. Moreover, the use of these lemmata need not be confined to pure functional reduction, but the full logic-programming paradigm can be applied, with unification instead of unidirectional matching.

The first-order program resulting from the compilation is a confluent Horn equational theory, therefore some form of paramodulation or narrowing (possibly together with resolution) should be used to perform equational reasoning. However, as was explained in section 3, under certain conditions, which are satisfied by definition by K-LEAF programs, SLD-resolution is equivalent to narrowing at a price of a further compilation step, and Prolog technology can be easily adapted to K-LEAF. The higher-order language has therefore been defined in such a way that the first-order program resulting from the first compilation step is a K-LEAF program.

4.2 The higher-order language IDEAL

The language IDEAL is (a sugared form of) a polymorphic lambda-calculus extended with data constructors, pattern matching, and logical operators. Conceptually, there are three distinct levels of the language corresponding to three different degrees of generality.

The highest level, IDEAL-3, is not an actual programming language: in agreement with the "naive" approach outlined in section 4.1, it could be described as a manysorted Horn theory with equality, which axiomatizes the convertibility and well-typing relations of a lambda-calculus enriched with Horn logics. Sorts correspond to syntactic categories of the object language; for example, *lambda-term*, *lambda-var*, *type*, etc. are distinct (metalanguage) sorts, lambda-variables are constants (or more generally ground terms) in the metalanguage, in a denumerable supply. Type-variables, in contrast, (due to our choice of an "implicit" polymorphism) are just logical variables of the sort *type*, i.e. ranging over ground types, which are those built from basic types (like *int*, *bool*, etc.) and type-constructors ($\rightarrow$, *list*, etc.). There will be predefined constructors for predefined object-language types, such as [] and [|] for lists, *true* for booleans, etc., and in addition the data constructors introduced by user-type definitions; each constructor comes with an arity, i.e. a fixed number of (typed) arguments. Moreover, for every n, there is an n-uple constructor, which enables the definition of uncurried functions. Observe that curried and uncurried versions of the same function may be defined, along with functions *curry* and *uncurry* to pass from one form to the other, as in Standard ML.

The user is allowed to define his own polymorphic data types, through a construct like the one suggested in Turner (1985):

typename(Typevar1,...,Typevarn) ::=

constructor1(Typename11,...,Typename1n_1);

....

constructorm(Typenamem1,...,Typenamemn$_n$

which declares data objects of type *typename*, the structures being identified by *constructor1*, ...,*constructorm*, each of the appropriate argument types. The predefined logical functions are:

and: bool $\rightarrow$ bool $\rightarrow$ bool

$\exists$: $\alpha \rightarrow$ bool $\rightarrow$ bool

$\equiv$: $\alpha \rightarrow \alpha \rightarrow$ bool

The more usual notation $\exists$ z.t may be used instead of $\exists\lambda$z.t if no ambiguity arises.

A brief grammar of the object-language is as follows.

(Lambda-) data terms or *patterns P* are lambda-terms built from constructors and lambda-variables:

P ::= lamvar | constr | constr pattuple

pattuple ::= (P1, P2, ... , Pn)

Terms are lambda-terms extended with pattern-abstraction and logical operators:

term ::= lamvar | abstr | appl | **true** | term1 **and** term2 | $\exists$term | term1≡term2

appl ::= term1@term2 | n-ary-constr (term1, ..., termn)

abstr ::= λlamvar.term | pattern-abstr | **rec-i** [lamvar1=term1, ..., lamvarn=termn] (with 1≤i≤n)

pattern-abstr ::= funpabs | predpabs

funpabs ::= λ{ P1.term1 :- boolexp1 || P2.term2 :- boolexp2 || ... || Pn.termn :- boolexpn}

where the sequence of patterns *(P1, P2, ..., Pn)* is *regular*, i.e.:

(1) Every *Pi* is linear, i.e. does not contain multiple occurrences of a same lambda-variable;

(2) *P1, ..., Pn* are superposition-free, i.e. are not unifiable (when lambda-variables are regarded as logical variables), and the *boolexpi* are expressions of type *boolean.*

predpabs ::= λ{P1.boolexp1 || P2.boolexp2 || ... || Pn.boolexpn}

"Single-pattern" abstractions *λP.term* or *λP.(term :-body)* are abbreviations respectively for

λ{*P.term :- true*} and λ{*P.term :- body*}

The *let...in* and *where* constructs, not explicitly mentioned, can be considered syntactic sugar for functional application, as in the untyped calculus, because we do not have a distinct typing rule for it; *letrec* $V_1=T_1,...,V_n=T_n$ *in exp* and *exp whererec* $V_1=T_1,...,V_n=T_n$ will analogously stand, as usual, for

let V_1 = *rec-1*[$V_1=T_1,...,V_n=T_n$], ..., V_n = *rec-n*[$V_n=T_n,...,V_n=T_n$] *in exp.*

A subtler differentiation, which do not show here, of syntactic categories (i.e. metalanguage sorts) and correspondingly of the object-language constructs would be necessary to be able to fully handle the definition of the object-language and its operational semantics in first order logic (Bosco *et al.*, 1989c).

The core of the equality (convertibility) theory is, of course, any axiomatization of beta-convertibility: for example, Revesz's system (Revesz 1985, Klop 1985), extended with rules handling substitution within the new constructs:

(β1) (λX.X)@T = T
(β2) (λX.Y)@T = Y ⇐ dif(X,Y)
(β3) (λX.T1@T2))@T = (λX.T1@T)@(λX.T2@T)
(β3c) (λX.c(T1,...,Tn))@T = c(λX.T1@T,...,λX.Tn@T) for any constructor c
(β3||) (λX. λ{ P1.T1 :- B1 || ... || Pn.Tn :- Bn})@T =
λ{ (λX.(P1.T1 :- B1))@T || ... || (λX.(Pn.Tn :- Bn))@T}
(β3:-) (λX.(P.Ti :- B))@T = (P.(λX.Ti)@T :- (λX.B)@T) ⇐
difpat(X,P), nonfreepatv(P,T) or nonfree(X,Ti)
(β3≡) (λX.T1≡T2)@T = (λX.T1)@T≡ (λX.T2)@T
(β3∃) (λX.∃T1)@T = ∃((λX.T1)@T)
(β4) (λX.λX.T1)@T2 = λX.T1
(β4p) (λX.(P.Ti :- B))@T = P.Ti :- B ⇐ in(X,Y)
(β5) (λX.λY.T1)@T2 = λY.(λX.T1@T2) ⇐ dif(X,Y),
nonfree(X,T1) or nonfree(Y,T2)
(β5p) (λX.(P.Ti :- B))@T = (P.(λX.Ti)@T :- (λX.B)@T) ⇐
difpat(X,P), nonfreepatv(P,T) or nonfree(X,Ti)

where capital letters denote logical variables, *difpat(X,P)* means that X is different from the lambda-variables occurring in the pattern P, *nonfreepatv(P,T)* means that the lambda-variables occurring in P are not free in T, *in(X, P)* means that the lambda-variable X occurs in the pattern P.

An alpha-rule is, of course, also necessary, Revesz's rule is

(α*) (λX.T) = λY.((λX.T)@Y) ⇐ nonfree(Y,T)

The clauses could be used as conditional rewrite rules to reduce lambda-terms (which are ground terms of the metalanguage), even though the uncontrolled renaming caused by rule α in this form would in any case prevent reduction from terminating. In solving (existential) equations between lambda-terms by paramodulation, uncontrolled alpha conversion can be eliminated by moving the alpha-axiom from the set of the rewriting rules to the set of clauses - like the reflexive axiom X=X - against which resolution is performed:

(α=) λX.T1 = λY.T2 ⇐ (λX.T1)@Z = (λX.T2)@Z, dif(X,Y), dif(Z,X), dif(Z,Y)

This use of the alpha-rule is, of course, also valid for purely functional reduction, if rewriting of a term *t* is viewed as one particular sequence of paramodulation and resolution among those starting from the equation *t* = Z.

Since in a lambda-term only identity or distinctness between lambda-variables matter, not their concrete individual names, these can always be replaced by logical variables, and the *dif* conditions in the rewriting rules can viewed as *constraints* which are incrementally added to the term being reduced, and checked for satisfiability, without actually instantiating logical "lambda" variables to lambda-variable names (i.e., in Prolog, without ever substituting upper-case with lower-case).

The inclusion of the typing system is obtained, in principle, by adding to each rewrite rule *T1* = *T2* a condition *well-typed(T1,type)*, where *well-typed* is a predicate defined by a Horn theory.

The reduction rules for the other constructs of the object-language are as one would expect. For example, omitting the type-checking part and disregarding formal details, the rules for the functional pattern-abstraction are:

λ\{ P1.T1 :-B1 || ... || Pn.Tn :- Bn\}@T = (λPi.Ti)•T ⇐ match(Pi,T), (λPi.Bi)•T = **true**
for $1 \leq i \leq n$

where the metalanguage operator • denotes reduction to a standard lambda-term application without pattern-abstraction, as defined by

(λc(P1,...,Pm).T)•c(T1,...,Tm) = (λP1...λPm.T)•T1•...•Tm
for every m-ary constructor *c*,
(λa.T)•a = T for every 0-ary constructor *a*;
(λX.T1)•T2 = (λX.T1)@T2

and where the predicate *match* has a similar obvious definition.

Analogous rules hold for predicate-abstractions:
\{λ P1.B1 || ... || Pn.Bn\}@T = (λPi.Bi)•T ⇐ match(Pi,T)

The reduction rule for the (mutual) recursion operator formally is, as usual,

rec-i [F1=T1, ..., Fn=Tn] =
= (λF1...λFn.Ti)@(**rec-1**[F1=T1, ..., Fn=Tn])@...@(**rec-n** [F1=T1, ..., Fn=Tn])

Specialized versions of the alpha-rule have to be introduced to perform renaming within pattern-abstractions (and rec-abstractions), for example:

\{λ P1.B1 || ... || Pi.Bi || ... || Pn.Bn\} = \{λ P1.B1 || ... || Pi'.Bi' || ... || Pn.Bn\} ⇐
λ Pi.Bi = λPi'.Bi'
λc(P1, ..., Pn).T = λc(P1', ..., Pn').T' ⇐ λP1 ...λPn.T = λP1' ...λPn'.T'

There is one clause for the logical conjunction:
and true true = true
The rule for the existential quantifier merely "copies" into the Horn metalanguage the object-language expression (conceptually replacing a lower-case lambda-variable with a new upper-case logical variable):

$\exists$(λX.T) = **true** ⇐ (λX.T)@Z = **true**

Analogously, the rule for equality could copy the object-language equality into the metalanguage equality: T1≡T2 = **true** ⇐ T1 = T2, or, equivalently:

X≡X = **true**
(λX.T1≡λY.T2) = ((λX.T1)@Z ≡ (λY.T2)@Z)⇐ dif(X,Y), dif(Z,X), dif(Z,Y)

We have instead chosen to restrict the equality test to convertibility between finite objects, i.e. between closed normal forms; this amounts to substituting the previous rules for ≡ with the following:

($\alpha\equiv$) (λX.T1 ≡ λY.T2) = **true** ⇐ ((λX.T1)@Z ≡ (λY.T2)@Z) = **true**, dif(Z,X), dif(Z,Y).

... (specialized versions of α for pattern abstractions and recursive definitions)

T1@T2 ≡ S1@S2 ⇐ T1 ≡ T2, S1 ≡ S2

c(X1,...,Xn) ≡ c(Y1,...,Yn) ⇐ X1 ≡ Y1, ... , Xn ≡ Yn for every n-ary constructor *c*.

a ≡ a for every 0-ary constructor (i.e. constant) *a*

For these strict equality rules to be complete, it must be assumed that for every type there exists in the language a constant that may be assigned that type, possibly with no other properties (which amounts to selecting an infinite subset of lambda-variables and forbidding abstraction on them).

An IDEAL-3 program is a ground metaterm of sort *lambda-term*, except that lower-case lambda-variables may be replaced by upper-case logical variables, and with the additional condition that it is a *closed* lambda-term. Moreover, there may be a set of global user-type definitions.

The model-theoretic semantics could be the one outlined in the introduction, with a minimal Herbrand model where every lambda-term simply denotes the class of all the lambda-terms convertible to it. We could also try to adapt one of the other available semantics for lambda-calculus, since equality in the model is not a predicate allowed to occur in the program: the only equality between terms that may be tested is the syntactic identity (modulo alpha-renaming) between closed normal forms.

We have, in any case, two notions of equality: (1) the metalanguage equality, coinciding with convertibility or with equality in some other model; (2) its restriction to normal forms, or strict equality, which is the only equality that may occur within a lambda-term.

For example, the two terms *rec f=c(f)* and *rec g=c(g)*, though being alpha-convertible to each other, are not strictly equal, since they are not normalizable. The terms *rec f=c(f)* and *rec g=c(c(g))* are neither strictly equal nor convertible, but generate the same "infinite structure" (their Boehm trees coincide).

As for the operational semantics, the execution of the program *t* is the reduction of the equality *t=R* by paramodulation with the clauses defining the language and with the functional reflexive axioms (plus resolution with X=X and α=, and with the clauses defining non-equational predicates). In practice, the use of resolution against X=X and α= will be disciplined by a strategy that avoids, for example, trivial answers *R:=t* when actually the reduction of *t* is desired.

(Oriented) paramodulation and resolution would be abstractly able, as noted in the introduction, to instantiate higher-order variables to newly-generated function definitions or predicate definitions, while dynamically type-checking them (though the type system, from a functional point of view, is, of course, completely static). Observe that in our first-order theory lambda-terms convertible (therefore, equal) to well-typed terms are well-typed, even though their subterms cannot be typed; oriented paramodulation, however, is not able to type them, which is probably just what we want, so in this case incompleteness is welcome (alternatively, if one insists on having the convertibility typing rule, the *well-typed* condition should be added to each rule T1 = T2 for term T2 instead of T1).

A simple example of an IDEAL program is:

```
letrec
        append = lambda {  [] . lambda L . L
                        ||  [X|U] . lambda L . [X | append@U@L] }
        reverse = ...
in  ∃ F. F@[1,1] ≡ [1,1]
```

We would get the type inference

append: list(A)-->list(A)-->list(A)
reverse: list(A)-->list(A)

and, among the answers,

F := lambda x.x; F := lambda x.[1,1]; F := reverse; F := append@[]; ...

while with the goal

∃ F@[1,2] ≡ [2,1]

we would only get, among the solutions,

F := lambda x.[2,1]; F := reverse; ...

Abstractly, if *append* and *reverse* had not been defined in the program, even their definitions would still be in the space of solutions of ∃ *F. F@[1,1] ≡ [1,1]*: one should find *F := letrec append = ...* in just the same way as *F := lambda x.x*, etc.; but this is, of course, not an answer to be realistically expected.

The second level of the language, IDEAL-2, in principle syntactically equal to IDEAL-3, is obtained by introducing a partial evaluation step which, for any given program, i.e. for any given global lambda-term *t*, replaces the above first-order axioms of the meta-interpreter with the set of theorems of the forms

(pe1) ∀var(term).∀X.(λX.term)@X = e
  (where *var(term)* are the logical variables in *term*)
(pe2) ∀var(Pi).λ{P1.t1:-b1||...||Pn.tn:-bn}@Pi = ti :- bi
  (where *var(Pi)* are the variables in the pattern *Pi*)
(pe3) (∃X.term) :- (λX.term)@Z
(pe4) **rec-i**[...] = e
where

(1) The lhs *λX.term* or *λ{P1.t1:-b1||...||Pn.tn:-bn}* or **rec-***i[...]* is a subterm of *t* that is an outermost abstraction, or is the rhs *e′* of another such theorem
(2) The rhs *e* in (pe1) or (pe4) results from reducing (i.e. paramodulating) with the axioms themselves the lhs until no further reduction is possible or, in case of recursion abstraction, after formally one reduction of the *rec* operator (which merely amounts to viewing the *rec* construct as a recursive logical definition instead of as a lambda-term); to paramodulate the universal goal *∀X.abstr@X* the variable X is first skolemized into a constant *x* (which may be a lambda-variable, as lambda-variables are meta-constants that do not possess any particular property) and then restored in the obtained theorem.

The definition is well founded because in each theorem *∀X.abstr@X=e* the term *e* contains one less abstraction than the term *abstr*, and *rec*s are only reduced once.

"Compiled" function definitions like

f P1 = t1 :- b1

...

f Pn = t :- bn

are directly allowed in the user syntax, as are first-order ordinary function definitions.

As in IDEAL-3, the model-theoretic semantics of an IDEAL-2 program could be given by the ordinary first-order Horn semantics. The Herbrand Universe is built from all the lambda-abstractions - viewed as constructors whose arity is given by the number and type of the free variables - that are contained in the program, besides built-in and user-defined constructors and the function @, plus possibly the first-order functions defined directly by the user. The Herbrand model is the set of equivalence classes of terms w.r.t. to the definitions contained in the program. The operational semantics could be, as before, oriented paramodulation.

Instead, an alternative approach can be followed, based on some useful properties of the conditional rewriting system made up by the above set of lemmas. Since for every rule *(pe1)* or *(pe4)* there is no other rule with the same lhs, the occurrences of @ in *t* may be considered as occurrences of a constructor @′, distinct from the function @, so that there is no functional composition in the lhs's of the rules; correspondingly, in the rhs of every rule the occurrences of @ within abstractions are to be substituted with occurrences of @′;
In this way, having the general rules for lambda-reduction (which are non-regular) been discarded, the whole rewriting system becomes regular due to the regularity conditions for pattern abstractions.
Conjuncts in bodies are predicates or strict equalities.

These conditions characterize K-LEAF programs or, more generally, IIIn systems in Bergstra and Klop's (1986) classification; K-LEAF model-theoretic and operational semantics can therefore be directly adopted, with "flattening plus resolution" instead of paramodulation. This amounts to removing functions - including @ - from the Herbrand Universe, and giving them an algebraic-cpo interpretation (recall that Scott's domains are algebraic cpo's with the *consistent completeness* condition, which can be discarded in first-order languages). Moreover, the equational theory of the highest level itself, IDEAL-3, can be translated into a K-LEAF program, as will be shown in section 6.1.

The program of the previous example, considered as an IDEAL-2 program, would be compiled into:

```
append@[] = lambda L.L
append@[X|U] = lambda L.[X | append@'U@'L]
(lambda L.L)@Z = Z
(lambda L.[X | append@'U@'L])@L = [X | append@U@L]
reverse@...
```

The execution of goal

?- F@[1,1] ≡ [1,1]

still yields the solutions

F := lambda X.X; F := reverse; ...

because *reverse* is a function defined explicitly in the program, and *lambda X.X* is implicitly defined, being an abstraction contained in the definition of *append.* On the other hand, the solution

F := lambda x.[1,1]

cannot be found, because it is not a definition contained in the program. The solution

F := append@[],

equivalent to *F := lambda X.X*, is explicitly generated by paramodulation, but not by narrowing or by flattening plus resolution.

If *append* is defined as an uncurried function

```
append([], L) = L
append([X|U], L) = [X | append(U, L)]
```

the solution *F := lambda X.X* is also lost, as this is no longer an implicitly defined function.

Finally, IDEAL-1 is IDEAL (-2 or -3) with the additional restriction that existential variables may only be first-order. For IDEAL-1 programs the operational semantics corresponding to IDEAL-2 is equivalent to that corresponding to IDEAL-3, i.e. replacing the general theory of lambda with the compiled code does not cause loss of solutions. The extended programming example reported in Section 2 is IDEAL-1. Simpler examples are shown in the next section.

4.3 The user level IDEAL

The actual syntax of IDEAL(-1) has been already implicitly introduced through the significant application described in Section 2. In this section the programming features offered by the implemented language are shown through specific examples. The following is the rephrasing in IDEAL of a well-known functional program taken from Turner (1985).

Example 4.1

```
        foldr@Op@Z = g

wherec
                g@[] = Z,
                g@[A|X] = Op@(A, g@X):
            :(α # β→β)→β→(list(α)→β).
```

An alternative definition of *foldr* is:

```
foldr@Op@Z = λ[]  .    Z,
          [A|X].  Op@(A, foldr@Op@Z@X).

    product = foldr@(*)@1.:list(int)→int
     sum = foldr@(+)@0.                :list(int)→int.
           sum@[1,2,3]                 % term to be evaluated
           :int        6        % result
```

Function and predicate definitions with patterns are powerful programming constructs: the very common function definitions by cases on the input structure can concisely and expressively be coded with patterns, instead of by nesting *if then else*s and data selectors. Unlike some other functional languages, patterns in IDEAL are not an extra feature of the language, rather they are a consequence of having integrated a logical and a functional language. In fact, the use of patterns in IDEAL is not restricted to data discrimination/selection (as happens when a pattern is matched against the actual parameters in a function call). Instead, IDEAL patterns are treated with unification, whereby the discrimination/selection/construction roles of a pattern component are not fixed but depend on the instantiation state of the data with which it is unified.

Both in top-level definitions and in embedded conditional lambda-abstractions, a condition *cond* may be added, with the effect of restricting the *application domain* of the functional clause. The application domain of a function defined with alternative clauses is the union of the individual domains of the single clauses (which do not overlap given the non-ambiguity restrictions). Informally, the application domain of a single clause *P=term :- cond* is defined as the set of all instances of the pattern which satisfy the condition *cond*. Therefore, in order for a rewriting of *F@Arg* to take place with a given clause *F@P=term:-cond*, the argument *Arg* must match the pattern P and the bindings thus created must satisfy *cond*.

With the extension of higher-order capabilities to predicates, definitions of predicate combinators and lexically scoped predicate definitions become possible, which greatly improves conciseness and modularization of logic programs, as suggested by the following example.

Example 4.2

comb@P@(X,Y) :- P@(Z,X),P@(Z,Y)
:(α # β→**truth-value**) →β # β →**truth-value.**

A type α → **truth-value** can be written as [α].

The type of the above expression is displayed as [α # β] →[β # β].

```
   non-disjoint = comb@member
  wherererec
              member@(X,[X|L]).
              member@(X,[Y|L]) :- member@(X,L)
 :[list(α) # list(α)].

    person ::= (a;b;c;d;...).                 % declares type person

    brothers = comb@parent
  where
              parent@(a,b),.
              parent@(c,d):   [person # person].
```

where *non-disjoint* is a predicate which succeeds when two lists are non-disjoint, while *brothers* succeeds when its two arguments have a common parent.

Though not handled by the formal semantics for obvious reasons, a metalevel construct *bag* is available for producing, in formally one step, the possibly empty list of all the *Term* satisfying *Cond*. The following definition of *quicksort*, derived by a widely known functional program built on functional set-expressions, is an example of the use of *bag*, which enables a more abstract specification of the algorithm with respect to the way the list is scanned.

Example 4.3

```
[] ++ L = L                  ; definition of append
[X|U] ++ L = [X|U++L].  :list(A)-->list(A)-->list(A)

gt@X@Y :- X > Y.        :A-->A-->bool
lt@X@Y :- X < Y.        :A-->A-->bool
gte@X@Y :- X >= Y.      :A-->A-->bool
lte@X@Y :- X =< Y.      :A-->A-->bool
inv(lt) = gte,
inv(gt) = lte.          :(A-->A-->bool)-->(B-->B-->bool)

qsort@p@[] = [],
qsort@p@[A|L] = qsort@p@bag(X,(member(X,L),p@X@A)) ++
                   [A|qsort@p@bag(X,(member(X,L),inv(p)@X@A))]
                        :(A-->A-->bool)-->list(A)-->list(A)
```

An example of the the logic part "calling" the functional one is the following goal, where the predicate *member* "calls" the function *map*, whose application occurs in one of the predicate arguments.

Example 4.4

```
map([],F) = [],
map([X|L],F) = [F@X|map(L,F)]:list(A)-->(A-->B)-->list(B)

member(X,map([1,2,3],lambda(x,x+1)));term to be evaluated

X:int  2;     3;     4
```

The values 2,3,4 are "alternative" values which in a sequential environment are obtained by "backtracking".

5. Execution mechanism for K-LEAF: the Outermost SLD-resolution

The computational methods that have been proposed for the execution of languages based on Horn-clause logic with equality are, in general, linear refinements of resolution and completion (i.e. SLD-resolution and narrowing, respectively). Among them we find conditional narrowing (Dershowitz and Plaisted, 1985; Fribourg, 1985) and SLDE-resolution (i.e. SLD-resolution with syntactic unification replaced by a E-unification (Goguen and Meseguer, 1986a; Subrahmanyam, 1986; Martelli *et al.*, 1987)).

The technique we have chosen is *flat SLD-resolution*, i.e. SLD-resolution on *flattened* programs augmented with the clause *x=x*. The flattening tranformation consists in eliminating functional composition by recursively replacing a term *f(t1,...,tn)* with a new variable *v* and adding the functional atom *f(t1,...,tn)=v* to the body. The original idea, in the theorem-proving domain, probably traces back to Brand (1975), while in the area of logic and functional programming it was first proposed in Barbuti *et al.*, (1984) and Tamaki (1984).

SLD-resolution on flat programs seems to be more adequate than narrowing, because:

(1) SLD-resolution was shown to be equivalent to "refined" narrowing (Bosco *et al.*, 1988a), with a considerable gain in efficiency with respect to "ordinary" narrowing (elimination of redundant solutions and, more generally, reduction of the search space);
(2) The full (relational + functional) language can be supported by a single inference mechanism;
(3) Conditional equations can easily be handled, without need of extensions;
(4) Sharing of subexpressions deriving from a common expression is obtained for free.

A selection rule corresponding in the unflattened program to an innermost rule can be easily implemented through the usual leftmost selection rule of Prolog (Bosco *et al.*, 1988a), provided the flat literals are put in the right order by the flattening procedure. This strategy has, however, a serious drawback in the unlimited possibility of resolving functional atoms with $x=x$, which results in a large amount of useless computation. The elimination of the reflexive clause causes the loss of completeness, unless functions are constrained to be everywhere defined, as in Fribourg (1985). The problem can be overcome by noting that the resolution of a functional atom $t=z$ with $x=x$ is only useful when the resolutions of the atoms in whose arguments z occurs bind z to variables (i.e., they do not require a value for z). This is in general not the case, and it cannot be determined statically.

The detection of this situation requires an *outermost* strategy, analogous to lazy evaluation in functional programming, which reduces a functional atom only when its output variable would be bound to a non-variable term by resolution of a consumer atom. Resolution with $x=x$ can then be profitably applied to the functional atoms whose output variables do not occur elsewhere in the goal, and may therefore be implemented as an *elimination rule* (which can also be viewed as an explicit garbage collection step). Moreover, when, in the resolution of an atom, unification attempts to instantiate a variable produced by another (functional) atom, resolution of the current atom is suspended and resolution of the producer is tried instead. The suspended goal is resumed after (one step of) resolution of (all) the activated functional atom(s).

Resolution with $\equiv$-clauses can also be handled in an *ad-hoc* way, so as to eliminate the infinite branches, by simply applying a sort of fictitious $x\equiv x$ clause in those cases (i.e. atoms of the form $x\equiv y$ with x and y non-produced) where the two sides of the strict equality will certainly not be bound to terms denoting infinite or undefined objects.

The strategy is similar to Reddy's (1985) *lazy narrowing* with the difference that, in unifying an expression e with a variable x, outermost SLD-resolution goes on "evaluating" until e becomes a data-term, while lazy narrowing immediately produces the substitution $\{x{:=}e\}$, which may not be a solution of the equation $e\equiv x$ in the intended semantics.

Outermost SLD-resolution also has the advantage over lazy narrowing that it obtains for free the sharing of subexpressions derived from a common expression.

To describe the execution algorithm, we need the definition of an *outermost atom* of a flattened goal. An outermost atom is

(1) A relational atom $p(d_1,...,d_n)$, or
(2) A strict-equality atom $d_1 \equiv d_2$, or

(3) A functional atom $f(d_1,...,d_n) = x$, whose produced variable x does not occur elsewhere in G.

The algorithm is the following. Let the *current-goal* be the initial flattened goal G.

Selection:

```
while the current-goal is not empty and there is no failure do
    - select-don't-care an outermost atom A in the current-goal G.
    - if A is a functional atom then eliminate it, i.e. current-goal := current-goal -{A}
              else
                   execute the demand-driven-resolution of A in G with the program
                   case - the demand-driven-resolution returns a new goal G':
                              current-goal := G';
                          - the demand-driven-resolution returns failure:
                              failure;
                   end case
      end if
end while
if the current goal is empty then success, and the solution (i.e. the answer substitution)
                         is the composition of all the mgu's used in the demand-driven-
                         resolution steps
```

Demand-driven-resolution
of an atom A in a goal G with a set P of (flat) program clauses:

- case A is a relational atom $p(d_1,...,d_n)$ or a functional atom $f(d_1,...,d_n) = x$:

```
    select-don't-know in P a clause cl such that A and the head of cl are unifiable
    if there is no such clause then return failure
         else let σ be the mgu;

              case σ does not bind to non-variable terms
                        produced variables occurring in A:
                           apply ordinary resolution to A and cl,
                           and return the goal thus obtained;

                   σ binds to non-variable term a variable z
                        produced by a functional atom t=z:
                           (resolution of A suspended)
                           execute demand-driven-resolution of t=z in G with P
                                case it returns failure: return failure;
                                     it returns a goal G' , where the atom A has been
                                     instantiated to some τA :
                                          execute demand-driven-resolution of τA in G'
                                          with {cl}
                                             case it returns failure: return failure;
                                                  it returns a goal G" : return G"
                                             end case
                                end case
              end case
    end if
```

A is a strict-equality atom $d \equiv d'$:
  case A is $c(d_1,...,d_n) \equiv c'(d_1',...,d_m')$:
      apply ordinary resolution to A and a ≡-*clause* ;
      if resolution fails then return failure
            else return the goal thus obtained
      end if
      (i.e. if c is the same constructor as c' return the goal
      $G - \{c(d_1,...,d_n) \equiv c'(d_1',...,d_n')\} + \{d_1 \equiv d_1',...,d_n \equiv d_n'\}$;
      if c and c' are different constructors, failure);

  A is $x_1 \equiv x_2$ where both x_1 and x_2 are non-produced variables:
      unify them (which results in a binding τ of x_1 to x_2 or vice versa)
        and eliminate A, i.e return the goal $\tau(G-\{A\})$

  A is $x \equiv c(d_1,...,d_n)$ or $c(d_1,...,d_n) \equiv x$,
        where x is a non-produced variable:
      apply ordinary resolution to A and a ≡-*clause*
        and return the goal thus obtained;

  A is $x \equiv d$ or $d \equiv x$,
        where x is a variable produced by a functional atom $t=x$:
      execute *demand-driven-resolution* of $t=x$;
      case
        it fails: return failure
        it returns a new goal G′, where the atom A has been
        instantiated to some τA:
          execute *demand-driven-resolution* of τA in G′ with P
          case it returns failure: return failure;
            it returns a goal G" : return G"
          end case
      end case
  end case
end case.

Example 5.1
Let the flat program be:

cl_1: $f(x,y,z)=a \leftarrow c(x) \equiv z.$
cl_2: $p(a).$
cl_3: $g(x) = c(v) \leftarrow g(x)=v.$

where a is a constant and c is a 1-adic constructor:

cl_4: $a \equiv a.$
cl_5: $c(x) \equiv c(y) \leftarrow x \equiv y.$

Let the flattened goal be

$\underline{p(v1)}$,$f(x,v2,z)=V1,g(y)=v2$

where $p(v1)$ is the only outermost atom. Its resolution with cl_2 suspends, as the mgu $\{v1:=a\}$ binds a produced variable (i.e. $v1$) with a non-variable term (i.e. a). Thus the resolution of the producer of $v1$ (i.e. $f(x,v2,z)=v1$) is performed, with the substitution $\{x':=x,\ y':=v2,\ z':=z,\ v1:=a\}$ as mgu. This resolution returns the goal:

$\underline{p(a)}$,$c(x) \equiv z,g(y)=v2$

The suspended resolution of $p(a)$ (the instantiation of $p(v1)$) with the clause cl_1 is reconsidered. This resolution succeeds and returns the goal:

$c(x) \equiv z,\ \underline{g(y)=v2}$

where both atoms are outermost. Let $g(y)=v2$ be the selected atom. The elimination rule can be applied because $v2$ is not consumed by any atom. Then the derived goal is:

$\underline{c(x) \equiv z}$

The goal $c(x) \equiv z$ is resolved through cl_5 with the mgu $\{x'':=x,\ z:=c(y'')\}$

$\underline{x \equiv y''}$

Since x and y'' are two non-produced variables, the resolution succeeds by binding y'' to x; thus the computed solution is: $\{z:=c(x)\}$.

The outermost strategy, unlike the innermost case, cannot be implemented by means of a trivial compilation, because the atom selection order is not known statically, but can only be established at run-time. A more complex control of the computation than the one needed for Prolog is therefore required. While the selection order of the relational atoms is immaterial, the choice of the functional atoms to be resolved must be performed within the unification algorithm. The efficiency of the strategy is thus related to the efficiency in recognizing the produced variables and in finding their producers.

As the design of an efficient sequential model is a preliminary step to any parallel implementation, first we have developed a K-LEAF abstract (sequential) machine (Bosco *et al.*, 1989a). It consists in a modification of the Warren Abstract Machine (WAM) (Warren, 1983) where, to implement the outermost strategy, the unification instructions are changed as follows:

(1) Functional atoms are represented as terms stored in the heap;
(2) To represent produced variables, a new kind of term is introduced which links the variable to its producer;
(3) Unification instructions collect all the (terms denoting the) functional atoms that produce the variables bound by the unification: these atoms are then resolved before body atoms.

Storing functional atoms as terms on the heap requires, to start their resolution, an efficient implementation of a meta-predicate similar to Prolog's *call.*

6. Mapping IDEAL into K-LEAF

This section describes some aspects of the "compiled" version of IDEAL. Lambda-lifting techniques (Johnsson, 1987; Hughes, 1983; Peyton Jones, 1985) already known in the functional language context, are derived here following an independent path without borrowing too much from the functional world, i.e. proceeding according the suggested methodology of the logic programming community, based on *partial evaluation of meta-interpreters* (Jones *et al.*, 1985; Sterling and Beer, 1986).

In our case, the meta-interpreter is the axiomatization of IDEAL in K-LEAF and the HO program is a non-saturated λ-expression which represents an IDEAL user program. The union of the two pieces represents a normal K-LEAF program, which can be partially evaluated as any other logic program. The path towards the actual implementation is shown on the subset of the language dealing with lambda abstraction and application, which are the kernel of any higher-order extension. More detailed issues related to the actual HO L+F integration (patterns, conditions and existential variables) can be found in Bosco *et al.* (1989b).

6.1 A partial-evaluation approach to compilation

The partial evaluation technique in the context of programming languages based on FO logic merely amounts (given a set of axioms) to trying to prove FO theorems. In our case, the theorems to be proved must be chosen in order to represent a sort of *precomputation* of an actual HO program. So, for example, if the actual program *Prog* is $\lambda x.\lambda y.x+y$, an interesting theorem from the efficiency point of view is $\forall a.\exists X.\ Prog@a = X$. This theorem, when proved with a constructive interpretation of the existential quantifier (as in K-LEAF or Prolog) gives us a lemma $\forall a.Prog@a = \lambda y.a+y$ (the *computed-substitution* for X), which embodies the precomputation of β-reduction on the first argument for the curried *plus* function.

The actual goal for the partial evaluation purpose will be: $?\text{-}\ Prog@a = X$, where a represents a skolemized universally quantified variable.

Now let us consider how the resulting lemmas fit the efficiency requirements. After reconverting Skolem constants into universal variables the actual clause to be asserted should be:

$$\lambda x.\lambda y.x+y@A = \lambda y.A+y. \qquad (1)$$

If we continued the process of partial evaluation, from the goal:

$$?\text{-}\ (\lambda y.A+y)@B = X.$$

we would obtain the final lemma:

$$(\lambda y.A+y)@B = A+B. \qquad (2)$$

These clauses each consist of a head defining the K-LEAF function @ and of an empty body (a body would appear if the original HO function were a conditional one). Each clause is responsible for taking an argument A of the curried function (which, apart from some unification details, can be regarded as being passed in a register) and for binding a "result variable" (a location referenced by a register) with the result of the application. Such a result structure ($\lambda y.A+y$ in the first clause), according to normal WAM compilation, when unified against an unbound variable, is built in the Prolog *heap* while accessing the input register at each occurrence of the input argument. It is worth noting that the most important aspect in supercombinator-based implementations of functional languages, namely the possibility of compiling such a building phase into abstract machine instructions (e.g. push, cons,... in the G-machine (Johnsson, 1985; Burn *et al.*, 1988)), is automatically offered by this mapping from HO to FO, supported by a Prolog-like compilation based on the well-known WAM. In fact the building of structures is made by sequences of *unify* instructions which, when working in a *write mode*, behave exactly in the same way.

The partial evaluation approach gives a sound basis for the compilation process. Any K-LEAF axiomatization of IDEAL can serve this purpose: for example, the following derived from the equational theory in section 4:

(β1) (λX.X)@T = T
(β2) (λX.Y)@T = Y ⇐ dif(X,Y)
(β3) (λX.T1@T2))@T = (λX.T1@T)@(λX.T2@T)
(β3c) (λX.c(T1,...,Tn))@T = c(λX.T1@T,...,λX.Tn@T) for any constructor c
(β3||) (λX. λ{ P1.T1 :- B1 || ... || Pn.Tn :- Bn})@T =
λ{ (λX.(P1.T1 :- B1))@T || ... || (λX.(Pn.Tn :- Bn))@T}
(β3:-) (λX.(P.Ti :- B))@T = (P.(λX.Ti)@T :- (λX.B)@T) ⇐
difpat(X,P), nonfreepatv(P,T) or nonfree(X,Ti)
(β3≡) (λX.T1≡T2)@T = (λX.T1)@T≡ (λX.T2)@T
(β3∃) (λX.∃T1)@T = ∃((λX.T1)@T)
(β4) (λX.λX.T1)@T2 = λX.T1
(β4p) (λX.(P.Ti :- B))@T = P.Ti :- B ⇐ in(X,Y)
(β5) (λX.λY.T1)@T2 = λY.(λX.T1@T2) ⇐ dif(X,Y),
nonfree(X,T1) or nonfree(Y,T2)
(β5p) (λX.(P.Ti :- B))@T = (P.(λX.Ti)@T :- (λX.B)@T) ⇐
difpat(X,P), nonfreepatv(P,T) or nonfree(X,Ti)

(α) λX.T1 = λY.T2 ⇐ (λX.T1)@Z = (λY.T2)@Z,

To apply this system a preliminary syntactic transformation of the program is required to convert all the @ in the scope of a lambda abstraction into the equivalent constructor @′. α strict equality extends K-LEAF strict equality and allows the resolution mechanism to obtain β-normal forms.

A more conventional and equivalent environment-based semantics can also be used. To get a compiler we should iterate the partial evaluation on, roughly speaking, all the abstractions in a program, as was indicated in the formulae *pe1-pe4* in section 4.2. We can try to embed the partial evaluation step directly into the axiomatization, thus obtaining a more efficient compiler. The following program is the result of such embedding and can be considered a kernel compiler. In the goal *peval(Form,Env) = Res*, *Form* is the λ-term to be transformed, *Res* is the result of the transformation, and *Env* is an environment binding λ-variables to logical variables, thus handling α-renaming.

```
peval(X,E) = search(X,E) :- atomic(X).
peval(A@B,E) = app(peval(A,E),peval(B,E)).
peval(lambda(X,B),E) = lemma(Alfa, peval(B,[(X,Alfa)|E])).
peval(A+B,R,E) = plus(peval(A,E),peval(B,E)).
..........................................................................

plus(A,B) = A+B.        where + is a constructor
app(A,B) = A@B.
..................

search(X,[]) = X.
search(X,[(Y,B)|L]) = if(eq(X,Y),B,search(X,L)).

lemma(Alfa,Beta) = lambda(Alfa,Beta) :-
        {**write this lemma somewhere** (lambda(Alfa,Beta)@Alfa = Beta) ***}.
```

Universally quantified variables are here implemented by "normal" new logical variables which are guaranteed not to be instantiated in the course of the program.

Some additional refinement is still due, in order to get a non-naive compiled implementation. First, let us consider clauses (1) and (2) of the previous example; their first arguments are of the form *Prog@A*, where *Prog* is the abstract syntactic term denoting a functional term in the program at some stage of λ-saturation. If we left it as it is, any matching phase for an application step would need to match the actual function *F* of the application *F@a* (that is, a complex λ-term) against another complex λ-term in order to identify the function to be applied. This problem is overcome by giving to each λ-abstraction a new name (i.e. by explicitly naming each functional node in the graph) equipped with the set of free variables at that level, i.e. the set of variables which should be already bound at the invocation of such a function. In our example the terms *λx.λy.x+y*, *λy.A+y* would change into *f1*, *f2(A)*, respectively, and the (K-LEAF) clauses would change accordingly:

```
f1@A= f2(A).
f2(A)@B= A+B.
```

6.2 Type inference

It has been shown by several authors how *type inference*, in functional languages, can be recast in a problem of abstract interpretation over type domains. Usually, at the operational level there is a loss of elegance of this approach, because the need to perform type unification imposes some changes from the source program and the program whose partial evaluation gives the type inference. In the logic framework, on the contrary, this method can be exploited in the most natural way, that is, no changes in the axiomatization are required, apart from the rules dealing with built-in domains. W.r.t. *peval*, here the change of domains is embodied in the use of "normal" existentially quantified logical variables, which act here as type variables over which unification implements type intersection and is reflected in the change of the rules for *plus* and *app* into the following:

```
plus(int,int) = int.
.................
app(lambda(Alfa,Beta),Alfa) = Beta.
```

where the type *lambda(Alfa,Beta)* is left here in place of the usual *Alfa -> Beta.*

6.3 An actual compiler

An extract of the actual IDEAL compiler, which derives from the methodology introduced in sections 6.1 and 6.2, is reported and commented on in the following. Although different policies could be chosen to accommodate *compilation* and *type inference*, we will illustrate a procedure which carries on both processes at the same time, i.e. it both constructs a list of flat functions (which constitutes the compiled code) and assigns to the program its most general type.

The procedure, moreover, generates *fully lazy supercombinators* (Hughes, 1983). To guarantee that a closed term is evaluated only once in the course of the computation, *maximally free expressions* in lambda terms are abstracted into new lambda variables in order to be shared through the normal graph representation. Despite the relative complexity of the problem the Prolog program is found to be quite compact and understandable. This is due to the full use of some logical capabilities. The original program for doing the same transformation, written in Prolog by Hughes, was so complex that even the author had problems in understanding it after some time (Bird, 1987).

The top-level procedure *eval* takes the following input parameters (the numbers in parentheses are the argument positions):

(1) The λ-*term* to be compiled;
(7) The *Environment*, i.e. an association list of the form *(Name, (Var, Vart))* where
Name: syntactic λ-variable
Var: α-renaming of the λ-variable
Vart: type variable represented by a Prolog variable;
(8) *Variable(list)* w.r.t which maximally free expression of *Term* are to be calculated.

Output parameters are as follows:

(2) Output syntactic representation with *type error information*:
If the program is type-correct this will be equal to the input term, otherwise the expected type will be inserted into the program, where there is a type clash;
(3) *Compiled version* of the input term;
(4) *Type* of the input term;
(5) (List of) *Maximally free expressions* in input term w.r.t. the input variable list;
(6) (List of) variables which have been substituted to MFE's in (3).

CASE 1: X is a logical (universal) variable

X has been already substituted for some syntactic λ-variable; it must be dealt with as a λ-variable, that is, if X is the latest abstracted variable it is not returned as a free variable. A new type variable "Ty" is returned as the type of the variable.

```
eval(X,X,X,Ty,Free,Free,Env,Var) :- var(X),!,
(is_abstracted(X,Var) -> Free=[];Free=[X]).
```

```
is_abstracted(X,Var) :- var(Var),!,X==Var.
is_abstracted(X,Var) :- member(X,Var).
```

CASE 2: X is a combinator name

```
eval(X,X,V,_,[X],[V],_,_) :- atomic(X),is_comb(X),!.
```

CASE 3: Builtins

```
unitype(Term,Term,Exp,Type) :- occur-check_on,Exp=Type, ! ,occur-check_off.
unitype(Term,error(Term,Exp,Type),Exp,Type) :-  occur-check_off.
```

unitype is assumed to take a type expression (third arg) and unify it with an expected type (fourth arg), provided that the occur-check test is enabled. If unification succeeds, the input syntactic term (first argument) is returned as unchanged (second parameter). Otherwise the term *error(input-term, type-expression, expected-type)* is returned for being able to give information about where there is a type clash. Now let us consider a few clauses about builtins.

```
eval(+,U,+,Type,[],[],_,_) :- !,unitype(+,U,(int,int)-->int,Type).
eval(eq,U,eq,Type,[],[],_,_) :- !,unitype(eq,U,(X,X)-->bool,Type).
eval(if,U,if,Type,[],[],_,_) :- !,unitype(if,U,(Bool,X,X)-->X,Type).
..............
```

CASE 4: Other atomic symbols

An atomic symbol corresponds to an occurrence of a λ-variable inside an expression. The environment must be searched to get the relative α-renaming Xr and type variable Xt. Xr is returned as a free variable if it is not directly in the scope of the Xr abstraction.

```
eval(T,U,Xr,Type,Free,Free,Env,Var) :- atomic(T),!,search(Env,T,(Xr,Xt)),
unitype(T,U,Xt,Type), (is_abstracted(Xr,Var) -> Free=[]; Free=[Xr]).
```

CASE 5: Lambda-abstraction:

First the body of the abstraction is processed in a new environment enriched with the association among the λ-variable X and two fresh logical variables *Newr*, *Newt* implementing α-renaming and type variable, respectively. The type of the abstraction (Type) is assigned with *Newt-->Tyb*, where *Tyb* is the resulting type of the body. Afterwards, the function relative to the current λ-abstraction is built: the head is obtained by creating a compound term whose functor is a newly generated name and whose arguments are the variables *Fvb* used to abstract the MFEs in the body (*Freeb*). Finally, the body of the function made with the same functor and the actual MFEs (*Freeb*) is processed.

```
eval(Lambda,U,R,Type,Free,Fv,Env,Var) :- Lambda=lambda(X,B),!,
eval(B,Bu,Br,Tyb,Freeb,Fvb,[(X,(Newr,Newt))|Env],Newr),
(B==Bu -> Lam1=Lambda; Lam1=lambda(X,Bu)),
unitype(Lam1,U,Newt-->Tyb,Type),
get_comb_pattern(Fvb,Head),myassert((Head@Newr = Br)),
Head=..[Cloname|_],Ris=..[Cloname|Freeb],
eval(Ris,_,R,_,Free,Fv,Env,Var).
```

This behaviour is shown in a simple example:

Term	Code	Type	Free	Fv	Env	V
λzxy.(x+x)+(z+z)		Z'->B'				
λxy.(x+x)+(z+z)		B'=X'->B''			[(z,Z,Z')]	Z [illegible]
λy.(x+x)+(z+z)		B''=Y'->B'''			[(z,Z,Z'), (x,X.X')]	X [illegible]
(x+x)+(z+z)	{c1(U)@Y = U}	Z'=X'=int	(X+X)+(Z+Z)	U	[(z,Z,i),(x,X,i), (y,Y,Y')]	[illegible]
c1((X+X)+(Z+Z))	{c2(K)@X = c1(X+X+K)}		(Z+Z)	K	[...	X [illegible]
c2(Z+Z)	{top@Z = c2(Z+Z)}		[]		[...	[illegible]

CASE 6: Pairing

Every compound term is converted into a cartesian product which is handled by the following clause. The only aspect worth noticing is the append operation which approximates the union operation over the MFEs of the two components of the pair.

```
eval(Pair,U,(A1r,B1r),(A1t,B1t),Free,Fv,Env,Var) :- Pair=(A,B),!,
        eval(A,Au,A1r,A1t,Freea,Fva,Env,Var),
        eval(B,Bu,B1r,B1t,Freeb,Fvb,Env,Var),
        append(Freea,Freeb,Free),append(Fva,Fvb,Fv),
        ((A==Au,B==Bu) -> U=Pair; U=(Au,Bu)).
```

CASE 7: Application

This is a special case of a builtin function.

```
eval(@,U,@,Type,[],[],_,_) :- !, unitype(@,U,(Alfa-->Beta,Alfa)-->Beta,Type).
```

CASE 8: Recursive definitions (*letrec([f1=b1,...fn=bn], Body)*)

The fixpoint equation $f = body(f)$ can be implemented in different ways. For example, in the G-machine (Johnsson, 1987) it leads to the run-time construction of a cyclic structure. While it could be possible to implement cycles in the underlying K-LEAF virtual machine (as in Prolog, this would merely amount to solving the goal *F=comp(F)* where, as for any other λ-abstraction, *F* is the α-renaming of *f* and *comp* represents the compilation of *body*), this would lead to a discrepancy between the implementation and the current semantics. So we chose to compile *letrecs* to a flat level by introducing, as for any other λ-abstraction, new function names.

The evaluation proceeds as follows. First (by the predicate *scandefs*), local function names are assigned α-renamings and type variables in a new environment. Then, the *letrec* structure is processed. This compiles the bodies by substituting the function names with their α-renamings. The resulting structures represent the equation:

[F1,...,F2]=[compb1(F1,...,Fn), ...,compbn(F1,...,Fn)]

for both compiled code and types. Finally the equations are solved, by just unification for the type case and by assigning the logical variables *F1,...,Fn* with *n* newly generated names (by *getnames*) for the compiled version.

```
eval(Letrec,U,Result,Type,FE,FEvars,Env,Var) :-
    Letrec=letrec(Def,Body),!,
    scandefs(Def,Env,Envnew,Forms,Varsr,Varst),
    eval((Body,Forms),(Bu,Fu),(Body1r,Forms1r),(Body1t,Forms1t),
            FE1,FEvars1,Envnew,Varsr),
    mk_list(Forms1r,Forms2r),mk_list(Forms1t,Forms2t),
    ((Forms==Fu,Body==Bu) -> Let1=Letrec; Let1=letrec(Fu,Bu)),
    getnames(Varsr,Newnames,FEvars1),
    unitype(Let1,Lu,Varst,Forms2t),          /* F_n-type = Body_n-type */
    unitype(Lu,U,Body1t,Type),
    Varsr=Newnames,              /* F_n = Body_n */
    lemmas(Forms2r,Newnames),
    FE1=FEvars1,
    eval(Body1r,_,Result,_,FE,FEvars,Env,Var).
```

CASE 9: Other compound terms

The argument list is first translated into a cartesian product, which is processed by the appropriate clause, then the type of the functor is equated to *Lty-->Type*, where *Lty* is the type of the product and *Type* is the type of the result. If the list of compiled arguments coincides with the list of MFE variables of the product (this means that every argument is a free expression (FE)) then the whole compound term is a FE, and so a new variable (*Newvar*) is returned for abstracting the FE. Otherwise a compound term built out of the functor and the returned compiled arguments is returned as the result and MFEs coming from the product are compacted into a set.

```
eval(T,U,R,Type,Mfree,Mfv,Env,Var):-
not(atomic(T)),T=..[F|L],mk_cart_prod(L,Lcart),
eval(Lcart,Lu,Lr,Lty,Mfs,Mfvs,Env,Var),
eval(F,Fu,_,Lty-->Type,_,_,Env,_),
mk_list(Lr,List),mk_list(Lu,Lur),
((Lcart==Lu,F==Fu) -> U=T; U=..[F,Fu|Lur]),
```

```
(Mfvs==List -> (Ris=..[F|Mfs],Mfree=[Ris],R=Newvar,Mfv=[Newvar]);
                (to_set([],Mfs,Mfree), to_set([],Mfvs,Mfv), R=..[F|List])).

to_set(Inl,[],Inl).
to_set(Inl,[Mf|Mfs],Outl) :- var(Mf),member(Mf,Inl),!, to_set(Inl,Mfs,Outl).
to_set(Inl,[Mf|Mfs],Outl) :- to_set([Mf|Inl],Mfs,Outl).
```

7. Parallelism in IDEAL/K-LEAF

Due to their declarative nature, logic and functional languages are widely recognized as good candidates for a "natural" move from sequential programming of algorithms to the situation where several processing elements can be made to co-operate in parallel for the solution of a problem. We deliberately exclude here the other, although very important, aspect of parallel/concurrent programming, typical of embedded systems, where the program must cope with "simultaneous" and "continuous" distributed changes of an external world. While the latter scenarios require real concurrency, i.e. at least some explicit notions of *merging* or *synchronization* at the user language level, in the first case it is just a matter of programming style whether to introduce an explicit notion of parallelism.

With logic and/or functional languages we can, at least in principle, exploit the sources of parallelism already *implicitly* present in their operational semantics (e.g. based on resolution or on reduction), with no need of explicit constructs to spawn/synchronize parallel computations. A first consequence of this fact is that the same semantic characterization fits both the sequential and the parallel versions of such languages: concepts like *logic consequence, computed substitution answer, resolution step, normal form, rewriting step,...* are independent of the (sequential/parallel) way they are proved or computed.

The computational model of pure logic languages suggests two aspects that can, in principle, be handled concurrently, the search rule and the computation rule. The OR-parallelism is related to the use of parallelism in the search rule (a parallel search rule is intrinsically fair). OR-parallelism in outermost SLD-resolution for K-LEAF is essentially similar to OR-parallelism in pure logic languages: it introduces the possibility of performing in parallel all the possible resolutions of the selected functional/relational atom against the set of clauses defining it. AND-parallelism is related to the use of parallelism in the computation rule: two or more atoms in a goal can be resolved in parallel.

Even simpler, the computational mechanism of functional languages, namely reduction, can be applied in parallel to several different redexes in a graph (or string), obtaining parallel evaluation of functional arguments along with function bodies.

In our approach the adoption of flat SLD-resolution as a uniform computational mechanism for integrated Logic-Functional languages implies that AND-parallel execution of atoms derived from the transformation of functional calls into functional atoms are equivalent to parallel functional reductions.

The main problem in designing parallel algorithms is to achieve the "right" balance of parallel versus sequential execution according to the actual features of the physical machine, namely number of processors, processor power, network throughput and latency, and others. Several methods can contribute to determine a good compromise. On the one hand we have to guarantee enough parallelism for exploiting the processing power. On the other, we must ensure that each process has a suitable lifetime to compensate the overhead due to process creation and communication.

The first constraint should be primarily solved by designing inherently parallel algorithms (for example, quicksort is "more" parallel than standard bubblesort). We are confident that the declarative and symbolic nature of logic and functional languages encourages the development of *divide and conquer* and *search-based* programs with great potential for parallelism. Other program analysis and transformation techniques, such as abstract interpretation (for strictness analysis; Burn, 1987), partial evaluation, etc. can further increase the degree of implicit parallelism without resorting to speculative parallelism (i.e. parallel evaluation of subproblems which are not guaranteed to eventually contribute to the solution of the overall problem, such as parallel evaluation of both branches of if-then-else) which is usually more difficult to manage. In many cases the resulting small granularity of potential parallelism does not fit the second constraint. A way of determining larger sequential parts of computation is needed. This can hardly be achieved by automatic tools. Our choice was to leave to the programmer such a responsability, by providing him with simple annotations by which to characterize sequential and parallel parts.

Thus our approach to parallelism could be called "controlled implicit parallelism" in the sense that all safe computations (resolution of equational goals which will be required in order to get the final solution) and by-definition eager computations (normal logical goals) could in principle be executed in parallel, but sometimes this would generate a lot of interacting processes wasting the architecture's computational power. For the sake of efficiency we introduce annotations whose basic purpose is to guarantee that the grain size of each subcomputation is "optimal" for the kind of processing elements (roughly, commercial microprocessors) which constitute our reference architecture. We chose to have a parallel annotation // having the following informal meanings:

(1) When put on the name of a predicate or function symbol in a definition it specifies that OR-parallelism is required for the resolution of a goal involving that name.
(2) When put on a goal it specifies that the resolution of such a goal must be spawned as a parallel (AND) process.

As a simple example let us consider the IDEAL program:

```
map@F@[] = []
map@F@[A|X] = [F@A|map@F@X]
goal(L,R) :- map@f@L=R.
goal(L,R) :- map@g@L=R.

f@X = long_computation(X).
g@X = short_computation(X).
:- goal([1,2,3,4,5],R).
```

A reasonable parallel modification of the program could be:

```
map@F@[] = []
map@F@[A|X] = [ (F@A)// | map@F@X ]
map_seq@F@[] = []
map_seq@F@[A|X] = [F@A|map_seq@F@X]
```

```
//goal(L,R) :- map@f@L=R.
//goal(L,R) :- map_seq@g@L=R.
f@X = long_computation(X).
g@X = short_computation(X).

:- //goal([1,2,3,4,5],R).
```

That is, //goal has to be executed by OR-parallelism; due to the complexity of *f* it is worth generating an AND-process for each application of *f* to a list element, while, for *g*, we estimate that sequential execution is better.

7.1 Completeness and OR-parallelism

It must be recalled that OR-parallel resolution of a goal against the defining clauses of the predicate provides a correct implementation of the abstract resolution strategy which requires for completeness a breadth-first search on the SLD-tree. Thus a problem arises with the annotated program, related to the "implicit" sequential reading of the non-annotated predicates. In fact, by leaving predicates "sequential" we would like to approximate the efficiency obtainable by the sequential Prolog models based on backtracking (and depth-first strategy, single environment). This could be a cause of incompleteness.

This is not a significant problem if the programming methodology requires us to start with a "sequential" version of the program which could be sufficiently tested on a Prolog-like environment. In this sense adding parallelism could only improve the correctness of the "sequential" implementation.

These arguments are not in favour of uncontrolled program development. Rather they merely stress the importance of a methodology and tools for achieving "correct" sequential IDEAL/K-LEAF programs. Run-time techniques to discover repetitions in a depth-first branch are available in the Prolog context, but at this stage we do not plan to incorporate such run-time checks into our executors. Also, we could use some methods for proving that an IDEAL/K-LEAF program is complete even with a depth-first strategy. The question of how to proceed when a completeness proof is lacking is a philosophical one. We could automatically consider the other predicates (those for which the completeness proof has not been achieved) as "OR-parallel" predicates or to blindly (and more practically) adopt a depth-first strategy trading the (limited) risk of incompleteness with the sequential efficiency.

7.2 Completeness and AND-parallelism

If an unconstrained form of AND-parallelism was adopted, no cause of incompleteness could be introduced by simply leaving the resolution of an AND conjunct to be performed sequentially. However, since we are interested in a combination of OR-parallelism and AND-parallelism, in order to enable an efficient implementation we are forced to restrict the general possible AND-OR interaction. This feeling is shared by many researchers in the field of parallel implementation of Prolog (Warren, 1987; Westphal *et al.*, 1987; Gabriel *et al.*, 1985; Hermenegildo, 1987). In fact the unrestricted AND-OR models, besides being quite difficult to understand from the user point of view, require us to share in a distributed architecture a growing cactus stack, with great complications in order to keep locality of sub-computations. Our choice has been to combine full OR-parallelism with deterministic AND-parallelism, i.e. only-AND conjuncts having at most one solution are "allowed" to be generated in parallel. Now the problem appears of how to detect such a "deterministic" nature. The only simple case where this could be done automatically while preserving completeness is when a functional goal (or part of a functional goal) is ground, so a "deterministic" tag (˜) could be automatically put on the related produced variable and propagated during the computation. Apart from this simple case corresponding to simple functional reduction, two ways are possible for a sound exploitation of AND-parallelism. (1) Use partial evaluation to try to discover the instantiation state of variables in the course of the computation; in this way we could enable more AND-parallel deterministic computations. (2) Automatically translate unrestricted AND-parallel programs into equivalent programs making use of (built-in) sound set-oriented-primitives (in the sense that they must allow us to "consume" solutions as soon as they are computed, in contrast with the usual set-primitives working only with finite solution spaces).

7.3 A simpler alternative: mapping AND-parallelism into OR-parallelism

The kind of AND-parallelism necessary to fully exploit the parallelism available in functional reduction (namely the possibility of running in parallel arguments and function bodies) requires the introduction of synchronization primitives, like the read-only variable annotation of Concurrent Prolog. For example, the program (which we assume to be executed by AND-parallelism):

```
f(X,Y) = g(X,Y,a)
g(a,a,a) = b.
h(a)=a.
?- f(h(a),U)=R.
```

should be implemented as:

```
f(X,Y) = R :-  g(X,Y,a) = R.
g(a,a,a) = b.
h(a) = a.
?- f(V?,U)=R,h(a)=V.
```

However, the capabilities usually present in any OR-parallel implementation allow simpler but quite useful forms of AND-parallelism, namely those related to the parallel evaluation of arguments of functions and data structures.

We investigated how *set* primitives offered by an OR-parallel abstract machine could be used to obtain various forms of AND-parallelism. A similar approach has been also recently taken by Argonne researchers in the context of the GigaLips project (Carlsson *et al.*, 1988), in contrast to more complicated AND-OR schemes requiring a highly sophisticated and complex virtual machines as in Westphal *et al.* (1987). It amounts to (syntactically) converting a problem of AND-parallelism into a program which only makes use of OR-parallel *set* primitives.

```
par_and(F,G) :-
    parsetof((parsetof(F,F,Fset) ; // (parsetof(G,G,Gset),(Fset,Gset),[(Fs,Gs),(Fs,Gs)]),
```

member(F,Fs),member(G,Gs).

Here *F* and *G* are evaluated in parallel (by the outermost *parsetof*) and each of them can lead to several OR-parallel solutions (computed by the innermost *parsetof* constructs). Afterwards the computation becomes sequential, and *member* calls perform the join of solutions in a backtrack way. Of course, in a parallel context the use of the AND-parallel results can be performed in OR-parallel provided that *member* is declared as OR-parallel.

In order to guarantee completeness, of course, the implementation must allow solutions in the set to be eagerly consumed. This implies a producer-consumer relationship among the set and *member*, which, again, requires synchronization at the implementation level. This actually is a case of mixing OR-parallelism with deterministic AND-parallelism, but as set-primitives (whose result is deterministic) are the only AND-parallel conjuncts, the overall implementation can be more specialized than the general treatment of read-only variables. This is also a feasible solution for achieving general AND-OR parallel computations.

8. The present state of IDEAL implementation and future work

IDEAL programs are transformed into Horn clauses: higher-orderness is eliminated through a variant of *lambda-lifting*: this technique was developed to compile functional programs into a set of program-dependent *supercombinators* (Hughes, 1983), which can be considered (first-order) rewriting rules, easily transformable into either Prolog (Bosco and Giovannetti, 1986) or K-LEAF clauses. We extended it to cope with the logical aspects of IDEAL (namely, patterns, logical variables and conditions).

A first implementation of IDEAL (mapping IDEAL into Prolog and then running the so-obtained programs) adopted a default eager (i.e. call-by-value) strategy; the comparison w.r.t. some compiled/interpreted LISP systems was quite satisfactory (see Bellia *et al.*, 1987). We have terminated a lazy version: it is obtained by transforming IDEAL into K-LEAF (Bosco *et al.*, 1989b) and executing the resulting programs according to the outermost strategy of K-LEAF, which is supported by an extended WAM (Bosco *et al.*, 1989a). Currently, such extended WAM is executed by a C-emulator.

The whole compilation from IDEAL to extended WAM is influenced by *strictness annotations*, in the form of labels ε, λ (eager, lazy, resp.) associated with the arguments of functions, predicates and constructors. Eager annotations generally lead to a more efficient code. However, there are cases where lazy annotations allow more efficient computations.

Extrapolations of the run-time figures obtained by the C-emulator versus efficient Prolog implementations (e.g. Quintus, BIM, etc.) show that the language can be easily made almost as efficient as the best implementations of modern lazy functional languages (i.e. in the range 1-2 slower than Lazy ML) and compete with conventional languages for some applications. In fact, by an assembly language level executor of the WAM, the *invertible* simulator, described in section 2, should be able to process about 1000 events per second on a MicroVax, i.e. twice as slow as *non-invertible* "industrial" simulators (written in C, Fortran) on the same machine.

The performance figures reported above refer to an "eager by default" compilation mode of the source program. If the opposite view (i.e. "lazy by default") is adopted, the simulation becomes about two times slower. The overhead is caused by the construction and exploration of delayed expressions: in the simulation queries, any delayed expression is eventually reactivated, hence the overhead is not reduced by savings in computation. In the fault-finding example, on the contrary, the lazy version of the program is far more efficient than the eager one; the difference increases exponentially as the size of the circuit grows, and for a 4-bit adder reaches a factor of 100. The fault-finding queries involve a generate&test process. Due to lazy evaluation, failures occur earlier (than in the eager computation) because the tests can be performed on partially computed structures. Moreover, when a failure occurs, backtracking only reconsiders the choice points which contribute to the failure, because of the unification-driven activation of suspended atoms employed in outermost resolution. A preliminary (compiled into WAM code) OR-parallel version of IDEAL/K-LEAF (that introduces the possibility of performing in parallel all the possible resolutions of a function/predicate call against the set of clauses defining it) has been also developed, based on the OR-parallel Prolog system developed in CSELT (Giandonato and Sofi, 1988; Merlo *et al.*, 1988). This was relatively straightforward due to the orthogonality among the extensions to cope with the outermost selection strategy and those for supporting OR-parallelism. We are currently testing such parallel implementation in an emulated environment, before installing it on our physical, Transputer-based, parallel architecture (Balboni *et al.*, 1987). Moreover, we are extending the current implementation to optimize the AND-parallel scheme shown in section 7.

9. References

G.P. Balboni, G.Giandonato and R.Melen, A parallel architecture for AI-based real-time applications, Proc. 1987 AFCEA European Symposium (Rome, 1987).

R. Barbuti, M. Bellia, G. Levi and M. Martelli, On the integration of logic programming and functional programming, Proc. 1984 Symp. on Logic Programming (IEEE Comp. Society Press, 1985), 160-166.

R. Barbuti, M. Bellia, G. Levi and M. Martelli, LEAF: A language which integrates logic, equations and functions, in Logic Programming: Functions, Relations and Equations, D. DeGroot and G. Lindstrom, Eds. (Prentice-Hall, 1986), 201-238.

M. Bellia and G. Levi, The relation between logic and functional languages: A survey, Journal of Logic Programming 3 (1986), 217-236 .

M. Bellia, P.G. Bosco, E. Giovannetti, G. Levi, C. Moiso and C. Palamidessi, A two-level approach to logic plus functional programming integration, Proc. PARLE Conference, LNCS 258 (Springer-Verlag, 1987), 374-393.

J.A Bergstra and J.W. Klop, Conditional rewrite rules: confluence and termination, J. of Computer and System Science 32 (1986), 323-362.

P.G. Bosco and E. Giovannetti, IDEAL: An Ideal DEductive Applicative Language, Proc. 1986 Symp. on Logic Programming (IEEE Comp. Society Press, 1986), 89-94.

P.G. Bosco, E. Giovannetti and C. Moiso, Refined strategies for semantic unification, Proc. TAPSOFT '87 , LNCS 250 (Springer-Verlag, 1987a), 276-290.

P.G. Bosco, E. Giovannetti, G. Levi, C. Moiso and C. Palamidessi, A complete semantic characterization of K-LEAF, a logic language with partial functions, in Proc. 1987 Symp. on Logic Programming (IEEE Comp. Society Press, 1987b), 318-327.

P.G. Bosco, E. Giovannetti and C. Moiso, Narrowing vs. SLD-resolution, J. of Theoretical Computer Science, Vol. 59, No. 1-2 (North-Holland, 1988a), 3-23.

P.G. Bosco, C. Cecchi and C. Moiso, Exploiting the full power of logic plus functional programming, Proc. 5th Int. Conference and Symposium on Logic Programming (MIT Press, 1988b), 3-17.

P.G. Bosco, C. Cecchi and C. Moiso, An extension of WAM for K-LEAF: a WAM based compilation of conditional narrowing (1989a). Submitted for publication.

P.G. Bosco, C. Cecchi and C. Moiso, Implementation of IDEAL (1989b). Submitted for publication.

P.G. Bosco, C. Cecchi, E. Giovannetti and C. Moiso, The language IDEAL, CSELT Int. Rep. (1989c).

D. Brand, Proving theorems with the modification method, SIAM J. Comput. 4 (1975), 412-430.

G. L. Burn, Abstract interpretation and the parallel evaluation of functional languages, PhD Thesis, University of London (1987).

G.L. Burn, S.L. Peyton Jones and J.D. Robson, The spineless G-Machine, Proc. of 1988 ACM Lisp and Functional Programming Conference (ACM, 1988).

M. Carlsson, K. Danhof and R. Overbeek, A simplified approach to the implementation of AND-parallelism in an OR-parallel environment, Proc. 5th Conference and Symposium on Logic Programming (MIT Press, 1988), 1565-1577.

N. Dershowitz and D.A. Plaisted, Logic programming cum applicative programming, Proc. 1985 Symp. on Logic Programming (IEEE Comp. Society Press, 1985), 54-66.

M. H. van Emden and R. A. Kowalski, The semantics of predicate logic as a programming language, J. ACM 23 (1976), 733-742.

M. Fay, First order unification in an equational theory, Proc. 4th Workshop on Automated Deduction (1979), 161-167.

L. Fribourg, Oriented equational clauses as a programming language, J. Logic Programming 1 (1984), 165-177.

L. Fribourg, SLOG: A logic programming language interpreter based on clausal superposition and rewriting, Proc. 1985 Symp. on Logic Programming (IEEE Comp. Society Press, 1985), 172-184.

J. Gabriel, T. Lindholm, E.L. Lusk and R.A. Overbeek, Logic programming on the HEP, in Parallel MIMD computation: HEP Supercomputer and its applications (MIT Press, 1985), 181-202.

G. Giandonato and G. Sofi, Parallelizing logic programming based inference engines, Proc. of the International Conference on Supercomputing (1988),282-287.

E. Giovannetti, G. Levi, C. Moiso and C. Palamidessi, Kernel LEAF: an experimental logic plus functional language - its syntax, semantics and computational model, ESPRIT Project no. 415, Subproject D, Deliverable D2 (1986).

E. Giovannetti and C. Moiso, A completeness result for a semantic unification algorithm based on conditional narrowing, Proc. Foundations of Logic and Functional Programming, LNCS 306 (Springer-Verlag, 1988), 157-167.

J.A. Goguen, J.W. Thatcher, E. Wagner and J.B. Wright, Initial algebra semantics and continuous algebras, J. ACM 24 (1977).

J.A. Goguen and J. Meseguer, Equality, types and generic modules for logic programming, in Logic Programming: Functions, Relations and Equations, D. DeGroot and G. Lindstrom, Eds. (Prentice-Hall, 1986a), 295-364.

J.A. Goguen, One, none, a hundred thousand specification languages, Proc. IFIP 86 (Elsevier Science Publishers, IFIP 1986b), 995-1004.

M.V. Hermenegildo, Relating goal scheduling, precedence and memory management in AND-parallel execution of logic programs, Proc. 4th Conf. on Logic Programming, (MIT Press, 1987), 556-575.

S.Hoelldobler, Equational logic programming, Proc. 1987 Symp. on Logic Programming (IEEE Comp. Society Press, 1987), 335-346.

S.Hoelldobler, From paramodulation to narrowing, Proc. 5th Int. Conference and Symposium on Logic Programming (MIT Press, 1988), 327-342.

J. Hughes, The design and implementation of programming languages, PhD Thesis, University of Oxford (1983).

J.-M. Hullot, Canonical forms and unification, Proc. 5th Conf. on Automated Deduction, LNCS 87 (Springer-Verlag, 1980), 318-334.

J. Jaffar, J.-L. Lassez and M.J. Maher, A theory of complete logic programs with equality, J. Logic Programming 1 (1984), 211-223.

J. Jaffar, J.-L. Lassez and M.J. Maher, A logic programming language scheme, in Logic Programming: Functions, Relations and Equations, D. DeGroot and G. Lindstrom, Eds. (Prentice-Hall, 1986a), 441-468.

J. Jaffar, J.-L. Lassez and M.J. Maher, Some issues and trends in the semantics of logic programming, Proc. of Third Int. Conf. on Logic Programming, LNCS 225 (Springer-Verlag, 1986b), 223-241.

T. Johnsson, Lambda-lifting: transforming programs to recursive equations, Proc. of Int. Conf. of Functional Programming Languages and Architectures, LNCS 201 (Springer-Verlag, 1985), 190-203.

N.D. Jones, P Sestoft and H. Sondergaard, An experiment in partial evaluation: the generation of a compiler generator, Proc. First Int. Conf. on Rewriting Techniques and Applications, LNCS 202 (Springer-Verlag, 1985) 124-140.

S. Kaplan, Fair conditional term rewriting systems: unification, termination and confluence, Technical Report no. 194, University of Orsay (1984).

J.W.Klop, Term rewriting systems, Notes for the Summer Workshop on Reduction Machines (Ustica, 1985).

J.W. Lloyd, Foundations of Logic Programming (Springer-Verlag, 1984).

A. Martelli, C. Moiso and G.F. Rossi, Lazy unification algorithms for canonical rewrite systems, Proc. of Colloquium on Resolution of Equations in Algebraic Structures, Lakeway, 4-6 May, 1987.

C. Merlo, C. Moiso, M. Porta and G. Sofi, Parallel Prolog for signal-understanding parallel machines: implementation and applications, ESPRIT Pilot Project no. 26, Deliverable 14b (Sept. 1988).

D. Miller and G. Nadathur, Higher-order logic programming, Proc. of Third Int. Conf. on Logic Programming, LNCS 225 (Springer-Verlag, 1986), 448-462.

R. Milner, A theory of type polymorphism in programming, Journal of Computer and System Sciences 17, 3 (Dec. 1978), 348-375.

S.L. Peyton Jones, An introduction to fully-lazy supercombinators, Proc. 13th Spring School of the LITP, LNCS 242 (Springer-Verlag, 1985), 176-208.

U.S. Reddy, Narrowing as the operational semantics of functional languages, Proc. 1985 Symp. on Logic Programming (IEEE Comp. Society Press, 1985), 138-151.

U.S. Reddy, On the relationship between logic and functional languages. In Logic Programming: Functions, Relations and Equations, D. DeGroot and G. Lindstrom, Eds. (Prentice-Hall, 1986), 3-36.

P. Rety, C. Kirchner, H. Kirchner and P. Lescanne, NARROWER: A new algorithm for unification and its application to logic programming, Proc. First Int. Conf. on Rewriting Techniques and Applications, LNCS 202 (Springer-Verlag, 1985) 141-157.

G. Revesz, Axioms for the theory of lambda-conversion, SIAM J. Comput. Vol. 14, No. 2 (1985).

L. Sterling and R.D. Beer, Incremental flavor-mixing of meta-interpreters for expert systems construction, Proc. 1986 Int. Symp. on Logic Programming (IEEE Comp. Society Press, 1986), 20-27.

P.A. Subrahmanyam and J.-H. You, FUNLOG: A computational model integrating logic programming and functional programming, in Logic Programming: Functions, Relations and Equations, D. DeGroot and G. Lindstrom, Eds. (Prentice-Hall, 1986), 157-198.

H. Tamaki, Semantics of a logic programming language with a reducibility predicate, Proc. 1984 Int. Symp. on Logic Programming (IEEE Comp. Society Press, 1984), 259-264.

D.A. Turner, MIRANDA: a non-strict functional language with polymorphic types, in Proc. of Int. Conf. of Functional Programming Lnguages and Architectures, LNCS 201(Springer-Verlag, 1985), 1-16.

D. H. D. Warren, An Abstract Prolog Instruction Set, Technical Note 309, SRI International (Oct.1983).

D.H.D Warren, The SRI model for OR-parallel execution of Prolog. Abstract design and implementation, Proc. 1987 Symp. on Logic Programming (IEEE Comp. Society Press, 1987), 92-103.

H. Westphal, P. Robert, J. Chassin and J.C. Syre, The PEPSys model: combining backtracking, AND- and OR-parallelism, Proc. 1987 Symp. on Logic Programming (IEEE Comp. Society Press, 1987), 436-448.

J.-H. You and P.A. Subrahmanyam, E-unification algorithms for a class of confluent term rewriting systems, Proc. ICALP'86, LNCS 226 (Springer-Verlag, 1986), 454-463.

Chapter 5

Principles of FP2: Term Algebras for Specification of Parallel Machines

Ph. Schnoebelen and Ph. Jorrand

Lab. Lifia-Imag, 46, av. Félix Viallet, 38000 Grenoble, France

In FP2, term rewrite rules are used to specify abstract data types and parallel processes. FP2 process specifications can be combined hierarchically and then syntactically flattened into elementary specifications. The use of rewrite rules has several advantages, including a clean declarative semantics and a simple rewrite-based interpreter.
We also illustrate how FP2 specifications lend themselves to formal analysis by describing a "symbolic model checking" procedure for properties expressed in a *CTL*-like temporal logic.

1 Introduction

This chapter presents the principles of FP2 ("Functional Parallel Programming"), a language where systems of parallel processes are described by means of a form of term rewrite rules.

Parallelism is clearly recognized as a major concept in computer science. Indeed it has always been part (often not explicitly) of computing machinery, and it is now expected to be the most important source of improvements in computing speed for the near future. Improvements of several orders of magnitude are often expected.

However, parallel programs are complicated objects and it is very difficult to reason correctly about them. It is also expected that a revolution in our thinking habits will prove necessary in order to use efficiently the power of parallel machines. What we need are models, notations, concepts, theories, proof methods, etc. for parallel programs.

In a famous paper, C. A. R. Hoare (1978) advocated the use of a model where parallel computations are described as a set of interconnected parallel modules (also called *processes*) having an independent activity of their own, and communicating through the explicit sending and receiving of messages: this gave rise to the CSP ("Communicating Sequential Processes") language. This model had the advantage over more primitive concepts (e.g. shared memory) to use as basic entities sequential processes that can be understood in isolation. The use of explicit message passing had the same conceptual advantage over the reading and writing of a shared memory location as, in classical programming languages, the invocation of side-effect-free procedures had over random assignments of global variables.

In addition, Hoare advocated the use of "*rendezvous*" as the synchronization mechanism for message passing. This mechanism ensures than ***when a message is sent, it is received "at the same time"***. This is a conceptually simple solution for it does not consider situations where a message is sent and not yet received. Now, for a message to be received, it has to be accepted, so that a sending process may be delayed until the receiving side is willing to communicate: while rendezvous is conceptually simpler to analyze, it is more difficult to realize in actual architectures.

Following CSP, several models and languages have been proposed and developed. Some researchers investigated the *semantics of parallelism*, trying to answer the question "What is a parallel process ?" Other computer scientists designed languages for parallel programs, aiming at both ease of use and clarity. A notable example is OCCAM (May 1983), derived from the original CSP.

One drawback of CSP is that it is still an *imperative* language, suffering from the corresponding problems: programs are easy to write, but proofs of programs are difficult. On the other hand, the advantage of so-called declarative languages for semantic simplicity is well known: (pure) Prolog is a famous example. Indeed, a definition which has often been given of a specification language is "any language with a declarative semantics". FP2 is simply a parallel language having a declarative semantics.

FP2 uses an algebraic framework and describes non-deterministic systems by means of transition rules, which are clauses stating what the possible changes of states are. Operationally, such rules may be used to interpret the program and to produce one of its possible behaviors: the specifications are executable and can be used interactively for prototyping. One important feature of these descriptions (we call them *presentations*) is that they can easily be analyzed statically in order to infer properties of the denoted programs: this stems from our use of a declarative semantics.

A process has some named communication ports (or connectors) and its transitions may involve communications along these connectors: we use the rendezvous mechanism so that the executability of transitions may depend on the willingness of a communicating partner to engage in the communication.

In addition, FP2 processes can be combined to form networks of parallel processes, and the connectors of these processes can be linked, allowing the exchange of messages among processes (following an arbitrary topology). One other important feature is that these combinations of processes can be *flattened*, that is, it is possible to compute a presentation describing a network of processes (themselves given by FP2 presentations). Of course, having this possibility induces some drawbacks, and several natural ways of combining processes cannot easily be incorporated into this framework. However, one important advantage is that it extends to networks the applicability of any formal tool developed around the concept of presentation.

This chapter contains only a clean and high-level survey of the FP2 language and its semantics. We did not include any exotic feature, or discuss implementation strategy, etc. The reader is referred to (Jorrand 1986) for an informal presentation of the language and to (Jorrand 1987, Schaefer & Schnoebelen 1987) for examples of specifications in FP2.

Section 2 presents the basic notions we use in our model. It is a kind of non-deterministic state transition system, where state transitions are labeled with arbitrary events. Then, events are specialized for representing a general view of communications, so that communicating systems can be viewed as a form of non-deterministic state transition systems, with operators for composing them.

In section 3, the classical definitions for multi-sorted algebras are introduced and used for defining process presentations. A declarative semantics for process presentations is given. It allows us to state the correctness of the flattening operations as well as the correctness of a simple rewrite-based interpreter. As already stated, we choose to concentrate on the kernel of FP2, omitting several extensions that can be found elsewhere. However, the rationale for several restrictions of the language is clearly detailed and described.

The rest of the chapter shows, through a long example, what can be obtained from our use of a simple declarative semantics based on term algebra. We propose a temporal logic for analyzing the behavior of FP2 processes and outline a possible approach towards an automated proof procedure for this logic. Section 4 introduces the underlying theoretical framework. A branching time temporal logic is defined for expressing properties of non-deterministic state transition systems. The principles of a model checker for this logic are explained, based on the computation of fixed points of predicate transformers. Then, in section 5, these principles are applied to the definition of a "symbolic" model checker for FP2 processes, taking advantage of the fact that FP2 is based on term algebras. The central issue was to choose a representation for elementary predicates of the logic so that union, intersection, negation and equivalence could be computed. The problem was, of course, negation and this led to choosing constrained terms (i.e. terms with disequations) for representing predicates. Then, results on unification and disunification can be applied, thus defining an appropriate calculus for an FP2 model checker, which gives rise to a semi-decision procedure for analyzing the temporal properties of FP2 processes. A major consequence of this approach is that verification is not limited to finite state processes.

2 An algebra of communicating systems

This section describes the mathematical model we use for parallel systems. The model is based on a special kind of transition system, designed for describing the exchange of values between communicating processes. After defining transition systems in section 2.1, we specialize them into communicating systems in section 2.2 and define systems combining operators in section 2.3. Then a natural equivalence relation is proposed in section 2.4, leading to the definition of "processes". The specific choice of this framework is discussed in section 2.5.

2.1 Basic notions

Transition systems are non-deterministic automata where transitions are labeled with some actions, understood as actions involving the external environment, that is, communications or synchronization events.

Definition 2.1 (Transition system)
A transition system *is a tuple* $\mathcal{P} = \langle Q, L, \rightarrow, I \rangle$ *where* $Q = \{q, q', \ldots\}$ *is a non-empty*

set of states, $L = \{e, \ldots\}$ *is a set of* actions *or* events, $\rightarrow \subseteq Q \times L \times Q$ *is a* transition relation *and* $I \subseteq Q$ *is a non-empty set of* initial states.

A triple $(q, e, q') \in \rightarrow$ denotes a change of state from q to q' through the action e; it is called a *transition* and is written $q \xrightarrow{e} q'$. The notation $q \xrightarrow{e} q'$ is also used as the proposition stating that (q, e, q') is an element of $\rightarrow$. If $q \xrightarrow{e} q'$ is a transition of $\mathcal{P}$, q' is called a *direct successor* of q and $q \xrightarrow{e} q'$ is a *possible step* from q. As there may be several possible steps from a same state q, the behavior of a transition system is non-deterministic. A transition system is *finitely branching* if for all $q \in Q$, the set $\{q \xrightarrow{e} q'\}$ is finite.

Given two transition systems $\mathcal{P}_i = \langle Q_i, L_i, \rightarrow_i, I_i \rangle$ $(i = 1, 2)$, we write $\mathcal{P}_1 \simeq \mathcal{P}_2$ if $\mathcal{P}_1$ and $\mathcal{P}_2$ are equivalent *as labeled graphs*, i.e. when $L_1 = L_2$ and there exists a bijective mapping $g : Q_1 \rightarrow Q_2$ s.t. $q \xrightarrow{e}_1 q'$ iff $g(q) \xrightarrow{e}_2 g(q')$.

Transitions may be chained: a *path* (of $\mathcal{P}$) is a sequence

$$s = q_0 \xrightarrow{e_1} q_1 \xrightarrow{e_2} q_2 \xrightarrow{e_3} q_3 \cdots$$

alternating states and events, such that all $q_i \xrightarrow{e_{i+1}} q_{i+1}$ are transitions of $\rightarrow$. A path is either infinite or it has length n and is terminated by a state q_n. We write $[s]_n$, the *truncation* of s at length n: $[s]_n = q_0 \xrightarrow{e_1} \ldots \xrightarrow{e_n} q_n$ if s had length at least n, else $[s]_n = s$.

Paths are partially ordered by the *prefix ordering*: given two paths s_1 and s_2, we write $s_1 \ll s_2$ iff either $s_1 = s_2$ or s_1 is finite with length n and $[s_2]_n = s_1$.

An *execution* of a transition system $\mathcal{P} = \langle Q, L, \rightarrow, I \rangle$ is a maximal (w.r.t. $\ll$) path $q_0 \xrightarrow{e_1} q_1 \xrightarrow{e_2} q_2 \cdots$ such that $q_0 \in I$. An execution is a possible behavior of the system, the maximality requirement implies that an execution may be finite only if it ends into a *final state*, that is a state with no possible successor. We write $Ex(\mathcal{P})$ for the set of all executions of $\mathcal{P}$.

The *trace* of an execution $s = q_0 \xrightarrow{e_0} q_1 \xrightarrow{e_1} q_2 \ldots$ is the sequence of events $tr(s) = e_0, e_1, \ldots$ A trace may be finite or infinite: it belongs to $L^* \cup L^\omega$. We write $Tr(\mathcal{P})$ for $\{tr(s) \mid s \in Ex(\mathcal{P})\}$ and we define $\sim_{Tr}$, the so-called "trace equivalence", by

$$\mathcal{P}_1 \sim_{Tr} \mathcal{P}_2 \text{ iff } Tr(\mathcal{P}_1) = Tr(\mathcal{P}_2)$$

A state (resp. a transition) is *reachable* if it belongs to an execution. If we write I^* $(= \rightarrow^* (I))$ for the reachable states of $\mathcal{P} = \langle Q, L, \rightarrow, I \rangle$, then we have $I \subseteq I^* \subseteq Q$ and we may define

$$Prune(\mathcal{P}) \stackrel{\text{def}}{=} \langle I^*, L, \rightarrow \cap (I^* \times L \times I^*), I \rangle$$

$Prune(\mathcal{P})$ is $\mathcal{P}$ where all non reachable states (and transitions) have been pruned out.

2.2 Communicating systems

In the definition of transition systems we just gave, actions are uninterpreted. If we want to deal with parallel programs exchanging values, we shall have to add some structure to our set of actions.

We assume that a transition system has a set $K = \{k, \ldots, A, B, \ldots\}$ of *connectors* (or communication ports). Exchanging values is sending or receiving values along some ports. We assume a given set $Val = \{v, \ldots\}$ of *message values* (or simply *values*) to be circulated along connectors and we define an event as a set of communications along a set of connectors.

Definition 2.2 (Communicating system)
A communicating system *is a transition system $\mathcal{P} = \langle Q, L, \rightarrow, I \rangle$ where L is $\mathcal{F}_p(K, Val)$, the set of all partial functions from K to Val. $\mathcal{P}$ is written*

$$\mathcal{P} = \langle Q, K, Val, \rightarrow, I \rangle$$

An event $e \in L$ has the form $\{(k_1, v_1), \ldots, (k_n, v_n)\}$ with distinct k_i's and is usually written "$k_1(v_1) \cdots k_n(v_n)$". Such an event denotes the communications, during a single transition, of the n values v_i along the n connectors k_i. As this actually denotes a set, the order of the terms is not relevant. We sometimes write "$k(v) + e$" to denote an event containing the communication $k(v)$, with e as the remaining part. We write $Dom(e)$ for the set $\{k_1, \ldots, k_n\} \subseteq K$ of connectors involved in event e. The *empty event*, written τ, is just an empty set of communications: $Dom(\tau) = \emptyset$. It is the only event which does not involve synchronization with the external environment. A transition $q \xrightarrow{\tau} q'$ is called a *τ-transition.*

Remark 2.3
In this presentation of FP2, we shall not consider τ as a non-visible event: one can consider that the occurrence of a τ event is indicated by some ticking signal. This limitation is for conceptual and technical simplicity. Note however that the τ event has the peculiarity of not needing to synchronize with the external environment.

Note that we did not introduce any distinction among communications between what would be called input and output communications. Indeed, this directionality does not exist in our framework: we shall sometimes use directed arrows to depict connectors (e.g. in Figure 6), but only as a support to our operational intuition.

From now on, we shall often speak of a *process* when referring to a transition system $\langle Q, L, \rightarrow, I \rangle$ where L is some $\mathcal{F}_p(K, Val)$. It will typically be written $\mathcal{P} = \langle Q, K, \rightarrow, I \rangle$ when Val is understood. We write $\mathbf{CS} = \{\mathcal{P}, \ldots\}$ for the class of all communicating systems.

Example 2.4
The simplest communicating system is

$$0_{CS} = \langle \{q\}, \emptyset, \emptyset, \{q\} \rangle$$

It has only one state, no connector and no transition.

Example 2.5
We depict in Figure 1 two processes S_1 and S_2. Formally, S_1 is given by $Q = \{q, q'\}$,

$K = \{A, B\}$, $Val = \{0, 1, 2, \ldots\}$, $\rightarrow = \{q \stackrel{A(0)}{\rightarrow} q', q' \stackrel{\tau}{\rightarrow} q\}$ and $I = \{q\}$. We do not make S_2 explicit. In the figure, the initial states have been circled and the connectors drawn. Each of these two systems has only one initial state and one possible trace: they are *deterministic*.

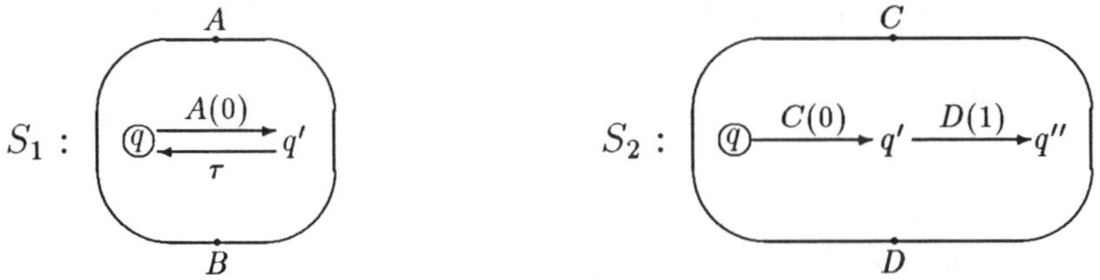

Figure 1: Two communicating systems

The only execution of S_1 is

$$q \stackrel{A(0)}{\longrightarrow} q' \stackrel{\tau}{\rightarrow} q \stackrel{A(0)}{\longrightarrow} q' \stackrel{\tau}{\rightarrow} \cdots$$

which is infinite. The only execution of S_2 is

$$q \stackrel{C(0)}{\longrightarrow} q' \stackrel{D(1)}{\longrightarrow} q''$$

which is finite.

2.3 Combining communicating systems

In this section, we present three process combining operators. These operators correspond to natural ways of combining and building programs in a hierarchical and modular way. The first operator, $||$, is used to put two processes "in parallel". The second, $+$, is used to link connectors, effectively allowing values to be exchanged between different processes which had been put in parallel. The third, $-$, is used to hide (or to forget) connectors, with the idea of abstracting from them once they have been used for connecting processes. Formally, these operators are written $||_c$, $+_c$ and $-_c$ to distinguish them from similar operators (to be introduced later) applying on other objects, but in this section there will be no danger of confusion, so we shall drop the "c" subscript.

Definition 2.6 (Parallel combination)
If $\mathcal{P}_1 = \langle Q_1, K_1, \rightarrow_1, I_1\rangle$ and $\mathcal{P}_2 = \langle Q_2, K_2, \rightarrow_2, I_2\rangle$ are two communicating systems (with K_1 and K_2 disjoint) we define $\mathcal{P}_1 \,||\, \mathcal{P}_2$ (read "$\mathcal{P}_1$ in parallel with $\mathcal{P}_2$") by:

$$\mathcal{P}_1 \,||_c\, \mathcal{P}_2 \stackrel{\text{def}}{=} \langle Q_1 \times Q_2, K_1 \cup K_2, \rightarrow_{1||2}, I_1 \times I_2\rangle$$

where $\rightarrow_{1||2}$, is defined by the following rules:

$$\frac{q_1 \in Q_1 \quad q_2 \stackrel{e_2}{\rightarrow}_2 q_2'}{q_1 q_2 \stackrel{e_2}{\rightarrow}_{1||2} q_1 q_2'} \qquad \frac{q_2 \in Q_2 \quad q_1 \stackrel{e_1}{\rightarrow}_1 q_1'}{q_1 q_2 \stackrel{e_1}{\rightarrow}_{1||2} q_1' q_2} \qquad \frac{q_1 \stackrel{e_1}{\rightarrow}_1 q_1' \quad q_2 \stackrel{e_2}{\rightarrow}_2 q_2'}{q_1 q_2 \stackrel{e_1+e_2}{\longrightarrow}_{1||2} q_1' q_2'}$$

and where $e_1 + e_2$ denotes the canonical sum of two partial functions over disjoint domains.

A state of $\mathcal{P}_1 \parallel \mathcal{P}_2$ is a pair (q_1, q_2), written q_1q_2, made of a state q_1 of $\mathcal{P}_1$ and a state q_2 of $\mathcal{P}_2$. A transition of $\mathcal{P}_1 \parallel \mathcal{P}_2$ when in state q_1q_2 is a transition of $\mathcal{P}_1$ when in state q_1, or a transition of $\mathcal{P}_2$ when in state q_2, or both a transition of $\mathcal{P}_1$ and a transition of $\mathcal{P}_2$.

Example 2.7
We show in Figure 2 the parallel combination of systems S_1 and S_2 from Figure 1. Some steps have not been labeled in the figure: for example, there exists an execution starting by:

$$qq \stackrel{A(0)\,C(0)}{\longrightarrow} q'q' \stackrel{D(1)}{\longrightarrow} qq'' \stackrel{A(0)}{\longrightarrow} q'q'' \cdots$$

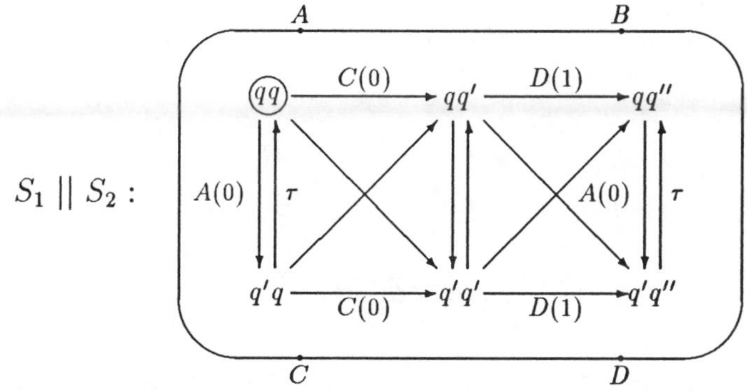

Figure 2: Parallel combination of S_1 and S_2

Elementary properties of $\parallel$ are:

$$\begin{array}{rcl} \mathcal{P}_1 \parallel \mathcal{P}_2 & \simeq & \mathcal{P}_2 \parallel \mathcal{P}_1 \\ (\mathcal{P}_1 \parallel \mathcal{P}_2) \parallel \mathcal{P}_3 & \simeq & \mathcal{P}_1 \parallel (\mathcal{P}_2 \parallel \mathcal{P}_3) \\ \mathcal{P} \parallel 0_{CS} & \simeq & \mathcal{P} \end{array}$$

Definition 2.8 (Connection)
If $\mathcal{P} = \langle Q, K, \rightarrow, I\rangle$ is a communicating system and $A, B \in K$ are two distinct connectors of $\mathcal{P}$, we define $\mathcal{P} + A.B$ (read "$\mathcal{P}$ with A connected to B") by:

$$\mathcal{P} +_c A.B \stackrel{\text{def}}{=} \langle Q, K, \rightarrow_{+A.B}, I\rangle$$

where $\rightarrow_{+A.B}$ is defined by the following rules:

$$\frac{q \stackrel{e}{\rightarrow} q'}{q \stackrel{e}{\rightarrow}_{+A.B} q'} \qquad \frac{q \stackrel{A(v)B(v)+e}{\longrightarrow} q'}{q \stackrel{e}{\rightarrow}_{+A.B} q'}$$

A state of $\mathcal{P}+A.B$ is a state of $\mathcal{P}$ and any transition of $\mathcal{P}$ is a transition of $\mathcal{P}+A.B$, but, in addition, every transition of $\mathcal{P}$ involving an event where the same value v is communicated along connectors A and B gives rise, in $\mathcal{P}+A.B$, to a transition where v

is exchanged between A and B, without communication with the external environment (which is why $A(v)$ and $B(v)$ no longer appear in the transition). Of course, e, the rest of the event, is unchanged and may still involve other external communications.

This definition is not standard (e.g. it allows a process to communicate or synchronize with itself). In most calculi, the parallel combination of processes automatically allows them to communicate, while ours conceptually needs two steps: we first combine processes, then we connect their connectors. In any case, the behavior is not different. Continuing the previous examples, $S_1 \parallel S_2$ having transition $qq \xrightarrow{A(0)\,C(0)} q'q'$, $S_1 \parallel S_2 + A.C$ [1] has transition $qq \xrightarrow{\tau} q'q'$ denoting the exchange between S_1 and S_2 of the value 0 along A and C.

Definition 2.9 (Hiding)
If $\mathcal{P} = \langle Q, K, \rightarrow, I\rangle$ is a communicating system and $A \in K$ is one of its connectors, we define $\mathcal{P} - A$ (read "$\mathcal{P}$ without A") by:

$$\mathcal{P} -_c A \stackrel{\text{def}}{=} \langle Q, K \setminus \{A\}, \rightarrow_{-A}, I\rangle$$

where $\rightarrow_{-A}$ is defined by the following rule:

$$\frac{q \xrightarrow{e} q' \quad A \notin Dom(e)}{q \xrightarrow{e}_{-A} q'}$$

A state of $\mathcal{P} - A$ is a state of $\mathcal{P}$ and all transitions of $\mathcal{P}$ which do not involve A in their events, are transitions of $\mathcal{P} - A$.

Example 2.10
Figure 3 contains the system $S = S_1 \parallel S_2 + A.C - A - C$. A possible execution of S is:

$$qq \xrightarrow{\tau} q'q' \xrightarrow{\tau} qq' \xrightarrow{D(1)} qq''$$

Note that we have not included the state $q'q$, now unreachable, only showing $Prune(S)$.

2.4 Communicating processes

We do not plan to take communicating systems as our model of parallel processes: they are not abstract enough. Rather we will consider as equivalent two transition systems having "the same" branching structure. This is formalized through the notion of (strong) bisimulation, due to Park (1981).

Definition 2.11 (Bisimulation)
Given two transition systems $\mathcal{P}_i = \langle Q_i, L, \rightarrow_i, I_i\rangle$ $(i = 1, 2)$, a relation $R \subseteq Q_1 \times Q_2$ is a bisimulation between $\mathcal{P}_1$ and $\mathcal{P}_2$, written $R : \mathcal{P}_1 \underline{\leftrightarrow} \mathcal{P}_2$, iff

(1) $I_1 \subseteq R^{-1}(I_2)$,

(2) $I_2 \subseteq R(I_1)$,

[1] We omit parentheses whenever possible, with a left-to-right precedence.

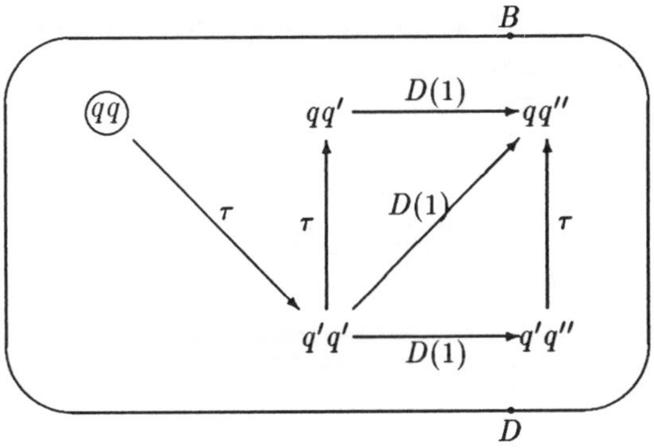

Figure 3: The system $S_1 \parallel S_2 + A.C - A - C$

(3) *for all transition* $q_1 \xrightarrow{e}_1 q_1'$ *of* $\mathcal{P}_1$ *and state* q_2 *of* $\mathcal{P}_2$ *s.t.* $q_1 R q_2$*, there exists a transition* $q_2 \xrightarrow{e}_2 q_2'$ *s.t.* $q_1' R q_2'$*,*

(4) *vice versa: for all* $q_2 \xrightarrow{e}_2 q_2'$ *and* q_1 *s.t.* $q_1 R q_2$*, there exists* $q_1 \xrightarrow{e}_1 q_1'$ *s.t.* $q_1' R q_2'$*.*

A consequence of this definition is that $Dom(R)$ contains all reachable states of $\mathcal{P}_1$ and $Im(R)$ all reachable states of $\mathcal{P}_2$. We write $\mathcal{P}_1 \underline{\leftrightarrow} \mathcal{P}_2$ when $R : \mathcal{P}_1 \underline{\leftrightarrow} \mathcal{P}_2$ for some bisimulation R and we say that $\mathcal{P}_1$ and $\mathcal{P}_2$ are *bisimilar*: for example, $\mathcal{P}$ and $Prune(\mathcal{P})$ are always bisimilar.

Proposition 2.12
For all transition systems $\mathcal{P}, \mathcal{P}_1, \ldots$ *of* **CS**:

(1) $Id_Q : \mathcal{P} \underline{\leftrightarrow} \mathcal{P}$,

(2) $R : \mathcal{P}_1 \underline{\leftrightarrow} \mathcal{P}_2$ *implies* $R^{-1} : \mathcal{P}_2 \underline{\leftrightarrow} \mathcal{P}_1$,

(3) $R : \mathcal{P}_1 \underline{\leftrightarrow} \mathcal{P}_2$ *and* $R' : \mathcal{P}_2 \underline{\leftrightarrow} \mathcal{P}_3$ *imply* $(R' \circ R) : \mathcal{P}_1 \underline{\leftrightarrow} \mathcal{P}_3$,

(4) $R : \mathcal{P}_1 \underline{\leftrightarrow} \mathcal{P}_2$ *and* $R' : \mathcal{P}_1 \underline{\leftrightarrow} \mathcal{P}_2$ *imply* $(R \cup R') : \mathcal{P}_1 \underline{\leftrightarrow} \mathcal{P}_2$.

(1), (2) and (3) imply that $\underline{\leftrightarrow}$ is an equivalence relation between transition systems, and (4) implies that whenever $\mathcal{P}_1 \underline{\leftrightarrow} \mathcal{P}_2$, there exists a largest R such that $R : \mathcal{P}_1 \underline{\leftrightarrow} \mathcal{P}_2$. Indeed, given a system $\mathcal{P} = \langle Q, K, \rightarrow, I \rangle$, we may define:

$$R_{\mathcal{P}} = \bigcup \{R \subseteq Q \times Q \mid R : \mathcal{P} \underline{\leftrightarrow} \mathcal{P}\}$$

Then $R_{\mathcal{P}} : \mathcal{P} \underline{\leftrightarrow} \mathcal{P}$ and $R_{\mathcal{P}}$ is an equivalence relation between states of Q, so that we may identify equivalent states and define

$$\mathcal{P}/_{\underline{\leftrightarrow}} \stackrel{\text{def}}{=} \langle Q/_{R_{\mathcal{P}}}, K, \rightarrow /_{R_{\mathcal{P}}}, I/_{R_{\mathcal{P}}} \rangle$$

with obvious definitions for $\rightarrow /_{R_{\mathcal{P}}}$. We have $\mathcal{P} \underline{\leftrightarrow} \mathcal{P}/_{\underline{\leftrightarrow}}$ and $\mathcal{P}/_{\underline{\leftrightarrow}}$ can be taken as a canonical representative of the equivalence class (modulo $\underline{\leftrightarrow}$) of $\mathcal{P}$:

$$\mathcal{P}_1 \underline{\leftrightarrow} \mathcal{P}_2 \text{ implies } Prune(\mathcal{P}_1)/_{\underline{\leftrightarrow}} \simeq Prune(\mathcal{P}_2)/_{\underline{\leftrightarrow}}$$

One important property of bisimulation equivalence is that it is a congruence for our three operators:

Proposition 2.13
For all processes $\mathcal{P}, \mathcal{P}_1, \mathcal{P}_2 \in \mathbf{CS}$,

$$\mathcal{P}_1 \underline{\leftrightarrow} \mathcal{P}_2 \text{ implies } \begin{cases} \mathcal{P}_1 \,||\, \mathcal{P} \underline{\leftrightarrow} \mathcal{P}_2 \,||\, \mathcal{P} \text{ and } \mathcal{P} \,||\, \mathcal{P}_1 \underline{\leftrightarrow} \mathcal{P} \,||\, \mathcal{P}_2 \\ \mathcal{P}_1 + A.B \underline{\leftrightarrow} \mathcal{P}_2 + A.B \\ \mathcal{P}_1 - A \underline{\leftrightarrow} \mathcal{P}_2 - A \end{cases}$$

In all three cases, the proof is by exhibiting the required bisimulation. We do not give it here.

In this presentation, a process is formally defined as *an equivalence class of communicating systems modulo bisimulation*. Bisimulation being a congruence w.r.t. $||$, $+$ and $-$, we may consider our three operators as being defined over processes, though we shall almost always consider a given representative of the equivalence class. As $\simeq$ is included in $\underline{\leftrightarrow}$, we inherit from $\simeq$ properties like associativity and commutativity of $||$. We may also compare $\underline{\leftrightarrow}$ with another "natural equivalence":

$$\mathcal{P}_1 \underline{\leftrightarrow} \mathcal{P}_2 \text{ implies } \mathcal{P}_1 \sim_{Tr} \mathcal{P}_2$$

This last proposition states that $\sim_{Tr}$ is compatible with $\underline{\leftrightarrow}$, that is, we may consider trace equivalence as an equivalence between processes, instead of simply between communicating systems. In fact, the operational semantics we shall consider in section 3.6 will not distinguish processes beyond $\sim_{Tr}$: when started a process $\mathcal{P}$ only produces one of its traces, that is, the trace of one of its executions. However there are several reasons for considering bisimulation as the natural equivalence for our processes, the most important will appear later (section 4) when we consider temporal logic. Furthermore note that $\sim_{Tr}$ is not a congruence w.r.t. $-$ (but it is a congruence w.r.t. $||$ and $+$). See e.g. (Brookes et al. 1984, Bergstra et al. 1988) for congruences based on trace equivalence.

Example 2.14
Consider the (paradigmatic) example in Figure 4. S_1 and S_2 are not bisimilar, though $Tr(S_1) = \{A.B, A.C\} = Tr(S_2)$ implies $S_1 \sim_{Tr} S_2$. However $Tr(S_1 - B) = \{A.C\} \neq Tr(S_2 - B) = \{A, A.C\}$.

This shows why it is not possible to compute $Tr(\mathcal{P} - A)$ from $Tr(\mathcal{P})$ alone. We shall not demonstrate how it is possible to compute $Tr(\mathcal{P} + A.B)$ and $Tr(\mathcal{P}_1 \,||\, \mathcal{P}_2)$ as a function of (resp.) $Tr(\mathcal{P})$, $Tr(\mathcal{P}_1)$ and $Tr(\mathcal{P}_2)$.

2.5 Some comments on communicating systems

The use of some kind of labeled transition systems as models for parallel systems is standard and (Keller 1976, Milner 1980) contributed to their widespread use. One advantage of them is that they are very simple. One problem with them is that they model independence by arbitrary interleaving. Suppose that two events e_1 and e_2 are independent (e.g. they come from different processes). Then this situation is modeled

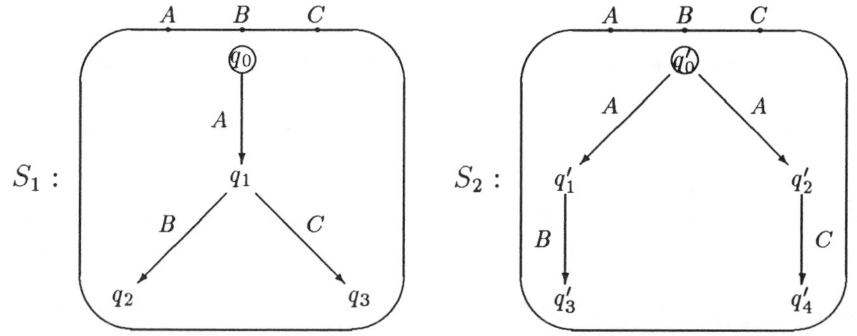

Figure 4: Trace equivalence and bisimulation

by saying that e_1 and e_2 may occur in any order. "In any order" refers to a global (and total) ordering of the events, as they occur in a trace, introducing a notion of global time and often failing to capture some liveness properties of parallel systems. Today, models lacking this problem are being investigated actively.

Even modulo bisimulation, our "communicating systems" are a very simple model. For example τ is not considered as a special *non-visible* event. These drawbacks are not important since our interest is not in the model itself but in the way systems are denoted by FP2 programs. Other equivalence relations could be used to identify processes provided they are congruences w.r.t. $||$, $+$ and $-$. Indeed, several well known models fulfill this condition, e.g. the acceptance trees of (Hennessy 1985, 1988), and the choice eventually rests on the intended applications.

Bisimulation is very well behaved and has been strongly advocated, see e.g. (Milner 1988, Bergstra and Klop 1989) (see also Abramsky (1987) for further arguments). It is also the natural equivalence to be considered in connection with branching time temporal logic (see e.g. Pnueli 1985). This point will be developed in section 4.

More importantly, our model is too simple from some other viewpoints. For example, it does not distinguish between deadlock and proper termination (this is not a problem as long as we do not consider the sequential composition $\mathcal{P}_1;\mathcal{P}_2$ of two systems). Adding such a structure to the model would, in principle, be more delicate than quotienting it by a well-behaved congruence. The (presumably simple) modification of the model would have to be raised to the level of the FP2 language, with the aim of retaining a declarative semantics, presentations combining operators and a simple rewrite-based interpreter, all of them in the style of Definitions 3.12, 3.16 and 3.20, with, of course, correctness properties similar to Propositions 3.17 and 3.21. This can easily be done for deadlock and sequential composition, but not for dynamic process creation.

The process combining operators of section 2.3 actually define an *algebra of processes*. Such an approach is widely used, and different calculus have been proposed (among which are CCS (Milner 1980, 1988), ACP (Bergstra & Klop 1986) and SCCS (Milner 1983)). These systems vary in two directions: the specific operators that are proposed and the underlying model. Our model (communicating systems with bisimulation) has already been discussed and our operators have been introduced in (Jorrand 1982).

In order to design a "real" language based on these constructs, several features should be added. For example, a renaming operator changing the names of the connectors of a process is clearly required in order to combine two copies of a single process. (Jorrand 1986) contains several other process-forming operators. They are (mostly) derived operators that could be expressed in terms of $||$, $+$ and $-$, and from a theoretical point of view they do not really add anything to the language. We have preferred not to include them in this presentation.

Other sets of operators can be found in the literature. They are all rather similar in spirit, simply some sets are more expressive than others. We have mentioned why our definition of *connection* is not standard. Note also that our *parallel combination* operator is different from an "asynchronous interleaving" generally found in other systems (e.g. CCS or ACP) and which is available in (Jorrand 1986). Our $||$ (taken from Jorrand 1981) allows synchronous events: it is used as a primitive in the Meije language (Austry & Boudol 1984).

3 A language for communicating systems

This section describes FP2, a language where communicating systems are defined through term rewrite rules. One of our objectives in this section is to clearly separate the declarative semantics of FP2 (Definition 3.12), the (so-called) flattening of presentations (Definition 3.16) and the rewrite-based interpreter of section 3.6. In fact, we only present a simplified subset of the FP2 language as it is described in (Jorrand 1986), but it would be easy to incorporate other constructs into this framework.

We first recall the necessary notions of algebraic specification (section 3.1) and term rewriting (section 3.2) underlying FP2 data types specifications (section 3.3): these notions are standard and can be found, e.g., in (Huet & Oppen 1980, Ehrig & Mahr 1985, Dershowitz & Jouannaud 1989). Then, in section 3.4, we show how communicating systems are defined in the FP2 language, before presenting, in section 3.5, how compound processes (i.e. networks) can be reduced to simple FP2 systems, allowing the definition of a straightforward interpreter for such processes (section 3.6). At first, section 3.1 may appear unnecessarily detailed, but all the concepts it describes will be required in section 5. Sections 3.4 and 3.5 pursue a direction already explored in (Pereira 1984, Jorrand & Pereira 1985).

3.1 Signatures, terms and equations

Definition 3.1 (Signature)
A many-sorted algebraic signature is a couple $\langle S, F\rangle$ where $S = \{s, \ldots\}$ is a non-empty set of sorts names *and $F = (F_{w,s})$ is a $S^* \times S$-indexed set of* function names *(with typical elements $f, g, \ldots$).*

A word w of S^* will be written $s_1, \ldots, s_n$ (or λ when $n = 0$), and a word w, s of $S^* \times S$ will be written $w \to s$ ($\lambda \to s$ or $\to s$ when $n = 0$). In practice, we shall always assume that all $F_{w,s}$ are sets, so that an arity function ρ can be defined. We shall write $\rho(f) = s_1, \ldots, s_n \to s$ instead of $f \in F_{s_1,\ldots,s_n \to s}$. A signature $\langle S, F\rangle$ will often be simply written F.

Given a many-sorted signature F, there is a standard notion of F-algebra, of F-homomorphisms and of F-congruences (see e.g. Ehrig & Mahr 1985). If F' is a sub-signature of F, any F-algebra can be seen as an F'-algebra by forgetting some carriers and some functions.

The term algebra T_F over a many-sorted signature F is constructed in the usual way. It is the least family $(T_{F,s})_{s \in S}$ such that:

(1) If $\rho(f) = \lambda \rightarrow s$ then $f \in T_{F,s}$,

(2) If $\rho(f) = s_1, \ldots, s_n \rightarrow s$ and $t_1, \ldots, t_n \in T_{F,s_1}, \ldots, T_{F,s_n}$ then (the string) $f(t_1, \ldots, t_n) \in T_{F,s}$.[2]

The elements of T_F are called *ground terms.* From now on, we only consider signatures F where all sorts are *inhabited*,[3] that is, where no $T_{F,s}$ is empty. This property is easy to check. Then T_F may be given the structure of an F-algebra by associating canonical interpretations to the function symbols: $f \in F_{s_1,\ldots,s_n \rightarrow s}$ denotes the function from $T_{F,s_1} \times \cdots \times T_{F,s_n}$ to $T_{F,s}$ which maps the tuple of n terms $t_1, \ldots, t_n$ to the string $f(t_1, \ldots, t_n)$. T_F can also be seen as the algebra of finite trees over F.

It is well known that T_F is the *initial F-algebra*, which means that for any F-algebra $\mathcal{A}$, there exists a unique F-homomorphism $i_{\mathcal{A}}$ from T_F into $\mathcal{A}$. We shall write $T = (T_s)_{s \in S}$ for T_F when F is understood.

Example 3.2
With signature $S = \{nat, bool\}$, $F_{\lambda \rightarrow bool} = \{true, false\}$, $F_{\lambda \rightarrow nat} = \{zero\}$ and $F_{nat \rightarrow nat} = \{succ\}$, we have:

$$\begin{array}{lcl} T_{bool} & = & \{true, false\} \\ T_{nat} & = & \{zero, succ(zero), succ(succ(zero)), \ldots\} \text{ (an infinite set)} \end{array}$$

We assume given an S-indexed family $X = (X_s)$ of *variables names.* Given an F-algebra $\mathcal{A}$, an $\mathcal{A}$-assignment is a (sort-preserving) mapping from X into $\mathcal{A}$, that is, an S-indexed family $\sigma = (\sigma_s)_{s \in S}$ of mappings $\sigma_s : X_s \rightarrow \mathcal{A}_s$.

The algebra $T_{F \cup X}$, written $T_F(X)$, is obtained by considering the variables as new constants; its elements are the *terms* and include the ground terms. A term where no variable appears more than once is a *linear term.* We write $Var(t)$ for the set of variables appearing in t, and more generally in any syntactic object.

$T_F(X)$ is the *free F-algebra generated by X*, which means that any $\mathcal{A}$-assignment $\sigma : X \rightarrow \mathcal{A}$ can be extended into a unique F-homomorphism, also written σ, from $T_F(X)$ to $\mathcal{A}$. A specific instance of this notion appears when $\mathcal{A}$ is $T_F(X)$ itself, in which case σ is called a *substitution.* When $\mathcal{A}$ is T_F, σ is called a *ground substitution.* We write $\Sigma = \{\sigma, \theta, \ldots\}$ (resp. Σ_g) for the set of all substitutions (resp. of all ground substitutions). The *domain* of a substitution σ, written $Dom(\sigma)$, is the set $\{x \in X \mid \sigma(x) \neq x\}$: for ground substitutions $Dom(\sigma) = X$. When $Y \subseteq X$, a *Y-ground* substitution is a substitution σ such that $Dom(\sigma) = Y$ and $\sigma(x)$ is ground for all $x \in Y$. A substitution is usually given under the form $\sigma = (x_1 \leftarrow t_1; \ldots; x_n \leftarrow t_n)$. $t(x \leftarrow t')$ denotes t where x has been substituted by t'.

[2] If op is binary, we shall sometimes write $t_1 \; op \; t_2$ instead of $op(t_1, t_2)$.

[3] Following a terminology from (Smolka et al. 87).

Two terms t_1 and t_2 are said to be *unifiable* when $\sigma(t_1) = \sigma(t_2)$ for some $\sigma \in \Sigma$, σ is called a unifier. It is well known that in such a case t_1 and t_2 admit a *most general unifier* (mgu) $g \in \Sigma$ such that any unifier σ is an instance of g: $\sigma = \theta \circ g$. Algorithms for computing mgus are well known (Robinson 1965, Huet 1976, Martelli & Montanari 1982, Lassez et al. 1986).

Definition 3.3 (Equation)
Given a many-sorted signature F, an (s-sorted) equation *over F is a couple (u, v), written $u = v$, of two terms of $T_{F,s}(X)$.*

An equational presentation *is a pair F, E of a signature F and a set E of equations over F.*

An algebra $\mathcal{A}$ *satisfies* an equation $u = v$, written $\mathcal{A} \models u = v$, if for every $\mathcal{A}$-assignment σ, $\sigma(u) = \sigma(v)$. This is also written $u =_{\mathcal{A}} v$ to emphasize that terms u and v are interpreted as polynomials over $\mathcal{A}$. This definition implies that variables appearing in an equation must be understood as being universally quantified.

Given a presentation F, E, we define a congruence $=_E$ on $T_F(X)$:

Definition 3.4
$=_E$ is the smallest congruence over $T_F(X)$ s.t.

(1) *$=_E$ contains E (i.e. $u =_E v$ whenever $u = v \in E$),*

(2) *$=_E$ is stable by replacement (i.e. $u =_E v$ implies $\sigma(u) =_E \sigma(v)$ for all substitutions σ).*

An F, E-algebra is an F-algebra $\mathcal{A}$ satisfying all equations of E (written $\mathcal{A} \models E$). It is well known that the quotient algebra $T_F/=_E$, written $T_{F,E}$, is initial in the class of all F, E-algebras.

3.2 Term rewriting

Equations are sometimes used as oriented *rewrite rules.* Applying them requires some syntactic manipulation.

The *positions* of a term t, written $Pos(t)$, are a subset of $\mathbf{N}_+^*$ inductively defined by:

(1) $Pos(x) = \{\epsilon\}$

(2) $Pos(f(t_1, \ldots, t_n)) = \{\epsilon\} \cup \{i.p \mid i = 1, \ldots, n \wedge p \in Pos(t_i)\}$

Thus $Pos(t)$ is a non-empty prefix-closed set of strings of positive integers, where ϵ denotes the empty string and . denotes concatenation.

Positions are used to denote paths to a subterm: if $p \in Pos(t)$, we write t/p for the subterm of t at position p, defined by $t/\epsilon = t$ and $f(t_1, \ldots, t_n)/(i.p) = t_i/p$. Subterm replacements are also defined relative to a position: if u and t/p are two terms of a same sort, we define $t[p \leftarrow u]$ by $t[\epsilon \leftarrow u] = u$ and $f(t_1, \ldots, t_i, \ldots, t_n)[i.p \leftarrow u] = f(t_1, \ldots, t_i[p \leftarrow u], \ldots, t_n)$. Clearly, t and $t[p \leftarrow u]$ have the same sort.

Definition 3.5 (Rewrite rule)
Given a many-sorted signature F, an (s-sorted) rewrite rule *over F is a couple (l, r), written $l \rightarrow r$, of two terms of $T_{F,s}(X)$ such that $Var(r) \subseteq Var(l)$.*

A rewrite system *is a pair F, R of a signature F and a set R of rewrite rules over F.*

Given a set R of rewrite rules and a term $t \in T_F(X)$ such that a subterm t/p of t equals $\sigma(l)$ for some rule $l \rightarrow r \in R$ and some substitution σ, we say that t is *reducible* and that t *rewrites into* u (where $u = t[p \leftarrow \sigma(r)]$). This is written $t \rightarrow_R u$. We write $\rightarrow_R^*$ for the reflexive transitive closure of $\rightarrow_R$ and $\leftrightarrow_R^*$ for the symmetric closure of $\rightarrow_R^*$. Now if we see R as a set of equations E, we clearly have $\leftrightarrow_R^*$ equals $=_E$ (see Definition 3.4).

Definition 3.6
We say that a rewrite system R is:

(1) Confluent *if whenever $t \rightarrow_R^* t_1$ and $t \rightarrow_R^* t_2$, there exists some t_3 such that $t_1 \rightarrow_R^* t_3$ and $t_2 \rightarrow_R^* t_3$,*

(2) Locally confluent *if whenever $t \rightarrow_R t_1$ and $t \rightarrow_R t_2$, there exists some t_3 such that $t_1 \rightarrow_R^* t_3$ and $t_2 \rightarrow_R^* t_3$,*

(3) Terminating *(or* noetherian*) if there exists no infinite chain $t_1 \rightarrow_R t_2 \rightarrow_R t_3 \cdots$,*

(4) Convergent *if it is both terminating and confluent,*

(5) Left-linear *if all rewrite rules have linear left-hand sides,*

(6) Overlapping *if there exist two left-hand sides l, l' in R and $p \in Pos(l')$ such that l and l'/p are unifiable non-variable terms,*[4]

(7) Regular *if it is both left-linear and non-overlapping.*

It is well known that if R is terminating and locally confluent, it is also confluent, and then convergent (this is "Newman's Lemma", see (Huet 1980) for a simple proof). It is also well known that if R is regular, then it is confluent (see Klop 1980, Huet 1980). Convergent systems are interesting because, if R is convergent, we may decide whether $t_1 =_R t_2$ simply by rewriting t_1 and t_2 until we reach irreducible terms $\downarrow t_1$ and $\downarrow t_2$ (this will eventually happen because R is terminating) and then checking whether these *normal forms* are identical: indeed $t_1 =_R t_2$ iff $\downarrow t_1 = \downarrow t_2$.

3.3 FP2 data types

In FP2, abstract data types are defined through *constructor-based* presentations. Following (Guttag & Horning 1978, Huet & Hullot 1982), this assumes that the signature F has been partitioned as $C + D$ where C is a signature by itself. The elements of C (resp. of D) are called *constructors*, (resp. *defined functions*).

Definition 3.7
A constructor-based *presentation is an equational presentation F, E where F is partitioned as $C + D$ and where the equations of E used as rewrite rules give a rewrite system R such that:*

---

[4] Of course, we do not consider trivial overlaps (at the root position) between two renamed copies of the same left-hand side.

(1) *R is terminating,*

(2) *R is left-linear,*

(3) *Left-hand sides have the form* $f(t_1, \ldots, t_n)$ *where* $f \in D$ *and* $t_i \in T_C(X)$ *for* $i = 1, \ldots, n$,

(4) *No two left-hand sides are unifiable,*[5]

(5) *Every term of* $T_F - T_C$ *is reducible by R.*

An immediate consequence of (3.7) and (3.7) is that R is non-overlapping, and then regular, and then convergent. Another consequence is that no term of T_C is reducible, which together with (3.7) implies that T_C is the set of ground normal forms w.r.t. R. This property is known as "sufficient completeness" of the specification. Now, R being convergent, T_C (seen as a F-algebra) is isomorphic to $T_{F,E}$.

Example 3.8
Figure 5 contains a presentation of boolean and positive integers, with several defined operations: addition, etc.

sorts
$nat, bool$
constructors
$true, false :\rightarrow bool$
$zero :\rightarrow nat$
$succ : nat \rightarrow nat$
functions
$+, * : nat, nat \rightarrow nat$
$eq : nat, nat \rightarrow bool$
variables
$n : nat$
equations
$zero + n == n$
$succ(n) + m == succ(n + m)$
$zero * n == zero$
$succ(n) * m == (n * m) + m$
$eq(zero, zero) == true$
$eq(zero, succ(n)) == false$
$eq(succ(n), zero) == false$
$eq(succ(n), succ(m)) == eq(n, m)$
end

Figure 5: FP2 presentation of booleans and natural numbers

Ascertaining whether a presentation $C + D, E$ is a constructor-based presentation is in general undecidable because of the termination condition, though there exist standard tools (Dershowitz 1987) that may be used (in our example, termination is easy

[5]Considering that they have different variables.

to prove). In practice, the termination requirement is often dropped: some computations may simply fail to terminate, but confluence is not affected, so that the behavior of the system remains consistent. Condition (3.7) is an instance of the inductive reducibility property, which is decidable in general (Plaisted 1985), and with very simple algorithms in our special case where there are no equations between constructors and where only left-linear rewrite rules are used (Thiel 1984).

The nature of constructor-based presentations allows us to see the algebra we define (i.e. $T_{F,E}$) as a set of typed values (the term algebra T_C, e.g. $\{true, false\}$ and $\{zero, succ(zero), \ldots\}$ in Example 3.8) over which some typed functions are defined (the functions of D, e.g. $+$, $*$ and eq in the same example). Indeed, in the following, we shall often speak of "values of T_C" with this interpretation in mind. Together with regularity, the "constructor discipline" enjoys many properties, making it well suited for programming languages (O'Donnell 1986). It is usually not felt as too strong a restriction: there exist automatic methods to translate more general presentations into "equivalent" ones respecting the discipline, see e.g. (Thatte 1985). However, note that the current trend is to infer automatically what are the constructors in an equational presentation (Comon 1988a, 1989a).

One important point is that "semantic" matching and unification in $T_{F,E}(X)$ (that is, matching and unification modulo E) are generally undecidable, though we shall need them in future sections. Fortunately, when we restrict ourselves to *constructor terms* (i.e. terms of $T_C(X)$), unification and matching become trivially decidable. This explains why constructor terms are used as subterms in left-hand sides of rules.

3.4 FP2 processes

Throughout this section, we assume given a constructor-based presentation $\langle S, C + D, E\rangle$. In such a context:

Definition 3.9 (Process signature)
A process signature *is a tuple* $\langle \Pi, K\rangle$ *where* $\Pi = (\Pi_w)$ *is an* S^**-indexed set of* state names *and* $K = (K_s)$ *is an* S*-indexed set of* connector names.

Such a signature allows us to define the syntactic basis we shall use for describing process behaviors. We first extend the arity function to state names: we write $\rho(Q) = w$ if $Q \in \Pi_w$. Given a process signature $\langle \Pi, K\rangle$, a *communication term* has the form $k(t)$ where $k \in K_s$ and $t \in T_{C,s}(X)$. We write $T_K(X)$ (resp. T_K) for the set of communication terms (resp. ground communication terms). Note that defined functions are not allowed in communication terms. A finite (possibly empty) set $\{k_1(t_1), \ldots, k_n(t_n)\}$ of communication terms with *distinct* k_i's is called an *event term*:, we write $T_{Ev}(X) = \{e, \ldots\}$ for the set of events terms and $Dom(e)$ for the set $\{k_1, \ldots, k_n\}$ of connector names used in event term e (resp. T_{Ev} for ground events). A *state term* is some $Q(t_1, \ldots, t_n)$ where $\rho(Q) = s_1, \ldots, s_n$ and $t_i \in T_{C,s_i}(X)$ for $i = 1, \ldots, n$. *Generalized* state terms allow t_i's from $T_{F,s_i}(X)$ instead of just $T_{C,s_i}(X)$. Ground generalized state terms also have unique normal forms: $\downarrow Q(t_1, \ldots, t_n) = Q(\downarrow t_1, \ldots, \downarrow t_n)$. Ground state terms (*not* generalized) are simply called *states*. The set of states is written T_Π: it is similar to the Herbrand base used in first-order logic.

Definition 3.10 (Transition rule)
Given a process signature $\langle \Pi, K \rangle$, *a* transition rule *is a triple* (p, e, p') *where* p *is a state term,* p' *is a generalized state term, and* e *is an event term.*

A transition rule is written "$p : k_1(t_1) \cdots k_n(t_n) \Rightarrow p'$". p and p' are respectively called the *precondition* and *postcondition* of the rule. Note that, in contrast with Definition 3.5, there is no restriction on the presence of variables, and that non-constructor functions may only appear in the postcondition. By extension, we write $Dom(p : e \Rightarrow p')$ for $Dom(e)$.

Transition rules are called "rules" for operational reasons that will only be clear in section 3.6. Until then, they are only used to define communicating systems (i.e. processes):

Definition 3.11 (Process presentation)
A process presentation *is a tuple* $\langle \Pi, K, TR, I \rangle$ *where* $\langle \Pi, K \rangle$ *is a process signature,* $TR = \{r_1, \ldots, r_n\}$ *is a (possibly empty) set of transition rules, and where* $I = \{p_1, \ldots, p_m\}$ *is a non-empty set of ground generalized state terms, called* initial states *or* initial rules.

An initial rule is written "$\Rightarrow p$". We write $\mathbf{PP} = \{P, \ldots\}$ for the set of all FP2 process presentations. Formally, the constructor-based presentation for data types should be included in the process presentation, but for simplicity we shall consider that these data types have been defined "globally".

A process presentation is a syntactic description of a communicating system:

Definition 3.12 (Declarative semantics of FP2 presentations)
A process presentation $P = \langle \Pi, K, TR, I \rangle$ *denotes the communicating system*

$$\mathcal{P}[\![P]\!] \stackrel{\text{def}}{=} \langle T_\Pi, K, T_{F,E}, \rightarrow_{TR}, \downarrow I \rangle$$

where

$$\rightarrow_{TR} \stackrel{\text{def}}{=} \{\sigma(p) \stackrel{\sigma(e)}{\longrightarrow} \downarrow \sigma(p') \mid \sigma \in \Sigma_g, (p : e \Rightarrow p') \in TR\}$$

and where $\downarrow I$ *is* $\{\downarrow p \mid p \in I\}$.

This declarative semantics $\mathcal{P}[\![.]\!] : \mathbf{PP} \rightarrow \mathbf{CS}$ is very simple and natural. With FP2 presentations, one easily describes any kind of non-deterministic behavior in term of states containing values. Consider the following example:

Example 3.13
Figure 6 contains a presentation (and a diagram) of an *ADD* process.

This process has a set of states $Q = \{X()\} \cup \{Y(n, m) \mid n, m \in \mathbf{N}\}$. Its only initial state is $X()$. A possible execution of $\mathcal{P}[\![ADD]\!]$ is

$$X() \stackrel{A(2)B(3)}{\longrightarrow} Y(2,3) \stackrel{\tau}{\rightarrow} Y(1,4) \stackrel{\tau}{\rightarrow} Y(0,5) \stackrel{C(5)}{\longrightarrow} X() \cdots$$

It is not difficult to see that *ADD* may only engage in executions where it starts in the $X()$ state, accepts two integer values n and m along its A and B connectors, internally computes the sum $n + m$ and then exchanges it through its C connector, finally reaching its $X()$ state and re-entering the loop.

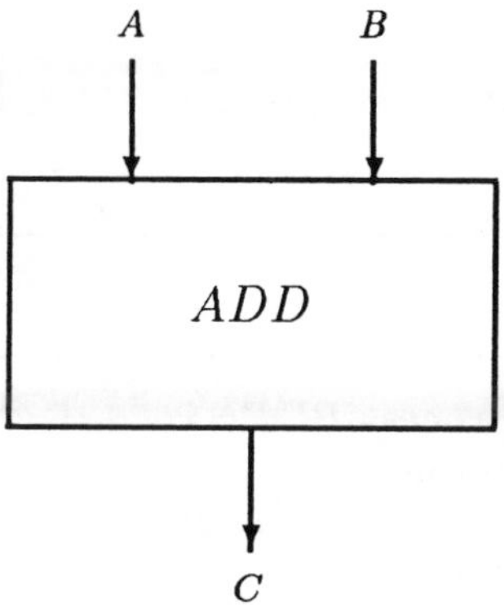


```
process ADD is
connectors
        A, B, C : nat
states
        X : –
        Y : nat, nat
variables
        n, m : nat
init
                                        ⇒ X()
rules
        X()               : A(n) B(m) ⇒ Y(n, m)
        Y(zero, n)        : C(n)      ⇒ X()
        Y(succ(n), m) :               ⇒ Y(n, succ(m))
end
```

Figure 6: FP2 definition of the ADD process

Example 3.14
Figure 7 contains another example of an FP2 process presentation. The $BUFF$ process is a one-place buffer for natural numbers that we will use in later examples.

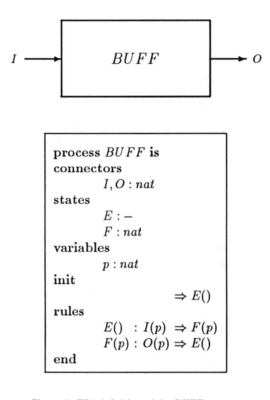

process $BUFF$ **is**
connectors
  $I, O : nat$
states
  $E : -$
  $F : nat$
variables
  $p : nat$
init
  $\Rightarrow E()$
rules
  $E() \ : I(p) \Rightarrow F(p)$
  $F(p) : O(p) \Rightarrow E()$
end

Figure 7: FP2 definition of the BUFF process

Definition 3.12 shows how the specific set of variables appearing in a rule is not relevant for the meaning of the rule. In particular, we shall always consider that *two different rules have disjoint sets of variables*, which can always be obtained by renamings, so that we will not have to bother about name clashes.

3.5 FP2 networks

We have presented a language for describing communicating systems (i.e. processes). The next step is to incorporate our three process combining operators (i.e. $||$, $+$ and $-$), giving rise to *network expressions*. Basically, an FP2 program is simply a presentation for data types followed by a list of process definitions. A process definition associates processes to identifiers (from a set Id), according to the following grammar:

$$\begin{array}{rcll} defn & ::= & \textbf{process}\ id\ \textbf{is}\ net & \\ net & ::= & P & (P \in \textbf{PP}) \\ & \mid & id & (id \in Id) \\ & \mid & net_1 \parallel net_2 & \\ & \mid & net + A.B & (A, B \in K) \\ & \mid & net - A & \end{array}$$

We write $\textbf{NET} = \{net, \ldots\}$ for the set of all network expressions. Note that $\textbf{PP} \subseteq \textbf{NET}$. We shall not detail the (obvious) conditions for well-formedness of network expressions and definitions, nor shall we give their (equally obvious) semantics. We shall write $\mathcal{P}[\![id]\!]$ without referring to an environment $env : Id \to \textbf{NET}$ which, formally, should be used and should be modified by process definitions.

Example 3.15
We may combine ADD and $BUFF$ into a process $ADD2$ which can perform the adding operation done by ADD and may store the result in its buffer component, thus being able to accept a new pair of naturals on input before outputting the first result. Here is a possible definition for $ADD2$ (shown in Figure 8):

$$\textbf{process}\ ADD2\ \textbf{is}\ ADD \parallel BUFF + C.I - C - I$$

simply defining $ADD2$ as the process:

$$\mathcal{P}[\![ADD2]\!] = \mathcal{P}[\![ADD]\!] \parallel_c \mathcal{P}[\![BUFF]\!] +_c C.I -_c C -_c I$$

where now $\parallel_c$, $+_c$ and $-_c$ are the operations we defined in section 2.3.

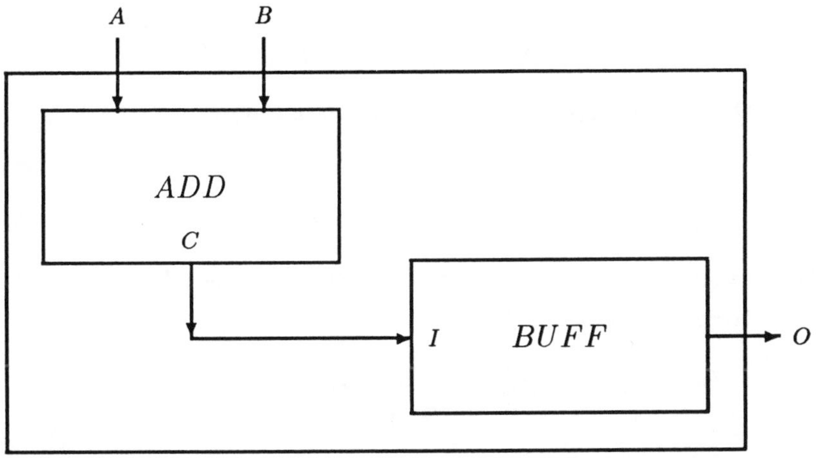

Figure 8: **process** $ADD2$ **is** $ADD \parallel BUFF + C.I - C - I$

One problem with these hierarchical constructions is that we lack a corresponding, so-called compositional, method for proving process properties. Indeed, in section 5 we shall present a temporal logic with an associated proof system that only applies to FP2 process presentations. In order to use such a system with networks defined as combinations of more elementary processes, we need a way to associate a process presentation to arbitrary FP2 networks.

One of the main characteristics of FP2 presentations is that it is possible to combine them in a manner which mimics hierarchical process compositions, that is, it is possible to define a *Flat* function from network expressions to process presentations with the property:

$$Flat(net) = P \;\Rightarrow\; \mathcal{P}[\![net]\!] = \mathcal{P}[\![P]\!]$$

and which behaves in a compositional way, that is, defined along the scheme:

$$\begin{array}{rcll} Flat(P) & = & P & (P \in \mathbf{PP}) \\ Flat(net_1 \mid\mid net_2) & = & Flat(net_1) \mid\mid_p Flat(net_2) & \\ Flat(net + A.B) & = & Flat(net) +_p A.B & \\ Flat(net - A) & = & Flat(net) -_p A & \end{array}$$

where the "p" subscript on $||_p$, $+_p$ and $-_p$ emphasizes the fact that these operations apply to process presentations. We shall sometimes omit this. Transforming a network expression into a single presentation is called *flattening*.

The existence of these $||_p$, $+_p$ and $-_p$ operations effectively turns the set **PP** of process presentations into an algebra where the $\mathcal{P}[\![.]\!] : \mathbf{PP} \rightarrow \mathbf{CS}$ function is an homomorphism.

Before defining the *Flat* function, we first introduce some product operations between state names, state terms and state rules. Given two presentations $\langle \Pi, K, TR, I \rangle$ and $\langle \Pi', K', TR', I' \rangle$ we define:

Product of state names:

$$\Pi \times \Pi' \stackrel{\text{def}}{=} \{Q.Q' \mid Q \in \Pi, Q' \in \Pi'\}$$

with $\rho(Q.Q') = \rho(Q)\rho(Q')$, the concatenation of arities.

Product of state terms:

$$Q(t_1, \ldots, t_n) \times Q'(t'_1, \ldots, t'_{n'}) \stackrel{\text{def}}{=} Q.Q'(t_1, \ldots, t_n, t'_1, \ldots, t'_{n'})$$

where we assume that the two state terms share no variables.

Product of transition rules:

$$(p : k_1(t_1) \cdots k_n(t_n) \Rightarrow q) \times (p' : k'_1(t'_1) \cdots k'_{n'}(t'_{n'}) \Rightarrow q') \stackrel{\text{def}}{=}$$
$$p \times p' : k_1(t_1) \cdots k_n(t_n)\; k'_1(t'_1) \cdots k'_{n'}(t'_{n'}) \Rightarrow q \times q'$$

where we assume that the two rules share no variables.

In order to be well formed, these definitions assume that K and K' are disjoint, which will always be the case. As usual, name clashes between variables are avoided through renamings.

We then introduce a (partial) function over rules: if A and B (of sort s) belong to $Dom(r)$, that is, if $r \in TR$ has the form:

$$r \equiv p : A(t_A)\, B(t_B)\, k_1(t_1) \cdots k_n(t_n) \Rightarrow p'$$

and if t_A and t_B are unifiable with mgu σ, we define $r_{+A.B}$ as:

$$r_{+A.B} \stackrel{\text{def}}{=} \sigma(p : k_1(t_1) \cdots k_n(t_n) \Rightarrow p')$$

Note that $r_{+A.B}$ is *not defined* when r does not use A or B or when t_A and t_B are not unifiable.

All these operations distribute over sets: $TR_{+A.B}$ is the set of all $r_{+A.B}$ (for $r \in TR$) which are defined. $TR \times TR'$ is $\{r \times r' \mid r \in TR, r' \in TR'\}$ and similarly for $I \times I'$. In order to further simplify our notations, we also introduce a hiding operation over a set of rules:

$$TR_{-A} \stackrel{\text{def}}{=} \{r \in TR \mid A \notin Dom(r)\}$$

and a product between transition rules and state names. If $Q \in \Pi_w$ and $(x_1, \ldots, x_n)$ is a tuple of distinct variables of X having sort w and not appearing in $p : e \Rightarrow p'$, then

$$Q \times (p : e \Rightarrow p') \stackrel{\text{def}}{=} Q(x_1, \ldots, x_n) \times p : e \Rightarrow Q(x_1, \ldots, x_n) \times p'$$

(and similarly for $(p : e \Rightarrow p') \times Q$). This also distributes over sets.

We now have enough notations to define $\|_p$, $+_p$ and $-_p$:

Definition 3.16 (Flattening of presentations)

(1) *Given two process presentations $P_i = \langle \Pi_i, K_i, TR_i, I_i \rangle$ $(i = 1, 2)$ with disjoint sets of connectors, the process presentation $P_1 \|_p P_2$ is:*

$$P_1 \|_p P_2 \stackrel{\text{def}}{=} \langle \Pi_1 \times \Pi_2, K_1 \cup K_2, (TR_1 \times TR_2) \cup (\Pi_1 \times TR_2) \cup (TR_1 \times \Pi_2), I_1 \times I_2 \rangle$$

(2) *Given a process presentation $P = \langle \Pi, K, TR, I \rangle$ and two connectors A, B of K_s (for a given sort s), the process presentation $P +_p A.B$ is:*

$$P +_p A.B \stackrel{\text{def}}{=} \langle \Pi, K, TR \cup TR_{+A.B}, I \rangle$$

(3) *Given a process presentation $P = \langle \Pi, K, TR, I \rangle$ and one connector A of K, the process presentation $P -_p A$ is:*

$$P -_p A \stackrel{\text{def}}{=} \langle \Pi, K \setminus \{A\}, TR_{-A}, I \rangle$$

Note that all three constructions are well defined: given two process presentations P_1 and P_2, the process presentations $P_1 \|_p P_2$, $P_1 +_p A.B$ and $P_1 -_p A$ are well formed (when P_1 and P_2 share no connectors, when A and B are two connectors of P_1 of a same sort).

The following result is the justification of all this section.

Proposition 3.17 (Correctness of flattening)
We have

$$\begin{aligned}\mathcal{P}[\![P_1 \parallel_p P_2]\!] &= \mathcal{P}[\![P_1]\!] \parallel_c \mathcal{P}[\![P_2]\!]\\ \mathcal{P}[\![P +_p A.B]\!] &= \mathcal{P}[\![P]\!] +_c A.B\\ \mathcal{P}[\![P -_p A]\!] &= \mathcal{P}[\![P]\!] -_c A\end{aligned}$$

whenever these expressions are defined.

This is clear enough and we shall not prove it formally here.[6] Note that what makes $\mathcal{P}[\![P +_p A.B]\!]$ equals $\mathcal{P}[\![P]\!] +_c A.B$ is the fact that $\sigma(p) \xrightarrow{e}\downarrow \sigma(p')$, where e is $A(\sigma(t_A))\,B(\sigma(t_B)) + e'$, has the form $q \xrightarrow{A(v)\,B(v)+e'} q'$ iff σ is a (ground) unifier of t_A and t_B, that is, an instance of their mgu.

Example 3.18
The flattened process presentation for $ADD2$ is given in Figure 9. Note how the use of unification in the definition of $+_p$ yielded the transition rule "$YE(zero, n) \Rightarrow XF(n)$" where the variable n in the precondition is part of "the contents" of the ADD process, while in the postcondition n is the contents of the $BUFF$ process. This transition rule describes how ADD and $BUFF$ may exchange a value through their connectors C and I.

3.6 Operational semantics of FP2

Most restrictions we imposed on FP2 process presentations were motivated by our goal of having a simple rewrite-based interpreter for FP2 processes. We now describe how this can be obtained. Basically, it only requires to "evaluate" values and then to "execute" process steps.

We assume given a constructor-based presentation $C + D, R$ and a process presentation $P = \langle \Pi, K, TR, I \rangle$. By definition, R is convergent, so that any ground term $t \in T_{C+D}$ (resp. any ground generalized state term p) has a unique normal form $\downarrow t$ (resp. $\downarrow p$) that can be computed by rewriting t or p with R.[7] $\downarrow t$ belongs to T_C (resp. to T_Π) and can be thought as "the value" of t: this accounts for the "functional programming" component of the language.

We may now define how transition rules are to be applied.

Definition 3.19 (Applicability of transition rules)
A transition rule $p : e \Rightarrow p'$ *is* applicable *in state* $q \in T_\Pi$ *through* $\sigma \in \Sigma_g$ *if* $q = \sigma(p)$.

Given a transition rule $p : e \Rightarrow p'$ applicable in state q through σ, $q \xrightarrow{\sigma(e)}\downarrow \sigma(p')$ is a transition of the process. Note that $\sigma(p')$ is a ground generalized state term: *applying* the rule (through σ) is simply computing $\downarrow \sigma(p')$.

---

[6] Formally, the first "=" should be a "$\simeq$".

[7] Confluence plus termination allow us to drop any restriction on the rewriting strategy but, as in many similar languages, all implementations of FP2 use a leftmost-innermost strategy (Schnoebelen 1986, 1988). This gives a "call-by-value" flavor to the implementation since, in practice, the termination requirement is not always fulfilled (see section 3.3).

connectors

$A, B, O : nat$

states

$XE : -$

$XF : nat$

$YE : nat, nat$

$YF : nat, nat, nat$

variables

$n, m, p : nat$

init

$\Rightarrow XE()$

rules

$XE()$	$: A(n)\ B(m)$	$\Rightarrow YE(n, m)$
$XF(p)$	$: A(n)\ B(m)$	$\Rightarrow YF(n, m, p)$
$YE(succ(n), m)$	$:$	$\Rightarrow YE(n, succ(m))$
$YF(succ(n), m, p)$	$:$	$\Rightarrow YF(n, succ(m), p)$
$XF(p)$	$: O(p)$	$\Rightarrow XE()$
$YF(n, m, p)$	$: O(p)$	$\Rightarrow YE(n, m)$
$XF(p)$	$: A(n)\ B(m)\ O(p)$	$\Rightarrow YE(n, m)$
$YF(succ(n), m, p)$	$: O(p)$	$\Rightarrow YE(n, succ(m))$
$YE(zero, n)$	$:$	$\Rightarrow XF(n)$

end

Figure 9: The presentation $ADD \parallel_p BUFF +_p C.I -_p C -_p I$

Given a presentation $P = \langle \Pi, K, TR, I \rangle$, a state $q \in T_\Pi$ and a transition rule $p : e \Rightarrow p'$ from TR, it is easy to find the σ's which make it applicable. This only requires a pattern-matching algorithm yielding a filtering substitution θ that can be completed into any ground substitution. This procedure gives all transitions of the process $\mathcal{P}[\![P]\!]$, as a consequence of Definition 3.12.

Now, a simple interpreter can be described.

Definition 3.20 (Rewrite-based interpreter for FP2)
We assume we are given a presentation $P = \langle \Pi, K, TR, I \rangle$.

Step 1: *Choose randomly an initial rule $\Rightarrow p$ of I and compute $\downarrow p$: this is an initial state q_0.*

Step 2: *In "current" state q_n, choose randomly a rule $p : e \Rightarrow p'$ of TR and a ground substitution σ which makes it applicable in state q_n.*

Step 3: *If no applicable rule exists, report termination and leave.*

Step 4: *If an applicable rule $p : e \Rightarrow p'$ exists, output the event $\sigma(e)$, compute $q_{n+1} = \downarrow \sigma(p')$ and let it be the new state. Go to step 2.*

This simple procedure is adequate in the following sense:

Proposition 3.21 (Adequacy of the interpreter)
*Given any presentation $P \in$ **PP**, the procedure described in Definition 3.20 may produce a trace $e_1, e_2, \ldots$ iff it belongs to $Tr(\mathcal{P}[\![P]\!])$.*

This is not difficult to see. It is nevertheless very important: the correctness of the interpreter is only meaningful w.r.t. the declarative semantics. The flattening operators of Definition 3.16 extend the scope of the interpreter to the whole language: it is therefore a possible implementation of FP2 processes (i.e. any *net* $\in$ **NET**), which has been used for prototyping (Schnoebelen 1986).

3.7 The "Alternating Bit" protocol in FP2

We now describe a more realistic example, based on a possible realization of the well known Alternating Bit protocol. This show how writing FP2 programs can be easy and natural (see Schaefer & Schnoebelen (1987) for another example). This example will also be used in section 5.

The Alternating Bit protocol is used to implement safe communication over a faulty line. The implementation we describe is first shown in Figure 10.

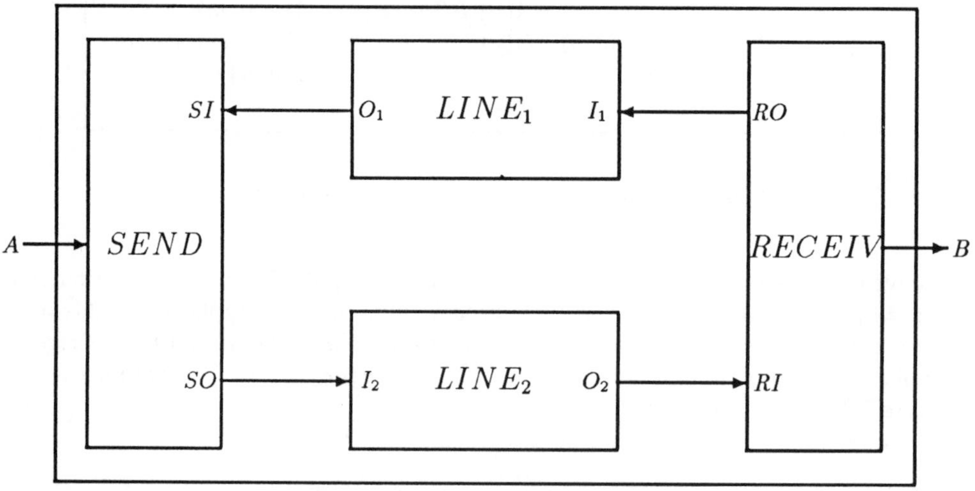

Figure 10: Alternating Bit protocol

Four processes are used to realize a safe transmission line with input A and output B. This network comprises a sender process, a receiver process and a bi-directional asynchronous communication line (here, two lines) which is supposedly not safe. "Not safe" means that we assume that the line may lose messages. Note that we assume that it cannot corrupt its messages.

Intuitively, the protocol can be described as follows. The sender process repeatedly sends its message, until it receives an acknowledgement. Messages are tagged so that an acknowledgement is understood as the reception of the current tag. The receiver process repeatedly accepts incoming messages and checks (via the tag) whether they have already been received successfully. It repeatedly acknowledges receipt of the last message.

We first describe the abstract data type of *messages* that will be exchanged between the four processes. A message is just a natural number, together with a tag (usually a simple bit, but we prefer to use a natural). This gives:

sorts
msg
constructors
$tag : nat, nat \rightarrow msg$
end

The simplest processes in the network are the $LINE$s. An FP2 presentation is given in Figure 11.

process $LINE$ **is**
connectors
$I, O : msg$
states
$E : -$
$F : msg$
variables
$m : msg$
init
$\Rightarrow E()$
rules
$E() \; : I(m) \Rightarrow F(m)$
$E() \; : I(m) \Rightarrow E()$
$F(m) : O(m) \Rightarrow E()$
end

Figure 11: FP2 presentation for the $LINE$s processes

The line is either empty (state $E()$) or contains a message (state $F(m)$). When it is empty, it accepts any message along its I connector, in which case it may (non-deterministically) store it (the first rule) or discard it (the second rule). Note that this choice is not influenced by the external environment. Once the message has been stored, it may only be sent along the O connector: it may not be lost.

A presentation for the $RECEIV$ process is given in Figure 12. In general, $RECEIV$ is in some state $Z(t)$ where t is the value of the last accepted tag. $RECEIV$ accepts (along its RI connector) tagged messages $tag(t', m)$ where t' may be equal to t. In this case, these messages are understood as being duplicated copies of the previously received message and they are ignored (see the first rule). When t' is a new tag (i.e. $t' = succ(t)$), the message is a new message: it is accepted, the value m is transmitted along B, and the stored tag is updated (see the second rule). In addition, $RECEIV$ is always willing to send its current "last tag" as an acknowledgement: this is described

process $RECEIV$ **is**
connectors
$B : nat$
$RI, RO : msg$
states
$Z : nat$
variables
$t, m : nat$
init
$\Rightarrow Z(zero)$
rules
$Z(t) : RI(tag(t,m)) \Rightarrow Z(t)$
$Z(t) : RI(tag(succ(t),m))\ B(m) \Rightarrow Z(succ(t))$
$Z(t) : RO(tag(t,zero)) \Rightarrow Z(t)$
end

Figure 12: FP2 presentation for the $RECEIV$ process

by the third rule.

The $SEND$ process is described in Figure 13. Its behavior is symmetric. Its state is some $S(t,n)$ where t is the last used tag and n is the value to be sent. When in state $S(t,n)$, acknowledgements are accepted along SI. If the acknowledgement contains the current tag (first rule), this is understood as a successful communication and new messages are accepted along A: the value m and the new tag $succ(t)$ are stored in the next state. If the acknowledgement contains the previous tag, it is just ignored (see the second rule). In addition, $SEND$ is always willing to send the current message (see the third rule).

There only remains to define the network by the following:

$$\text{process } AB \ \ \textbf{is} \ \ SEND \,||\, LINE_1 \,||\, LINE_2 \,||\, RECEIV \\ +SO.I_2 + O_2.RI + RO.I_1 + O_1.SI$$

and by hiding all internal connectors. The resulting network can be flattened into a presentation of twenty transition rules. We do not give them here.

3.8 Some comments on FP2

Some comments on this section are called for. Restricting communications to constructor terms (in Definition 3.10) was motivated by our use of unification in Definition 3.16. Of course, one would like to be able to drop this restriction which forbids us to send "computed" values, but this is not an easy problem: if we allow arbitrary communication terms and equations, flattening connection requires semantic unification, which is generally undecidable. We can only hope to handle restricted cases or be forced to modify our definitions of communication.

```
process SEND is
connectors
        A : nat
        SI, SO : msg
states
        S : nat, nat
variables
        t, n, m, p : nat
init
                                                 ⇒ S(zero, zero)
rules
        S(t, n)       : SI(tag(t, p)) A(m)  ⇒ S(succ(t), m)
        S(succ(t), n) : SI(tag(t, p))       ⇒ S(succ(t), n)
        S(t, n)       : SO(tag(t, n))       ⇒ S(t, n)
end
```

Figure 13: FP2 presentation for the $SEND$ process

A possible solution to this problem is to introduce some asymmetry into event terms. Suppose that we partition the set K of connectors into K_{in} and K_{out}: the "input" and the "output" connectors. If we only allow variables $x \in X$ in "input" communication terms: $k(x)$, we may use any term $t \in T_F(X)$ in "output" communication terms: $k'(t)$. Then connecting k and k' requires the unification of x and t, which is trivial. If we want to turn this into an algebra of presentations, it is necessary that these syntactic restrictions are preserved by $+_p$. This is not the case unless we further require that the x variable used in an input communication appears only once in the rule: then we obtain a possible definition to be used in place of Definition 3.10, enjoying all the properties we aimed at. It makes communication more similar to conventional message passing, but it is not really more expressive: in fact it does not even require unification. A further inconvenience is that only one-to-one communications from one output connector to one input connector can take place. The definition used in this chapter (only constructor terms in communications) is a good compromise which introduces no asymmetry between sending and receiving: indeed we did not even have to mention such notions. It immediately generalizes to interconnections of arbitrary sets of connectors (not just pairs).

The other restriction of Definition 3.10, allowing generalized state terms in postconditions only, is there to allow applicability of transition rules to be effective, so that the interpreter of Definition 3.20 is correct and complete.

The only difficulty with the interpreter is that, when in state q_n, it has to non-deterministically choose a grounding instance σ of the matching substitution θ between q_n and the precondition p of the applicable rule $p :\Rightarrow p'$. σ can be obtained by non-deterministically choosing arbitrary values for variables of p' which do not appear in p. This potentially involves unbounded non-determinism and processes not having the finite branching property.[8] This may motivate the following definition:

Definition 3.22 (Strong boundedness)
$P = \langle \Pi, K, TR, I \rangle$ *is* strongly bounded *if for all transition rules* $p : e \Rightarrow p'$ *of* TR, *we have* $Var(e) \cup Var(p') \subseteq Var(p)$.

Strong boundedness is preserved by all three flattening operations, so that we may consider the sub-algebra of strongly bounded presentations. Clearly, if P is strongly bounded, then $\mathcal{P}[\![P]\!]$ is finitely branching.[9] We may even bound the number of different transitions (in some state) by the number of rules in TR. Of course, the difficulty with the interpreter disappears if we restrict ourselves to strongly bounded presentations.

However, it would be unrealistic to restrict the language itself to strongly bounded processes because such processes may be obtained from non-strongly bounded ones: indeed, ADD and $BUFF$ (from Examples 3.13 and 3.14) are not strongly bounded while $ADD2 - A - B$ is.

A different "finite branching" property was studied in (Schnoebelen 1985), namely that for all states q and events e, the set $\{q' \in Q \mid q \xrightarrow{e} q'\}$ is finite. This property exactly corresponds to the usual notion of finite branching (see e.g. Hennessy & Milner 1985). In FP2, this property can be enforced syntactically (i.e. by restrictions upon presentations) but it is not preserved by the connection operator. Essentially the same problem arises in other systems, which explains why most researchers do explicitly consider models without any finite branching assumption (Bergstra & Klop 1989).

We may conclude this section on FP2 by comparing it with LOTOS (ISO 1985, Logrippo et al. 1988). Most notably, FP2 and LOTOS share their use of algebraic data types for specifying values and functions to be used in parallel processes. But while in FP2 both abstract data types and processes have a similar declarative semantics and an operational semantics based on rewriting, processes in LOTOS have CCS-like definitions. We see LOTOS as a sum (a product ?) of two different formalisms, and this situation causes serious problems when one wants to (automatically) validate programs. Basically one is left with a difficult choice between concentrating on one "side" of the language, effectively ignoring the other, or combining two different paradigms for program validation. On the other hand, we believe that it is possible to analyze FP2 processes without giving up their use of abstract data types. This is the point we exemplify in the remainder of this chapter.

Another point of comparison is the set of process combining operators that are allowed in a given language. LOTOS allows recursive definitions with dynamic creation of processes (i.e. definitions $x = t[x]$ where $t[x]$ contains occurrence of parallel combinations) while FP2 only allows static architecture to be defined. It is not clear what is the gain in expressive power (but see Liskov et al. 1986, Parrow 1989). However, it is well known that dynamic creation of processes is a major problem with the compilation of LOTOS and most implementations of LOTOS do not allow it. This is also a problem when building interpreters for LOTOS. While one has to apply the expansion

[8] To our knowledge, this problem has not been dealt with in the operational semantics of LOTOS (ISO 1985).

[9] This is not a necessary condition because some variables may range over sorts with a finite carrier, but it would be easy to refine the criterion into a necessary property.

theorem for each step of a LOTOS process in order to choose between possible moves, the flattening of an FP2 presentation needs only be performed once before invoking the interpreter.

4 A temporal logic for communicating systems

This section describes *CTL* ("Computation Tree Logic"), a temporal logic for reasoning about parallel programs and more generally, about non-deterministic systems. Lamport (1980) and Pnueli (1977) initiated the widespread use of temporal logics to reason about and to specify non-deterministic systems. Lamport (1980) also initiated a debate about whether one should prefer so-called "branching time" or "linear time" temporal logics. We shall not enter this debate. *CTL* is paradigmatic in the field of branching time temporal logic because it admits efficient decision procedures while remaining very expressive (Clarke & Emerson 1981, Emerson & Halpern 1982, Clarke et al. 1983). It can even describe a restricted kind of fairness constraints (see Queille & Sifakis 1983) which are often useful when reasoning about programs. It can be argued that *CTL* is not the best possible temporal logic one could design. However, we are not interested in *CTL* itself: in this chapter, *CTL* will only be used as an example of how rewriting techniques can be used to prove temporal properties of processes described through FP2 presentations. It should be clear that almost any (branching time) temporal logic could have been used as an example (all we need is a result similar to Proposition 4.6). See (Emerson & Srinivasan 1989) for a survey of other possibilities.

We define *CTL*'s syntax and semantics in sections 4.1 and 4.2. In section 4.3 we present some basic definitions and results about predicate transformers, which allow us, in 4.4, to present a "model checking" algorithm for the logic.

The developments of this section will not consider the specific events that may appear in a transition system $\mathcal{P} = \langle Q, L, \rightarrow, I\rangle$ so that, for simplicity, we shall ignore the L part. Events will reappear in the next section.

Remark 4.1
From now on, we shall only consider finitely branching transition systems, that is systems where for any $q \in Q$, the set $\{q' \mid q \rightarrow q'\}$ is finite.

4.1 Syntax of *CTL*

We assume given one set $Prop = \{a, \ldots\}$ of atomic state formulas (propositions). We define the language *CTL* of temporal formulas by the following grammar:

$$(CTL \ni f, g) \ ::= a \mid \top \mid f \wedge g \mid \neg f \mid \mathbf{EX}\, f \mid \mathbf{A}\, f\, \mathbf{U}\, g \mid \mathbf{E}\, f\, \mathbf{U}\, g$$

where the specific notations are inspired by (Browne 1986).

We also introduce the following syntactic abbreviations:

$$\begin{array}{rcl}
f \vee g & \equiv & \neg(\neg f \wedge \neg g) \\
f \Rightarrow g & \equiv & \neg f \vee g \\
f \Leftrightarrow g & \equiv & (f \Rightarrow g) \wedge (g \Rightarrow f) \\
\bot & \equiv & \neg \top \\
\mathbf{AX}\, f & \equiv & \neg \mathbf{EX}\, \neg f \\
\mathbf{AF}\, f & \equiv & \mathbf{A}\, \top\, \mathbf{U}\, f \\
\mathbf{EF}\, f & \equiv & \mathbf{E}\, \top\, \mathbf{U}\, f \\
\mathbf{AG}\, f & \equiv & \neg \mathbf{EF}\, \neg f \\
\mathbf{EG}\, f & \equiv & \neg \mathbf{AF}\, \neg f
\end{array}$$

These formulas apply to states. Informally, a state q satisfies **EX** f if f holds in some (immediately) next state, **AX** f means that f holds for all next states. **U** is the "until" operator: **A** f **U** g means that f will always hold for future states until g is eventually satisfied, while **E** f **U** g means that there is a possible behavior where f holds for all states until g eventually holds. **AF** f means that along every path (starting with the current state), f will eventually hold (i.e. f is *inevitable*), **EF** f means that there is a path along which f will eventually hold (i.e. f is *possible*), **AG** f means that f holds at every state of every possible path (i.e. f holds *globally*) and **EG** f means that there exists a path along which f holds at every state. These intuitions are formalized in Definition 4.3.

4.2 Semantics of CTL

The structures in which we interpret our temporal logic follow the now classical Kripke framework for modal logics. They are transitions systems augmented with an interpretation for the atomic propositions of *Prop*.

Definition 4.2 (Model)
A model *(or Kripke structure) is a pair $\langle \mathcal{P}, \mathcal{L} \rangle$ where $\mathcal{P} = \langle Q, \rightarrow, I \rangle$ is a transition system and where $\mathcal{L} : Prop \rightarrow 2^Q$ is an interpretation for atomic propositions.*[10]

As models, we only consider transition systems where all states are reachable. A model $\langle \mathcal{P}, \mathcal{L} \rangle$ is often written simply as $\mathcal{P}$. Given a system (i.e. a model) $\mathcal{P} = \langle Q, \rightarrow, I \rangle$ we define a *satisfaction* relation $\models$ between states of $\mathcal{P}$ and formulas of CTL by induction over the structure of the formulas. The notation "$\mathcal{P}, q \models f$" means that in system $\mathcal{P}$, state q satisfies formula f. When $\mathcal{P}$ is understood, we only write $q \models f$.

Definition 4.3 (Semantics of CTL)
We define $\models$ inductively by the following:

$q \models a$	*iff* $q \in \mathcal{L}(a)$
$q \models \top$	*always*
$q \models f \wedge g$	*iff* $q \models f$ *and* $q \models g$
$q \models \neg f$	*iff* $q \not\models f$
$q \models \mathbf{EX}\, f$	*iff there exists one step* $q \rightarrow q'$ *s.t.* $q' \models f$
$q_0 \models \mathbf{A}\, f\, \mathbf{U}\, g$	*iff for all executions* $q_0 \rightarrow q_1 \rightarrow \cdots, \exists i \geq 0, q_i \models g$ *and* $\forall j < i, q_j \models f$
$q_0 \models \mathbf{E}\, f\, \mathbf{U}\, g$	*iff for one execution* $q_0 \rightarrow q_1 \rightarrow \cdots, \exists i \geq 0, q_i \models g$ *and* $\forall j < i, q_j \models f$

[10] or, equivalently, a labeling of states with atomic propositions.

We write $\mathcal{P} \models f$ (or simply $\models f$) when $q \models f$ for all $q \in Q$. We define an interpretation function for formulas of CTL:

Definition 4.4
The interpretation of $f \in CTL$ (w.r.t. model $\mathcal{P}$) is the set:

$$Sat[\![f]\!] \stackrel{\text{def}}{=} \{q \in Q \mid q \models f\}$$

A logic such as CTL provides a very rich language in which it is simple to write the kind of properties we are typically interested in when reasoning about transition systems. These may be the presence (or absence, or possibility) of deadlock, liveness of certain events, etc.

Example 4.5
Typical statements will be

(1) $q \models \mathbf{AX}\ \bot$, which holds if q is a final state,

(2) $q \models \mathbf{AF}\ \mathbf{AX}\ \bot$, which holds if $\mathcal{P}$ will eventually stop if started in state q,

(3) $q \models \mathbf{AG}\ \mathbf{EX}\ \top$, which holds if $\mathcal{P}$ will not stop if started in state q,

(4) $\models (\mathbf{AG}\ \mathbf{EX}\ \top) \wedge (a \Rightarrow \mathbf{AG}\ \mathbf{AF}\ b)$, which holds if $\mathcal{P}$ cannot avoid being infinitely often in a state satisfying b once it has been in a state satisfying a (note that non-termination has to be specified),

It will be possible to interpret CTL formulas over FP2 processes even though processes are only defined modulo bisimulation. Indeed the adequacy of branching time temporal logic with respect to bisimulation semantics is well known: bisimilar states satisfy exactly the same temporal formulas [11] (Hennessy & Milner 1985, Brookes & Rounds 1983, Hennessy & Stirling 1985, Pnueli 1985). The converse holds for finitely branching systems, and these results are true of most proposed branching time logics, from minimalistic ones such as the so-called Hennessy-Milner logic of (Hennessy & Milner 1985) to the larger CTL^* of (Emerson & Halpern 1986). FP2 processes are in general not finitely branching: we refer to (Brookes & Rounds 1983, Schnoebelen & Pinchinat 1989) for a study of adequacy in this framework.

An important consequence is that we cannot freely decide to use a different semantics for our parallel programs while sticking to CTL: if the semantic equivalence is broader than bisimulation, the logic cannot meaningfully be understood as "speaking about processes". A possible way out is to develop new logics suited to different semantics of processes. As an example, (Graf & Sifakis 1985) describes a temporal logic suited to the acceptance models of (Hennessy 1985).

4.3 Predicate transformers

This section on predicate transformers follows (Sifakis 1982). The objective is to develop an algorithm for computing the interpretation of formulas of CTL. Throughout this section, we consider a given transition system $\mathcal{P} = \langle Q, \rightarrow, I \rangle$.

[11] provided the formula contains no atomic proposition, or more adequately provided we use a straightforward refinement of bisimulation which require that bisimilar states satisfy the same atomic propositions.

A subset of Q is called a *predicate*. Examples of predicates are all $Sat[\![f]\!]$ for $f \in CTL$. The set of all predicates is 2^Q, the powerset of Q. It is a complete lattice w.r.t. the subset ordering with set intersections and unions as glbs and lubs. It is also a boolean algebra so that we may combine predicates with the boolean connectives. If A and B are two predicates, $A \wedge B$, $A \vee B$ and $\neg A$ stand respectively for $A \cap B$, $A \cup B$ and $Q \setminus A$.

A mapping from 2^Q into itself is a *predicate transformer*. In a natural way, these predicate transformers also form a boolean algebra: let F and G be any two predicate transformers, and A any predicate. We define $F \wedge G, F \vee G, \neg F$ by:

$$\begin{aligned}
(F \wedge G)(A) &= F(A) \wedge G(A) \\
(F \vee G)(A) &= F(A) \vee G(A) \\
(\neg F)(A) &= \neg(F(A))
\end{aligned}$$

For any predicate transformer F, we also define F^*, $F^\times$ and $\widetilde{F}$ by:

$$\begin{aligned}
F^*(A) &= A \cup F(A) \cup F(F(A)) \cup \cdots \\
F^\times(A) &= A \cap F(A) \cap F(F(A)) \cap \cdots \\
\widetilde{F}(A) &= \neg F(\neg A)
\end{aligned}$$

F^* and $F^\times$ are called "F starred" and "F crossed", $\widetilde{F}$ is "the dual of F".

We shall sometimes need to use a predicate B as a constant predicate transformer: for example, $F \wedge B$ is the predicate transformer satisfying $(F \wedge B)(A) = F(A) \cap B$. Thus B seen as predicate transformer is defined by $B(A) = B$ and then $\widetilde{B}(A) = \neg B(\neg A) = \neg B$, that is, $\widetilde{B}$ is $\neg B$.

We define two specific predicate transformers, $pre_{\rightarrow}$ and $post_{\rightarrow}$, by:

$$\begin{aligned}
pre_{\rightarrow}(A) &\stackrel{\text{def}}{=} \{q \in Q \mid \exists q' \in A, q \rightarrow q'\} \\
post_{\rightarrow}(A) &\stackrel{\text{def}}{=} \{q \in Q \mid \exists q' \in A, q' \rightarrow q\}
\end{aligned}$$

When the transition relation $\rightarrow$ is understood, we drop the subscript and simply write *pre*. We shall not use *post*, which is simply pre^{-1}.

Intuitively, $pre(A)$ is the set of all states of Q that can be followed (according to $\rightarrow$) by a state belonging to A while $\widetilde{pre}(A)$ is the set of all states that cannot be followed by a state out of A, that is, all states that can only be followed by states of A, or that cannot be followed at all. The set of all states which can and must be followed by a state of A is $pre(A) \cap \widetilde{pre}(A)$, that is, $pre \wedge \widetilde{pre}(A)$. Similarly, $post(A)$ contains all states which can follow a state of A, so that $post^*(I)$ is the set of all reachable states in $\mathcal{P} = \langle Q, \rightarrow, I \rangle$.

Some basic distributivity properties of *pre* will be used in the next section. For all $A, \ldots \subseteq Q$:

$$pre(\bigcup_i A_i) = \bigcup_i pre(A_i)$$

and, writing $\rightarrow$ for $\rightarrow_1 \cup \rightarrow_2$:

$$pre_{\rightarrow}(A) = pre_{\rightarrow_1}(A) \cup pre_{\rightarrow_2}(A)$$

We may now relate the semantics of CTL and the computations based on predicate transformers through the following:

Proposition 4.6
For all $f, g \in CTL$:

$$\begin{array}{llcl}
(1) & Sat[\![\top]\!] & = & Q \\
(2) & Sat[\![f \wedge g]\!] & = & Sat[\![f]\!] \cap Sat[\![g]\!] \\
(3) & Sat[\![\neg f]\!] & = & \neg Sat[\![f]\!] \ (= Q \setminus Sat[\![f]\!]) \\
(4) & Sat[\![\mathbf{AX}\ f]\!] & = & \widetilde{pre}(Sat[\![f]\!]) \\
(5) & Sat[\![\mathbf{EX}\ f]\!] & = & pre(Sat[\![f]\!]) \\
(6) & Sat[\![\mathbf{E}\ f\ \mathbf{U}\ g]\!] & = & (pre \wedge Sat[\![f]\!])^*(Sat[\![g]\!]) \\
(7) & Sat[\![\mathbf{A}\ f\ \mathbf{U}\ g]\!] & = & (Id \vee pre \wedge \widetilde{pre} \wedge Sat[\![f]\!])^*(Sat[\![g]\!])
\end{array}$$

This proposition is the result which makes us say that "**AX** is $\widetilde{pre}$", that "**E** f **U** is $(pre \wedge f)^*$", ... (1) to (5) are obvious from Definition 4.3, (6) is almost as clear. (7) is more difficult to prove because it explicitly requires the finite branching assumption.

Remark 4.7
To see that (7) requires finite branching, consider as a counter-example the system (shown in Figure 14) where $Q = \{p, q_0, q_1, q_2, \ldots\}$ and where $\rightarrow = \{q_{i+1} \rightarrow q_i \mid i \in \mathbf{N}\} \cup \{p \rightarrow q_i \mid i \in \mathbf{N}\}$. If now $Sat[\![g]\!] = \{q_0\}$ we have:

$$\forall n \in \mathbf{N}, (Id \vee pre \wedge \widetilde{pre})^n Sat[\![g]\!] = \{q_0, \ldots, q_n\}$$

implying

$$(Id \vee pre \wedge \widetilde{pre})^* Sat[\![g]\!] = \{q_i \mid i \in \mathbf{N}\} \neq Q$$

while $Sat[\![\mathbf{A} \top \mathbf{U}\ g]\!] = Q$.

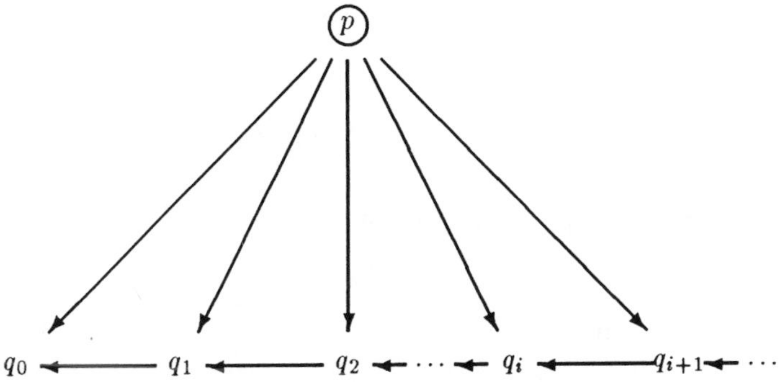

Figure 14: An infinitely branching system

4.4 Model checking

These results allow us to describe a model checker for CTL. A model checker is a procedure for deciding whether a given formula f holds for a transition system $\mathcal{P}$, that is, a decision procedure for sentences of the form $\mathcal{P} \models f$. We may also use model checkers to decide whether a given sentence $\mathcal{P}, q \models f$ is true. The main point is that $\mathcal{P}$, the model, is fixed and that we only check truth w.r.t. some $\mathcal{P}$. This approach to the automatic verification of parallel programs has been widely used since it was first proposed and its feasibility demonstrated (Queille & Sifakis 1982, Clarke et al. 1983).

Basically, a model checking algorithm just considers the state graph of the program to be verified and marks all states satisfying a given temporal formula. This relies on Proposition 4.6. For example, in order to mark all states satisfying $f \wedge g$, the model checker simply marks states for f and for g and then combines the markings. Fixed points are computed iteratively: in order to mark states for $\mathbf{E}\ f\ \mathbf{U}\ g$, the model checker first marks all states for g and for f, then states marked for g are used to initialize the states for $\mathbf{E}\ f\ \mathbf{U}\ g$ and the transition relation (the edges of the graph) is used backwards, marking all states (verifying f) from which it is possible to reach an (already marked) state for $\mathbf{E}\ f\ \mathbf{U}\ g$. Stabilization is used as the halting criterion: when no new states are added to the marked set, the computation is finished.

These explanations may seem naive, but they are the simplest way of describing the graph-walking procedure. For every similar logic, one relies on a result similar to Proposition 4.6, and the graph marking part is just an implementation of it (see Emerson & Lei (1986) for a very similar presentation). Of course, much ingenious thinking has been invested into algorithmic refinements, but this is not our concern here.

The main limitation with this approach is that it is restricted to finite state systems: the state graph is handled extensionally. For processes denoted by FP2 programs, we consider a "*symbolic* model checking" approach. Such an approach requires a symbolic notation for sets of states (i.e. predicates) and, in order to compute $Sat[\![f]\!]$ for arbitrary f of CTL, we only need to be able:

(1) To compute $Sat[\![\, a\,]\!]$ for atomic formulas $a \in Prop$,

(2) To compute unions, intersections and complements of sets of states,

(3) To compute *pre* over sets of states,

(4) To compute fixed points obtained by crossing or starring predicate transformers.

This is exactly what we shall explain now for systems described through FP2 presentations. There is one difficulty with item (4) of the previous task list: computing fixed points by successive iterations of monotonic predicate transformers may fail to terminate when the state graph is not finite and, consequently, our symbolic model checker will sometimes fail to return an answer. Note that this problem cannot be solved in our general framework where we cannot expect completeness: the halting problem (say) can be expressed in CTL so that the set of formulas holding in a given model $\mathcal{P}$ is in general not recursively enumerable.

A similar problem appears when we are dealing with systems without the finite-branching property. In this case, item (7) of Proposition 4.6 must be weakened into

$$Sat[\![\, \mathbf{A}\ f\ \mathbf{U}\ g\,]\!] \supseteq (Id \vee pre \wedge \widetilde{pre} \wedge Sat[\![\, f\,]\!])^*(Sat[\![\, g\,]\!])$$

which may still prove useful it we take advantage of various monotonicity properties of our basic predicate transformers. For simplicity, we will discontinue our exposition of predicate transformers, but note that several distributivity and continuity (w.r.t. both $\subseteq$ and $\supseteq$) properties of pre, $\widetilde{pre}$, F^* and $F^\times$ (see Sifakis 1982) can be used to improve the efficiency of the approach.

5 Symbolic model checking in FP2

This section describes a symbolic model checker for FP2 presentations, with no restriction to finite-state systems. The main idea is to use *constrained terms* (see below) for symbolic manipulation of sets of states. This idea has been introduced in (Schnoebelen 1987) and it relies entirely on *disunification*, a new method due to H. Comon (Comon 1988b, Comon & Lescanne 1989) for dealing with negation in so-called equational problems. Sections 5.1 and 5.2 are taken almost literally from (Comon & Lescanne 1989, Comon 1988a). They introduce the reader to equational problems and constrained terms with as few formalism as possible. Then section 5.3 proposes a temporal logic for FP2, based on the framework we developed in section 4 and adapting it to processes denoted by FP2 presentations: disunification allows us to obtain effective procedures for handling predicates (sets of states). Section 5.4 deals with some simple examples: as could be expected, we are faced with some of the usual problems of temporal logics.

Remark 5.1
In this section we only consider process presentations *without defined functions*, that is, we assume we are working with a presentation $C + D, E$ where both D and E are empty. Nevertheless, we still refer to F as our signature. This sublanguage is sometimes called "FP2 with constructors only" and all our examples of FP2 processes so far (ADD, $BUFF$ and the "alternating bit" network) were written in it. It is expressive enough to define any Turing machine as an FP2 process (Pereira 1984).

5.1 Disunification

Definition 5.2 (Disequation)
An (s-sorted) disequation *is a couple (u, v), written $u \neq v$, of two terms of $T_{F,s}(X)$.*

Disequations are the logical negation of equations. Variables in equations are implicitly universally quantified, but the introduction of negation cannot be done without making explicit these quantifications. This explains the following definition:

Definition 5.3 (Equational problem)

(1) *An (equational)* system *is an equation $u = v$, or a disequation $u \neq v$, or a conjunction of systems $P_1 \wedge \cdots \wedge P_k$, or a disjunction of systems $P_1 \vee \cdots \vee P_k$.*

(2) *An* equational problem *is a formula*

$$\exists w_1, \ldots, w_m, \forall y_1, \ldots, y_n : P$$

where $w_1, \ldots, w_m, y_1, \ldots, y_n$ are distinct variables and where P is a system.

Empty conjunctions and disjunctions of systems are allowed: we write them $\top$ and $\bot$ and they are neutral elements for (resp.) $\wedge$ and $\vee$. The free variables of $\exists w_1,\ldots,w_m,\forall y_1,\ldots,y_n : P$ are the variables of P that are not some w_i or some y_j. They are called the *principal unknowns* of the problem and we use $\mathcal{I} = \{x_1,\ldots,x_p\}$ to denote them. The y_j's are the *parameters* of the problem.

Example 5.4
The following problem:

$$P_0 \equiv \forall y_1, y_2 : x_1 = f(x_2, 0) \wedge (y_1 \neq x_1 \vee f(y_1, y_2) \neq f(x_2, x_1))$$

is an equational problem with parameters y_1, y_2 and with unknowns x_1, x_2. (In this and the following examples, we assume the signature $F = \{f : s, s \rightarrow s;\ 0 :\rightarrow s\}$.)

Definition 5.5
Given an F-algebra $\mathcal{A}$, an $\mathcal{A}$-assignment σ validates a system P if

(1) *P is an equation $u = v$ and $\sigma(u) =_{\mathcal{A}} \sigma(v)$, or*

(2) *P is a disequation $u \neq v$ and $\sigma(u) \neq_{\mathcal{A}} \sigma(v)$, or*

(3) *P is a conjunction $P_1 \wedge \cdots \wedge P_k$ and σ validates every P_i, or*

(4) *P is a disjunction $P_1 \vee \cdots \vee P_k$ and σ validates at least one P_i.*

Intuitively, an $\mathcal{A}$-solution of an equational problem $\exists w_1,\ldots,w_m,\forall y_1,\ldots,y_n : P$ is an $\mathcal{A}$-assignment σ assigning values to the free variables of the problem in such a way that there exists an assignment for the existentially quantified w_i's so that the system is validated whatever values are taken by the parameters (the y_j's). For technical reasons, the exact definition is rather complicated, so we give only a simplified definition which fits our restricted case where we only consider solutions in T_F.

Definition 5.6 (Solution of equational problems)
A substitution σ is a solution *(w.r.t. T_F) of a problem $\exists w_1,\ldots,w_m,\forall y_1,\ldots,y_n : P$ if*

(1) *σ is a $\mathcal{I}$-ground substitution,*

(2) *There exists a $\{w_1,\ldots,w_m\}$-ground substitution ρ such that for all ground substitution θ, $\theta \circ \rho \circ \sigma$ validates system P.*

When an equational problem admits at least one solution, we say that it is *satisfiable* (w.r.t. T_F). We write $Sol(P)$ to denote the set of solutions of problem P (and $Sol_{\mathcal{A}}(P)$ when we consider solutions w.r.t. algebra $\mathcal{A}$).

Example 5.7
$\sigma_0 = (x_1 \leftarrow f(0,0); x_2 \leftarrow 0)$ is a solution of P_0. Indeed $\sigma_0(x_1)$ equals $\sigma_0(f(x_2, 0))$ and for every ground substitution θ, either $\theta(y_1)$ is different form $f(0,0)$ or $\theta(f(y_1, y_2))$ is different from $f(0, f(0,0))$.

We give in Figure 15 (a sample of) the transformation rules for equational problems first proposed in (Comon 1988b, Comon & Lescanne 1989). These rules may be used to transform an equational problem P into a set $\{P_1,\ldots,P_k\}$ of other, hopefully

Elimination of parameters

$$(EP_1)\quad \forall y_1,\ldots,y_n : P \wedge (d \vee y_i \neq u) \;\mapsto\; \forall y_1,\ldots,y_n : P \wedge d(y_i \leftarrow u)$$

$$(EP_2)\quad \forall y_1,\ldots,y_n : P \;\mapsto\; \forall y_1,\ldots,y_{i-1},y_{i+1},\ldots,y_n : P \quad [\text{ if } y_i \notin Var(P)\,]$$

Clashes and Decompositions

$$\begin{array}{lll} (C_1) & f(t_1,\ldots,t_n) = g(u_1,\ldots,u_m) \mapsto \bot & \\ (C_2) & f(t_1,\ldots,t_n) \neq g(u_1,\ldots,u_m) \mapsto \top & [\text{ if } f \not\equiv g\,] \end{array}$$

$$(D_1)\quad f(t_1,\ldots,t_n) = f(u_1,\ldots,u_n) \;\mapsto\; t_1 = u_1 \wedge \ldots \wedge t_n = u_n$$

$$(D_2)\quad f(t_1,\ldots,t_n) \neq f(u_1,\ldots,u_n) \;\mapsto\; t_1 \neq u_1 \vee \cdots \vee t_n \neq u_n$$

Replacement

$$(R)\quad x = t \wedge P \;\mapsto\; x = t \wedge P(x \leftarrow t) \quad \left[\begin{array}{l} \text{if } x \in \mathcal{I},\ x \notin Var(t),\ x \in Var(P). \\ \text{And, if } t \in X, \text{ then } t \text{ must occur in } P \end{array}\right]$$

Elimination of trivial equations and disequations

$$(T_1)\quad t = t \;\mapsto\; \top$$

$$(T_2)\quad t \neq t \;\mapsto\; \bot$$

Occur checks

$$\begin{array}{lll} (O_1) & x \neq u \mapsto \top & \\ (O_2) & x = u \mapsto \bot & [\text{ if } x \in Var(u) \text{ and } x \not\equiv u\,] \end{array}$$

Non deterministic choice

$$(N_C)\quad P \wedge (P_1 \vee P_2) \;\mapsto\; P \wedge P_1 \quad [\text{ if } P_1 \text{ or } P_2 \text{ does not contain any parameter}\,]$$

Figure 15: Some transformation rules for equational problems

simpler, problems. We did not include an important, so-called "Explosion" rule, for it is difficult to state precisely. It is best explained by saying that it allows us to perform case analysis. Suppose that x is a variable of sort Nat occurring in problem P. Then it is possible to assume that x is either $zero$ or some $succ(x')$ (where x' is a new variable). The Explosion rule allows us to transform P into the two problems $P \wedge x = zero$ and $P \wedge x = succ(x')$. The conditions for applicability are complicated because of both correctness and termination requirements.

Example 5.8
Problem P_0 from Example 5.4 can be transformed into:

$$\begin{array}{lll} P_0 & \mapsto_{D_2} & \forall y_1, y_2 : x_1 = f(x_2, 0) \wedge (y_1 \neq x_1 \vee y_1 \neq x_2 \vee y_2 \neq x_1) \\ & \mapsto_{EP_{1,2}} & \forall y_2 : x_1 = f(x_2, 0) \wedge (x_1 \neq x_2 \vee y_2 \neq x_1) \\ & \mapsto_{EP_{1,2}} & x_1 = f(x_2, 0) \wedge x_1 \neq x_2 \\ & \mapsto_{R} & x_1 = f(x_2, 0) \wedge x_2 \neq f(x_2, 0) \\ & \mapsto_{O_1} & x_1 = f(x_2, 0) \end{array}$$

which is irreducible (no rule applies). This last problem can be seen as the substitution $(x_1 \leftarrow f(x_2, 0))$, of which the solution σ_0 from Example 5.7 is a ground instance.

This is a general behavior. The rules given in (Comon 1988b, Comon & Lescanne 1989) are such that their non-deterministic application over any problem P always terminates, giving irreducible problems $P_1, \ldots, P_k$ such that $Sol_{\mathcal{A}}(P) = \bigcup_{i=1,\ldots,k} Sol_{\mathcal{A}}(P_i)$.

In certain cases, e.g. when $\mathcal{A}$ is the term algebra or the algebra of rational trees, these rules will eventually lead to so-called problems *in solved forms*, which generally are irreducible problems with interesting properties (e.g. one can immediately extract solutions from them). There are several possible definitions for solved forms (with several possible sets of rules and/or strategies) depending on the kind of applications one has in mind, and we cannot list them here (see Comon (1989b) for a survey). The one we shall use is fit for solutions in T_F:

Definition 5.9 (Definition with constraints) (Comon & Lescanne 1989)
An equational problem is a definition with constraints *if it has the form:*

$$\exists w_1, \ldots, w_m : x_1 = t_1 \wedge \cdots \wedge x_p = t_p \wedge z_1 \neq u_1 \wedge \cdots \wedge z_n \neq u_n$$

where:

(1) *The x_i's are distinct variables and appear only once in the problem,*

(2) *The z_i's are variables,*

(3) *For $i = 1, \ldots, n$, z_i is different from u_i,*

(4) $Var(z_1, \ldots, z_n, u_1, \ldots, u_n) \subseteq Var(t_1, \ldots, t_p)$.

The $x_1 = t_1 \wedge \cdots \wedge x_p = t_p$ component is exactly like the *unification solved forms* of (Martelli & Montanari 1982). It clearly denotes an idempotent substitution. The $z_1 \neq u_1 \wedge \cdots \wedge z_n \neq u_n$ component is called a *constraint*. One property of definitions with constraints is that they always have some solutions [12] (see Comon & Lescanne 1989).

Our interest in definition with constraints stems from the following:

Theorem 5.10 (Comon 1988b)
The transformation rules of (Comon & Lescanne 1989) give an algorithm transforming any equational problem P into a set $\{P_1, \ldots, P_n\}$ of definitions with constraints such that $Sol(P) = \bigcup_{i=1,\ldots,n} Sol(P_i)$.

For example, the irreducible problem of Example 5.8 is a definition with constraints (with an empty constraint). One can find similar results in (Maher 1988) where the solved forms have a different definition (e.g. they may denote empty sets).

5.2 Constrained terms and predicates

Definition 5.11
An (s-sorted) constrained term *is a pair (t, d) where:*

(1) *t is a term of $T_{F,s}(X)$,*

(2) *d is a conjunction of disequations $z_i \neq u_i$ where $z_i \in Var(t)$ and u_i is a subterm of t not containing z_i.*

The constraint, d, is just a special case of a definition with constraints. (t, d) is written $t \,\&\, z_1 \neq u_1 \wedge \cdots \wedge z_n \neq u_n$ or $t \,\&\, d$. We simply write t when d is empty.

Constrained terms are used to denote subsets of T_F:

Definition 5.12 (Semantics of constrained terms)
An (s-sorted) constrained term $t \,\&\, d$ denotes

$$[\![t \,\&\, d]\!] \stackrel{\text{def}}{=} \{\sigma(t) \mid \sigma \in Sol(d)\} \quad (\subseteq T_{F,s})$$

where d is solved with $Var(t)$ as principal unknowns.

Note that, as we mentioned earlier, $[\![t \,\&\, d]\!]$ is never empty. Note also that with our definition of $Sol(d)$, $\sigma(t)$ must be ground and that $[\![t \,\&\, d]\!]$ does not change when we (bijectively) rename variables in $t \,\&\, d$.

Constrained forests are finite sets of s-sorted constrained terms. The constrained forest $f = \{t_1 \,\&\, d_1, \ldots, t_n \,\&\, d_n\}$ denotes $\bigcup_{i=1,\ldots,n} [\![t_i \,\&\, d_i]\!]$. (For simplicity, our presentation does not allow multiple sorts in constrained forests.) By extension, a constrained forest is any subset of $T_{F,s}$ that can be denoted by a finite set of constrained terms. The empty set is simply denoted by an empty forest.

Theorem 5.13 (Comon 1988b)
Constrained forests are stable by complementation, finite unions and intersections. Furthermore, there exists effective algorithms to compute these operations.

This is the main result which allows us to use constrained forests to compute with subsets of $T_{F,s}$. The following is a brief description of the algorithm:

---

[12]Provided that all sorts have an infinite carrier in T_F. If this is not the case, the definition can be modified (which we shall not do) so that the same results hold.

Union: This is trivial: one just has to take the union of the constrained forests.

Intersection: Intersection is distributive w.r.t. unions so that we only need to intersect s-sorted constrained terms $t_1 \,\&\, d_1$ and $t_2 \,\&\, d_2$. We assume that t_1 and t_2 share no variables, which can always be obtained by renaming. We write $Y = \{y_1, \ldots, y_m\}$ for $Var(t_1) \cup Var(t_2)$ and assume that $x \notin Y$ is a new variable of X_s. The problem

$$\exists y_1, \ldots, y_m : x = t_1 \wedge x = t_2 \wedge d_1 \wedge d_2$$

has x as principal unknown. It can be reduced to the definitions with constraints $P_1, \ldots, P_k$. These solved forms have the form $P_i \equiv \exists w_1, \ldots, w_m : x = u_i \wedge c_i$. Then:

$$[\![t_1 \,\&\, d_1]\!] \cap [\![t_2 \,\&\, d_2]\!] = \bigcup_{i=1,\ldots,k} [\![u_i \,\&\, c_i]\!]$$

Complementation: Here also it is enough to know how to compute the complement of a single s-sorted constrained term $t \,\&\, z_1 \neq u_1 \wedge \cdots \wedge z_n \neq u_n$. We assume $Var(t) = \{w_1, \ldots, w_m\}$ does not contain $x \in X_s$. Then the problem

$$\forall w_1, \ldots, w_m : x \neq t \vee z_1 = u_1 \vee \cdots \vee z_n = v_n$$

has x as principal unknown and can be reduced to the definitions with constraints $P_1, \ldots, P_k$. The P_i's all have the form $P_i \equiv \exists w_1, \ldots, w_m : x = u_i \wedge c_i$. Then:

$$T_F - [\![t \,\&\, z_1 \neq u_1 \wedge \cdots \wedge z_n \neq u_n]\!] = \bigcup_{i=1,\ldots,k} [\![u_i \,\&\, c_i]\!]$$

Example 5.14
Suppose we want to compute the complement of $[\![f(w,w)]\!]$. We reduce $P \equiv \forall w : x \neq f(w,w)$. Explosion gives the two problems:

$$P \mapsto_{Explosion} \begin{cases} P' \equiv \forall w : x \neq f(w,w) \wedge x = 0 \\ P'' \equiv \exists z_1, z_2 \forall w : x \neq f(w,w) \wedge x = f(z_1, z_2) \end{cases}$$

Now the possible reductions are:

$$\begin{array}{lll} P' & \mapsto_R & \forall w : 0 \neq f(w,w) \wedge x = 0 \\ & \mapsto_{C_2} & \forall w : x = 0 \\ & \mapsto_{EP_2} & x = 0 \end{array}$$

and

$$\begin{array}{lll} P'' & \mapsto_R & \exists z_1, z_2 \forall w : f(z_1, z_2) \neq f(w,w) \wedge x = f(z_1, z_2) \\ & \mapsto_{D_2} & \exists z_1, z_2 \forall w : (z_1 \neq w \vee z_2 \neq w) \wedge x = f(z_1, z_2) \\ & \mapsto_{EP_{1,2}} & \exists z_1, z_2 : x = f(z_1, z_2) \wedge z_1 \neq z_2 \end{array}$$

These two problems are definitions with constraints. We deduce that:

$$T_F \setminus [\![f(w,w)]\!] = [\![0]\!] \cup [\![f(z_1, z_2) \,\&\, z_1 \neq z_2]\!]$$

as expected.

The (very natural) idea of using terms of $T_F(X)$ to denote subsets of T_F has always had to deal with the complicated problem of the complementation operation. Indeed, if one only considers "unconstrained" terms, it is impossible to denote the complement of some $[\![t]\!]$ as some $\bigcup_i [\![t_i]\!]$ when t is non-linear (see our previous example); this was proved in (Lassez & Marriott 1987).

Solutions to these complement problems were known for the linear case. It is found that if t_1 and t_2 are linear, $[\![t_1]\!] \cap [\![t_2]\!]$ can be denoted as some $[\![t]\!]$ where t itself is linear, so that the subclass of linear unconstrained forests (having the form $\bigcup_i [\![t_i]\!]$ with linear t_i's) is also stable for complementation, union and intersection. This is exploited in e.g. (Thiel 1984, Schnoebelen 1988). Unfortunately, the application we have in mind cannot be restricted to linear terms.

Given a process presentation $P = \langle \Pi, K, TR, I \rangle$, predicates (in the sense of section 4.3) can be denoted by constrained terms. Indeed $\Pi + F$ can be seen as a many-sorted signature if we introduce a new sort *state*, and predicates are just subsets of T_Π (i.e. T_{state}). We shall sometimes speak of *constrained predicates* instead of constrained forests of sort *state*.

Theorem 5.13 directly applies here and allows us to compute intersections, unions and complements of constrained predicates. We still have to show how to apply *pre* on constrained predicates. This is easy: *pre* being distributive, it suffices to compute $pre_r([\![p \,\&\, d]\!])$ for a single transition rule $r \equiv p' : e' \Rightarrow p''$ and a single constrained term $p \,\&\, d$. We may assume that p and $p' : e' \Rightarrow p''$ do not share variables. We write $Y = \{y_1, \ldots, y_m\}$ for $Var(p, p', p'')$ and assume that $x \notin Y$ is a new variable of sort *state*. The problem

$$\exists y_1, \ldots, y_m : x = p' \wedge p = p'' \wedge d$$

can be reduced to the definition with constraints $\{P_1, \ldots, P_k\}$ as already seen. These P_i's have the form $\exists w_1, \ldots, w_m : x = p_i \wedge d_i$. Then:

$$pre_r([\![p \,\&\, d]\!]) = \bigcup_{i=1,\ldots,k} [\![p_i \,\&\, d_i]\!]$$

This result is a special case of the general form of Theorem 5.13 in (Comon 1988a).

5.3 A temporal logic for FP2

We may now define a temporal logic for FP2 processes simply by instantiating the general framework we presented in section 4. Instantiating means choosing some set *Prop* of atomic state formulas, together with their interpretations. We assume we are given an FP2 process presentation $P = \langle \Pi, K, TR, I \rangle$. We define *Prop* by the following grammar:

$$(Prop \ni)\ a \ ::= \ p \ \mid \ \textbf{enable}\ e \ \mid \ \textbf{after}\ e$$

where $p \in T_\Pi(X)$ is any state term (not necessarily ground) and $e \in T_{Ev}(X)$ is any event term. This it parameterized by the process presentation P at hand. We call $CTL[P]$ the resulting logic.

A canonical interpretation can be associated with the process presentation:

Definition 5.15
The model denoted by $P = \langle \Pi, K, TR, I\rangle$ *is the pair* $\langle \mathcal{P}, \mathcal{L}\rangle$ *where* $\mathcal{P} = \mathcal{P}[\![P]\!] = \langle T_\Pi, K, T_{F,E}, \rightarrow_{TR}, \downarrow I\rangle$ *as in Definition 3.12, and where* $\mathcal{L}$ *is given by:*

$$\begin{aligned}
\mathcal{L}(p) &\stackrel{\text{def}}{=} \{\sigma(p) \mid \sigma \in \Sigma_g\} \quad (= [\![p]\!]) \\
\mathcal{L}(\textbf{enable}\ e) &\stackrel{\text{def}}{=} \{q \in T_\Pi \mid \exists \sigma \in \Sigma_g, \exists q' \in T_\Pi, q \xrightarrow{\sigma(e)} q'\} \\
\mathcal{L}(\textbf{after}\ e) &\stackrel{\text{def}}{=} \{q' \in T_\Pi \mid \exists \sigma \in \Sigma_g, \exists q \in T_\Pi, q \xrightarrow{\sigma(e)} q'\}
\end{aligned}$$

Example 5.16
Assume we are dealing with process ADD from Figure 6. Then:

(1) "$Y(zero, x)$" means "when ADD is in some state $Y(t_1, t_2)$ with $t_1 = zero$".

(2) "**enable** $C(zero)$" means "when ADD may send $zero$ along C", we have

$$Sat[\![\,\textbf{enable}\ C(zero)\,]\!] = \{Y(zero, zero)\}$$

(3) "**enable** τ" means "when ADD may perform a silent step", we have

$$Sat[\![\,\textbf{enable}\ \tau\,]\!] = [\![\,Y(succ(n), m)\,]\!]$$

(4) "**after** τ" means "when ADD just performed a silent step", we have

$$Sat[\![\,\textbf{after}\ \tau\,]\!] = [\![\,Y(n, succ(m))\,]\!]$$

It is clear how these propositions can be used. The idea behind **after** e and **enable** e is that we want to be able to refer to events in state formulas. Thus, to express that once values 2 and 3 have been received by ADD, their sum cannot fail to appear along connector C, we can write $ADD \models \textbf{after}\ A(2)\ B(3) \Rightarrow \textbf{AF}\ \textbf{after}\ C(5)$.

There is one difficulty here. If we want to interpret **after** e as a formula about states, the states of a system should contain information about how they have been reached. Indeed, our intuition of **after** e is that it does not refer to states in an automaton (a graph), but to states along a computation sequence (an execution of the automaton). Formally, when we consider "**after** e" propositions, the models of CTL are not graphs but trees where a state contains complete information about the way it is reached from the root. Thus an FP2 presentation should be interpreted as the tree made from all its executions.

This solution is not compatible with the symbolic verification algorithm we have in mind: as we shall soon see, the algorithm uses the state graph directly denoted by an FP2 presentation. However, one can remark that "conflict-free" graphs are acceptable models, where conflict-free means that whenever the graph contains two steps $q_1 \xrightarrow{e_1} q$ and $q_2 \xrightarrow{e_2} q$ leading to a same state, we have $e_1 = e_2$. If we further require that the initial states have no predecessors (the graph is root-acyclic), our definition of $q \models \textbf{after}\ e$ matches the intuition. It turns out that it is easy, given any FP2 presentation P, to tell if $\mathcal{P}[\![P]\!]$ is conflict-free (in which case we say that the presentation is conflict-free), allowing us to use the symbolic verification method. For the general case, there exists an algorithm transforming any presentation into a logically equivalent conflict-free one (see Pinchinat (1989) for details). Consequently, from now on we shall always be in one of the two situations: 1) we consider a conflict-free presentation, or 2) we do not use "**after** e" propositions.

A further detail is that the graph $\mathcal{P}[\![P]\!] = \langle T_\Pi, K, T_{F,E}, \rightarrow_{TR}, \downarrow I\rangle$ may contain unreachable states. The solution is to use a formula $INIT$ characterizing initial states, i.e. such that $q \models INIT$ iff $q \in \downarrow I$. Then, we define $P \models f$ by $\forall q \in T_\Pi, q \models INIT \Rightarrow \mathbf{AG} f$.

It is now clear how an FP2 process presentation denotes a model of our temporal logic. There remains to show how, given any presentation $P = \langle \Pi, K, TR, I\rangle$ and any formula $a \in Prop$, it is possible to express $Sat[\![a]\!]$ as some constrained predicate over $\mathcal{P}[\![P]\!]$. First $Sat[\![p]\!]$ is just $[\![p]\!]$ as Definition 5.15 stated. Then $Sat[\![\textbf{enable } e]\!]$ is obtained as easily: if $\{p_i : e_i \Rightarrow p'_i \mid \sigma_i = mgu(e, e_i)\}$ is the subset of TR containing all transition rules having an event unifiable with e (assuming distinct variables) then

$$Sat[\![\textbf{enable } e]\!] = \bigcup_i [\![\sigma_i(p_i)]\!]$$

expressing $Sat[\![\textbf{enable } e]\!]$ as a constrained predicate. $Sat[\![\textbf{after } e]\!]$ is computed in exactly the same way: we consider the same subset $\{p_i : e_i \Rightarrow p'_i \mid \sigma_i = mgu(e, e_i)\}$ of TR but then use the postconditions:

$$Sat[\![\textbf{after } e]\!] = \bigcup_i [\![\sigma_i(p'_i)]\!]$$

5.4 Analysis of FP2 processes: some examples

We present in this section some examples of how the techniques we described can be used to analyze processes described by FP2 presentations. As the necessary computations are often tedious (and meant to be performed by a computer!) we only consider simple examples and often skip part of the actual computation. The main interest is to demonstrate the symbolic verification method.

Throughout the section, we assume we are working with a presentation $\langle \Pi, K, TR, I\rangle$. As a first example, we compute terminal states. These states are often called *sink* states and we shall write *Sink* for the set of sink states. We saw in Example 4.5 that $Sink = Sat[\![\mathbf{AX} \perp]\!]$. Now, Proposition 4.6 gives

$$Sat[\![\mathbf{AX} \perp]\!] = \widetilde{pre}(Sat[\![\perp]\!]) = \neg pre(Sat[\![\top]\!]) = \neg pre(Q)$$

Q, i.e. T_Π, is $[\![x]\!]$ where x is any variable of sort *state*, then $pre(Q) = pre([\![x]\!])$ is $\bigcup_i [\![p_i]\!]$ where the p_i's are the preconditions of the rules $p_i : e_i \Rightarrow p'_i$ of TR.

For *ADD* (see Figure 6) we have:

$$pre(T_\Pi) = [\![X(), Y(zero, n), Y(succ(n), m)]\!]$$

which implies

$$\begin{aligned} Sat[\![\mathbf{AX} \perp]\!] &= \neg[\![X()]\!] \cap \neg[\![Y(zero, n)]\!] \cap \neg[\![Y(succ(n), m)]\!] \\ &= [\![Y(n, m)]\!] \cap [\![X(), Y(succ(n), m)]\!] \cap [\![X(), Y(zero, m)]\!] \\ &= [\![Y(succ(n), m)]\!] \cap [\![X(), Y(zero, m)]\!] \\ &= \emptyset \end{aligned}$$

Then $Sink = \emptyset$ (for ADD), i.e.

$$ADD \models \neg \mathbf{AX} \perp$$

which proves that ADD cannot be blocked.

A similar computation would show that $ADD2$ (see Figure 9) has no sink states. It is interesting to compute the sink states of $ADD2 - O$ (i.e. $ADD2$ without its O connector). Its transition rules are:

$$\begin{array}{lll} XE() & : A(n)\ B(m) & \Rightarrow YE(n,m) \\ XF(p) & : A(n)\ B(m) & \Rightarrow YF(n,m,p) \\ YE(succ(n),m) & : & \Rightarrow YE(n,succ(m)) \\ YF(succ(n),m,p) & : & \Rightarrow YF(n,succ(m),p) \\ YE(zero,n) & : & \Rightarrow XF(n) \end{array}$$

Now

$$pre(T_\Pi) = [\![XE(), XF(p), YE(succ(n),m), YF(succ(n),m,p), YE(zero,n)]\!]$$

implying

$$Sat[\![\mathbf{AX} \perp]\!] = \neg pre(T_\Pi) = [\![YF(zero,n,m)]\!]$$

Thus $ADD2 - O$ is blocked iff it is in a state having the form $YF(zero,n,m)$, that is, when ADD in state $Y(zero,n)$ is ready to output value n while $BUFF$ in state $F(m)$ already contains an integer and cannot accept another one.

Returning to the "Alternating Bit" example from section 3.7, we may consider several properties we would wish to prove about the AB network. All computations have to be performed upon the twenty transition rules of the flattened presentation (not included): we shall skip the actual computation and only give some results.

First

$$AB \models \neg \mathbf{AX} \perp$$

which means that AB cannot be blocked. This does not mean that there is effective progress (at the conceptual level of the transmission line). This progress is expressed by saying that when some value enters along A, it will eventually be output along B, what we write "**after** $A(x) \Rightarrow$ **AF after** $B(x)$". Note that the two occurrences of x are not connected, so that the previous formula reads "*after some value enters along A, some value will eventually be output along B*" and is logically equivalent to **after** $A(x) \Rightarrow$ **AF after** $B(y)$. This problem cannot be avoided in a propositional logic like ours: the best we can do is to specialize the previous formula for some particular value, e.g. **after** $A(3) \Rightarrow$ **AF after** $B(3)$, reading "*after value 3 has been input along A, it will eventually be output along B*". Unfortunately, it turns out that

$$AB \not\models \textbf{after } A(x) \Rightarrow \textbf{AF after } B(y)$$

This is because nothing prevents the lines from constantly loosing the messages. Clearly, the property cannot be proved without including a fairness assumption. CTL

can be used to describe some kind of fairness constraints (see e.g. Queille & Sifakis 1983) but these possibilities are not sufficient in our example: we need a more expressive logic, e.g. CTL^*.

At this point we will discontinue our criticisms regarding CTL. As we previously stated, we only choose CTL as an example of symbolic manipulation over FP2 programs. We believe that more expressive logics are still amenable to the symbolic techniques based on constrained predicates.

6 Conclusions

This chapter has given a thorough exposition of the principles underlying the FP2 language. The touchstone of the approach is the use of term algebras to denote non-deterministic communicating systems, allowing a clear declarative semantics for FP2 process presentations. In particular, we have tried to clearly distinguish the origins and motivations of the several restrictions we put in the language: our motivations were mainly

(1) The use of a declarative semantics,

(2) The existence of correct flattening operators for presentations,

(3) The existence and adequacy of a rewrite-based interpreter for functions,

(4) The existence and adequacy of a rewrite-based interpreter for processes.

Variations along these lines will be investigated in the future. At the moment, it is not clear what are the limits of the framework.

The interest of our approach is demonstrated by the possibilities it offers to the "symbolic" analysis of processes, as is shown by the symbolic model checking application of section 5. An important point is that the flattening operators are essential to give its whole scope to this kind of analysis. As a consequence, we do not feel free to add a new process combining operator in the language if there does not exist a corresponding flattening operator.

7 Acknowledgements

We would like to thank Z. Belmesk, H. Comon, X. Pandolfi, S. Pinchinat and the FP2 group in general, for useful, valuable, patient (and numerous !) discussions, comments, remarks, etc. about this chapter. H. Comon deserves special thanks for his constant willingness to hear about parallelism.

This work has been supported, in part, by ESPRIT Project 415 and by CNRS Project C^3.

8 References

Abramsky, S. (1987). Observation equivalence as a testing equivalence. *Theoretical Computer Science*, **53**, 225–241.

Austry, D. and Boudol, G. (1984). Algèbre de processus et synchronisation. *Theoretical Computer Science*, **30**(1), 91–131.

Bergstra, J. A. and Klop, J. W. (1986). Algebra of communicating processes. In J. W. de Bakker et al., editor, *Proc. CWI Symp. Math. and Comp. Sci.*, North-Holland.

Bergstra, J. A. and Klop, J. W. (1989). Process theory based on bisimulation semantics. In *Linear Time, Branching Time and Partial Order in Logics and Models for Concurrency*, Noordwijkerhout, LNCS 354, pages 50–122, Springer-Verlag.

Bergstra, J. A., Klop J. W. and Olderog, E.-R. (1988). Readies and failures in the algebra of communicating processes. *SIAM Journal on Computing*, **17**(6), 1134–1177.

Brookes S. D., Hoare, C. A. R. and Roscoe, A. W. (1984). A theory of communicating sequential processes. *Journal of the ACM*, **31**(3), 560–599.

Brookes, S. D. and Rounds, W. C. (1983). Behavioural equivalence relations induced by programming logics. In *Proc. 10th ICALP*, LNCS 154, pages 97–108, Springer-Verlag.

Browne, M. C. (1986). An improved algorithm for the automatic verification of finite state systems using temporal logic. In *Proc. 1st IEEE Symp. Logic in Computer Science*, Cambridge, Mass., pages 260–266.

Clarke, E. M. and Emerson, E. A. (1981). Design and synthesis of synchronization skeletons using branching time temporal logic. In *Proc. IBM Workshop on Logics of Programs*, LNCS 131, pages 52–71, Springer-Verlag.

Clarke, E. M., Emerson, E. A. and Sistla, A. P. (1983). Automatic verification of finite-state concurrent systems using temporal logic specifications: a practical approach. In *Proc. 10th ACM Symp. Principles of Programming Languages*, Austin, Texas, pages 117–126.

Comon, H. (1988a). An effective method for handling initial algebras. In *Proc. 1st Workshop on Algebraic and Logic Programming*, Gaussig, LNCS 343, Springer-Verlag.

Comon, H. (1988b). *Unification et Disunification: Théorie et Applications*. Thèse de Doctorat, I.N.P. de Grenoble, France.

Comon, H. (1989a). Inductive proofs by specifications transformation. In *Proc. Rewriting Techniques and Applications 89*, Chapel Hill, LNCS 355, pages 76–91, Springer-Verlag.

Comon, H. (1989b). *Disunification*. To appear.

Comon, H. and Lescanne, P. (1989). Equational problems and disunification. *Journal of Symbolic Computation*, **7**, 371–425.

Dershowitz, N. (1987). Termination of rewriting. *Journal of Symbolic Computation*, **3**(1), 69–115.

Dershowitz, N. and Jouannaud, J.-P. (1989). *Rewrite systems*. To appear in the *Handbook of Theoretical Computer Science*.

Ehrig, H. and Mahr, B. (1985). *Fundamentals of Algebraic Specification 1. Equations and Initial Semantics*. Volume 6 of *EATCS Monographs on Theoretical Computer Science*, Springer-Verlag.

Emerson, E. A. and Halpern, J. Y. (1982). Decision procedures and expressiveness in the temporal logic of branching time. In *Proc. 14th ACM Symp. Theory of Computing*, San Francisco, pages 169–180.

Emerson, E. A. and Halpern, J. Y. (1986). "Sometimes" and "Not Never" revisited: on branching versus linear time temporal logic. *Journal of the ACM*, **33**(1), 151–178.

Emerson, E. A. and Lei, C. (1986). Efficient model checking in fragments of the propositional mu-calculus. In *Proc. 1st IEEE Symp. Logic in Computer Science*, Cambridge, Mass., pages 267–278.

Emerson, E. A. and Srinivasan, J. (1989). Branching time temporal logic. In *Linear Time, Branching Time and Partial Order in Logics and Models for Concurrency*, Noordwijkerhout, LNCS 354, pages 123–172, Springer-Verlag.

Graf, S. and Sifakis, J. (1985). *From Synchronization Tree Logic to Acceptance Model Logic.* Research Report 526, LGI-IMAG, Grenoble.

Guttag, J. V. and Horning, J. J. (1978). The algebraic specification of abstract data types. *Acta Informatica*, **10**, 27–52.

Hennessy, M. (1985). Acceptance trees. *Journal of the ACM*, **32**(4), 896–928.

Hennessy, M. (1988). *Algebraic Theory of Processes.* MIT Press.

Hennessy, M. and Milner, R. (1985). Algebraic laws for nondeterminism and concurrency. *Journal of the ACM*, **32**(1), 137–161.

Hennessy, M. and Stirling, C. (1985). The power of the future perfect in program logics. *Information and Control*, **67**, 23–52.

Hoare, C. A. R. (1978). Communicating sequential processes. *Communications of the ACM*, **21**(8), 666–677.

Huet, G. (1976). *Résolution d'équations dans les langages d'ordre* $1, 2, \ldots \omega$. Thèse d'Etat, Univ. Paris 7.

Huet, G. (1980). Confluent reductions: abstract properties and applications to term rewriting systems. *Journal of the ACM*, **27**(4), 797–821.

Huet, G. and Hullot, J.-M. (1982). Proofs by induction in equational theories with constructors. *Journal of Computer and System Sciences*, **25**(2).

Huet, G. and Oppen, D. C. (1980). Equations and rewrite rules: a survey. In R. Book, editor, *Formal Language Theory: Perspectives and Open Problems*, pages 349–405, Academic Press.

ISO. (1985). *Information processing systems - Open systems interconnection - LOTOS - A formal description technique based on the temporal ordering of observational behavior.* Draft proposal.

Jorrand, Ph. (1981). Bases for the specification of communicating processes. In *Proc. 6th Int. Computing Symp.*, London, pages 124–133, Westburg House.

Jorrand, Ph. (1982). Specification of communicating processes and process implementation correctness. In *Proc. 5th Int. Symp. on Programming*, Turin, LNCS 137, pages 242–256, Springer-Verlag.

Jorrand, Ph. (1986). Term rewriting as a basis for the design of a functional and parallel programming language. A case study: the language FP2. In *Fundamentals of Artificial Intelligence*, LNCS 232, pages 221–276, Springer-Verlag.

Jorrand, Ph. (1987). Design and implementation of a parallel inference machine for first order logic: an overview. In *Proc. PARLE 87, vol. I: Parallel Architectures*, Eindhoven, LNCS 258, pages 434–445, Springer-Verlag.

Jorrand, Ph. and Pereira, J. M. (1985). *A Formal Language for Specification of Communicating Processes.* Research Report 527, LIFIA-IMAG, Grenoble.

Keller, R. M. (1976). Formal verification of parallel programs. *Communications of the ACM*, **19**(7), 371–384.

Klop, J. W. (1980). *Combinatory Reduction Systems.* Mathematical Centre Tracts 127, Mathematisch Centrum, Amsterdam.

Lamport, L. (1980). "Sometimes" is sometimes "Not Never". In *Proc. 7th ACM Symp. Principles of Programming Languages*, Las Vegas, pages 174–185.

Lassez, J.-L. and Marriott, K. G. (1987). Explicit representation of terms defined by counter examples. *Journal of Automated Reasoning*, **3**(3), 1–17.

Lassez, J.-L., Maher, M. J. and Marriot, K. G. (1986). Unification revisited. In *Proc. Workshop on Found. of Logic and Functional Programming*, Trento, LNCS 306, Springer-Verlag.

Liskov, B., Herlihy, M. and Gilbert, L. (1986). Limitations of synchronous communication with static process structure in languages for distributed computing. In *Proc. 13th ACM Symp. Principles of Programming Languages*, St. Petersburg Beach, Florida.

Logrippo, L., Obaid, A., Briand, J. P. and Fehri, M. C. (1988). An interpreter for LOTOS, a specification language for distributed systems. *Software - Practice and Experience*, **18**(4):365–385.

Maher, M. J. (1988). Complete axiomatizations of the algebras of finite, rational and infinite trees. In *Proc. 3rd IEEE Symp. Logic in Computer Science*, Edinburgh, pages 348–357.

Martelli, A. and Montanari, U. (1982). An efficient unification algorithm. *ACM Transactions on Programming Languages and Systems*, **4**(2), 258–282.

May, D. (1983). OCCAM. *SIGPLAN Notices*, **13**(4).

Milner, R. (1980). *A Calculus of Communicating Systems. LNCS 92*, Springer-Verlag.

Milner, R. (1983). Calculi for synchrony and asynchrony. *Theoretical Computer Science*, **23**, 267–310.

Milner, R. (1988). *Operational and Algebraic Semantics of Concurrent Processes.* Research Report ECS-LFCS-88-46, Lab. for Foundations of Computer Science, Edinburgh. To appear in the *Handbook of Theoretical Computer Science.*

O'Donnell, M. J. (1986). *Equational Logic as a Programming Language.* MIT Press.

Park, D. (1981). Concurrency and automata on infinite sequences. In *Proc. 5th GI Conf.*, Karlsruhe, LNCS 104, pages 167–183, Springer-Verlag.

Parrow, J. (1989). The expressive power of simple parallelism. In *Proc. PARLE 89, vol. II: Parallel Languages*, Eindhoven, LNCS 366, pages 389–405, Springer-Verlag.

Pereira, J. M. (1984). *Processus Communicants: un Langage Formel et ses Modèles. Problèmes d'Analyse.* Thèse de Doctorat, I.N.P. de Grenoble, France.

Pinchinat, S. (1989). *Logique Temporelle pour FP2.* Rapport de DEA, Univ. Grenoble.

Plaisted, D. (1985). Semantic confluence tests and completion methods. *Information and Control*, **65**, 182–215.

Pnueli, A. (1977). The temporal logic of programs. In *Proc. 18th Symp. Foundations of Computer Science*, Providence, pages 46–57.

Pnueli, A. (1985). Linear and branching structures in the semantics and logics of reactive systems. In *Proc. 12th ICALP*, Nafplion, LNCS 194, pages 15–32, Springer-Verlag.

Queille, J. P. and Sifakis, J. (1982). Specification and verification of concurrent systems in CESAR. In *Proc. 5th Int. Symp. on Programming*, Turin, LNCS 137, pages 337–351, Springer-Verlag.

Queille, J. P. and Sifakis, J. (1983). Fairness and related properties in transition systems. A temporal logic to deal with fairness. *Acta Informatica*, **19**, 195–220.

Robinson, J. A. (1965). A machine-oriented logic based on the resolution principle. *Journal of the ACM*, **12**(1), 23–41.

Schaefer, P. and Schnoebelen, Ph. (1987). Specification of a pipelined event-driven simulator using FP2. In *Proc. PARLE 87, vol. I: Parallel Architectures*, Eindhoven, LNCS 258, pages 311–328, Springer-Verlag.

Schnoebelen, Ph. (1985). *The Semantics of Concurrency in FP2.* Research Report 558, LIFIA-IMAG, Grenoble.

Schnoebelen, Ph. (1986). *μ-FP2. A Prototype Interpreter for FP2.* Research Report 573, LIFIA-IMAG, Grenoble.

Schnoebelen, Ph. (1987). Rewriting techniques for the temporal analysis of communicating processes. In *Proc. PARLE 87, vol. II: Parallel Languages*, Eindhoven, LNCS 259, pages 402–419, Springer-Verlag.

Schnoebelen, Ph. (1988). Refined compilation of pattern-matching for functional languages. *Science of Computer Programming*, **11**(2), 133–159.

Schnoebelen, Ph. and Pinchinat, S. (1989). *On the Weak Adequacy of Branching-Time Temporal Logic.* To appear.

Sifakis, J. (1982). A unified approach for studying the properties of transitions systems. *Theoretical Computer Science*, **18**, 227–258.

Smolka, G., Nutt, W., Meseguer, J. and Goguen, J. (1987). Order-sorted equational computation. In *Proc. Coll. on the Resolution of Equations in Algebraic Structures*, Lakeway.

Thatte, S. R. (1985). On the correspondence between two classes of reduction systems. *Information Processing Letters*, **20**, 83–85.

Thiel, J.-J. (1984). Stop loosing sleep over incomplete specifications. In *Proc. 11th ACM Symp. Principles of Programming Languages*, Salt Lake City, Utah, pages 76–82.